God and Man in the Law

God and Man in the Law

The Foundations of Anglo-American Constitutionalism

Robert Lowry Clinton

University Press of Kansas

© 1997 by the University Press of Kansas

Published by the University Press of Kansas (Lawrence, Kansas 66049),
which was organized by the Kansas Board of Regents and is operated and
funded by Emporia State University, Fort Hays State University, Kansas State
University, Pittsburg State University, the University of Kansas, and Wichita
State University

Library of Congress Cataloging-in-Publication Data

Clinton, Robert Lowry.
    God and man in the law : the foundations of Anglo-American
constitutionalism / Robert Lowry Clinton.
        p.   cm.
    Includes bibliographical references and index.
    ISBN 0-7006-0841-9 (alk. paper)
    1. Constitutional law—United States—Interpretation and
construction.   2. Constitutional law—United States—Religious
aspects.   3. Constitutional history—United States.   I. Title.
KF4552.C57   1997   97-11020
342.73—DC21

British Library Cataloguing in Publication Data is available.

Printed in the United States of America

10 9 8 7 6 5 4 3 2 1

For my parents,

Robert L. Clinton

and

Wanda Lowry Clinton

Reason, indeed, in all domains, appears as the rule and measure of what is done, so that law, if it is really nothing but the formula of this rule, presents itself at once as an obligation founded upon the demands of reason. This is a definition which we note is at least founded upon custom and in accord with conscience universally. The unreasonable prescriptions of a tyrant may well usurp the title of laws but are not real laws; wherever reason is lacking, there can be neither law nor equity, but pure and simple iniquity.

Etienne Gilson, *The Philosophy of St. Thomas Aquinas*

Contents

PREFACE   xi

1. Introduction   1

Part One: The Origin and Development of
Judicialized Constitutionalism in the United States   11

2. Problems in Contemporary Constitutional Theory   13

3. Constitutional Interpretation and Judicial Review   23

4. Judicial Supremacy and Judicial Review   34

Part Two: The Anglo-American Constitutional Experience   45

5. Constitutionalism in a Liberal Democracy   47

6. Written and Unwritten Constitutions   58

7. Law and Morality   73

Part Three: The Legacy of the British Constitution   89

8. The British Constitution and the Common Law   91

9. Intentionalism and the Rules of Interpretation in English and
American Practice   104

10. The Rules of Interpretation, Stare Decisis, and Legal Fiction in
Constitutional Law   118

Part Four: The Normative Force of Tradition   129

11. Political Philosophy   131

12. Law and Jurisprudence   144

13. Natural Law and the Constitution   157

Part Five: Constitutional Gnosticism and Constitutional Theism   171

14. The Gnostic Alternative   175

15. The God of the Cosmos as a Whole   191

16. The God of the Cosmos and Its Parts   201

17. The Implications of Belief and the Continuity of the Western
    Legal Tradition   216

NOTES   229

BIBLIOGRAPHY   267

INDEX   281

Preface

This study is a defense of traditional jurisprudence—"legal knowledge," as it was defined by Immanuel Kant—in its application to American constitutional law. It begins with judicial politics and ends with political theology, traveling through constitutional theory and history, political philosophy, epistemology, and metaphysics on the way. The whole project is founded on the supposition that traditional jurisprudence, which involves parts of each of the subject areas listed above and more, is a body of real, objective knowledge about law—a fountain of collective wisdom that is entitled to a strong and legitimate claim on constitutional and legal analysis and thus cannot simply be rejected as blind adherence to the past.

Since American constitutional law has become largely "judicialized" in the twentieth century, the subject of constitutional interpretation has become central to the study of American constitutionalism. Though the written Constitution has its own principles, which bind the courts when they are applicable and clear, it does not mandate rules of interpretation and does not provide case-specific guidance for judges regarding the ways in which they are to settle the meaning of disputed provisions. Since the Constitution is not complete within itself, it must be supplemented by the common law tradition—which itself embodies understandings inherited from the Western legal tradition more generally.

I argue in this book that judges interpreting the Constitution should reclaim the traditions of a concrete past rather than attempt to lead American democracy into an abstract future backed by blind faith in its resulting justice. These traditions include, first, a way of thinking about a constitution as the political foundation of legal order necessarily resting upon an underlying social consensus that cannot be completely encapsulated in a written document yet cannot be ignored by judges. Such an order is conservative insofar as it guarantees a large role for convention in the determination of the proper relation between law and such other constitutionally relevant fields as religion and morality.

Second, our traditions also include an understanding of English common law as the basis of American constitutionalism, especially its doctrine of precedent and the rules for the interpretation of written legal instruments that were developed by common law courts during the formative periods of English law. It is true that American constitutionalism departs from British constitutionalism in important ways, such as vesting sovereignty in the people rather than in the legislature (though an American legislature—even the Congress—is not as broadly representative of the American polity as Parliament is of the English polity). But none of these departures involves the traditional rules, principles, or methods that the courts are to use in their application of constitutional law in actual cases.

Third, our traditions include an understanding of the common law as reflecting not merely a discordant jumble of cases but an underlying legal reality—the reason of the law—that ultimately rests upon a natural law foundation. The practical reason of the common law serves as a needed check upon the abstract reason characteristic of modern liberal individualism in a Hobbesian political world. However much individuals count under a liberal constitutional order, law is nonetheless an instrument whose main purpose is to institutionalize social and political order—even if an ultimate goal of that order is promotion of individual well-being.

Finally, our traditions presuppose an epistemological realism that grants real existence to things in the external world, including such purely intelligible realities as historical experience, tradition, and law itself. This kind of realism works in tandem with a naturalistic approach to law grounded in the experience of a divine source of order that is reflected in legal institutions and practices. It is thus incompatible with legal positivism, which truncates legal experience by defining a large class of legally relevant experiences out of existence. It is also incompatible with judicial supremacy, which allows judges to sever the bonds of legal tradition and so to disregard external constitutional reality when deciding particular cases.

The debts I have incurred during the preparation of this book are too many and too varied to acknowledge in complete detail; but I must make note of some of the larger ones. The first of these is owed to the University of Malta, which provided the facilities for the reading and thinking necessary to get the study off the ground. Special thanks go to Professor Rene Cremona, Dean of the Faculty of Laws, and to Professor Ian Refalo, with whom I joined in a year-long course of lectures on comparative constitutional law in 1991–92, and to the class of first-year law students who represented an educational world so different than the only one I had been previously familiar with. Thanks also to the Fulbright program, which provided the funding for the opportunity to spend a year among the godly people of the world's first Christian nation.

Closer to home, though in the more distant past, I should note my gratitude to Professors Clarke Cochran and Lawrence Mayer of Texas Tech University, and to Russell Wheeler of the Federal Judicial Center, from whom I gained an early interest in political theory, comparative government, and constitutional law, respectively—interests that not only have never subsided but also that figured largely in this project. To Professor Cochran, who nurtured my early interest in religion and politics, I owe an additional debt of gratitude.

Wallace Mendelson, of the University of Texas at Austin, has been for many years the consummate mentor and friend, a true giant among scholars whose example is an ever-present reminder of the seriousness of that enterprise. Malcolm MacDonald, also of the University of Texas at Austin, is due heartfelt thanks for providing direction and focus for my study of jurisprudence. Thomas Schwartz, of the University of California at Los Angeles, gave impetus to my study of empirical (formal) political theory—a study that figures largely in several sections of this book.

Matthew J. Franck, of Radford University, and Paul Kens, of Southwest Texas State University, have contributed much to this study through many conversations and correspondences on subjects related to the project. Sylvia Snowiss, of California State University at Northridge, and James R. Stoner, Jr., of Louisiana State University, read and commented upon an early version of some of the ideas that ultimately made their way into this book. Lane V. Sunderland, of Knox College, and Christopher Wolfe, of Marquette University, read and commented upon the penultimate version. To each of these reviewers goes my sincere thanks for their many useful comments and suggestions, though I did not follow them all and thus must absolve them of responsibility for any part of the final work that resulted from my failure to do so.

I am also indebted to my colleagues at Southern Illinois University at Carbondale, who have put up with me for longer than I deserved during completion of this project. Thanks are due especially to Uday Desai, whose chairmanship of our department has provided essential resources, and whose friendship has provided essential support. John Hamman has been both a supportive friend and an exciting and perceptive commentator on many aspects of the project from its inception to its completion. Richard Dale and Patrick Kelly have each contributed to this project in a variety of ways. Susan Collins has been especially helpful in answering many impertinent questions about difficult matters of political theory. Thanks also to Rhonda Musgrave and Marilyn Farthing, who helped greatly in the preparation of manuscript drafts throughout the project and took on many other chores during my preoccupation with it.

To my wife, Margaret-Anne, and to my children, Winter and Tucker, go love and gratitude for all the sacrifices they have been forced to make in order to see this project to completion. Margaret-Anne not only provided stimulating conversation about subjects closely related to the book, but also edited the whole manuscript prior to final copyediting by the press. I wish also to make special note of the strong religious faith of both Margaret-Anne and her mother, Lois Ann Pugh, which has long been a source of inspiration to me, and which found its way into this book in a multitude of ways. Thanks also to my brothers, Dave and Ron Clinton, whose steady support and friendship has meant so much to me for so many years. To my father, Robert L. Clinton, who suggested the title of this book, and my mother, Wanda Lowry Clinton, I owe the largest debt of all, and I dedicate this book to them. In his *Prolegomena to the Law of War and Peace* (p. 7), Hugo Grotius quotes from Philo's commentary on the Fifth Commandment: "Children have as their own nothing to which their parents do not possess a prior claim; their parents have either given them what they have, or have furnished to them the means of acquisition."

1·Introduction

JUSTINIAN'S DICTUM

According to Justinian, "Learning in the law entails knowledge of God and man, and mastery of the difference between justice and injustice."[1] The conjunction of these two ideas in the opening lines of the West's most important law book is not accidental; it arises from a profound sense of an intimate connection which acknowledges that, to be fully secure, human justice must be grounded in a larger order of things. Justice can be "an unswerving and perpetual determination to acknowledge all men's rights" only if such rights are real, knowable, and universal, and only if the will of man is susceptible to a determination by a universal, knowable reality.

The wisdom expressed in Justinian's terse formula was not seriously questioned until the sixteenth and seventeenth centuries, when the medieval consensus, most thoughtfully expounded in the *Summa Theologica* of Thomas Aquinas,[2] which fused theology and anthropology with politics and law, began to break apart under the pressure of socioeconomic and political forces. Those forces ultimately would lend plausibility to such reductive intellectual enterprises as that of Thomas Hobbes, who founded modern constitutionalism upon the twin assumptions of social atomism and philosophical materialism.[3]

The resulting secularization of law, despite having commenced several centuries ago in Europe, has developed to its fullest in the United States during the present century. It was not until the Gilded Age in America that Hobbesian metaphysics and social philosophy clearly may be seen to have carried the day against its main rivals, and it was not until the mid-twentieth century that the U.S. Supreme Court set in motion an ongoing process of constitutional secularization that continues unabated at the present time.

This process should be a concern, not only for religious fundamentalists (the so-called Christian Right, who want to see "God in the classroom"), but also for all who wish to see the Constitution and its law standing upon the surest possible

1

foundation. Modernity has seen the collapse of constitutional theism along with the breakdown of philosophical realism, legal naturalism, conventional morality, and the common law foundation of American constitutionalism.

Few people would now question that in addition to those losses there has been a corresponding loss of any sense of mastery over justice and injustice, and few would deny that conviction about the relationship between God and man has been severely shaken as well. Put more cryptically, we appear to have lost both our reason and our faith. Consequently, divine and human justice have been thoroughly divorced in the public mind. This separation has kept religion out of our public life and has effectively robbed the law of its most essential philosophic support, leaving in its trail a jurisprudence of skepticism and doubt.

Yet since a "jurisprudence of doubt" is, in an important sense, either an empty or an incoherent jurisprudence, certainly intolerable and perhaps even oxymoronic, it is natural that an intellectual enterprise has arisen to fill the ensuing void and to rationalize the fallout from the effort. That enterprise has come to be known as "constitutional theory," which can be described as an attempt to provide some reasonably coherent theoretical foundation for constitutional legality along the lines of fundamental principle.

Lacking the provision of such fundamentals by God or nature, the appeal must be to human artifice, to those events from which modern polities are said to have been "constituted." In consequence, during the past century, the language of justice and injustice has become more and more a "constitutional" language; and constitutional language, during that same period, has become increasingly the exclusive province of lawyers, judges, and courts.

If law has been thus "constitutionalized," and if the Constitution has been "judicialized," then any book about the fundamentals of modern legal reality must be a book on constitutional jurisprudence and thus about the judiciary. This is, then, a book about constitutional jurisprudence, that is, about the underlying logic and essential features of constitutionalism in its relationship to the wider fields of legal history and legal theory (jurisprudence), political philosophy, and theology. It is also a book about constitutional interpretation and judicial review, the treatment of which has been necessitated largely by the modern judicialization of public law in general, and constitutional law in particular, by the U.S. Supreme Court.

My purpose will be to place the judicialized constitutionalism of the modern era in the larger context provided by study of the Western legal tradition and classical legal theory. In this respect, my approach is explicitly conservative, founded on the belief that a real constitution can be sustained only by perpetual recovery and conservation of the best traditions that it embodies and presupposes. Since the most important of our underlying constitutional traditions are incompatible with judicial supremacy, it follows that the judicialization of constitutional law threatens constitutional order.

Before moving on to a more detailed elaboration, I shall summarize the underlying logic that informs the book from beginning to end and that determines the order of discussion.

OVERVIEW

Constitutional jurisprudence in the United States, at least in the present century, has been so largely a function of U.S. Supreme Court decisions as to make it virtually impossible to begin a discussion of constitutional theory without first treating the subjects of constitutional interpretation and judicial review. In Part One, consisting of Chapters 2–4, I consider the origins and historical development of the Court's hegemony in modern constitutional law, emphasizing the relationship between judicial finality and judicial freedom in constitutional interpretation and some of the consequences of judicial supremacy for contemporary constitutional theory.

In the three chapters in Part Two, I explore some of the problems and issues that have arisen from the institutions described in Part One. Among these issues are the relationship of constitutional to other kinds of law and the role of consensus in classical and modern constitutionalism (Chapter 5), the distinction between written and unwritten constitutions and the role of constitutional symbolism in relation to constitutional experience (Chapter 6), and the role of morality in the law, including the place of realism and conventionalism in both law and morals (Chapter 7).

In Part Three (Chapters 8–10), I proceed from the assumption that law generally, and constitutional law particularly, is institutionalized history and cannot be understood without a grasp of its historical foundations and subsequent historical development. The most immediate historical background relevant to a study of American constitutionalism is that of British constitutionalism and the English common law. The most vital features of the U.S. Constitution are derived straightforwardly from the British model, and the rules for its interpretation are drawn even more directly from the common law.

In Chapter 8, I consider the influence of the common law and the British Constitution on the U.S. Constitution particularly and on American constitutionalism more generally. In Chapter 9, I explicate the most important rules of interpretation derived from English practice and demonstrate the applicability of these rules in the early American constitutional context. I then explore the ideas of precedent and legal fiction in English and American practice in Chapter 10. The underlying argument is that the constitutional theory developed in Part Two fully implies the historically derived model of constitutional interpretation described in Part Three.

The constitutional jurisprudence advanced in Parts Two and Three is vulnerable to a charge of "historicism" unless it is adequately grounded in a wider theory of law that is not subject to such an attack. It is my purpose in Part Four, comprising Chapters 11–13, to advance such a theory. Since theories of law are necessarily grounded in political philosophy, which in turn presupposes an epistemological foundation, in Chapter 11 I shall consider the most important presuppositions of jurisprudential thought stemming from these fields. In Chapter 12, the two most important answers that have been given historically to the question concerning the nature of law—natural law and legal positivism—are contrasted in the thought of Thomas Aquinas and John Austin. The U.S. Supreme Court will be revisited in Chapter 13 in order to rehash the old argument about the Court's alleged use of "natural law" to decide constitutional cases. I shall also examine some of the underpinnings of modern liberal constitutional jurisprudence, best illustrated in the thought of John Stuart Mill.

The underlying argument in Part Four is that legal naturalism, when given a classical interpretation, is the most comprehensive and comprehensible philosophy of law, but it cannot justify imposition of "natural law," "fundamental values," or "moral rights" by the Supreme Court in constitutional cases. Positivism, on the other hand, results in a truncated idea of law that, when combined with judicial freedom and finality in constitutional law, leads inexorably to unprincipled judicial activism, aggrandizement of the legal profession, and tyranny of the legal establishment. Such an oxymoronic "constitutional order," when brought under the sway of Millian political principles, generates anarchy, debauchery, a debased society, and, finally, a return to the Hobbesian state of nature.

Classical natural law, unlike its modern counterpart, is grounded in full and explicit recognition of the centrality of spirituality, and hence divinity, in the legal order. The denial of this centrality, having received its most recent and articulate exposition in the constitutional thought of William Harris (see Chapter 14), is at the heart of much contemporary constitutional theorizing. This denial has resulted in a prevailing constitutional theory that is best described as "constitutional gnosticism," a doctrine rooted in the belief that man, not God, is primary ruler of the legal cosmos.

In Part Five, comprising Chapters 14–17, I examine the theological basis of the classical natural law approach, contrasting gnostic constitutional order (Chapter 14) with an alternative order derived from the assumption that God, not man, is ruler of the legal cosmos (Chapters 15 and 16). In Chapter 17, I address the implications of the book for jurisprudence generally and for the Western legal tradition particularly.

The underlying argument of Part Five is that a crossroads has now been reached in contemporary constitutional theory, and a choice between starkly contrasting alternatives must be made. Down one road lies the way to constitutional regeneration through recovery of faith in a divinely constituted legal order that imparts meaning to "historical events, beliefs, and practices."[4] Down the other road lies the path to constitutional degeneration through continued denial of such an order and of the relevance of tradition as the most significant record of its humanly experienced force. No doubt the latter road will be less bumpy at the start, but its end does not seem promising. The former road will make for difficult traveling at the outset, but its ultimate destination makes the initial effort worthwhile.

In sum, the assertion of faith in a divinely constituted cosmos implies the existence of a legal order with transcendent structure and requires attribution of juridical significance to legal traditions conceived as efforts to institute universalizable legal norms based on a human nature that is ordered by a transcendent source (Part Five). Such a theistic conception entails a naturalistic jurisprudence and forms the basis for a type of "natural law" founded on common experience rather than on intellectual abstraction (Part Four). A naturalistic jurisprudence imparts meaning and legal effect to historical events, beliefs, and practices and renders fully normative, for American constitutionalism, many of the historical practices derived from the British Constitution and the English common law (Part Three). These practices, when combined with an adequate conception of the nature of a constitution (Part Two), preclude a "judicialized" constitutionalism of the kind that has developed in the United States during the past century (Part One).

Reasoning the other way, the continuing viability of our modern judicialized Constitution (Part One) depends crucially on the continued rejection of the underlying logic of constitutionalism itself (Part Two) and the legal significance of its historical foundation in the common law in the case of the United States (Part Three). The continued rejection of the common law basis depends, in turn, on the rejection of any jurisprudence that ascribes meaningfulness and that gives legal effect to historical events, beliefs, and practices; this position requires embracing legal positivism and rejecting legal naturalism (Part Four). Finally, the only worldview that ultimately will support the truncated legal positivism of the modern era is the gnostic perspective in which man replaces God as primary ruler of the legal cosmos (Part Five).

SOME QUALIFICATIONS

It is necessary now to take note of some matters that might seem relevant to this book but that nonetheless will not be addressed in the usual manner. First, though I refer to some of the works of contemporary constitutional theorists whenever they help to illuminate particular features, I make no attempt to engage in a systematic critique of these works, taken as a whole. In other words, I shall not classify contemporary commentators and discuss them under such headings as "textualism," "intentionalism," "originalism," "interpretivism," "noninterpretivism," and the like, though these approaches will be noted and discussed at appropriate points.

My purpose is to expound and develop a constitutional theory, not to debunk (or celebrate) existing ones. Moreover, given the prevailing assumptions that undergird today's legal and constitutional order, most theories of constitutionalism, constitutional interpretation, and judicial review that have been advanced during the past several decades are at least plausible readings of constitutional reality. Since it is my position that the assumptions are wrong (not necessarily any particular implications drawn from them), my purpose will have been accomplished if I can succeed in calling those assumptions into question. Issues concerning whether particular theories or results follow, as a matter of logic or fact, from the questioned assumptions are beyond the scope of this book.

Second, astute readers will notice that I have elected to pass over (some critics may say I have glossed over) certain issues that might seem relevant, issues with which modern scholars are preoccupied and which are thus central in the contemporary secondary literature of several academic subfields. Examples might be the extent of compatibility (or incompatibility) between virtue ethics and quandary ethics and the extent to which either (or both) of them can be reconciled with American constitutionalism; the extent to which Platonism may be viewed as precursive of Christianity; the precise contours of the conflict between Plato and Aristotle over the nature of the "forms"; the bearing of Hobbes's doctrine on the Lockean liberalism that seems to have been one of its most important results; the extent to which Locke was a "Hobbesian"; the extent to which Blackstone was a "Lockean"; or the extent to which the American Founding was "liberal" or "republican."

In response, I can say only that such omissions are the inevitable result of the wide range of materials consulted and topics covered in this book; they should not be read as representing an opinion that such issues are unimportant or irrelevant. That said, it is also fair to note that most of these issues (and others of a similar kind) are tangential to the larger perspective I wish to encourage. For example, it is not necessary to conclude the issue of Plato's precursive Christianity or of Hobbes's atheism in order to assert confidently that, whatever the personal religious scruples of Plato or Hobbes, it is reasonable to think that Platonic philosophy is more compatible than Hobbesian philosophy with any kind of theistic constitutionalism. Likewise, it is unnecessary to resolve the issue of Plato versus Aristotle on the question of whether the "real" existence of the "forms" requires their embodiment in matter to conclude reasonably that, both for Plato and for Aristotle, the "forms" at least *exist* (whatever their embodiment) in a way that they do not exist either for Hobbes or for Hume.

A third closely related observation concerns the way in which I have used the works of thinkers representative of different philosophical traditions without first trying to resolve the incompatibilities or inconsistencies that may exist between them. For example, on the one hand I have borrowed freely from the ideas of Plato, Augustine, and Eric Voegelin—thinkers who plausibly may be held to represent a "Christian Platonist" tradition. On the other hand, I have borrowed freely from the works of Aristotle, Thomas Aquinas, Etienne Gilson, and Mortimer Adler—all of whom would be considered "Aristotelians" of a certain stripe.

Again, I can say only that the fundamental complementarity of these traditions seems far more important than the distinctions that may be drawn between them. Indeed, even the distinctions often may be read as complementary, as in the case of the different positions that tend to be held by, say, Christian Platonists and Thomists on the relationship between empirical evidence and the resolution of philosophical and theological issues.

I would also take the position, with the classical tradition as a whole, that the real is a unified whole and that knowledge about it, "science," if there is to be such, must at least strive to capture a semblance of that unity. The contemporary academic division of labor has become a serious problem here. Constitutional theory, at its best, is a branch of political philosophy, a discipline founded in the West by Plato and Aristotle and developed subsequently by a host of other thinkers across vast reaches of space and time. It also has close ties with legal history, political science, and several other academic disciplines.

Any work attempting to propound a constitutional theory worth taking seriously must itself take seriously its antecedent historical and theoretical underpinnings. This approach requires taking into account the best thinking and writing that has been done on the subject of constitutionalism at all times and in all places, without reliance on a spatio-temporal statute of limitations that could have been set only arbitrarily. For example, some of the best writing on constitutionalism has been done by Thomas Aquinas, Kenneth Arrow, and Frederic William Maitland; yet it is doubtful that many scholars specializing in any of the academic subfields suggested by these names are familiar with the works of more than one of them, and some contemporary commentators may be unfamiliar with any.

If academic overspecialization has become a serious problem for intellectual activity in general, and for constitutional studies in particular, the resulting narrowness of perspective can be overcome only by attempting to gain a larger view, which requires an approach that sacrifices some detail by the deliberate exclusion of peripheral material. Since one of the larger purposes of this book, negatively speaking, is to establish that acquiescence in modern judicialized constitutionalism requires wholesale rejection of many of the most important philosophical, historical, jurisprudential, and theological traditions of Western law and that such acquiescence usually involves little serious effort to confront those traditions and defeat them openly, it is necessary to paint the constitutional landscape in bold strokes with a rather large brush. Of course, as any good painter knows, large brushes are clumsy, and a bold stroke is dangerous; some oversimplification of the landscape surely will result. I can only hope that the gain in perspective on the forest will compensate adequately for some loss of focus on the trees.

ACADEMIC SPECIALISM IN CONTEMPORARY CONSTITUTIONAL THEORY

I believe that current understanding in the fields of enquiry bearing most directly on constitutional decisionmaking has become seriously truncated through academic overspecialization. A preponderance of books and articles now appearing on such subjects as constitutional theory, constitutional interpretation, constitutional politics, or judicial review (to name only four divisions that themselves are yet being continually subdivided) are being written by four groups of scholars.

First are lawyers specializing in constitutional law, many of whom are skilled in the analysis of case law but notably ill-trained in methods of historical analysis (hence the popular reference to "lawyers' history"). They often neglect to draw upon other, larger, fields of legal experience, perhaps because of advancing specialization in the legal profession. Second are political scientists specializing in public law (a group to which I belong), who tend to be either well-grounded in political theory or well-trained in the use of quantitative methods of investigation (though not usually in both) but who often ignore more traditional modes of legal analysis in their efforts to explain constitutional phenomena. Third are professional philosophers specializing in social or legal philosophy, ethics, or moral philosophy, who sometimes neglect the bearing of institutional history, political science, and legal history upon their primary subject area. Fourth are historians specializing in constitutional or legal history, who often neglect moral and political philosophy, political science, and sometimes philosophy of history as well.

Though this description is hardly adequate in presenting the full range of problems stemming from Balkanization of the fields pertinent to constitutional study, it will suffice further to clarify my undertaking, in which I hope to demonstrate four points. First, constitutional law cannot be understood fully apart from a corresponding understanding of its roots in the legal tradition from which it springs (and of which it is only a part) and consequently of its relation to the law of procedure, contract, tort, property, crime, and so on. Second, public law cannot be understood fully apart from an understanding of its relationship to the ancient private law from which it springs and to the traditional methods of legal analysis that have emerged during that development. Third, academic ethics and moral philosophy are not fully comprehensible as separate fields of enquiry pertinent to constitutional study without a thorough grounding in theology, metaphysics, and epistemology—i.e., theories of the right or the good presuppose theories of the real and the knowable and often presuppose views about the presence or absence of divinity. Fourth, constitutional history cannot be understood fully without an understanding of legal history, and neither constitutional nor legal history can be understood apart from a philosophy of history that convincingly attributes meaning to historical events, beliefs, and practices.

Though time and space will not permit pursuing here the details of such a comprehensive view, a start must nonetheless be made, for surely only the most cynical among us would hold that reality necessarily conforms to the demands of academic specialism, and just as surely only inveterate Panglossians would claim that the contemporary academic division of labor provides sufficient assurance that disciplinary boundaries will receive adequate attention. Indeed, it may be a guarantee that the walls that represent such boundaries will become so high as to dissuade even the hardiest of climbers.

Yet constitutional theory cannot be penetrated by an exclusive focus on the American Constitution, or on the Supreme Court's glosses upon it, or on written constitutions generally, or even on modern constitutions taken as a whole. Many of the problems that constitutions address are fundamental problems of political and social order that necessarily transcend any given constitutional approach. Some of these problems are unique to particular societies; others are universal. In order even to begin a fair consideration of constitutional order in a particular society, it is necessary to distinguish the particulars from the universals. This approach requires paying attention to the wisdom afforded by the individuals who have thought through constitutional problems in other times and places.

Since no one can be an expert (at least by current academic standards) in all the areas pertinent to constitutional study, it follows that the effort of traversing some disciplinary boundaries is required. In constitutional theory, close attention to the problems generated by these artificially created boundaries seems doubly crucial. The normal myopia brought about by specialism occurs when scholars form tiny communities clustered about such topics as "judicial review" or "constitutional interpretation" or "constitutional history in the Taney era" and so forth, become experts in the specialties, and then pontificate to everyone outside the field. This myopia is exaggerated in constitutional theory because constitutional scholars are also constitutional citizens, with important interests at stake in the outcome of constitutional decisions. It should not be surprising, for example, that most people who make their living reading and writing (including constitutional theorists) tend to like J. S. Mill's *On Liberty,* though the average constitutional citizen might find the attraction puzzling.

One of the most important consequences of this "double aspect" of constitutional scholarship and constitutional citizenship has been to produce a seemingly pervasive attitude of contempt among academics for constitutional citizens other than constitutional scholars, perhaps reflected in Soterios Barber's judgment that "if academics can't hope to know what the Constitution means, no one else can."[5] Such a statement reflects an insensibility to the extent to which academicians, by professional interest as well as by inclination, are wedded to particular (and sometimes doubtful) constructions and interpretations of the Constitution. And it also reflects an insensibility to the fact, regarded by students of bureaucracy as a truism, that "expertise" is no guarantor of good sense.

Yet in the last analysis, Barber's judgment is probably in perfect synchrony with the requirements of a thoroughly judicialized constitutional order. In my view, the only way that government by judges can survive for long in the American context is through an ignorant, demoralized citizenry that has forgotten (or "unlearned") Plato's maxim that self-government begins and ends, not in the courts, but in the souls of men.

Part One · The Origin and Development of Judicialized Constitutionalism in the United States

No study of constitutional law, constitutional history, or constitutional theory in the United States can avoid confronting the reality that, in the contemporary American context, courts are, and are widely regarded to be, primary guardians of our fundamental law. Though my ultimate objective is to propose a constitutional theory that is theistic (Part Five), naturalistic (Part Four), historical (Part Three), and consensual (Part Two), that proposal must be understood as an alternative to the "judicialized" constitutionalism that is currently dominant on the American scene.

My purpose in Part One is to examine the elements that have given rise to the current situation. In Chapter 2, I consider some of the ways in which contemporary constitutional theory has both contributed to and been victimized by today's judicialized constitutionalism. I pay special attention to the tendency of many constitutional theorists to treat the Constitution as little more than a malleable written text (a "blueprint") devoid of meaningful traditions that determine its content independently of what judges say about it.

In Chapter 3, I examine the relationship between constitutional interpretation and judicial review, showing how judicial supremacy arises from the combination of judicial freedom in the choice of rules of interpretation and judicial finality in court review of the acts of other government agencies. I also examine the distinction between "constitutional interpretation" and "constitutional construction" as well as the history of the "interpretivism-noninterpretivism" debate among contemporary constitutional theorists.

In Chapter 4, I explore the idea of judicial supremacy in greater depth, focusing on the myths that support it and the constitutional historiography that made its emergence possible. I also examine the judicialization of administrative law that has occurred in recent years, suggesting that judicialization of constitutional law is only part of a larger trend toward judicialization of public law more generally in the United States.

2 · Problems in Contemporary Constitutional Theory

In a previous book I have described the historical process in which legal practitioners, legal academics, social reformers, and other interested political actors in late nineteenth- and early twentieth-century America used constitutional and legal doctrine to initiate the process I have termed the "judicialization of constitutional law" in the United States.[1] Some of the current practical effects of the resulting judicialized constitutionalism are nicely summarized by Robert F. Nagel:

> Today federal courts control more important public decisions and institutions in more detail and for more extended periods than at any time in our history. Constitutional interpretations have important influence over a vast range of policies, including those relating to marriage, parent-child relations, abortion, zoning, public administration, police practices, aid to private education, commercial advertising, defamation, criminal penalties, aliens, women, jury selection, voting, affirmative action, and state taxation. There is no way to be sure how many school districts are significantly controlled by federal judges, but a reasonable estimate would put the figure at more than six hundred. In the few years since the theory of a "conditions of confinement" lawsuit was first created, judges have ordered pervasive prison reforms in more than thirty states and suits are pending in others. There have been decrees affecting some 270 local jails, with hundreds of cases pending. Mental health systems and public housing have been under judicial control in some states, and of course the judiciary has been responsible for numerous legislative apportionment plans. There have been decrees that govern welfare programs, and the courts are now beginning to restructure state and local personnel policies in an effort to dismantle patronage systems. This unprecedented use of judicial power is not a response to specific and limited necessity or emergency. The power is exercised in every state and on a wide variety of social issues. Moreover, there is considerable potential for growth of judicial involvement in the governmental process. Even a relatively "conservative" Supreme Court seems transfixed; recent decisions, such as those dealing with the legislative veto and political gerrymandering, illustrate the Court's continuing insistence that almost no public is-

13

sue should be excluded from judicial oversight. Fertile minds in academia and the practicing bar are always at work generating legal theories that would "reinvigorate" provisions, like the clause prohibiting impairment of contracts or the clause guaranteeing the state a republican form of government, that had previously been relatively quiescent. Heavy reliance on the judiciary—in various ideological directions—is fast becoming an ingrained part of the American system; already it is difficult for many, whether in or out of the academy, even to imagine any alternative.[2]

It might be added that the passage just quoted is an understatement. It says nothing, for instance, about the extent to which all the business of contemporary legislative bodies and administrative agencies is conducted under a cloud of uncertainty about the constitutional legality of every act. When one adds this anticipatory factor to the ever-growing list of judicial intrusions into areas of activity historically governed by other institutions, it becomes clear that it is no longer possible to question the observation that we are, in many of the most vital aspects of life in the American polity, governed primarily by judges. Nagel's metaphor is that of "addiction": American society has grown "dependent" on the omnipresent, omnicompetent federal judge, who appears to have supplanted the priest of earlier times.[3]

Nagel concludes that "excessive reliance on judicial review" undermines long-term support for basic constitutional principles, impairs the "general health of the political culture," and works against "both the preservation and the healthy growth of our constitutional traditions."[4] I concur with these conclusions and, to an extent, with Nagel's location of blame in the intellectual habits of lawyers and judges.[5] Judges are unfit by temperament and unqualified by training to govern the American republic in most of the areas Nagel notes. At the same time, it cannot be denied that the intellectual habits of legal professionals are firmly grounded in the intellectual orientations of the more general culture; and as the analogy with the priest suggests, the "routinization" of judicial power, as Nagel refers to it, is a problem with deep roots.

One of the most important results of judicialization has been to turn virtually all discussions about the Constitution into discussions about the role of judges in its interpretation. Thus Soterios Barber, one of the few contemporary constitutional theorists who has tried hard to establish that the constitutional text "has to mean something that is independent of what anyone might want or believe it to mean,"[6] nonetheless states flatly that the primary dilemma of "mainstream scholars" is that of "justifying a strong and unapologetic exercise of judicial power in constitutional cases."[7]

An even more pointed illustration is offered by Michael Perry, whose *Morality, Politics, and Law* was the main subject of Barber's remarks.[8] Perry argues in his review of Barber's *On What the Constitution Means:*[9]

Barber insists that we must resolve the question how to conceive of the Constitution before going on to face the question what role the judiciary (and the other branches of government) should play. Yet, in a society, like American society, in which it is axiomatic that the judiciary should enforce the Constitution, the choice among competing conceptions of the Constitution is (in part) precisely a choice among competing conceptions of judicial role. In resolving the question how to conceive of the Constitution, we are resolving the question what role the judiciary should play. In that sense, the two questions are really one question: What conception of "Constitution/judicial role" ought we to choose?"[10]

Perry's equation of Constitution with court is pervasive in contemporary constitutional theory and has led to the idea, expressed by Mark Tushnet, that judicial review is "an 'all or nothing' proposition." According to Tushnet, "Either one allows judges to do whatever they want or one allows majorities to do whatever they want. Either choice is deeply anticonstitutional—which means, I suppose, that constitutionalism is self-contradictory."[11]

Constitutionalism may be a contradiction under any regime in which judicial review is "all or nothing"; but judicial review is "all or nothing" only under a theory of judicial supremacy that, by equating review with supremacy, presses opponents of the latter to deny the legitimacy of review itself. Yet judicial supremacy is neither inevitable as a matter of constitutional theory nor generally compelling when considered in the wider context of constitutional history. As was demonstrated in *Marbury v. Madison and Judicial Review*, the Supreme Court itself did not claim finality for its own constitutional interpretations until 1958,[12] nor did constitutional commentators until the early twentieth century.[13] And the Court did not assert any power to control the boundaries of constitutional authority assigned to other agencies of government until the late nineteenth century, except in "cases of a judiciary nature."[14]

Moreover, all presidential vetoes of congressional acts prior to the 1830s were justified on constitutional grounds and were accompanied by explicit, uncontested assertions of executive authority to interpret the fundamental law.[15] Further, most of the great debates in Congress during the antebellum period were arguments over the meaning of constitutional provisions, the record of which is permeated by assertions of legislative duty to interpret the Constitution both rightly and in accordance with accepted canons of construction.[16] Finally, in *Marbury and Review* the process by which the American legal establishment encouraged the development of judicial supremacy in the late nineteenth and early twentieth centuries, an encouragement that hardly would have been necessary had judicial supremacy always existed, was spelled out in graphic detail.[17]

Barber, apparently largely accepting the constitutional historiography presented in *Marbury and Review*,[18] questioned whether that history could be of any use in addressing the pressing constitutional problems of our time, given the absence in the book of a normative analysis of constitutionalism and democracy (among other things) and my alleged assumption of a readership that shares an "unexamined conception of democracy and finds normative significance in historical events, beliefs, and practices."[19]

There is much irony in Clinton's critique of academic moral relativism. Instead of defending the possibility of principled (and therefore "judicial") judgment in controversial cases, Clinton would narrow the scope of judicial review on the assumption that such a narrowing is necessary to avoid policy making (a "legislative" function) by judges. . . . This assumption suggests the moral skeptic's contention that policy choices are unavoidable in hard cases. In addition, moral conventionalism, a form of moral relativism, seems implicit in Clinton's preference for constitutional reasoning through historical research and the citation of precedent rather than the activity of fresh moral argumentation. . . . Clinton fails to confront arguments that conventionalist conceptions of constitutional meaning (and corresponding restrictions on judicial power) are inconsistent with the moral realism of the founding generation, *The Federalist's* elevation of substantive ends over institutional forms, and Marshall's preference for legal argumentation directed more to the practical commonsense of his readers than to their respect for formal authority.[20]

Although Barber is right to be concerned about the prevalence of relativism and skepticism in morals, his implicit equation of these attitudes with conventionalism, per se, is unfounded. There is a difference between law and morality, and a corresponding distinction between moral and legal conventionalism, that Barber and many other commentators appear to ignore. One may be a legal conventionalist without being a moral conventionalist (see Chapter 7).

Nor is moral conventionalism necessarily "a form of moral relativism"; the matter depends entirely on the basis of the convention(s) in question. There are principled reasons for adherence to tradition in certain fields of activity, in which instances the justification for following the conventions associated with such traditions will not itself be "conventional." And nowhere is this statement more apropos than in the field of Law. To say that the authority of traditions embodied in moral, legal, or social conventions rests upon a foundation no more secure than "the moral skeptic's contention" is, in effect, to deny that human beings have learned (or can learn) anything from millennia of documented (or documentable) collective experience.

Since democracy is a tradition that presupposes acceptance of a number of important conventions, to suggest, essentially without argument, that anyone who finds "historical events, beliefs, and practices" normatively significant thereby exhibits an "unexamined conception of democracy" is to beg fundamental questions about the extent to which particular conceptions of democracy (and other forms of government) are themselves rooted in historical events, beliefs, or practices. On the relation between tradition and democracy, G. K. Chesterton probably said it best:

It is obvious that tradition is only democracy extended through time. It is trusting to a consensus of common human voices rather than to some isolated or arbitrary record. . . . If we attach great importance to the opinion of ordinary men in great unanimity when we are dealing with daily matters, there is no reason why we should disregard it when we are dealing with history or fable. Tradition may be defined as an extension of the franchise. Tradition means giving votes to the most obscure of all classes, our ancestors. It is the democracy of the dead. Tradition refuses to submit to the small and arrogant oligarchy of those who merely happen to be walking about. All democrats object to men being disqualified by the accident of birth; tradition objects to their being disqualified by the accident of death. . . . We will have the dead at our councils. The ancient Greeks voted by stones; these shall vote by tombstones. It is all quite regular and official, for most tombstones, like most ballot papers, are marked with a cross.[21]

Barber's explicit identification of "principled" and "judicial" judgment, with its clear implication that only judges are capable of making principled judgments "in controversial cases" (or, alternatively, that if principled decisions are to be made at all, then judges will have to do it), though characteristic of much contemporary constitutional theorizing, is fundamentally wrong. It is at least arguably true that the modern Supreme Court, largely through unprincipled decisionmaking, has done as much as, if not more than, any other institution of government to foster the skepticism and relativism that Barber deplores. Had the Court, during the past century or so, taken more seriously the "normative significance of historical events, beliefs, and practices," especially in such areas as religion clause or equal protection jurisprudence, things might have turned out better.

Though Barber wishes to distinguish thinking about the Constitution from thinking about what the Supreme Court says about it, he betrays this distinction by refusing to take seriously the beliefs and practices that make up the larger part of the Constitution's history. Still, Barber's observation that in *Marbury and Review* I did not attempt to ground constitutional history in constitutional theory is essentially correct; hence one of my primary goals is to answer that objection. This book is an outgrowth of *Marbury and Review* in the sense that in it I did not attempt to address the issue of why anyone should regard the legal or constitutional history expounded in it as determinative for contemporary constitutional decisionmaking.

JUDICIAL POWER AND CONSTITUTIONAL THEORY

Constitutional law in the United States is an especially difficult problem for constitutional theorists today primarily because of the Court's advancing monopoly over constitutional interpretation. That is to say, ever since the Court's initial assertion, in 1958, of the conclusiveness of its own constitutional readings upon the other branches of government, the most controversial and widely discussed feature of American constitutionalism has been the role of the Court, not the meaning of the Constitution.

Although the preoccupation of scholars with the Court during the past four decades has been both inevitable and thoroughly justified, it is nonetheless true that this preoccupation has tended to obscure other important issues in constitutional law. For example, court-watching has led political scientists to an undue emphasis on judicial behavior and academic lawyers to an equally unproductive constitutional legalism. Emphasizing judicial behavior in relation to the legal formulas that are its natural result leads in turn to an unjustifiable preoccupation with the justiciable meaning of the written constitutional text, to the exclusion of the underlying nonjusticiable traditions and conventions that are presupposed by the text.

Preoccupation with the "writtenness" of the Constitution then serves, over time, to obscure certain questions. What is the degree of consensus required to differentiate a truly "constitutional" principle from any other kind of law (see Chapter 5)? What are the nature and extent of the unwritten practices, principles, and conventions required to sustain a viable constitutional order under a written constitutional instrument? What is the relationship between the words of the Constitution, viewed *in abstracto*, and the thoughts and experiences that produced those words (see Chapter 6)? What is the distinction between legal and moral rules and the bearing of this distinction upon constitutional order (see Chapter 7)?

Preoccupation with the judiciary has also led constitutional commentators to overemphasize "interpretation" and has made possible the recent rise of various forms of "textualism" in constitutional theory. Although the language of the constitutional text is rightly viewed as the point of departure for any inquiry into its meaning, prompting one of the cardinal rules of legal interpretation (see Chapter 9), it remains true that textual interpretation, narrowly conceived, is only one of several legitimate ways to understand constitutional reality. Moreover, under traditional approaches, a written legal text is not authoritative, per se; rather, it is considered useful because it is often the most reliable guide available for understanding its authors' intentions and purposes, which then constitute "the law."

Since words are spoken with the intent to convey meaning, and indeed have no meaning apart from such intentions, viewing a constitutional text, per se, as controlling the law effectively deconstructs the text. This view reduces the Constitution to a plethora of empty words and phrases with ever-changing content, useful perhaps as a set of general guidelines or a kind of blueprint, within or upon which courts or other deconstructive interpreters are expected to graft substantive rules and principles in order to keep an essentially meaningless text "in tune with the times."

Indeed, the blueprint metaphor has become so common among modern constitutional commentators as to have entered into the very *definition* of the term "constitution." For example, Michael S. Moore, a prominent contemporary constitutional theorist, defines "constitution" as "simply a political philosophy written down . . . a blueprint of the good society, and those who draft it should do so with just such a vision of what they are doing."[22]

Taken at face value (for what it *says*), Moore's statement seems harmless enough. On the other hand, if treated as a definition in the strict sense, where due regard must be paid to what it does *not* say (what it leaves aside as well as what it implies), it begins to appear overly parochial (not all constitutions are written), overbroad (the framers held differing conceptions of the Good), and dismissive (even if a constitution is a "political philosophy," it is surely not "simply" that, for no real political philosophy is "simply" anything).

The most important problem with conceiving a constitution as a written set of general guidelines whose interpretive possibilities are to be exploited subsequently by judges is that such an approach overemphasizes the prescriptive, future-oriented malleability of a constitution while denigrating its descriptive, historical givenness. Holding both these features in balance is essential to any viable constitutionalism; indeed, without such a balance, there is arguably no constitution at all.

At the same time, however defective the blueprint conception may seem from a logician's or a linguist's point of view, it undeniably captures the essence of a certain popularized contemporary impression of the Constitution that has been left in the wake of several decades of political and judicial manipulation. As such, it may be useful at this point to examine the impression more closely.

BLUEPRINT CONSTITUTIONALISM

Inasmuch as any viable constitution expresses, at some fairly general level, the fundamental principles of order in a political society, it follows that constitutions are best viewed as both prescriptive and descriptive. Constitutional rules cannot simply be made up by some group of sociopolitical elites functioning in the manner of an architect who draws a blueprint for a house. In Eric Voegelin's words, "The order of a society is not a blueprint to be translated, with good will, into reality. It must be discovered."[23]

Voegelin illustrates the point in his own discussion of the relationship between legal order and social reality in the genesis of the U.S. Constitution:

> The procedure by which the Constitution of 1789 was created had not been provided by the Articles of Confederation. In terms of procedural validity the Philadelphia Convention was a revolutionary assembly and the continuity of the legal order had been broken. Nevertheless, while the term *revolution* ordinarily is used in connection with events of 1776 and after, it is very little used in connection with the events of 1789—in spite of the fact that the constitutional continuity was broken and that not all the means for achieving ratification of the new Constitution in the several states fell under the heads of sweetness and reason. The peculiarity will become intelligible if the whole period, from the beginning of the movement for independence to the making of the Constitution of 1789, is considered one social process in which the growing nation, winding its way through the difficulties of intercolonial and interstate relations and the labors of the war, gained its power physiognomy and, after the unsatis-

factory experiments with the Continental Congress and the Articles of Confederation, at last found the Constitution that was valid and at the same time expressive of the authoritative power structure of the new nation. The genesis of the American Constitution in the events between 1776 and 1789 furnishes perhaps the finest object-lesson for the growth of authoritative power in a new society, accompanied as it was by superb craftsmanship in devising legal forms for the stable structure. The case is of special importance . . . because the protraction of the social process and the manner in which the questions of legality and constitutionality are subordinated to the questions of creating and ordering the nation leave no doubt whatsoever on which side the weight of the complex phenomenon of law lies.[24]

To define a constitution simply as a political philosophy congealed into a blueprint for a philosopher's vision of the good society or as a set of guidelines to be translated later "with good will, into reality" is to distort—or even to destroy—the underlying reality the term "constitution" is linguistically designed to represent. This underlying reality is essentially historical, relating the artificial symbolism of a written constitutional text to the real constitutional experiences from which that symbolism arises. The relationship is composed in a way that recognizes the tension between the constitutionally "given" and the constitutionally "made."

Moore's definition reflects a serious misunderstanding (and a somewhat cavalier usage) of the idea of "political philosophy." If philosophy *(philos + sophia)* is love of wisdom, and political philosophy is love of wisdom about right order in the polis, then the very concept of political philosophy fully presupposes the real or possible existence of a rightly ordered constitutional polity to be wise about. In *Minos,* Socrates queries, "What is Law, for us?" The reply: "Law is the discovery of what is."[25] Modern predilections aside, this much is as true for Hobbes as for Plato.

Thus a political philosophy, in any sense worthy of the name, is a larger perspective founded upon a notion of reality (even though kept in the background) from which are generated, and against which are measured, all efforts to frame political institutions, including "legal" and "constitutional" ones. In this sense, the constitutional system of any polity is derivative from, and thus subordinate to, its overall legal order (whether the constitution is a written legal instrument or not). And the legal order, in its turn, is fully subject to political ordering in the manner suggested by Voegelin.

To indicate that such a perspective might simply be "written down" is grossly to understate the range of political philosophy and grossly to overstate the range of constitutional legalism. If true, its effect would be to extend the range of constitutional legalism to the whole of political existence or, alternatively, to restrict the range of political philosophy to that which can be constitutionalized, legalized, or perhaps even trivialized. Indeed, the blueprint conception seems already to reflect a certain debasement of political theory in modern times, in which political philosophy is taken to stand for little more than anybody's (or any group's) favored set of "policy preferences." This way of talking gains support from the prevailing skepticism about ultimate values in today's academic establishment, from the ascendancy of behavioralism in modern political science, and from the vested interests of the legal establishment in promoting litigation.

In any case, not only is it impossible to reduce a political philosophy to a few pages of written text, but it is also impossible for a single writing (or multiple ones, for that matter) to capture fully the whole of a society's constitutional principles. At best, the provisions of a written constitution can provide an incomplete list of such principles and thus can be just a more or less adequate reflection of that society's real constitution. This observation becomes clear immediately upon traveling beyond our own borders into the larger constitutional universe. As Sir Henry Maine once said of John Austin's analytical jurisprudence, that it says far too much about far too little, so the same may be said of the parochialism of blueprint constitutional jurisprudence.[26] Just as Austin's notion of law tends to become incoherent when applied outside the domain of post-Roman Western European legal systems (see Chapter 12), so blueprint constitutionalism breaks down when applied outside the domain of American-style written constitutions.

It collapses because there is no distinction between written and unwritten constitutions sufficiently sharp to support its apparent disregard for constitutional traditions other than our own, even those upon which our constitutionalism unarguably draws, such as the English tradition. That the distinction is artificial may be shown most clearly by reflecting on the origins of the American Constitution, most of the salient features of which are anything but novel.

The blueprint definition also reflects, by implication, the error of assuming that the Framers were in full agreement on the particular blueprint that would constitute the good society. Perhaps they were, if by "blueprint" one means only to refer to the minimal, mostly procedural, provisions that structure the federal system and its government and that are largely apparent from the text itself. But if one goes beyond the text to substantive "values" (which most of those who espouse this conception of constitutionalism clearly mean to do), the assumption of such an agreement becomes questionable. If, as has been amply demonstrated by historical research, the Constitution was a "bundle of compromises," then it is plain that the Framers could not have been of one mind on all the issues pertinent to a substantive vision of the good society.

Even if they had been, since they were not authorized to institute the good society in the sense of importing their own substantive values into the Constitution for all time, it follows that, if blueprint constitutionalism is correct, then the Constitution is illegitimate. The Framers had no power to bind subsequent generations to their constitutional principles if such principles were nothing more than their subjectively preferred "blueprint of a just society." Indeed, arguably it was Jefferson's apparent adoption of such a view that led him to think the Constitution should be overturned every generation or so. Only if "constitution" is defined as a set of fundamental precepts so widely shared as to "constitute" the society over large stretches of time and thus be overturnable solely by extraordinary consensus does one generation have authority to bind another.

The distinction between procedural and substantive constitutional principles points to another, yet closely related, distinction between truly "constitutional" rules (e.g., first-order "decisional" rules) and substantive policy rules that happen to be "in the Constitution" either expressly, impliedly, or by judicial decision. Rules of the former kind are "rules about rule-making" and include rules of interpretation of the sort that I will pay closest attention to (see especially Chapters 9 and 10). Unlike substantive policy rules, procedural decision rules do tend to command general assent over long spans of time, largely because they can claim the support of long-standing traditions at the point of their subsequent explicit incorporation into a written constitution (i.e., they are generally "given") and thus do not reflect as many contingent factors as do substantive legal rules. The blueprint metaphor papers over this distinction much as it does that between procedural and substantive law.

Finally, since blueprint constitutionalism emphasizes writing rather than consensus as the essence of a constitution, it tends to obscure the all-important distinction between constitutional lawmaking and any other exercise in lawmaking for which it could be said plausibly that its drafters had a "vision," "blueprint," or "political philosophy" in mind; and this might be said of almost any exercise in lawmaking, under appropriate conditions. Taken to the limit, this view ultimately implies that a "constitution" is just like any other "law" and thus may be abrogated just as easily as any other law (i.e., without any showing of special consensus, such as the "special majorities" required for formal constitutional amendment in the United States) when its provisions are found inconvenient.

This idea is not completely novel. Jefferson appeared at times to espouse it, as did Edward S. Corwin a century later.[27] But in general it has been soundly rejected throughout two centuries of our national existence, and it is not difficult to see why. Adoption of any conception of the Constitution that blurs the line between constitutional and other kinds of law eliminates the need for the term "constitution" at all, and Americans have never been disposed to view their basic governing instrument as superfluous.

It may be concluded that contemporary constitutional theory is preoccupied with a constitutional text not regarded as historically compelling, meaningful per se, representative of a multigenerational historical consensus in the American polity, or symbolic of a wider constitutional experience. Rather, it pursues the idea of a general blueprint, the details of which must be filled in on a continuing ad hoc basis, combined with an "addiction" to judicial government. Such an approach effectively enthrones the judiciary as a kind of constitutional monarchy, overthrowing the republican form of government instituted at the Founding.

3 · Constitutional Interpretation and Judicial Review

Despite the recent overemphasis on the "writtenness" of the Constitution, the resulting undeserved prominence of textualism in contemporary constitutional theory, and other problems (see Chapter 2), it remains true that one of the most distinctive characteristics of the constitutional polity in the United States is its steady reliance for more than two centuries on a single written constitutional instrument. This feature of American constitutionalism virtually ensures not only that there will be continuing controversy about the way in which key terms in the Constitution are to be defined—usually termed the problem of "constitutional interpretation"—but also that the controversy will assume the shape of an argument between more or less "rigid" and "flexible" approaches.

Critics of modern judicial activism tend to argue in favor of more restrictive, or rigid, readings of constitutional provisions as a check on judicial innovation; supporters tend to favor more flexible readings so as to render the Constitution more malleable. Neither side is correct; or perhaps more precisely, both are partly right and partly wrong. On the one hand, the fact that the Constitution is Law leads to a justifiable demand for consistent application in cases over time, which in turn can lead to rigidity. On the other hand, the Constitution is also a governing instrument, which means that care must be taken to ensure that the ever-accumulating case law (and the courts that administer it) does not paralyze legitimate governmental functions, as many observers believe has happened in consequence of the individual rights–driven constitutional jurisprudence of the past forty years. Two obvious examples are the erosion of the political questions doctrine and the relaxation of traditional requirements regarding standing to sue.

Perhaps some additional clarity can be gained by attending to one of the realities of constitutional development, captured in a distinction between constitutional interpretation and constitutional construction that forms the basis of an excellent forthcoming study by Keith E. Whittington.[1] According to Whittington, the function of interpretation is to give effect to determinate constitutional meaning; the function of construction is to supply meaning for indeterminate portions of the constitutional text.[2] Though I will not follow Whittington's terminology in subsequent sections of this book, it will be wise to keep in mind the underlying constitutional reality that his terms represent.

Since interpretation is essentially a literary activity, it is especially well-suited for development by lawyers and judges. Thus it has tended to become the province of courts to "say what the law is" (adapting John Marshall's famous phrase) where the plausible determinacy of constitutional language has made possible a variety of purely interpretive approaches. Yet where the indeterminacy of certain portions of the constitutional text has required provision of constitutional meaning through the interplay of nonjudicial political forces, the result has been a kind of extralegal constitutional construction that, albeit principled, is nonetheless primarily a political activity necessarily involving nonjudicial actors and agencies. Thus it is largely unsuitable for courts. Examples would include the establishment of a national executive administration in the 1790s; the interposition, nullification, and secession controversies of the antebellum period; some famous impeachment controversies; or the recent conflict over the reach of executive power in foreign and military affairs.

Attention to the ubiquity and importance of constitutional constructions throughout American constitutional history makes it clear that constitutional development in the United States has been very much a "departmental" affair, involving the political branches and the administration of the national government as well as the states. (Whittington provides a long list and several in-depth case studies.[3]) That said, it may also be noted that much (probably most) of this developed during the first century of our national existence; tellingly, three of Whittington's four major case studies occur before 1870.[4] Whether or not those cases were selected by Whittington with this in mind, their symbolic import can hardly be denied in the face of Robert Nagel's observations, the modern erosion of the political questions doctrine and the rules of standing, and the Court's own pronouncements regarding its constitutional hegemony during the past forty years.

In any case, Whittington's study suggests that if, during the past 100 years, our constitutional system has been steadily progressing (or declining) toward judicial supremacy, it may be at least partly because courts increasingly have been entering the domain of constitutional construction and attempting to preempt other agencies of government by calling the activity "interpretation." But when judges go beyond the activity of applying determinate legal texts, where all the resources of traditional legal practice are available both to circumscribe their efforts and to justify their results, they enter an area in which they have neither special claim nor special competence.

Ironically, arguments in favor of judicial control of the Constitution are weighty only where the Constitution is fully "interpretable," i.e., where the courts can be chained to the rules of traditional legal practice that are directly applicable in the context of a determinate legal text. Thus textual indeterminacy should be considered fatal for any argument attempting to support an ultimate judicial guardianship of the Constitution. Yet arguments from the alleged "indeterminacy" of the constitutional text have most often been heard from proponents of judicial supremacy, not the other way around.

The whole point seems to have been lost in contemporary constitutional theory, where most commentators have failed to acknowledge any semblance of a distinction between the activity of drawing meaning from a determinate legal text and the very different activity of supplying meaning where no determinate text exists. Instead, the distinction appears to have been collapsed in contemporary constitutional theory through overextension of the domain of interpretation, resulting in a myopic preoccupation with interpretation in the narrower sense and a corresponding impression that all constitutional questions may (and should) be answered by courts. When one adds to this mixture the oft-acknowledged American penchant for converting conflicts of interest that are essentially political into legal disputes, and the plain self-interest of lawyers in assisting such conversions, perhaps it becomes easier to see why so many people find it difficult to imagine any alternative to government by judges.

CONSTITUTIONAL INTERPRETATION IN THE UNITED STATES

Throughout American history the meaning of important constitutional provisions and concepts, and sometimes the structure of the document as a whole, has been the subject of intense controversy. At least two of these controversies have had a lasting impact on the character and vocabulary of constitutional discourse in the United States and thus should be noted as background for any discussion of contemporary constitutional theory.

The earliest of the controversies originated in the ratification struggle between proponents and opponents of the Constitution and continued throughout the entire antebellum period. The terminological rubric was "strict construction" versus "liberal construction" and was most clearly applicable as a matter of judicial interpretation when confined to readings of the congressional power-granting provisions of Article 1 in conjunction with the necessary and proper clause. The most graphic illustration of the controversy may be found in the debate surrounding the Supreme Court's decision in *McCulloch v. Maryland*.[5] The Court, on the basis of a liberal interpretation of the necessary and proper clause, upheld the constitutionality of the Second Bank of the United States and denied the authority of Maryland to tax the bank's operations.

Viewing the implied powers of the national government on a continuum running from "most expansive" ("appropriate") at one end to "most restrictive" ("absolutely necessary") at the other, "strict interpretation" meant "more restrictively" and "liberal interpretation" meant "more expansively." The distinction began to break down after the Civil War, partly because the constructive outcome of the war gave force to the Court's earlier interpretive resolution of the controversy in favor of "more expansive" and partly because the Court in the laissez-faire era muddled the distinction by combining dual federalism (a perverse form of strict interpretation limiting the power of the national government through the Tenth Amendment) with substantive due process (an expansive reading of the Fourteenth Amendment limiting state power through "liberty of contract").[6]

The second of the controversies, "judicial activism" versus "judicial restraint," arose from this muddling of the distinction between strict and liberal interpretation (both liberty of contract and dual federalism representing forms of judicial activism) amid the "government versus business" ethos of the Gilded Age. Traceable perhaps to James Bradley Thayer's "reasonableness" rule, first advanced in the 1880s and later popularized by the Holmes-Brandeis wing of the Supreme Court, restraint became the maxim of most liberal constitutional theorists of the New Deal era and the hallmark of the Roosevelt Court.[7] It later became the hallmark of conservative thinkers who opposed the liberal activism of the Warren Court and remains viable today in the constitutional thought of commentators such as Wallace Mendelson, Christopher Wolfe, and Lino Graglia.[8]

The theory of constitutional interpretation underlying the doctrine of judicial restraint is quite complex, involving considerations of text, intentionality, rules concerning standing and justiciability drawn from Article 3's case/controversy provision, historic legal conventions, and prudential considerations.[9] The most important point to note here is that calls for restraint, like Thayer's rule, are conceivable only in an age of activism. To the extent that restraint means "self-restraint," it could not have been the main device intended by the Founders to curb judicial overreaching of the Constitution.[10]

However contentious the controversies surrounding issues of constitutional interpretation may have been during the first century and a half of national existence in the United States, in recent years the subject seems to have taken on added complexity. In the past two decades, a bewildering array of theories has emerged, generating debates on such issues as "structuralism," "originalism," "interpretivism," "textualism," "aspirationalism," and the like.[11] This recent interest in constitutional interpretation has resulted primarily from a sea change in the way the Supreme Court views its own role in constitutional adjudication and secondarily from the way in which contemporary constitutional commentators have responded to the Court's newly minted role.

During the antebellum period, constitutional interpretation was performed continuously by the three branches of the federal government. In the 1790s, debates in Congress on the meaning of key provisions in Articles 1, 2, and 3 shaped the contours of the federal government as it was to exist for a century and a half subsequently.[12] At the same time, during the first half-century of the Republic, presidential vetoes of congressional acts were exercised almost solely on constitutional grounds.[13] Finally, in *Marbury v. Madison* (1803), the Supreme Court successfully asserted its power to construe authoritatively constitutional provisions in such a way as to make possible their application as law, at least in the decision of cases involving the performance of judicial functions.[14]

In this early period, questions about constitutional meaning were not generally regarded as solely, or even primarily, judicial. Tocqueville's famous aphorism, according to which all political questions sooner or later developed into judicial ones, described a tendency rather than a reality, as had the earlier arguments of the Antifederalist Brutus.[15] When Jeffersonian Republicans and Jacksonian Democrats launched early attacks on the Court, they did so on the basis of a widespread belief that congressional or presidential interpretations of the Constitution were entitled to as much respect as those of the judiciary.[16] When Populists and Progressives of the late nineteenth and early twentieth centuries attacked the courts, their primary target was the institution of judicial review itself, not a particular theory of constitutional meaning.[17]

More recently, and especially during the past forty years, the Court has pressed its claim to be the primary organ of constitutional interpretation in the United States with increasing frequency, intensity, and success. The Court's assertion of constitutional guardianship has resulted partly from pressure from its leading constituents, partly from a growing legalization of American institutions generally, partly from abdication of constitutional responsibility by the political branches of government (usually for political reasons), partly from judicial aggrandizement, and partly from tendencies inherent in liberal democracy.

The first doctrinal assertion of this role came in 1958 when, in *Cooper v. Aaron* (the Little Rock school desegregation case), the Court claimed, for the first time in American constitutional history, judicial finality for its readings of the Constitution, thus in effect equating its own constitutional interpretations with the Constitution itself.[18] The legal peg that supported this maneuver was the Court's declaration that its own constitutional decisions, along with constitutional provisions, national laws, and federal treaties, possessed Article 6 "supreme law" status.[19]

The most important result of the Court's claim, supported by a growing number of legal scholars who engaged themselves in an effort to make the claim good, has been the emergence of judicialized constitutionalism. By now, nearly two generations of Americans have been brought up to regard Supreme Court decisions as virtually coterminous with the Constitution.[20]

JUDICIAL FINALITY AND JUDICIAL FREEDOM

Ironically, judicial monopolization of constitutional law has had the almost certainly unintended effect (at least for its adherents) of making the question of interpretive methodology even more urgent than it otherwise would have been. If constitutional interpretation, in the ultimate sense, is to be the exclusive province of a few federal judges who are not subject to the normal external constraints of democratic processes, it becomes even more essential that these judges be constrained to perform their interpretive function in accordance with high standards of internal accountability. That is to say, if politics is not to provide the required accountability, then the law itself must do so. Otherwise, judicial discretion will find its limit only in personal "will" rather than in "judgment" (borrowing Hamilton's phrase from *Federalist* No. 78), and judges will not be "under the law."[21]

The resulting paradox is this: precisely to the extent that judicial finality in constitutional law exists, arguments supporting judicial freedom in constitutional interpretation are correspondingly weakened. Conversely, to the extent that judicial freedom is maintained, especially in the choice of interpretive method, precisely to that extent is the assertion of judicial hegemony in constitutional matters rendered suspect. Judicial finality destroys judicial freedom by removing the external limits on judicial authority that make judicial freedom meaningful. Put another way, judicial finality destroys judicial accountability, and freedom without accountability is license in an individual and tyranny in a government.

That the Supreme Court has not been immune to the effects of this paradox has been recently (and aptly) noted by Justice Antonin Scalia, while dissenting from a portion of the Court's opinion in *Planned Parenthood of Southeastern Pennsylvania v. Casey* (1992).[22] Answering the objections of the now-famous "joint opinion" to continuing political attacks on the Court resulting from its abortion decisions, Scalia remarks that

> [as] long as this Court thought (and the people thought) that we Justices were doing essentially lawyers' work up here—reading text and discerning our society's traditional understanding of that text—the public pretty much left us alone. Texts and traditions are facts to study, not convictions to demonstrate about. But if in reality our process of constitutional adjudication consists primarily of making value judgments; if we can ignore a long and clear tradition clarifying an ambiguous text, [if our] pronouncement of constitutional law rests primarily on value judgments, then a free and intelligent people's attitude towards us can be expected to be (ought to be) quite different. The people know that their value judgments are quite as good as those taught in any law school—maybe better. If [the] "liberties" protected by the Constitution are

[undefined] and unbounded, then the people should demonstrate, to protest that we do not implement their values instead of ours. Not only that, but confirmation hearings for new Justices should deteriorate into question-and-answer sessions in which Senators go through a list of their constituents' most favored and most disfavored alleged constitutional rights, and seek the nominee's commitment to support or oppose them. Value judgments, after all, should be voted on, not dictated; and if our Constitution has somehow accidently [sic] committed them to the Supreme Court, at least we can have a sort of plebiscite each time a new nominee to that body is put forward.[23]

Scalia's remarks suggest that the recent preoccupation of legal academicians with theories of constitutional interpretation is the result of the modern fusion of judicial finality with judicial freedom in constitutional law, a fusion that has no basis in traditional legal practice. They also suggest that contemporary controversies over originalism, textualism, or interpretivism are best viewed as part of a larger, more significant historical struggle about the role of traditional practices generally in constitutional law. After all, originalism, textualism, and interpretivism are derived from a more general class of traditional rules, the justification of which must form the basis of any attempt to vindicate such approaches in the constitutional sphere.

Moreover, no theory of constitutional interpretation can be reasonably advocated without a fully articulate, complementary theory of judicial review. If, as Justice Scalia believed with respect to *Casey*, the Court is deciding constitutional cases that it does not have the legal authority to decide, its claim of power to determine the rules according to which the Constitution will be applied to the case (i.e., to engage in constitutional interpretation at the most fundamental level of exercising choice among first-order interpretive principles) is not a claim of right. It is a self-serving assertion of naked power and may be contested appropriately by extralegal (political) means.

Thus constitutional interpretation is not a matter that safely may be left exclusively to the courts, if this means that judicial applications are to be regarded as conclusive upon all other agencies of government no matter what the constitutional issue involved and that courts are entitled to determine without constraint the interpretive rules according to which such applications are to be made. Any theory of interpretation that affirms simultaneously both of these propositions is essentially a call for judicial supremacy. Such assertions fail to address the crucial question as to whether, and in what kinds of cases, judicial power to exercise constitutional review exists at all. In the language of modern statistics, judicial review and constitutional interpretation are highly intercorrelated variables with tightly woven circular effects.

For example, from the standpoint of constitutional legitimacy, a broad-gauged power of review that would authorize courts to overturn the acts of any other agency of government in any kind of case could hardly be joined sensibly with a noninterpretivist theory of meaning without substantially undermining the balance of constitutional forces underlying the separation of powers. Yet a theory of review that confined the judiciary's constitutional role to the protection of courts from the incursions of nonjudicial agencies (i.e., to "cases of a judiciary nature," to use Madison's phrase) would necessarily give wider latitude to judicial interpretations in the relevant cases.

Reasoning the other way, constitutional interpretation may be viewed as an independent variable with differential effects on the scope and extent of judicial review. For example, the textual foundation of judicial review is found in the conjunction of Article 3—which extends federal judicial authority to cases arising under the Constitution, laws, and treaties of the United States—and Article 6— which subordinates state laws to the same class of federal acts. Yet the respective meanings of Articles 3 and 6 are themselves matters of constitutional interpretation.

INTERPRETIVISM AND NONINTERPRETIVISM

If constitutional interpretation and judicial review are related in the way(s) that I have suggested, then a conception of review that authorizes the judiciary to overturn acts of other agencies of government with finality in virtually any type of case naturally implies a theory of interpretation that restricts judicial freedom to determine the rules of interpretation according to which constitutional meanings are supplied. The point is an important one because the terms of contemporary debate on constitutional interpretation have been shaped largely by the onset of the kind of broad-gauged, "final" judicial review that appeared initially in the 1950s. This is especially true of the controversy between interpretivists and noninterpretivists—a distinction that would have been virtually unthinkable in earlier times. Even though "strict versus liberal interpretation" and "restraint versus activism" were matters of controversy long before the advent of broad-gauged modern review, "interpretivism versus noninterpretivism" was not.

As Michael Perry has suggested, noninterpretive review became an issue only after the Supreme Court began to decide cases on the basis of values that could not plausibly be regarded as having been "constitutionalized by the framers."[24] Indeed, at least one prominent authority has suggested that the entire edifice of contemporary constitutional theory has been erected solely for the purpose of attempting to justify *Brown v. Board of Education* (1954) and its progeny.[25]

Whether or not contemporary constitutional theory is largely an apologetic for advancing judicial power, there does seem to be a measure of consensus among those commentators who presently disagree about the "right" way to interpret the Constitution that the scope of modern judicial review is very wide. Yet it is also true that the number and variety of constitutional decisions that cannot be justified under the logic of traditional interpretive rules are still comparatively small. And noninterpretivist judges have never constituted a majority of the Supreme Court's membership, even in its most activist phases.

Nor does it seem inevitable that the presence of a few decisions that go beyond the text or history of the Constitution, all confined to a particular era, signals a revolution in the underlying logic of our constitutional polity or requires trashing the fruit of centuries of accumulated legal experience by throwing out the traditionally employed rules of interpretation that are incompatible with those decisions. After all, we have long been forced to live, at least for short periods of time, with "bad" judicial decisions (and, in at least some instances, with legal academicians who thought they were "good"). *Dred Scott, Plessy v. Ferguson, E. C. Knight, The Income Tax Case, Lochner v. New York,* and *Hammer v. Dagenhart* come readily to mind.[26]

In some of the cases, reversal came about through constitutional amendment,[27] in others, through subsequent judicial decision.[28] The important point is that in most (if not all) such instances, the "bad" decisions were founded upon departures from traditional interpretive rules, and their subsequent reversal thus brought about a restoration of traditional constitutional principle.[29] Never did the question arise as to whether traditional practices ought to be scuttled in order to "save" the controversial decision.

Some observers will doubtless point out that most of the "bad" decisions were conservative ones protecting individual or institutional property rights against "good" regulations in the public interest, distinguishing those old decisions from such new, liberal ones as *Brown v. Board of Education, Griswold v. Connecticut,* and *Roe v. Wade,* which are said to protect more fundamental or important personal rights against unwarranted (i.e., "bad") governmental intrusions.[30] But this distinction is unfounded. As to the alleged fundamentality of personal (as opposed to property) rights, both logic and history cut against this distinction. Historically, property rights, broadly conceived, are the foundation of all other rights, without which there would be no existing institutions that could be adapted for the defense of such personal rights as privacy, equal treatment, or freedom of expression. Logically, all personal rights may be recast as rights of property. Indeed, to whatever extent such personal rights are legally relevant, they are nothing else than properties in those aspects of personhood deemed worthy of legal notice.

In Roman law, the distinction between persons and property is derived entirely from private law and is rooted in the difference between "persons" (who are capable of rights and duties) and "things" (which are the rights and duties themselves). With respect to the law of actions, the third main branch of Roman private law, the distinction is purely jurisdictional, expressing the difference between modes of attachment, between jurisdiction *in personam* and jurisdiction *in rem.*[31] English law, while preserving the jurisdictional distinction (e.g., in Blackstone's *jura personarum* and *jura rerum*), adds a substantive dimension in its distinction between real and personal property but has no separate category of rights that are conceived as purely personal and thus as nonproprietarian.[32]

The alleged contemporary opposition between personal and property rights, at least as this opposition is understood by most people nowadays, is thus without foundation either in nature or in law. In the constitutional field, the distinction is largely a result of the Supreme Court's political retrenchment in the wake of the New Deal crisis of the 1930s. In other words, the difference is wholly artificial and can claim neither a logical nor a historical warrant.

In answer to the argument that the old property rights were those of privilege and the new ones those of the underdog, not even this much can be granted. By far the largest part of the history of English common law is a story of the progressive development of legal institutions that would render the property rights and interests of feudal tenants more secure.[33] The story is one of hard-fought struggle, and the institutions therein devised cannot be cast aside without threatening the rights and interests of newer claimants as well. As Martin Shapiro has noted, many of the most controversial decisions of the modern era, especially those involving entitlements, are really "property rights" decisions masquerading as "human rights" decisions, thus collapsing the distinction between property rights and personal rights relied upon so heavily by proponents of modern judicial activism.[34]

On the public interest aspect of the distinction, the argument cuts both ways. Surely it is as plausible to argue, for example, that a decision having the effect of legitimizing up to 2 million abortions per year is not in the public interest as it is to argue that it is not in the public interest to allow employees to contract with employers for unlimited hours of labor. Just as surely, it is plausible to argue that the old system of segregated black schools did a better job of educating blacks than today's public school system does of educating anyone.

Even *Brown*, the sacred cow of contemporary constitutional law, has been subjected recently to a measure of critical scrutiny,[35] and its progeny has never really been regarded as sacrosanct.[36] For example, black scholars recently have questioned whether the ultimate effects of school desegregation have been favorable to black children[37] and whether affirmative action has been helpful or hurtful to the prospects of aspiring black professionals.[38]

It is simply too early to tell whether decisions like *Griswold* or *Roe* will suffer the same fate as *Lochner* and *Hammer*. Even if they do not, the recent "joint opinion" in *Casey*, however flawed, suggests that such decisions can be saved only by incorporation into traditional legal practice (i.e., only if they ultimately can be justified along the lines of traditional legal analysis).[39]

These considerations suggest that, despite the prevailing view among legal academicians that broad-gauged judicial review is a fait accompli, the jury is still out on the question. Though much of the discussion in subsequent chapters takes for granted the wide scope of modern review and thus focuses more heavily on the issue of interpretation, the fact that the question is not concluded on the scope of review, and the existence of the close relationship between scope of review and style of interpretation, demands that the former not be lost sight of during these discussions.

As I have argued before, I believe that restricting the scope of review is a more effective way to restrain judges than telling them how to interpret the Constitution.[40] Yet the persistence of those commentators who argue for noninterpretive modes of constitutional application despite the existence of broad-gauged judicial review necessitates a brief examination of contending versions of the origin and development of judicial review in historical perspective. This examination, with other arguments, should help further to clarify the historical basis of current disputes about the "right" way to interpret the Constitution.

4 · Judicial Supremacy and Judicial Review

JUDICIAL SUPREMACY IN CONSTITUTIONAL LAW

Constitutional interpretation and judicial review are inversely correlated. A conception of review that authorizes the judiciary to overturn acts of other agencies of government with finality in virtually any type of case naturally implies a theory of interpretation that restricts judicial freedom to determine the rules of interpretation according to which constitutional meanings are supplied. The possibility of "noninterpretive interpretation" of the Constitution was not advanced, and would hardly have been comprehensible, prior to the 1950s. The Supreme Court did engage in noninterpretive review before the 1950s, but until then, the Court did not claim judicial *supremacy* in constitutional law.

In earlier periods the Court had construed constitutional provisions in ways not authorized by the Framers, but since the Court did not combine these erroneous constructions with corresponding claims of judicial hegemony in constitutional interpretation, the ensuing controversies remained disputes about the meaning of particular constitutional provisions. More general questions concerning whether, and under what conditions, courts are entitled to depart from traditional rules for interpreting constitutional language did not arise. In other words, the rules of interpretation were taken for granted as was the inevitability of judicial mistake in their application.

But when the Court, in the 1950s and 1960s, began to claim judicial supremacy in constitutional law, scholars began to search for ways to constrain (and to empower) judges engaged in the performance of their newly asserted role of "supreme expositor of the Constitution." This search began with the work of Alexander Bickel and other commentators in the wake of the Supreme Court's decision in *Brown v. Board of Education* (1954). Among the more prominent ideas generated in the course of the search are Bickel's own "fundamental values," Herbert Wechsler's "neutral principles," Charles Black's "underlying structures," John

Hart Ely's "representation-reinforcement," and Jesse Choper's "structural-func-
tionalism."[1]

These efforts can fairly be described as attempts to provide a supportive theoretical framework for modern judicial supremacy by showing that judicial interpretation of the Constitution plausibly may be constrained according to some rule,
principle, or general interpretive approach. More recently, some scholars have
questioned whether these earlier "interpretivist" efforts will bear objective scrutiny and have openly advocated more subjective or noninterpretivist approaches.[2]
At the same time, with a few notable exceptions, interpretivists and noninterpretivists alike appear to have rejected, for the most part, at least one historic cardinal rule of interpretation: the maxim that a written legal instrument ought to be
read in accordance with the will of its maker(s)—in the constitutional field, the
rule of "original intent." There are at least two major reasons for this rejection.

First, as was demonstrated in *Marbury v. Madison and Judicial Review,* a limited
form of constitutional judicial review is firmly grounded in Articles 3 and 6 of the
constitutional text; yet no plausible reading of the relevant provisions will yield a
definition of judicial supremacy as a combination of judicial finality and judicial
freedom. Thus any constitutional theorist advocating both judicial supremacy and
originalist interpretation would appear to be arguing that a judge should follow
the Framers' intent except in regard to those provisions of Articles 3 and 6 that
are the textual basis of that judge's power to interpret the Constitution authoritatively in the first place. When even judicial conservatives have a hard time imagining any alternative to judicial supremacy, intentionalist interpretive approaches
become more difficult to defend.

The second reason already has been suggested in the discussion of blueprint
constitutionalism. The blueprint model effectively empties the Constitution of
historical meaning by a kind of deconstruction of the text. If the Constitution has
historical meaning, that meaning must be comprised—at least in part—in the mes-
sages its makers intended to convey. It follows that, to the extent that the blueprint
metaphor is influential in constitutional theory, the historicity, or "givenness," of
the Constitution will be seriously compromised thereby. Since the Constitution's
most important historical content is the meaning intended by its makers to control
the law, compromising the document's historicity defeats the intentions of the
makers.

To push these points a bit further, it will be helpful to examine briefly the history of judicial review in its relation to constitutional interpretation in the United
States. Since either the initiation or early development (if not both) of judicial
review is usually thought to have been chiefly a creature of *Marbury* and the Marshall Court, that case and Court will provide a convenient starting point for the
examination.

According to the prevailing view of American constitutional history, the problem of constitutional judicial review was settled in 1803 when, in *Marbury v. Madison*, the Supreme Court declared itself to be the primary organ of constitutional interpretation.[3] The theory that appears to be most widely accepted currently is that review was established in *Marbury* on the basis of a weak, but nonetheless existent, historical foundation composed of scanty but insufficient, or "inconclusive," justificatory materials in the pre-Founding, Founding, and early constitutional periods (i.e., the 1790s).[4] According to this theory, modern (broad-gauged) judicial review is explained and justified as an original "creative" fashioning by the Marshall Court that was later expanded by subsequent Courts in response to the demands of individuals and groups for judicial supervision of states, executives, and Congresses in accord with the growing "needs" of American society.

The problem of constitutional interpretation, on the other hand (so the story goes), was deemed solved by the judiciary's reading into the sometimes vague language of the Constitution "substantive values" or "fundamental principles" derived from natural law, the main purpose of which in the early nineteenth century was to protect vested rights of property.[5] According to this view, the "natural law/natural rights/property rights" approach to constitutional interpretation survived the Civil War, albeit becoming increasingly controversial between the 1870s and 1930s as American legal realism undermined its foundations.

Then, amid the 1930s Court fight over New Deal policy, the original constitutional consensus broke down, as the Supreme Court thoroughly repudiated the jurisprudence of laissez faire—which, some observers say, had been merely the latest manifestation of the earlier "natural rights" approach to constitutional decisionmaking.[6] The full implications of this breakdown, however, were not recognized completely until the 1950s, when Alexander Bickel and other scholars began to point toward a new era of constitutional adjudication based on the idea of "fundamental rights and liberties."

Though certainly not identical with it, this historical perspective owes much to the constitutional revisionism that was produced by certain controversies of the Progressive Era, some of which involved the legitimacy of judicial review itself. According to the progressive view in general, the U.S. Constitution was a product of the class interests of economic elites during the Founding era who feared the rise of a participatory democracy. They sought to insulate their property by the institution of a Madisonian system of government that would both minimize the political effects of the age-old cleavage between rich and poor and maximize the extent of legal protection afforded to wealth by a system of courts conditioned to guard vested interests under private law.[7]

Not surprisingly, due to its nonelective aspect, the Supreme Court has often been thought a ready-to-hand example of the Constitution's allegedly "undemocratic" character.[8] The Marshall Court's "establishment" of judicial review has likewise been regarded as an attempt to consolidate the Federalist program for protecting property rights in the wake of that party's defeat in the election of 1800.[9]

Historically, the progressive theory has led to two opposing views regarding the legitimacy of judicial review. The first, prominent among some early twentieth-century critics of the Court, regards judicial review to be completely illegitimate, a usurpation wholly unjustified by Founding-era practices and principles.[10] The second view is fashionable among many contemporary commentators and holds that, though review cannot be justified on legal or constitutional grounds, neither can any other practice—including nonreview. Thus review is just another political practice like any other kind of policymaking and need only be justified accordingly.[11]

From the latter view, we get the idea that modern judicial review is essentially "legislative" rather than "adjudicative" or "interpretive."[12] From the former view, we get the familiar impression that judicial review—even though we may like it—was nonetheless "conceived in sin" and thus is in need of continual justification. From the confluence of these views comes the idea that judicial review—and the constitutional law that follows from it, whatever its "real" constitutional basis—is largely a judicial creation, the application of which therefore must be a matter of judicial discretion.

From the standpoint of constitutional interpretation, the most significant feature of the constitutional picture that emerges from these views is that of a written text that is seen (by contemporary constitutional theorists) to be, throughout the entirety of American constitutional history, a plethora of procedural (i.e., non-substantive) forms and ambiguous substantive phrases. Of course, these phrases are nonetheless really nonsubstantive because, strictly speaking, they have no definite content.

Nonetheless, since the courts must apply the Constitution as law *(Marbury)*, its provisions must contain enough substance to resolve concrete disputes. This, in turn, requires a continual infusion of meaning from some source external to the Constitution itself. The two main alternative sources are, in all eras, either rules of traditional practice (external to the Constitution but internal to the common law) or prevailing social, economic, moral, or political ideologies (external both to the Constitution and to the common law).

Since most contemporary constitutional theorists seem to think that ideology has played a larger role than legal practice in American constitutional history, the basic structure of our constitutional situation is determined, according to this view, by the coexistence of empty constitutional forms and extralegal substantive principles. Our constitutional problem thus becomes that of supplying the "right" set of principles derived from the "appropriate" source, which, according to many commentators, is exactly what the courts have been doing (or trying to do) from the beginning.

This conception of American constitutional history is fundamentally wrong.

First, the early development of judicial review in the United States cannot be regarded plausibly as a usurpation of legislative authority because, as Christopher
Wolfe has persuasively demonstrated, judicial review in the Founding era was not
regarded as "legislative" in any sense.[13] And if review was not legislative, then it
cannot have been justified on grounds of policy (contra modern critical legal theorists and behavioralistic political scientists).

Second, judicial review was not conceived in sin. There are ample historical
materials available to show that review, when appropriately constrained by limitations inherent in the judicial function, was (or at least was in the process of rapidly
becoming) a well-accepted institution by the time of the drafting and adoption of
the Constitution and certainly by 1800.[14] Moreover, modern, aggressive judicial
review clearly did not develop in the incremental, "progressive" manner claimed
by many of its adherents. Rather, the history of its development occurred in an
uneven fashion, characterized by fits and starts, and its crucial points may be found
in 1895 and 1954.[15]

Thus modern, broad-gauged review cannot be justified as a normal outgrowth
of common-law decisional processes, or on policy grounds, or on the nihilistic
ground that, since nothing at all can really be "justified," judicial review does not
need to be justified either. Neither can it be vindicated on the skeptical ground that
constitutional meaning is, and always has been, unclear (and so interpretation is
always debatable).

JUDICIAL REVIEW IN THE UNITED STATES

Sylvia Snowiss has persuasively argued in a recent book that judicial review was
already established by 1800 but only as to relatively "clear cases."[16] *Marbury v.
Madison* did not alter this but established a clear precedent for the Court's power
to disregard congressional laws in cases "of a judiciary nature"—i.e., cases in
which judicial functions were threatened by application of a questionable statutory
provision.[17] *Marbury* "established" only that the judiciary would play an important
role in constitutional interpretation, not that it would be the sole, or "ultimate,"
constitutional interpreter. The idea that some single organ of government has to
possess such authority is a product of the late nineteenth and early twentieth centuries, the Supreme Court never claiming for itself such an authority before the
1950s.[18]

Moreover, after *Marbury* the Court did not invalidate another act of Congress
until the 1850s.[19] Neither did it cite *Marbury* in support of judicial review before
the 1880s nor in support of broad-gauged review until the 1950s.[20] Between the
1890s and the 1930s, the Court did invalidate both federal and state laws in larger
numbers, with greater frequency, and according to constitutional meanings not
fairly attributable to the Framers. But as Christopher Wolfe has aptly noted, in this
"transitional era," though the Court

established a new form of judicial review by elevating one phrase of the Constitution (the due process clause) to a high level of generality and permitting the judges to engage in broad policy-making by their application of that provision to economic regulation . . . because they identified the Constitution with a particular understanding of "natural law" (and its applications), the judges who brought about and employed this new form of judicial review seem to have been convinced that they were simply carrying on the traditional era's principle of faithful interpretation of the Constitution. The more definitive change in the nature of judicial review did not occur until judges not only employed a broad legislative form of the power, but also did so on the basis of a new theoretical understanding of it.[21]

This "new theoretical understanding" emerged in the 1950s and gave rise to the contemporary controversy over constitutional interpretation—a controversy that is not only about the "right" way to interpret constitutional provisions but also about whether courts should be confined to basing constitutional applications on legitimate "interpretations" at all.

As to natural law, even though the turn-of-the-century Court might have thought that its reading of the due process clause(s) was founded upon eighteenth-century natural law principles, its reading of history was palpably mistaken. On the one hand, the laissez-faire judges ignored precedent. Natural law (even in its eighteenth-century form) was never an explicit, generally acknowledged source of constitutionally justiciable principles for the Court; it was rather a collection of highly general theoretical principles that were no doubt subscribed to by almost everyone—just because of that generality.

On the other hand, such principles, by themselves, would have been but of little use to courts trying to resolve concrete legal disputes because their implications for particular controversies were not clear enough to render such applications uncontroversial. Judicial application of natural law in actual cases accordingly would have resulted in an intolerable indeterminacy in constitutional litigation. Though a few justices flirted with a "natural rights/fundamental law" approach in the 1790s, the Marshall Court's early rejection of such an approach in the first decade of the nineteenth century was thus largely inevitable.[22]

An example may serve to illustrate some of these points. It has often been thought that the Court's liberty of contract decisions of the laissez-faire era can be viewed plausibly as extensions of an earlier American commitment to economic liberty derived from natural law. To be sure, this commitment was grounded in a much broader notion of liberty in general that was characteristic of natural law thinking in the eighteenth century (as contrasted to that which emerged later in the nineteenth century). Likewise, it is probably fair to say that there was a strong influence of a certain type of natural law thinking on the late nineteenth-century Supreme Court.

The trouble is that the kind of natural law theory to which the late nineteenth-century Court was responsive had little to do with the natural law ideas that had been prominent a century earlier. Natural law in the age of industrialization, reflecting the ultimate triumph of Hobbesian atomistic materialism in the United States, was rather the peculiarly truncated version associated with the Social Darwinist ideology of Herbert Spencer and his followers, as was cogently pointed out by Justice Holmes in several famous dissenting opinions.[23] It was exactly this truncation that enabled the Court to implement certain features of the laissez-faire program when deciding constitutional cases and that has subsequently enabled contemporary commentators and judges to ascribe to that program a natural law basis.

However well-intentioned the judges who put laissez-faire justice into effect, it was nonetheless the program of a relatively small group of lawyers, businessmen, and intellectuals who were able to enlist federal judges for a time in what was essentially a project of self-aggrandizement.[24] The ultimate failure of the Supreme Court to recognize that the project had little to do with constitutional principle, properly understood, was one of the most important factors leading to the constitutional crisis of the 1930s. That crisis, in its turn, led to the creation of the *Carolene Products* jurisprudence of the post–New Deal era, with its double-tiered standards of review and artificial distinctions, e.g., between personal and property rights.

The fact that well-meaning judges could so easily have mistaken class interest for constitutional principle points with some clarity to the main thesis of this book, at least as to the problem of the judicial role in constitutional law. It comes to this: the best way to ensure judicial accountability in a constitutional system governed by a nonelective judiciary is by tying judicial interpretation of the Constitution very closely to traditional modes of legal analysis. Alternatively, if traditional rules of interpretation are rejected, then fidelity to our constitutional system requires rejection of an ultimate judicial guardianship of the Constitution.

THE MYTHICAL CHARACTER OF THE PROGRESSIVE REVISION

The judicial behavior that has come to be known as laissez-faire justice, and that led to the court-packing crisis of the 1930s, also sparked the development of a major reinterpretation of American constitutional historiography, accomplished by progressive historians in the early twentieth century, and made it seem a plausible account of the American Founding. The progressive revision, predominant in various forms throughout most of the present century, has bred much cynicism as well as some myths that support such an outlook.

For instance, it has become commonplace to think that "constitutions are political documents," that "judges are policy-makers—especially when deciding constitutional cases," and that constitutions are not "really" fundamental laws. After all, if the framers themselves were just another gaggle of fearful politicians seeking to secure their power, prestige, and possessions against the unbridled envy of the masses, it is hard to imagine that any other group of constitutional elites would be any different.

This set of impressions is a distortion of reality brought about by a subtle method of converting statements that contain small grains of truth into generalizations that are flatly false. Widespread belief in the truth of such generalizations ultimately raises such statements to the status of full-blown, destructive myths about the way in which our polity and its citizenry are constituted.

Foremost among these myths is the proposition that written constitutions are "political documents." The sense in which this statement is true is obvious, pointing to the distinction between interpretation and construction already discussed. There are always political forces involved in the promulgation of a constitution since the main purpose of such an enterprise is the establishment of a structured polity. The representation and slavery compromises at the Philadelphia Convention in 1787 are obvious examples.

But the declaration of such an obvious truth is not the sense in which the "political document" statement is normally uttered; indeed, there would be little sense in uttering it at all if that was the intended meaning. Rather, something like the following is usually meant: "Constitutions, even more than ordinary laws, represent the efforts of some elite group in society to perpetuate its long-term political and/or economic interests at the expense of other groups and, as such, should be regarded with an even larger measure of suspicion than, say, statutes (i.e., constitutions are less lawlike than other kinds of law). Thus courts are entitled to approach the interpretation of constitutional provisions with a greater degree of latitude than when interpreting other laws."

Whereas the first statement, proposing the meaning almost never intended by the "constitution as political document" is true, the second statement, proposing a large measure of suspicion and the consequent judicial latitude, which is the meaning almost always intended, is false. Constitutions, which embody fundamental substantive principles and first-order procedural rules, generally represent a far wider consensus of political opinion in society than do ordinary laws, and the compromises effected thereby operate at a higher level of generality. Thus constitutions are *more* lawlike than less general forms of lawgiving, and deviation from settled constitutional rules will inevitably have more far-reaching repercussions in the polity than will deviation from rules of lesser generality. If this is not true, then it would indeed be fair to say, with Mark Tushnet,[25] and in accordance with the logic of constitutionalism already outlined, that our notion of constitutionalism itself is a destructive myth and should be discarded. We should, then, devalue constitutional rules in direct proportion to their judicially mandated changeability.

Another pervasive contemporary myth in constitutional law holds judges to be "policymakers" or courts to be "policymaking institutions." As in the "political document" example, the truth in the statement, that judicial decisions have important policy implications, is trivial and thus is almost never its intended meaning.

Rather, the usual point being made by the commentators who assert this proposition is far stronger (and more questionable). In their view, judges are conceived as utterly incapable of deciding cases on any grounds other than underlying "policy preferences" derived from social, economic, or professional class interests, political party affiliation, diet, race, gender, or almost any other nonlegal motive that may be conceived as an independent variable in a regression equation (whether or not the judges in question are aware of the underlying motivation). The point is to convey a general impression that judges are incapable of deciding cases "according to law" and thus that constitutional judicial decisions are invariably "subjective."

The notion that constitutions are not really fundamental laws is obviously wrong in at least two senses. First, some constitutional principles command near-universal assent and thus may serve as the basis for a consensual constitutionalism, even if not all provisions "in the Constitution" can do so. Second, the continued existence of those extraordinary majorities required to put new provisions into (and to remove old provisions from) the Constitution suggests that our society is not yet prepared formally to collapse its constitutional law into other types of law and that it is not yet inclined to regard the Founders as just another legislative body (even if a superlegislature) bent on writing its own class interests into the fundamental law.

THE JUDICIALIZATION OF ADMINISTRATIVE LAW

Judicialized constitutionalism presupposes widespread acceptance of the judicial monopoly in constitutional law as well as uncritical acceptance of certain myths. If the Supreme Court has sole and final authority to determine the meaning of all (or nearly all) federal constitutional provisions, as well as freedom to choose the rules of interpretation that will aid in that determination, then we have government by judges in the sense that, though Congress and state legislatures continue to enact statutes that affect individuals and groups through executive officials and administrative agencies, the lines of authority that circumscribe these efforts are increasingly determined by courts.

The preceding discussion, however, should not be taken to mean that judicialization has been confined solely to the field of constitutional law. Given the pervasive (and often undifferentiated) effects of constitutional law in contemporary American society due to the high visibility of important constitutional cases, it is hardly surprising that such judicialization has not been confined to the constitutional arena. It has spilled over into other areas of the law, especially that of administrative law—its closest relative.

Administrative law in the United States is largely a development of the last half-century (though its foundations were laid much earlier). An early twentieth-century struggle between common lawyers (who wanted to prevent the rise of administrative adjudication) and regulators (who wanted to forestall judicial supervision of administrative agencies) resulted finally in the passage of the Administrative Procedure Act of 1946.[26] The act adopted a compromise solution that allowed agencies to adjudicate, subject to judicial review by the regular courts on final agency decisions, but only on legal—not factual—issues.[27]

The act also featured a bifurcated standard of review. For adjudication, an agency determination was to be upheld unless "substantial evidence on the record as a whole" indicated otherwise, but an agency *rule* was to be upheld unless "arbitrarily and capriciously" made (one version of the famous "lunacy test").[28] Moreover, the act's standards governing rulemaking proceedings were primarily those of notice, comment, and publication.[29]

The compromise did not endure for long. In the 1960s and 1970s, the federal courts (especially the District of Columbia Circuit Court, which sooner or later deals with most appeals involving federal agencies) began to effect a shift away from the restrictive approach of the act, imposing evermore stringent requirements on agencies, especially in rulemaking. This change was accomplished largely through judicial development of the idea of "agency deliberation."[30]

Agency deliberation developed primarily as a gloss upon the original notice, comment, and publication requirements of the act. First, standing to participate in rulemaking proceedings, and to challenge in court rules already enacted, was expanded. Second, the notice requirement was expanded so as to increase the effectiveness of comments. Third, a "dialogue" requirement was introduced, forcing agencies to respond to all "significant" comments by "interested" or "affected" parties. Fourth, in order to formalize and enforce the dialogue requirement, courts imposed the additional requirement of a "rulemaking record." Finally, the courts imposed a requirement that agencies take a "hard look" at all the evidence bearing upon a proposed regulation (the so-called "hard look" doctrine) and then further required that agencies actually base their decisions on that evidence (the so-called "reasoned decision" criteria).[31]

As Martin Shapiro has aptly noted, the effect of these measures has been the imposition by courts on agencies of nothing less than a completely new style of decisionmaking.[32] Shapiro terms it "synoptic," to contrast it sharply to the traditional, customary style that has characterized most agency decisionmaking in the past, which is termed "incremental."[33]

Shapiro also notes the main problem with this kind of judicial intrusion. Since synopticism is based on a philosopher's style of "discourse" and is therefore "elitist," the imposition of such a strategy on agencies, which are already in a tenuous position from a constitutional standpoint, further exacerbates the constitutional problems of the so-called "fourth branch."[34] Moreover, since the new approach is being imposed not by electorally accountable policymakers but by independent federal judges, the problem of agency responsibility is transferred to the "third branch" as well—hence, the title of Shapiro's book, "*Who Guards the Guardians?*"[35]

It is true that Congress by now has legitimized most of the judiciary's agency deliberation agenda by writing more expansive standing, notice, and record requirements directly into statutes creating agencies and programs.[36] But the more important point is that these statutes were not innovative; they merely imposed standards developed by courts while glossing the Administrative Procedure Act, and thus they have generated a largely judge-made (i.e., judicialized) administrative law.

The process of judicialization that has occurred in administrative law during the past three decades is a compressed version of that which has taken place in constitutional law during the past century. Just as administrative law has been employed to bring agencies under the control of courts, constitutional law has been used to bring legislatures under their control. Just as the act's procedural requirements in adjudication have been extended in many respects to rulemaking, so have procedural requirements of the Constitution been extended in many respects to lawmaking (e.g., as in the modern development of substantive due process). Just as the courts have used administrative law to control the character and scope of agency rules, so have they used constitutional law to control the character and scope of congressional delegations of rulemaking authority. Just as the courts have used administrative law to control jurisdictional boundaries within the administrative state, so have they used constitutional law to control the boundaries of power between executive and legislative institutions generally.

The pervasive influence of the judiciary in the late twentieth century is apparent in virtually every phase of American life. Some of this influence has been salutary; some, in my view, has been disastrous. Yet whatever one thinks of these results, the difficulty of squaring the method by which we have reached them with the institutions of a democratic republic is and always has been patently obvious. To the examination of this difficulty we shall now turn.

Part Two · The Anglo-American Constitutional Experience

In Part One, my purpose was to describe how judicialized constitutionalism developed from the relationship between judicial review and constitutional interpretation. Judicial supremacy is defined as the power to determine with finality (i.e., with conclusive effect on other agencies of government) both the mode of constitutional interpretation and the meaning of constitutional provisions. Judicial supremacy is thus described as the conjunction of judicial finality in constitutional law with judicial freedom in constitutional interpretation.

The rise of judicial supremacy has in turn encouraged among constitutional commentators a way of thinking about constitutions that includes an image of the Constitution as a written blueprint to be manipulated and imposed by judicial interpretation. This model, which stems largely from an overemphasis on the writtenness of the constitutional text, leads to fluctuating extremes of rigidity and fluidity in constitutional law and undermines some of our most important constitutional traditions.

In Part Two, I explore the theoretical foundations of such an approach and contrast it to the main alternative in Anglo-American constitutional jurisprudence: the British Constitution, which is consensual, traditional, and unwritten.

In Chapter 5, I contrast classical constitutional theory (also consensual, traditional, and unwritten) to modern liberal democratic constitutional theory, using Kenneth Arrow's famous impossibility theorem to critique the latter. Many of our recent constitutional troubles stem from a failure to understand that a radically individualized decision process in regard to the choice of what kind of life is good for human beings is fundamentally incompatible with certain minimal requirements of democracy. Judicial supremacy in any extreme form also brings the polity uncomfortably close to a variant of Arrovian dictatorship.

The focus of Chapter 6 is on the important distinction between written and unwritten constitutions. A modern American conception of constitutional law, as a series of judicial glosses on a written constitutional text, is contrasted to a more traditional English conception, represented by the definition of A. V. Dicey, as the set of rules affecting the distribution of sovereign power. Our current preoccupation with the writtenness of the Constitution is ahistorical. It was not even subscribed to by John Marshall, who is often held to have been an archetypical constitutional literalist (see *Marbury v. Madison* on the "nature of a written constitution"). It is also self-defeating and leads to a wooden, formulaic constitutional jurisprudence that, by selectively overextending some constitutional symbols while neglecting the experiences that caused their adoption, generates constitutional instability.

In Chapter 7, the important distinction between law and morality will be considered, with an emphasis on the way in which the distinction plays out in debates over the public and the private in law and over the real versus the conventional in both law and morals. Contemporary constitutional theorists who recommend that judges scuttle conventional morality in constitutional and other kinds of cases, imposing instead more recently minted, personally favored moral values, are obligated to demonstrate that such impositions are fully justified because they are founded in a theory of human nature powerful enough to gain wide acceptance. Few, if any, such commentators have come close to meeting such a demand.

In Part Two, I argue that text-preoccupied, judicialized, blueprint constitutionalism is theoretically bankrupt. It cannot provide the groundwork for a truly viable constitutionalism, which must respect tradition, convention, and the dominant social consensus.

5 · Constitutionalism in a Liberal Democracy

In the deepest sense, constitutional principles are so widely shared in a particular society that their general application and acceptance is part of that society's self-definition, its "character." Put etymologically, such principles literally "constitute," or "make up," an authoritative social order. In this sense, all societies that have attained reasonably high levels of sociopolitical self-definition have "constitutions."

As Plato once taught, a similar logic applies to individuals, to whom we often refer, for example, as having distinctive "characters" or as possessing "strong" or "weak" constitutions. After describing the constitution of a tyrannical city, Plato turns to the individual whose psyche is representative for such a polis:

> Then if man is like city, . . . there must be the same arrangement in him; his soul must be laden full of slavery and ungenerousness, and those parts of the soul which were most decent are enslaved, but the small part most mad and abominable is master. . . . Is not, then, the harvest of evils much greater for that man to reap who has an evil constitution in himself, the tyrannical man whom you have just judged to be most miserable, if he does not live out his life as a private person, but if he is compelled by some chance to be tyrant himself, and tries to rule others when he cannot be master of himself? It is just as if one sickly in body, and so not master of himself, should be compelled to live his life not in private but always contending with other bodies, at war his whole life long.[1]

The undeniably political component in such attributions refers to the ways in which different individuals respond to, and attempt to control, environmental forces. Such responses usually, if not always, involve decisionmaking (however inchoate) at some level of the psyche, suggesting that individual constitutions, no less than political ones, are, at bottom, predispositions to make decisions in distinct, particular ways. Moreover, it is the continuity and consistency of such personal constitutions that provide the individual integrity and identity without which social life would be impossible.

On the other side of Plato's anthropomorphic equation stands the well-constituted state—the continuity, consistency, integrity, and identity of which is the groundwork of the personal security that makes individual freedom and its derivatives possible. Just as the well-constituted individual is an extraordinary and continuous confluence of otherwise dissolute passions governed by reasoned habituation in the psyche, so the well-constituted society is an extraordinary and continuous consensus of otherwise fragmented interests governed by reasoned habits of deliberation and decision. The essence of a constitution, whether personal or social, lies in this consensus of forces. For Plato,

> The tyrannical man would be in one likeness with the city under a tyrant, and the democratical man with the city under democracy, and so with all the others. . . . Then what city is to city as to virtue and happiness, that man is to man.[2]

Here it is important to stress that, under Plato's analysis, there is no "conflict," in the modern, Hobbesian sense, between the "individual" and "society" (see Chapter 11). That alleged conflict is a fiction of modern political science that arose from the necessity of providing a theoretical justification for the early absolutism of the modern nation-state. For Plato, there is no "society" with "interests" that stand opposed to those of a hypothetical, abstracted "individual."

The relationship between the individual and society is best described as a "tension" within the soul of every individual between interests held in common with others and interests that are particular. There are no merely "social" interests separate from the individuals who are interested in them, nor are there merely "individual" interests devoid of social implications. The balance of forces comprised in this tension may surely differ from one to another individual, just as the balance of aggregates may differ from one society to the next.

The criminal's particular interest in escaping punishment, at least temporarily and from his own point of view, may outweigh his more generally shared interest in living in a peaceful, orderly society; yet the criminal, as much as the law-abiding citizen, needs safe streets in order to thrive. Moreover, he needs effective punishment (for Plato a combination of retribution and rehabilitation—see the *Laws*) so as to bring the psychic conflict between his own purely particular and his more general interests into equilibrium. The constitutional problem, par excellence, is the need to effect a stable resolution of the natural tension between individual and social interests—a symbiosis the balance of which may lie on the side of conflict or consensus, depending on the cultural milieu in the given instance.

ARROW'S CONSENSUAL CONSTITUTIONALISM

Plato's constitutional anthropomorphism, perhaps somewhat surprisingly, finds a measure of confirmation in the politico-economic analysis of Nobel laureate

Kenneth J. Arrow. According to Arrow, there are basically three general types of social choice process: (1) the rule of authority, or dictatorship, based on the "will of one"; (2) the rule of custom, tradition, or convention, based on the "will of all"; and (3) the system of capitalist democracy, based on the will of many, whether political (voting) or economic (the market).[3]

Neither authority nor custom presents a problem for the constitutional theorist, so long as priority is given to the determinateness of the social choice. In the case of authority, only one will counts in the determination of the social choice; and, in the case of tradition, individual wills are presumed not to be in conflict. Democracy, however, presumes conflict among individual wills while conceding the necessity for resolving such conflict by some procedure that both results in a determinate social choice and is faithful to the preferences, tastes, and values of the conflicting individual wills.

These requirements, taken together, generate the fundamental question Arrow poses in his celebrated *Social Choice and Individual Values:* Is it possible to construct a procedure for translating known individual tastes, values, preferences, and so on into social decisions without the choice being either imposed (e.g., by custom, convention, or tradition) or dictatorial (e.g., by authority)?[4] Using a set of reasonable assumptions concerning the rationality of the decision process, together with some minimalist constraints on the environment in which decisions are made, Arrow proves that the answer to the question is negative.[5]

If Arrow's analysis is correct, it follows that constitutional decision procedures, even in modern pluralist democracies based on voting, cannot, at least in some sense, escape being either imposed or dictatorial. This result in turn suggests that it may be necessary, in the last analysis, to consider whether the relevant aspects of imposition or those of dictatorship are preferable in the establishment of constitutional procedures for a democratic society. However, it will be useful first to examine Arrow's result more closely.

The reasonableness of Arrow's assumptions and conditions is easy enough to demonstrate. Arrow assumes a polity in which individuals vote sincerely (not strategically) according to tastes, values, or preferences that are autonomously chosen (not a function of the decision process itself) and expressible as a weak ordering (i.e., they need not be interpersonally comparable).[6]

If any of these assumptions does not hold, then elements of imposition or dictatorship are already present in the social choice process. If individuals vote strategically rather than sincerely, the outcome will be subject to determination by the set of voters who possess a higher degree of strategic competence in the manipulation of electoral outcomes. If individual preferences are not autonomous, then they are heteronomous and thus imposed by something (or someone) other than the individuals whose preferences it is the business of democratic elections faithfully to register. If individual preferences are not expressible even as a weak ordering, then they are self-contradictory and thus automatically irrelevant to any rational decision process.

Arrow expresses the last in his statement of the following "axioms of individual rationality":[7]

Axiom I: For any alternatives x and y, x is preferred or indifferent to y, or y is preferred or indifferent to x (connectedness).

Axiom II: For any alternatives x, y, and z, if x is preferred or indifferent to y and y is preferred or indifferent to z; then x is preferred or indifferent to z (weak transitivity).

In other words, by Axioms 1 and 2, we always have at least a weak ordering of any set of alternatives for a given individual.

The problem is to construct a decision process for society as a whole that is both responsive to autonomously chosen individual preferences and determinate in its outcomes. Arrow expresses these requirements in the following definition of a social welfare (choice) function, where R is the relation of either preference or indifference, and n is the number of individuals:

> a process or rule which, for each set of individual orderings R1, . . . , Rn for alternative social states (one ordering for each individual), states a corresponding social ordering of alternative social states, R.[8]

Formally, $R = f(R1, . . . , Rn)$. Informally, the social choice is simply a function of individual preferences, whether "utilitarian" (in which instance preferences would be interpreted as representing "tastes"), or "liberal" (in which case they would be taken to represent "values").[9] The definition, in effect, applies Axioms 1 and 2 to society as a whole.

By contrast, a Platonic Realist model, which would require that choices be based on an idea of the Good (which might differ from what pleases individuals or what they value), could not be based on preferences at all. This kind of function would be "one which assigns the same social ordering for every set of individual orderings" and so would be, in an important sense, imposed.[10]

Arrow establishes five additional conditions on the choice function. The first of these lays down a requirement that would appear to be overly minimalist for any society claiming to be both liberal and pluralistic, requiring only that a "true social ordering" be obtainable from "some sufficiently wide range" of individual orderings.[11] It is presumed that advance (a priori) knowledge about individual preferences is incomplete, "to the extent that there are at least three among all the alternatives under consideration for which the ordering by any given individual is completely unknown."[12] In other words, from the set of all conceivable social states, there is at least one subset of three or more admissible alternatives that can be ordered in any logically possible way. This condition has often been referred to as "unrestricted domain," and it is a crucial one, as we shall see.

The second of Arrow's conditions, called "positive association," is somewhat trivial in a democratic polity, requiring that "if one alternative social state rises or remains still in the ordering of every individual without any other change in those orderings, we expect that it rises, or at least does not fall, in the social ordering."[13] In other words, the social choice function does not respond perversely to changes in individual orderings.

Arrow's third condition, the so-called "independence of irrelevant alternatives," complements positive association, requiring that the social ordering of alternatives in the feasible set (S) be completely independent of the existence (or, perhaps more aptly, the nonexistence) of alternatives not in S. This means that the social choice C(S) is solely a function of the preferences of individuals for feasible alternatives (those in S). So long as the individual preferences between any two admissible alternatives remain the same from one situation to the next, the social ordering between those two alternatives remains fixed. By confining the decision process to pairwise comparisons, this rule also ensures that some kind of voting will be the preferred method of social choice, though some forms of voting would violate the condition (e.g., rank-order, or Borda rule, voting).[14]

The fourth and fifth conditions are those of nonimposition and nondictatorship. The fourth requires that, if x is preferred to y by everyone in some situation, then x is socially preferred to y in that situation (not necessarily in any other). More formally, a social choice function is imposed if, for some pair of distinct alternatives in S, C(S) is the same no matter what the preferences of the individual voters.[15] The fifth condition simply rules out the possibility that there might be a single individual voter whose preferences determine the social choice regardless of the preferences of all the other voters. Again, more formally, a social choice function is dictatorial if there is an individual (i) such that "for all x and y, xP_iy implies xPy" where P_i stands for i's preference ordering and P stands for the social ordering.[16]

As Arrow notes, the five conditions, taken together, assuming also Axioms 1 and 2 and the definition of a social choice or welfare function, "express the doctrines of citizens' sovereignty and rationality in a very general form, with the citizens being allowed to have a wide range of values."[17] The conditions could hardly be objectionable to a proponent of modern liberal democracy in a pluralist setting.

Yet Arrow demonstrates that the five conditions are collectively inconsistent. If no prior assumptions are made about the nature of the individual orderings, then there is no method of voting that will remove the Condorcet Effect (the so-called "paradox of voting"), thereby ensuring collective rationality.[18] Put differently, the only way of passing from individual tastes, values, or preferences to social decisions that are both rational and tolerant of a wide range of individual orderings is either imposed or dictatorial.[19]

What is true for a system of voting is no less true for a market, considered as a method of achieving an "optimal" or "maximal" state of satisfaction (e.g., a state in which the marginal rate of substitution between any two commodities is the same for all consumers) according to the theory of consumer choice. Any such optimal state that is derived from the assumption that each individual orders alternative social states (say, x, y, and z) solely in accordance with the commodities he receives under each alternative will necessarily violate one of the five conditions. The same result follows from any other set of purely individualistic assumptions.[20]

What may be concluded from these results? Arrow himself answers:

> If we wish to make social welfare judgments which depend on the values of all individuals, i.e., which are not imposed or dictatorial, then we must relax some of the conditions imposed.[21]

But which condition(s)? Axioms 1 and 2 together with the definition of a social choice function merely require that there be a social ordering based on individual preferences that are weakly ordered in a non–self-contradictory way. The second and third conditions add only that the social choice function should be sensitive to changes in individual preferences, so long as such preferences are for feasible alternatives. The fourth and fifth conditions rule out only imposed or dictated solutions. The idea of an allegedly "democratic" system of voting that fails to conform to these standards appears to be an absurdity.

We are left with the first condition, which allows a "wide range of individual orderings" or a "diversity of values with respect to alternative social states" while disallowing a priori assumptions about the nature of such values so long as there are three or more alternatives, as the only available candidate for relaxation. The other assumptions and conditions describe features pertaining directly to "democracy," but the first condition generates a "liberal" gloss upon those features. The impossibility of instituting all the democratic features at once without relaxing the liberal one confirms the inherent tension between the two approaches.

Examples of this tension abound in modern political life. There is the oft-noted "instability" of multiparty systems as measured against the greater "stability" in two-party ones. Indeed, majority rule satisfies all the conditions (except the first) so long as the number of alternatives is restricted to two.[22] This would be cold comfort, however, to devotees of multiparty politics (including third-party supporters in the United States), who would doubtless tend to view such a restriction as a kind of "imposition."

Another way of relaxing the requirements of the first condition so as to render the other conditions collectively consistent is to make certain a priori assumptions about the allowable tastes, values, and preferences of individuals for alternative social states. In other words, we could require, in advance, "that the tastes of individuals fall within certain prescribed realms of similarity."[23]

One such attempt has been made by Duncan Black, who showed that restricting the range of possible orderings to those that are "single-peaked," or conditioned by "a fundamentally similar attitude toward the classification of the alternatives," yields a social choice function that conforms to Arrow's remaining conditions.[24]

Another example may be found in the thought of such modern political thinkers as Rousseau and Kant, who insisted on a sharp distinction between the preferences of individuals that are based on self-interest (the "particular will" for Rousseau or the "pragmatic imperative" for Kant) and those that are based on a rational conception of the social good (the "general will" for Rousseau or the "moral imperative" for Kant).[25] According to Arrow, "Voting, from this point of view, is not a device whereby each individual expresses his personal interests, but rather where each individual gives his opinion of the general will."[26]

We are now in a position to return to the earlier discussion of Plato's anthropomorphic consensual constitutionalism, informed by the intervening consideration of Arrow's theorem. Arrow's result strongly suggests that a constitutionalism based on the joinder of liberalism and democracy is illusory, unless it can be presumed that a reasonably wide consensus on the allowable shape of admissible individual preference orderings for alternative social states exists.

In Plato's time, such a consensus was rightly presumed, because the modern opposition of the individual and society that lays the foundation for liberal democracy was unknown. In our time, however, it cannot be presumed and so must either exist in its own right or be fabricated by construction of some such constitutional fiction as the "general will." Yet, by Arrow's theorem, the resources of consensus cannot be found within liberal democracy itself. Indeed, liberal democracy is the problem; for liberalism undermines consensus by continually widening the domain of allowable individual preferences (thus exacerbating the violation of Arrow's first condition). Democracy undermines it still further by continually expanding the range of individuals whose preferences count in the making of social choices.

If the institutions of liberal democracy cannot reasonably be expected to produce consensus, then it must be either imposed or dictated. To pose the issue in this manner, though it may seem rather stark, makes possible the understanding of a heretofore unsatisfactorily explained aspect of American constitutional history: the paradoxical rise to supremacy of a politically unaccountable federal judiciary in the making of fundamental constitutional social choices for a liberal democratic republic.

During the antebellum period, a tolerably strong consensus on the shape of most important constitutional issues existed in the United States, thereby rendering social choices both determinate and reasonably well-grounded in similarly shaped individual attitudes toward social decisions. Between the end of the Civil War and the onset of the Great Depression, however, this consensus was eroded both by social and economic forces and by the political forces inherent in liberal democracy itself.

The most important of the latter was the gradual acceptance, throughout the latter half of the nineteenth century, of a Millian libertarian liberalism (see Chapter 13), which radically widened the domain of individual preferences for alternative social states. Combined with this was a concomitant slow expansion of the suffrage, which broadly extended the range of relevant decisionmakers in the American polity. As the original consensus weakened, increasingly paralytic political institutions began to yield ground to the courts, which are small deliberative bodies better positioned to make decisive choices in a society riven with conflict. This process has culminated in widespread deference to the judiciary (particularly to the U.S. Supreme Court) on constitutional issues and, as a result, the judicialized constitutionalism of contemporary times.

The drift toward government by judges is perhaps explicable from the standpoint of efficacious decisionmaking, but it raises serious problems for constitutional democracy. Since judicial supremacy vests control of fundamental social choices in a division of the government that is several degrees removed from the personal constitutions of the people upon whom the real constitution of any polity ultimately must be founded, the prospect arises that areas of consensus that do exist in society at large will be undermined rather than reinforced by the Court.

This problem has been exacerbated further in the United States by the failure of even the Supreme Court itself to achieve consensus on many controversial constitutional questions. When the Court fails to achieve consensus, it risks falling into something approaching Arrovian dictatorship. For example, whenever there is a 5-to-4 split on an important constitutional ruling, one justice effectively determines the social choice for all of society, regardless of anyone else's preferences. That this situation is generalizable in accordance with Arrow's fifth condition is shown by the fact that, under judicial supremacy, such a possibility is always present. A perusal of the Court's leading constitutional opinions during the last forty years reveals that this situation is no longer a rare occurrence, though it was in earlier periods. In Arrow's words, a social choice function is dictatorial

> if there exists an individual i such that, for all x and y, xPiy implies xPy regardless of the orderings R1, . . . , Rn of all individuals other than i, where P is the social preference relation corresponding to R1, . . . , Rn.[27]

To the extent that judicial supremacy is aptly described by Arrow's definition, it is violently incompatible with the institutions of liberal democracy. It should be remembered that judicial supremacy consists of two main components: judicial finality (the power to decide all—or nearly all—constitutional cases, including those that determine the constitutional authority of other agencies of government) and judicial freedom (the power to select the interpretive rules according to which such cases will be decided—even if the rule is "noninterpretive").

One way of ensuring that constitutional judicial review does not become Arrovian dictatorship is to deny the Court final power of review in all cases that require a determination of the constitutional authority of other agencies of government. In essence, that was the solution I proposed in *Marbury and Review*. Another approach—the alternative emphasized in this book—is to bind judges to traditional interpretive rules in the decision of all constitutional cases. Although judicial finality and judicial freedom combined (judicial supremacy) leads, potentially, to a kind of Arrovian dictatorship, judicial finality without judicial freedom involves a form of Arrovian imposition.

THE SUPERIORITY OF IMPOSITION OVER DICTATORSHIP

According to Arrow, a social choice function is said to be imposed "if, for some pair of distinct alternatives x and y, xRy for any set of individual orderings R1, ..., Rn, where R is the social ordering corresponding to R1, ..., Rn."[28] Under one interpretation of this definition, imposition corresponds to "the type of social choice in which decisions are made in accordance with a customary code" and in which the implied restraints "are not felt as such but really are part of the tastes of the individuals."[29] Under an alternative interpretation, in which the "true desires of the individual members of the society" are "in conflict with the custom of the group," the definition is "a correct formalization of the concept of conventionality."[30]

Though Arrow rules out imposition along with dictatorship as incompatible with democratic choice, his own theory implies that some elements of one or the other must necessarily be present in any liberal democracy. Since all forms of dictatorship, including judicial supremacy, should be ruled out if there are milder forms of imposition available, we are left with the forms of custom and convention.

Obviously custom is the milder imposition, since its restraints are not felt; in convention, they are. Yet even convention is preferable to any form of dictatorship, since convention does not allow imposition of the arbitrary will of a single individual. Nevertheless, if there is a way to move from convention to custom, thereby reconciling the conflict between the individual and the group, it ought to be done.

The best way to make this move, in the constitutional arena, is by confining judges to traditional rules of legal interpretation, no matter what their views on substantive constitutional issues. Rule by tradition, at least in the interpretive arena, is an acceptable form of imposition because rules of interpretation plausibly can be regarded as embodied in the tastes and values of most people. Any impression to the contrary has been brought about by the efforts of persons wishing to effect substantive results at variance with outcomes that would have been obtained by adherence to such rules.

Rule by tradition is, as G. K. Chesterton said, an extension of the franchise. It represents the widening of democracy in the strongest possible sense, the democracy to which a constitution most fundamentally and directly applies, that which is embodied in the "We the People" of the Constitution's preamble. Arrow's result suggests that the only way to achieve consensus and democracy at the same time is by the tradition defined in terms of Chesterton's "democracy of the dead." If a tradition is sufficiently long-standing, the votes of the dead will almost always outweigh the votes of the people who happen merely "to be walking about."

Law generally, and constitutional law particularly, is more than a collection of "rules of the moment"; it is the institutional record of the human attempt to secure order, through self-understanding, in history. Donald R. Kelley puts it even more strongly:

> Historically, the principal questions, terminology, and lines of investigation of the study of humanity have been, over two millennia and more, the "science of law" . . . especially in the western legal tradition.[31]

If we free judges from the obligation to honor that study in the most fundamental of decisions, then we can hardly expect that anyone at all will honor it in lesser ones. They will surely not do so if they are under the sway of libertinistic political principles that allow no interference with individual preferences for alternative social states. That is exactly the point expressed by Plato's anthropomorphism. As Arrow notes, Platonic Realism, similar to custom as a form of imposition, is a set of constraints upon social choices drawn from prior assumptions about the nature of allowable individual preferences (see the *Laws*).[32] As we shall see in subsequent chapters, the real and the customary have even more in common than this.

The liberal policy of removing traditional, customary, or conventional restraints on individual preferences, tastes, and values, in the expectation that social choices, as a result, somehow will be less socially determined, expresses a vain hope. Such a policy is itself a social choice, and Arrow's result calls into serious question the prospect of easy movement from individual to social choices once a wide array of individual orderings is reached by the removal of the constraints that make up a society's underlying constitutional traditions.

In constitutional law, the distinction between explicit constitutional principles (conceived as social choices that are deliberately arrived at and recorded) and underlying constitutional traditions is expressed in the difference between written and unwritten constitutions. My argument is that a written constitution, divorced from the firm support of the underlying constitutional traditions from which it springs, will ultimately prove a failure. An apt organic analogy is available here, that of the plant that may grow and remain healthy only so long as the ground underneath it is tended.

A society cannot escape the outworkings of its own past or the demands of its own Good any more than an individual can. It can, however, in the attempt to bury its past or abolish its Good, distort the natural consequences of these determinations by misreading or ignoring the historical reality that conditions them. There is an honored tradition in Anglo-American jurisprudence, expressed by John

Locke: "The end of law is not to abolish or restrain, but to preserve and enlarge freedom."[33] Yet if the natural tendency to enlarge the sphere of freedom is not fully complemented by the recognition, institution, and conservation of the conditions under which freedom is possible, the result of the distortion will be license, not liberty.

6 · Written and Unwritten Constitutions

American-style written constitutions are relatively modern, yet constitutions in the wider sense are ancient. Since any written constitution may be conceived as representative of an underlying constitution in the wider sense, the writtenness of a constitution cannot be its essence; its essence must be its function in constituting a polity. The most important features of the American Constitution, the origins of which are firmly rooted in written and unwritten principles and practices of British constitutionalism (see Chapter 8), are derived from the English model, a model not written in the American style but a collection of texts, traditions, customs, and conventions governed by long-accepted methods of legal analysis.

Americans of the Founding era uniformly presumed the applicability of such methods to the federal and state constitutions they adopted. Sharply distinguishing written from unwritten constitutions and then applying such a distinction in an effort to understand early American constitutions is to treat our constitutions as if they were conceived in a vacuum and thus had no history. Moreover, interpreting a constitutional text without respecting its underlying traditions progressively will rob that text of any meaning.

The most famous elaboration of a distinction between written and unwritten constitutions is by implication in Chief Justice John Marshall's opinion for the Court in *Marbury v. Madison*.[1] Addressing the issue of whether a legislative act repugnant to the Constitution is void, Marshall says that the purpose for which constitutional limitations are committed to writing is to ensure "that those limits may not be mistaken, or forgotten."[2] Answering the question as to whether the courts are obligated to enforce a constitutionally invalid law, Marshall then declares that an affirmative response "would subvert the very foundation of all written constitutions."[3]

Though commentators have sometimes used Marshall's remarks to suggest that writtenness is somehow essential to the constitution of any society governed by a written constitutional instrument, it is doubtful that the great chief justice was making a theoretical statement of this kind. Marshall does not say that constitutional limits are committed to writing in order to create such limits *ex nihilo;* rather, he says that the limits are penned so that they will not be "mistaken" or "forgotten," suggesting that the limits are preexistent.

Similarly, Marshall's argument against an alleged obligation of courts to enforce concededly unconstitutional laws is aimed at showing that, if judges are not allowed to treat a written constitutional instrument as law while deciding cases, they would be put in the position of violating their oaths of office because the Constitution is law, and courts are entitled only to decide cases "according to law." Sylvia Snowiss points out that one of Marshall's most significant contributions to American constitutionalism was his successful effort to assimilate the written constitution to a *preexisting* body of law in such a way as to make it amenable to traditional rules of interpretation used in the analysis of other legal instruments.[4]

Marshall has often been regarded as a textualist in matters of interpretation, yet his textualism is almost always circumscribed by intentionalism, that is, by an assertion that written constitutional language is usually the best indicia of what the Framers intended. Such a view implies that the "real" constitution is comprised not in its written language but in the underlying predispositions of its authors, conditioned by historical experience.

If this were not so, if the essence of a written constitution could be fully contained in its writtenness, then a constitution could not be "real" at all in any meaningful sense; it would be merely "nominal," a constitution in name only. Examples of such constitutions might be those propaganda documents of totalitarian states that, upon superficial reading and an unfamiliarity with the underlying constitutional traditions of such polities, would probably convince almost anyone that the societies represented were profoundly libertarian. In short, the only constitutions the mere writtenness of which make up their essence are empty abstractions, window dressings that fail to reflect the underlying real constitutions of the societies from which they spring.

Etienne Gilson, following Aristotle and Thomas Aquinas, has provided a useful description of the constitution of Being as a composite of formal essence and actual existence.[5] Essence, a category that comprises the formal qualities of a being, consists in the attributes that render its actual existence logically possible and without which its real existence would be impossible. The two most fundamental requirements of any being's essence are self-identity and the absence of inner contradiction among the primary constituents of that being. For example, the essence of a round square renders impossible the actual existence of such a being, but the essence of an equilateral triangle, whose primary constituents are threeness and equality, renders the existence of that kind of being logically possible.

Fullness of being, however, requires more than the purely formal attributes of a merely possible existence. It requires that a being actually exist as well, and the question of the actual existence of any being is entirely separate from the question of that (or any other) being's defining characteristics. The possible existence of an equilateral triangle does not guarantee the actual existence of any particular triangle. Existence adds to essence a radical "givenness" that is not reducible to the purely formal primary constituents of any actually existing being. And the fact that no combination of essences is fully sufficient to guarantee the real existence of any being makes this givenness appear so radical as to constitute the fundamental mystery of existence as we experience it. Thus the question is raised to which religion seems to provide the only answer: "Why is there anything rather than nothing?"

The constitution of any polity is a being that reflects the dominant underlying decisional predispositions of that polity's citizenry. The constitution of a polity is thus a composite of that polity's formal essence and its actual existence. Since the essence of any being is that which ensures that being's self-identity and lack of internal contradiction, the essence of a constitution, whether of a polity or of an individual, is that which ensures the self-identity and internal coherence of that polity or individual.

As such, the essence of a constitution is no different from the essence of any other being, for "constitution" is just a name for that which imparts to an existing society continuous political representation in historical time.[6] Just as the essence of any being's constitution is that which enables us to ascribe formal identity to it and to regard it as self-consistent over time, so the essence of any polity's constitution is that which enables us to identify it and to recognize it as self-consistent polity over time.

But essence does not guarantee existence for a constitutional polity any more than for any other being. The hypothetical libertarian constitution for a totalitarian state, though formally conceivable, like the round square, is existentially impossible and thus can bear no relation to the underlying constitutional predispositions of any actual polity. Since the constitutional symbols in such a text cannot correspond to the constitutional experience of an existing society, they are not "given" in reality.

A real constitution, as distinct from a paper constitution, is, by definition, that by which existing things are really "constituted," in which things really cohere, by which things are made really continuous and thus receive their real identity from one moment to the next. It is what binds together you yesterday, you today, and you tomorrow in such a way as to make it meaningful (not absurd) for me to refer to you at those three times by the same name. It is what ties Americans in their political and legal capacity in 1992 to Americans in their political and legal capacity in 1792.

Any truly viable constitutionalism presupposes the idea of constitutional being as a composite of formal essence and actual existence. Thus the true value of any written constitutional instrument is comprised in the extent to which it represents adequately the continuous, identifiable historical existence of its corresponding polity: its "adequation" to constitutional reality. Since this adequation is a long-term affair, involving beings both "in" and "not in" actual existence (e.g., citizens who have died and citizens yet unborn), any viable constitutionalism must be grounded in constitutional history.

This kind of viable constitution is also a binding, not a loosing, force, an ordering, not a liberating, force. There are some critics, enamored of modern judicial "updating" of the Constitution, who will object that a constitution also embodies change—not merely continuity, and difference—not merely identity, perhaps citing Chief Justice Marshall's famous dictum in *McCulloch v. Maryland* that "it is a constitution we are expounding."[7] This objection is both a mistake of logic and a misinterpretation of Marshall's statement. Marshall meant that constitutional purposes are large, not that such purposes are subject to the continuing variability of judicial sentiments. Marshall knew well that change will occur with or without a constitution but that legal continuity, social cohesion, and national identity will not. We do not need a constitution to bring about change; we need a constitution to confine change within acceptable bounds. That is what Marshall's *McCulloch* dictum is about.

Sound constitutional theory fails to provide support for the kind of sharp distinction between written and unwritten constitutions found at the root of the blueprint conception. But it would be a mistake to think that there are no important differences at all between written and unwritten constitutions. It is the attempt to articulate a society's self-defining character in a written constitutional text that gives rise to the problems of constitutional interpretation (*how* the written instrument is to be construed) and judicial review (*who* is to construe it). Constitutional interpretation and judicial review are problematic largely because no written constitution can articulate fully a polity's underlying constitutional principles.

To suppose that the written U.S. Constitution fully articulates the underlying constitutional principles of the American polity would require ignoring crucial features of American constitutionalism. Such features include the allegedly extra-constitutional (some would even say contraconstitutional) growth of the administrative sector ("fourth branch") of the federal government and the administrative law that circumscribes it; the development of certain unwritten constitutional conventions that surround the electoral college due to the possible appearance of "faithless" electors;[8] the growth (and subsequent decline) of political parties in American constitutional history without even a word of constitutional text; and the struggle between common lawyers and regulators over the control of liability for personal injury in tort that occurred in the early twentieth century and that ultimately was one of the major factors leading to the institution of the administrative state in the 1930s and 1940s[9] and subsequently to the contemporary decline of political parties. This list is hardly complete.

If even a written constitutional text cannot fully articulate a polity's underlying constitutional principles, it goes without saying that a judicial decision that inter-prets language in a constitutional text cannot do so either. It is likely that such an interpretation, if freed from the shackles of historically honored rules that circum-scribe interpretive innovation, will be farther off the mark than an interpretation constrained by such rules. The history of judicialized constitutionalism in the United States provides many examples of zealous judges abandoning both tradi-tional rules of interpretation and underlying constitutional consensus in order to dictate results that they prefer on grounds other than legal or constitutional ones. The list includes most, if not all, of the "bad" decisions of the *Lochner* era men-tioned in Chapter 3.

It may be useful at this point to provide an illustration of the idea of consensual constitutionalism constrained by traditional rules of interpretation by reference to one of the most contentious substantive constitutional issues of our time. In 1973, the U.S. Supreme Court, in *Roe v. Wade*, decided that a pregnant female had a nearly absolute constitutional right to terminate her pregnancy by abortion of a nonviable fetus.[10] In part, this decision was reached on the basis of the Court's refusal to determine the issue of "when human life begins," a refusal that appeared to lead to a de facto resolution of the entirely separate issue of whether a fetus was a "person" within the meaning of the Fourteenth Amendment's due process clause.[11]

Critics of *Roe* often suggest that the Constitution, the Court, and the country would have been better off had the Court reached the ontological issue regarding the humanity of the fetus instead of leaving that question aside in favor of the remaining empirical grounds. The idea seems to be that the Court's failure to confront certain "fundamental" (i.e., "metaphysical") issues will lead it to make "unprincipled" decisions.

Although *Roe* may have been an unprincipled decision that the Court and the country would have been better off without, I do not see how the Court's answer-ing the question about the beginning of human life (especially if it did not know the answer) would have helped matters much from a strictly *constitutional* stand-point. A truly "constitutional" principle must be so widely acknowledged and ac-cepted as to form a significant part of a society's self-definition.

With this in mind, suppose that 98 percent of Americans believed, at the time of *Roe*, that a nonviable fetus is a "human life," certainly a reasonable assumption, since even a nonviable fetus is both "alive" and not a dog or a tomato. Suppose further that 98 percent of Americans believed likewise when the Fourteenth Amendment, the Bill of Rights, and the Constitution itself were adopted. In this scenario, it would be plausible to regard the proposition that a nonviable fetus is a human life as a kind of substantive constitutional principle. But this does not nec-essarily resolve the issue between the parties in *Roe* because the Constitution ex-tends due process protection only to "persons," not to "human life."

Now suppose that the Court extends its analysis of conception to that of "personhood" and declares that all human lives are persons within the meaning of the due process clause, thereby arguably defeating the *Roe* abortion right. Will the "principle" of the latter decision be a truly "constitutional" one? It will be so only for one who believes that anything the Supreme Court happens to call a "constitutional principle," and can defend on some plausible ground, really *is* one.

There is certainly no strong consensus in the United States on the legal personality of a fetus (though probably there is such a consensus on its life or humanity). For the Court to have imposed such a "solution" in the absence of a textual or historical warrant would simply have been to ignore constitutional reality. It would have been to impose, de jure, the constitutional opinion of the Right upon everyone, much as its de facto resolution of the same issue in *Roe* did impose the corresponding opinion of the Left.

But the Constitution is neither of the Right nor of the Left, and the very sincerity of current pretensions that constitutional opinion can be constitutional truth suggests an intellectual deformation that calls for serious reexamination of the nature of constitutional order. This reexamination requires excursions into political philosophy and legal history, and recovery, in some measure, of the classical tradition from which those disciplines spring. In the end, the reexamination will show that constitutional adjudication tied closely to traditional practice is the only viable alternative to constitutional disorder when constitutional consensus is not present.

This is so not because traditional legal practices comprise a package of fundamental values that are better than those contained in alternative packages. It is so because such practices are the historic methods employed by legal institutions to test and filter ideas originating outside the legal process and that thereby allow true consensus to develop within the law. They are not merely "ideas" competing with other "ideas" for preeminence. They are features of experience and therefore of reality. It is the loss of the sense of this distinction between abstract ideas and concrete experiences that is at the root of many present constitutional troubles.

More examples could be added to this list, but the point should be clear without belaboring the obvious: the traditional legal practices are the result of the growth and development of unwritten constitutional conventions. Moreover, these conventions bear much the same relation to American law as the conventions of the British Constitution bear to English law.[12] Most important, none is instituted by constitutional text and none is enforced (or enforceable) by courts. These practices are, in part, the "traditions" complementing the "text" noted by Justice Scalia in his *Casey* dissent. The existence of these traditions, arising from the institutions of an underlying unwritten constitution, raises important questions about the relationship between written constitutional symbols and underlying constitutional experiences.

SYMBOLS AND EXPERIENCE

Because no written constitutional document can fully articulate a society's underlying constitutional commitments, faithful constitutional interpreters must be aware of the extent to which written constitutional symbols are closely tied to the underlying constitutional experiences they represent.[13] The problem concerns the relationship between history—the record of experience in the realm of actual existence—and theory—the product of human reflection upon that experience through the use and manipulation of symbols. The latter activity takes place in the realm of "essences."

People who reject the authority of traditional legal practices in constitutional law appear to assume not only that constitutional symbols may be analytically distinguished from constitutional experiences (which is true) but also that the results of analyses based on this distinction may be synthetically applied, straightforwardly and unproblematically, to everyday constitutional decisionmaking (which is false). Nontraditionalist constitutional theorists assume that they (or judges) can abstract from experience symbols conducive to analysis, subject those symbols, divorced from their formative experiences, to formal manipulation by deductive processes, and then apply the resulting conclusions to the resolution of concrete legal disputes.

This procedure leads naturally to the type of judicialized constitutionalism I have described, that is, to a situation in which it becomes plausible to define a constitution as little more than a collection of judicial glosses on a written text. A cursory glance at the contents of any contemporary casebook will show that most commentators would now define the phrase "constitutional law of the United States" as the set of Supreme Court opinions about the meaning of key constitutional provisions. But this can no more be an adequate description of our constitutional law than can a mere writing adequately comprise our constitution.

By way of contrast, one might consider the definition of constitutional law advanced by A. V. Dicey as the set of "all rules which directly or indirectly affect the distribution or exercise of sovereign power."[14] A moment's reflection should be sufficient to remind the reader of a fact that might seem startling at first glance because it seems to have been so long forgotten: that Dicey's definition is a more accurate description of constitutional law *even in the United States* than is the judicialized definition. It is more accurate because Dicey's claim is staked upon the ground of underlying constitutional experiences, not upon mere words.

Most written constitutions are peculiarly dramatic and highly focused attempts to symbolize the experience of political reality in the language of a legal document. They are attempts to legalize aspects of political experience that are deemed particularly fundamental by their framers. The American Constitution, in its project of making life in a Hobbesian world more livable, does so by establishing a delicate balance among and between a number of tensional forces through their symbolization in its written text.

It is important to note that these tensional forces are experienced as *real*. The symbols chosen by the makers of the Constitution to represent the tensions inherent in modern political life reflect primary experiences of reality in the realm of actual existence. They are not to be treated as logical contradictions to be resolved in the realm of essences but as tensions of real existence that must be contained or controlled. They are not to be regarded as contradictions either in the Constitution or in our constitutionalism. They are contradictions of political life more generally that cannot be resolved at all; that is why we need a Constitution to contain them.

Since the symbols chosen reflect primary experiences of reality and thus are not independent of that reality, it follows that the symbols themselves are fully intelligible only when read in the context of the experiences from which they are derived. There is no known or generally agreed-upon vantage point outside experience from which to judge abstractly whether the balance of forces symbolized by the constitutional language has in fact been enhanced, preserved, eroded, or destroyed by subsequent application of this language in a concrete instance.

Since the experiential realities at the core of the constitutional arrangement are expressed in the language of tension and balance, the overall constitutional project must be viewed as an effort to maintain equilibrium between conflicting forces. The most obvious danger in such a system is that the equilibria established at the outset may be disrupted later if one or the other side of a constitutional antinomy is construed as self-subsistent (hypostatic) and allowed to overcome its opposing polarity. Whenever this occurs, the symbols involved are torn from their experiential moorings, and the constitutional balance is eroded.

CONSTITUTIONAL OVEREXTENSION

By way of example, consider the development of the doctrine of liberty of contract by the U.S. Supreme Court in the late nineteenth and early twentieth centuries. In the 1870s, the leaders of the newly organized American Bar Association (ABA) launched an effort that would ultimately prove to be a successful campaign to persuade the American judiciary to intensify legal protection for the developing American free enterprise system.[15]

Beginning with the famous—though at the time unsuccessful—argument of former justice Campbell before the Supreme Court in the *Slaughterhouse Cases*,[16] members of the conservative bar pressed upon the Supreme Court, lower federal courts, and state courts the theory that the Fourteenth Amendment of the Constitution embodied a notion approaching an absolute transactional liberty in economic matters. For more than two decades after the Court's initial rejection of this theory in *Slaughterhouse*, its proponents could find only a few state and lower federal judges to support their view. They were joined by Justices Field and Bradley on the Supreme Court, whose dissenting opinions in several cases further grounded the theory in that most abstract (and thus contentless) provision of the Declaration of Independence, the "pursuit of happiness."[17]

Mostly due to changes in the membership of the Supreme Court, and wholly in the absence of any judicial development of the sort that one might expect to find among judges reared in the traditions of the common law, the Court, in 1897, read the logic of the Field-Bradley dissents into the Fourteenth Amendment's due process clause.[18] Nor was there any incremental development of the idea of liberty of contract in the four decades following, which might have served to limit the scope of the doctrine in accordance with other common law doctrines that it, in effect, overthrew.[19]

Instead of finding a comfortable place within the evolving structure of American law, liberty of contract joined with dual federalism and other alien doctrines just in time to defeat much of the New Deal recovery program in the mid-1930s.[20] Then, as abruptly as they had emerged, these doctrines were summarily dismissed.[21] Some comments of Guido Calabresi regarding the necessity of striking a workable balance between continuity and change in a legal system are relevant:

> Continuity and change are essential attributes of a legal system. . . . Abrupt changes . . . can create deep ruptures in society, ruptures that slower, more organic change would avoid. Different legal-political systems have balanced the need for continuity and change in different ways, some giving more weight to one, some to the other. In the nineteenth century the United States is said to have developed a unique solution to meeting the two requirements. The principal instruments of this system were the common law courts, for most law was court-made. Legislatures did, of course, possess the ultimate authority, subject to constitutional requirements, to make law; however, that authority was exercised sparingly, by modern standards, and in largely revisionary capacity. In such a world, the law could normally be updated without dramatic breaks through common law adjudication and revision of precedents. Change occurred because the doctrine of *stare decisis* was adhered to in a relatively loose fashion and precedents were not, even nominally, ultimately binding. The changes that did occur tended to be piecemeal and incremental, organic if one wishes, as courts sought to discover and only incidentally to make the ever-changing law. The system, despite its reliance on judges whose relation to the electorate was at best problematical, could at bottom be called democratic because the requirements of the legal process, of "principled" decision-making, tended to limit the scope of judicial authority. The incremental nature of common law adjudication meant that no single judge could ultimately change the law, and a series of judges could only do so over time and in response to changed events or to changed attitudes in the people.[22]

The world Calabresi describes is the world of nineteenth-century America before the advent of liberty of contract and its companion dogmas of substantive due process, substantive equal protection, and dual federalism. Had Calabresi's passage been written in the era he describes, it surely would have been prophetic, for the "abrupt changes" wrought by the rise and fall of liberty of contract did in fact create "deep ruptures" in American society that "slower, more organic change" perhaps would have avoided. These ruptures were the inevitable consequence of the doctrine's lack of foundation in the Constitution, in the common law, and in American experience generally.

The experience that the doctrine symbolized was not that of the Framers, or the ratifiers, or nineteenth-century Americans, or "conventional morality" in any form; rather, it symbolized the interest of a small group of economic and social elites who were able to enlist a small but influential group of lawyers and judges in their support. At the purely formal level, its lack of fruitfulness as a legal concept that could be subsequently fitted somehow to the evolving American experience and thus to the fabric of the common law may perhaps best be understood by recalling a remark of Justice Cardozo in reference to legal principles generally:

> The tendency of a principle to expand itself to the limit of its logic may be counteracted by the tendency to confine itself within the limits of its history.[23]

Unfortunately, liberty of contract could not "expand itself to the limit of its logic" because, logically, it had no limits. Indeed it can be read to support legal or constitutional protection for almost anything anyone can get anyone else to agree to. At the same time, it could not have been confined "within the limits of its history" because it had no history. If I may be allowed a bit of irony, I would say that such principles are in fact unprincipled. At the very least, Kant's suggestion that "the inscrutable wisdom through which we exist is not less worthy of veneration in respect to what it denies us than in what it has granted" is applicable here.[24] In Kenneth Arrow's language, constitutional principles without limits simply cannot be in the feasible set.

To bring this digression into current context, it is only necessary to point out that many of the substantive values that contemporary nontraditionalists wish to have imported into the Constitution by judicial decision have the same logical and historical character as that of liberty of contract. And those values are no more rooted in the constitutional experience of the American people than were the dogmas of laissez-faire constitutionalism. The most striking example is that of personal privacy.

Upon a virtually nonexistent constitutional and historical foundation, the U.S. Supreme Court, beginning in 1965, began the development of a constitutionally protected "zone of privacy," which was held at the time to include the decision of a married couple to use birth control.[25] Soon thereafter, the category was extended to encompass birth control for nonmarried couples,[26] private use of pornography,[27] access to birth-control information for minors,[28] and first-trimester abortions on demand for pregnant females.[29] After the Court's fashioning of this last "right," its effect was held to bar virtually all state-imposed restrictions on access to abortion: e.g., second-trimester hospitalization requirements,[30] parental consent laws applied to minors,[31] spousal consent laws applied to husbands,[32] physician "second opinion" requirements,[33] viability-testing requirements,[34] fetal protection laws,[35] and so on.

With respect to the general category, the Court has made notable efforts to restrict its scope to matters involving "family, marital, and reproductive" rights[36] and more recently has softened its initial position on such issues as parental consent for minors seeking abortions.[37] But if I am right, notwithstanding these qualifications, the restrictions will not hold up so long as the Court stops short of a wholesale overthrow of the underlying principle because, like liberty of contract, the logic of personal privacy ultimately does not admit of any principled limits. Thus all judicial efforts to restrict the scope of the category will seem arbitrary, as homosexuals and other groups are now plausibly contending.

With respect to abortion, the virtual limitlessness of the principle of *Roe v. Wade* has been amply demonstrated. It has generated a policy more extreme than that of any other civilized country in the Western world (in its nearly absolute protection of access to abortion in derogation of the acknowledged state interest in protecting the unborn).[38] It has thereby produced political and social instability of the sort that makes even its flat overruling not completely out of the question.[39]

That the overruling of *Roe* is considered a real possibility, at least by the proponents of abortion, has been transparently obvious in several recent Supreme Court confirmation hearings before the Senate Judiciary Committee. Calabresi, who sees the polarization resulting from *Roe* as a problem caused by the Court's possibly hasty invalidation of an obsolete statute, suggests that it might have been avoided had the Court initially treated the issue as one of statutory interpretation:

> It is . . . possible that a politically viable compromise might have emerged even if none seems plausible now. Once a question has polarized into an issue of my fundamental value against yours, it is hard to back down from the confrontation. But if the question has not yet become polarized, inconsistent views can sometimes coexist. For example, states once allowed abortions in order to save lives, even though that was a compromise of sorts among views. What this shows is not that compromising on deeply held values is the right thing to do. . . . Rather, it suggests that sometimes an accommodation among the sets of values can be reached if the issue is not polarized, if a confrontation of competing sets of values is avoided.[40]

CONSTITUTIONAL POLARITY

None of this turmoil should be surprising when we recall the previous discussion of symbols and experience. The recognition of constitutional polarity as the pervasive reality at the heart of the Framers' achievement implies the corollary that a cardinal mistake in constitutional interpretation is the effort to absolutize fa-vored constitutional symbols. When such a project is effectively accomplished, not only is the polar opposite of the absolutized symbol destroyed, but the absolutized symbol itself loses intelligibility and thus is deprived of its effective constitutional force. As Heraclitus warned more than two millennia ago, "One of a pair of op-posites cannot exist without the other."[41]

In the domain of constitutional history, this paradox results from the fact that the absolutized symbol has no independent meaning in the constitutional frame-work aside from its relation to its tensional counterpart in the constitutional bal-ance, since it is that counterpart from which its real, substantive limitations—and therefore its real, substantive possibilities—are derived. Concepts such as liberty of contract or personal privacy tend to lose their intelligibility in a process of case-by-case adjudication over time because the process gradually exposes this inherent limitlessness through the subjection of the concept to a variety of appli-cations in the real world.

Words may be defined arbitrarily or operationally; symbols must be defined in accordance with the things or experiences that they symbolize. If, in a process of constitutional revisionism, the symbols of the initial constitutional order are torn from their experiential moorings, and if the resulting redefined symbols are then analyzed in relation to the remaining unredefined ones embodied in the original constitutional language—as was done in the liberty of contract cases and is now being done in the personal privacy cases—the result will be a distortion in the relationship between constitutional text and constitutional tradition. This indeed happened in the late nineteenth and early twentieth centuries. In absolutizing the idea of economic liberty by using constitutional provisions not designed to protect economic liberty, the Court made nonsense of those provisions that are designed to protect economic liberty and of those power-granting provisions designed to restrict it at the same time.

The examples I have discussed point to one of the key dangers of trying to govern a polity by a written constitutional instrument. Through exploitation of the linguistic possibilities contained in the text, interpreters may come to regard the text as determinative of the entire universe of constitutional existence, thereby extending the reach of textual meaning over the entire range of constitutional experience and aggrandizing the position of the interpreters. This danger has re-cently been given a quiet but thorough articulation in the constitutional thought of William Harris (see Chapter 14).

Let us return for a moment to Dicey's definition of constitutional law as com-prising all rules affecting the distribution or exercise of sovereign power. Dicey divides British constitutional rules into the categories of *laws,* which are enforce-able by courts, and *conventions,* which are not.[42] According to Dicey, the primary function of the conventions, maxims of political morality that prescribe the ways in which the discretionary powers of the government (of which the courts are a part) may be exercised, is to ensure that political sovereignty resides in the people and not in any part of the government. If these maxims were enforceable by the courts, then political sovereignty would reside in the judiciary.[43]

A similar distribution was effected by the courts in the early days of the American Republic, most notably by the Marshall Court's advancement of the doctrine of political questions.[44] But because, over time, the range of constitutional provisions naturally in tension with the political functions guarded by the doctrine has been extended, the doctrine itself has been substantially eroded. An example is state control of congressional apportionment giving way to judicially mandated reapportionment according to the dictates of wooden mathematical formulas derived from an artificial conception of equality and a truncated notion of representation, leading to an erosion of balanced government, federalism, and separation of powers.[45]

Just as the constitutional symbol "due process," designed to protect individuals against arbitrary impositions of government in the field of criminal procedure, was overextended when applied to the field of economic regulation, as in the liberty of contract cases, so is the constitutional symbol "equal protection," designed to guard individuals against invidious or unfair treatment based on unreasonable classification schemes by government, overextended when applied in the context of republican representation. Regulation and representation are not primarily about individuals. As Lane Sunderland has suggested recently, the price of such overextension of constitutional language ultimately may be governmental paralysis.[46]

The historical distortions in constitutional interpretation that were effected in the late nineteenth century and that are being effected in a different context today resulted largely from the process of symbolic manipulation. They are examples not only of a natural tendency to manipulate legal language for purposes ulterior to law but also of a natural tendency to logical abstraction in thinking, to thinking in terms of formal essence rather than of actual existence, to thinking "words," not "things." Such distortions are understandable in view of what Etienne Gilson has aptly termed "the irrepressible essentialism of the human mind,"[47] resulting in countless efforts to purify, or to "sterilize being by reducing it to an abstract concept."[48] Indeed,

> All real essences are known through abstraction, yet their abstraction does not entail their separation from existence. Such a separation never occurs until essentialism begins to deal with them as with abstractions from abstractions. Essences then become *entia tertiae intentionis,* and they are dead.[49]

No contemporary constitutional theorist could have penned a better description of the "separation from existence" of such constitutional abstractions as liberty of contract or personal privacy. Due process is an intelligible abstraction knowable only through the real, historical experiences from which its essential character is derived. By contrast, liberty of contract, devoid of essential historical character, is an "abstraction from an abstraction," *entia tertiae intentionis,* a nonexistent, dead essence. The constitutional provisions the penumbras from which Justice Douglas drew emanations of personal privacy in *Griswold v. Connecticut* are intelligible abstractions knowable only through the real, historical experiences from which their essential characters are derived. By contrast, personal privacy, devoid of essential historical character, is "abstraction from abstraction," *entia tertiae intentionis,* nonexistent, and dead.

These tertiary abstractions represent hypostatic attempts to purify constitutional reality by treating a small, dependent part of that reality as an independent, self-subsisting whole. Again Gilson supplies the corrective:

> All such attempts are bound ultimately to fail, because concreteness is but another name for essential impurity. All that which is concrete is metaphysically impure. In human experience there are no such things as pure self-subsisting essences, and man himself is far from being one: mind and body, forms and matter, substances and accidents are simultaneously given in actual complexes of mutual determinations. Each concrete essence is a sharing in several different essences, and it is not from looking at them in particular that we can see how they can fit together. Existence is the catalyser of essences. Because it itself is act in a higher order than that of essences, it can melt them together in the unity of a single being.[50]

I do not believe that the Constitution ultimately can survive such metaphysical distortion. Much of the constitutional symbolism adopted by the Framers was a reflection not merely of contingent political or economic interests, contra the prevailing progressive historiography, but of insights real and true into the structure of fundamental political and social order under modern conditions. Some of the theoretical and historical underpinnings of the Framers' achievement have been recently well described in a masterful treatise by James R. Stoner, Jr.[51]

According to Stoner, American constitutionalism is appropriately conceived as a marriage of liberal political philosophy, the foundations of which are most clearly articulated in the thought of Thomas Hobbes, with English common law, most clearly exemplified in the jurisprudence of Sir Edward Coke.[52] Such a marriage requires (among other things, to be sure) a frank acknowledgment of the modern reality of life in a Hobbesian world, with its emphasis on the "rational" calculation and "enlightened" self-interest of individuals. Yet this recognition must be coupled with a willingness to temper calculation and self-interest with a large dose of historical experience, in reliance upon the collected wisdom of ages past.

Though the Founders exhibited confidence in the capacity of human reason to aid in the design of political institutions, this confidence seems always to have been accompanied by a corresponding awareness of the limitations of individual rationality. Witness their reluctance to incorporate a Bill of Rights into the main text of the Constitution, or their deliberate structuring of governmental institutions to counteract the ambitions of men who are not angels, or their attention to the design (and ultimately, the fate) of ancient republics.[53]

In other words, the constitutional achievement of the Framers is, in no small measure, the recognition of the need to institutionalize, and thereby confine (or check), the calculating reason and enlightened self-interest of liberal individualism. Although institutional design was perhaps the most obvious path to this end, the Founders' institutional analysis was conducted, from beginning to end, against the background of English common law and British constitutionalism—both of which had been claimed as the birthright of the colonists. And it was the denial of this claim that precipitated the American Revolution.

The joinder of liberalism with common law, under the social and political conditions of the Founding era, was an easy match. To the English-trained and English-influenced lawyer of late eighteenth-century America, the common law was seen less as a check on (or a counter to) individual rights than as the very fountain of those rights that needed to be constrained. Thus the natural (preexistent) relationship between liberalism and common law is simultaneously an affinity and a polarity. Once established, neither of the two can easily be sustained or dispatched without the other.

The present dominance in academic circles of positivist intellectual conceit, its main project being to concretize the denial of objectivity in the sociopolitical field, has thoroughly obscured the extent to which the insights of the Founding generation may be understood to reflect noncontingent political reality.[54] The antinomies in the constitutional language of the Framers symbolize antinomies in political experience generally. Their vision might best be characterized as one of life in a constitutional *metaxy* (an "in-between" of existence), a concept introduced by Heraclitus and Plato, reintroduced by Augustine and Aquinas, and most recently applied by Eric Voegelin and his followers.[55] Application of this wisdom demands embracing—not resolving—those tensions of political experience that cannot be abolished. And it necessitates acknowledgment that any constitutional polity is subject to a long fall into social and individual disorder if that demand is not met.

7 · Law and Morality

The written Constitution of the United States is best conceived as an effort to symbolize a more general experience of life in a constitutional *metaxy:* a field of tensions that cannot be resolved because they embody fundamental conflicts of sociopolitical existence. The most important of these unresolvable tensions derives from the classical parallelism of psyche and polis which conceives the individual and society to be mutually reflective parts of an essential unity. In modern (post-Hobbesian) political thought, this presumed natural unity is replaced by the assumption of an opposition that can be resolved only by artifice, by some kind of social contract (see Chapter 11).

Since the tensional forces that characterize the modern constitutional *metaxy* are not regarded as susceptible to a natural resolution, they can be held only in a more or less precarious balance to prevent a fall into disorder. Thus the ancient, concrete symmetry of psyche and polis gives way to the modern conflict between a hypothetical, abstracted individual and an equally abstract society. This conflict is reflected in the written Constitution of the United States by the familiar counterpoise of principles embodied in provisions addressing individual rights and governmental powers. Yet the essential parallelism is not overcome; for, as we have seen in the maxim of Heraclitus, "One of a pair of opposites cannot exist without the other."[1]

Ironically, the sharpness of the Hobbesian conflict has been blunted considerably in Hobbes's own native land, primarily because, in England, the rights of individuals, like other aspects of British constitutionalism, have been regarded historically as derived from common law, defined by Blackstone as the "custom of the realm."[2] The constitutionally protected "rights of Englishmen" are a matter of conventional morality, part of the same fabric of constitutional rules and principles that restricts individual rights in the name of public order and common decency. The result of this way of thinking is that, under British constitutionalism, the extent of the exercise of individual rights is strongly conditioned by, and firmly grounded in, a conception of constitutional order that is widely regarded as that which makes the exercise of those very rights both possible and necessary. In turn, the conventional status of rights tends to blur but not to collapse the distinction between law and morals when these are regarded from a constitutional standpoint.

By contrast, individual rights in the United States nowadays are seen as derived from specific written constitutional provisions under the special guardianship of particular "rights-sensitive" institutions, the courts. The courts, then, engage in periodic battles with other, presumably less rights-sensitive institutions that are empowered by other constitutional provisions. These latter institutions tend to be viewed as seeking always to trample on individual or group rights at the behest of self-interested majorities.

This way of thinking has led to an overly sharp distinction between law and morals in the United States that tends, paradoxically, to collapse altogether in some instances, as in the well-known cliché about the impropriety of "legislating morality," a phrase that presupposes a distinction between law and morals so sharp as to eliminate any relationship whatever between them. Whenever an instance of legislating morals is charged, it is almost always part of an effort by some individual or group to claim high moral ground for themselves against social convention, whether or not the challenged legislative imposition has anything to do with morals as commonly understood.

Consequently, courts are often led to seek, find, and articulate moral grounds of decision outside conventional morality (and thus outside the common law) since conventional morality is usually the subject under attack by the individuals or groups seeking special constitutional protection against legislative majorities. But if courts are driven to seek guidance from sources of law outside convention merely because of their own institutional role, then that role itself must be firmly grounded either in constitutional text or constitutional tradition. And it is grounded in neither of these. Thus it often appears that conventional morality has been summarily dismissed without argument, and one is entitled to ask why.

Because of this conception of the relationship between law and morality, the law-morals distinction often tends to be confused with another: that between the "public" and the "private." If we think of morals as encompassing those areas of activity that are not (or should not be) subject to public regulation because they are regarded as essentially private and of law as encompassing the areas that are (or should be) subject to public regulation, then it is easy to see that the character of the law-morals distinction is intimately related to the public-private constitutional antinomy that is easily unbalanced where the distinction is drawn either too sharply or too narrowly.

For example, in the development of the Supreme Court's liberty of contract doctrine, a near-absolute transactional freedom in private business relationships was allowed to overcome the need for public economic regulation in the early twentieth century. Yet in the end the gain for economic liberty was short-lived, as the Court renounced all judicial supervision of economic regulatory schemes in the late 1930s as a result of the famous "switch in time that saved nine."

In the 1890s, however, the belief was widely shared among academic and social elites that public regulation of private business activity was immoral. That view led to an overly sharp distinction between law and morality and to the formulation of overly abstract legal doctrines to implement that distinction. The resulting intellectual incoherence in legal doctrine led ultimately to a complete collapse of that very distinction in the economic field.

Its collapse in turn has led to a set of legal doctrines as untenable as the earlier ones, including the unrealistic distinction between economic and personal rights. The Court's doctrine of personal privacy may represent a similar type of constitutional overextension, though it is still too early to tell whether the ultimate outcome will be the same. In these instances, an erosion of constitutional symbols resulted from the unbalancing of crucial constitutional antinomies established in order to balance public power against private rights. This unbalancing was caused largely by the importation into constitutional law of supposedly moral doctrines alien to the common law and its traditional interpretive practices. Two of these doctrines are Social Darwinism in the liberty of contract cases and, for lack of a better label, Lifestyle Liberalism in the modern privacy cases.

Lifestyle Liberalism arises from the idea that individual decisions concerning how life is best lived are sacrosanct. One of the earliest and most influential modern formulations of this outlook can be observed in the libertarian thought of John Stuart Mill. Millian liberalism necessarily involves skeptical presuppositions about the existence of an authoritative and knowable Good for human beings that is reflected in human nature and derived from a transcendent source of order (see Chapter 13).

Mill's main concern was *individual* liberty in its relation to majoritarian tyranny, the right to be let alone. In more recent times, however, his concern for individuals has given way to a focus on group identity generated by the sharing of particular lifestyles in which unimpaired participation is conceived as a kind of constitutional entitlement by the group's members. In today's pluralistic political atmosphere, where groups must compete in a Hobbesian political marketplace for government provision of greater security against real or imagined threats, an absolute right to be let alone easily becomes an absolute right to organize and recruit for the purpose of marketing a given lifestyle as widely as possible. In a Hobbesian world, the only real security against a violent end is the absolute power to bring others to such an end first.

When the call for absolute individual freedom to choose one's own plan of life—essentially, a right of privacy—is conceived as a *moral* obligation by all others to refrain from interfering with the absolute right of a group to propagate the given lifestyle as a viable alternative social state in Arrow's sense, then the natural boundary that distinguishes private right from public power is eroded, for the range of allowable social orderings is preeminently a public business. Confusing the public and the private in this manner exacerbates the problem of collective irrationality that arises from a relatively unrestricted domain of allowable individual preferences. As Arrow has shown, this lack of restriction makes democratic decisionmaking, in a sense, "impossible." Elevating the idea of individual choice with respect to one's own good into a supreme political principle treats the human Good (a public matter) as if it were merely a fragmented collection of individual (private) goods.

This confusion is not limited to cases in which essentially public matters are treated as private ones. Once the natural boundary dividing the public and the private is no longer visible, it should not be surprising to find problems that seem to travel in the other direction. A remarkable illustration of Lifestyle Liberalism's effect on the law with regard to such confusion is provided by Graham Walker in his discussion of two cases used by Michael Moore to exemplify the kind of decision that judges would be likely to make if only they would eschew conventional morality and instead "take a peek" at what Moore claims (without argument) to constitute *real* "moral reality."

In the second of the cases described by Walker, Moore's prescription, had it been followed by Judge Learned Hand, would have amounted to treating an essentially public matter (the conditions under which mercy killing is an appropriate response to financial exigency) as if it were private. And in the first case, Moore asks an Iowa judge to abandon a widely shared consensus (not just in Iowa) that the way in which children are raised (within some rather obvious limits) is a private matter and to impose instead, as a matter of public policy, a judicially created right to a "creative and stimulating environment."

> The examples [Moore] gives are not constitutional cases, but illustrate the point. An Iowa judge, says Moore, should have ignored a conventional consensus in rural Iowa about a child's need for a stable environment, and should instead have awarded custody to a California parent who could have guaranteed the child's "right" to a "creative and stimulating environment." Federal judge Learned Hand, if he had been Moore's kind of moral realist, could have seen the need, when faced with a case involving a father's mercy killing of his financially burdensome retarded child, to affront "conventional moral judgment" and acquit the father.[3]

In Chapter 13 I shall examine more thoroughly the philosophical underpinnings of the point of view that underlies Moore's position. It seems, in one instance, curiously to value the quality of life over life itself, and in the other, somewhat arbitrarily to elevate the value of an urban lifestyle over that of a rural one as a matter of law. But next I wish to examine more closely the views of those individuals who would encourage the abandonment of conventional morality in the manner of Moore's exemplary judge.

MORALS AND METHODS

Though there are important differences between and among the commentators who oppose reliance on traditional interpretive methods in constitutional law, many appear to have in common the conviction that judges should apply the moral and methodological conclusions of contemporary constitutional theory rather than the rules of traditional practice in the decision of cases. Since the latter derive mainly from English common law, it follows that the call for substitution of other rules amounts, in effect, to a denial of the authority of the common law foundation of American constitutionalism. Modern judicial activism is largely a result of the American judiciary's acceptance of this calling.

Contemporary constitutional theory, however, has thus far provided no viable, agreed-upon substitute for common law methodology. With respect to rules of interpretation, though a variety of interpretive strategies has been advanced in the works of contemporary theorists, their general tendency has been toward advocacy of what I have referred to as judicial freedom—leaving to individual judges, perhaps constrained by some very broad guidelines, the choice of which interpretive rules to employ in particular situations.[4]

Judicial freedom to create and select rules of interpretation is, in turn, methodologically prerequisite for wide judicial application of morally preferred outcomes, since no traditional interpretive approach, whether based on text or history, if faithfully carried out, would leave room for many such innovations. As to substantive law, the common law approach generally has been to restrict judicial innovation either to cases of first impression or to circumstances in which existing rules have been so completely overtaken by time, disuse, or changing social conventions as to be "absurd, unreasonable, or impossible to perform" were a court to attempt their application.[5]

Allowing courts to base particular judicial decisions on any approach conceived and developed external to the common law would be problematic enough in a common law jurisdiction, even if there existed a generally accepted alternative approach. But where there is no agreed-upon interpretive method, even among members of the "reasoning class," and where the views on substantive morality dominant in that class do not represent the views of society as a whole, the problems are exacerbated.[6] They are further exacerbated in constitutional law, where the effect of judicial decisions is greatly magnified, thus making it even more critical that existing social consensus be preserved. Again, authentic constitutional principles are by nature so widely agreed upon as to render their general application and acceptance part of a society's self-definition.

It is therefore appropriate to demand that any theory of constitutional interpretation reliant upon the infusion of external sources of constitutional principle specify the means by which widespread agreement plausibly may be presupposed. If no set of extralegal principles has been widely acknowledged enough to form a true constitutional consensus with sufficient clarity in its everyday implications to compose a viable source of law for judges engaged in constitutional interpretation, then the use of such principles will raise a question: Are judges indeed applying the favored principles of some social, political, or intellectual elite that has deluded itself into believing that its favored principles are (or ought to be) everyone else's, too?

Since the divorce of contemporary constitutional theory from conventional morality and the common law has produced the dismissive attitude of so many constitutional theorists toward ordinary citizens, it is not surprising to find a similarly dismissive attitude directed at conventional morality and the common law itself. The examples furnished by Moore are a case in point. Whatever one's views on mercy killing or child-rearing, it is surprising that anyone would trot out such cases as exemplary of the obvious. Yet Moore apparently thinks the right decisions in these cases so clear that he uses them in the belief that his audience will find their mere statement reason enough for allowing judges generally to scuttle moral or social conventions whenever they want to.

Moore suggests strongly that personal values, so long as these are the result of a process of moral truth-seeking in which a judge has been "in session with himself," ought *always* to trump conventional morality in the decision of constitutional cases. And he further suggests that the antidote for the plausible fear of "serious moral mistakes being imposed on hapless litigants," which he rightly suspects would arise from the widespread use of such an approach, is simply "better moral theory" administered by judges who are "sensitive moral beings" with "personal involvement"—in short, judges who are not "moral lepers."[7]

One might have expected at this point that Moore would make some attempt to explicate the "better moral theory" he has in mind; instead he merely points to the mercy killing and child-rearing examples while defending concededly antidemocratic "moral truth-seeking" on the bench. In the end, Moore appears to be satisfied with saying only that "given the present occupants of the bench," judges nowadays are not likely to be "moral lepers" who make decisions that are "morally awful." Without a shred of evidence, Moore concludes his brief discussion of the topic with these observations: "The danger of the wildly erratic judge with the bit in his teeth, charging down some morally outrageous path, is the real myth here. The worst we get from bad judges is conventional moral judgments of a woodenheaded sort."[8]

If my discussion of Moore seems a caricature, it is not meant to be. Moore's attitude is typical of the alarming extent to which modern academic elites have uncritically embraced the dominant role of judges in contemporary policymaking and the judicialized constitutionalism that complements that role. Social critic John Ralston Saul finds this unsurprising. Commenting on the judge as a "mythological" figure in modern bureaucratic society, a "prince of reason" who tries to decide cases "with the general good in mind," Saul notes that "the judge is precisely what the descendants of reason—technocrats in all their forms—have always wanted . . . the sort of individual that they have laboured to make our entire civilization feel it ought to want."[9]

Saul observes that our age seems to be operating under an "essential misunderstanding" that reason itself possesses moral authority, when, in truth, it is "nothing more than a disinterested administrative method." According to Saul, our "renewed and intense concentration on the rational element" has so eclipsed "the other more or less recognized human characteristics—spirit, appetite, faith and emotion, but also intuition, will and, most important, experience"—as to have produced "a degree of imbalance so extreme that the mythological importance of reason obscures all else and has driven the other elements into the marginal frontiers of doubtful respectability."[10]

Saul's comments suggest, contrary to the views of Moore and many other contemporary constitutional theorists, that judges engaged in moral philosophizing on the bench may indeed be more prone than others to regard the moral authority of modern rationalism somewhat uncritically, thus mistaking the worldview of a neo-Hegelian intellectual elite for a social consensus. Even if one grants the connection between rationality and judgment noted and criticized by Saul, and even if one grants further, with Moore and others, that judges are more likely to be "reasonable" than other decisionmakers, it is nonetheless a remarkable faith that would grant such decisional freedom to judges, in blatant disregard of historical practice and without even a smattering of serious argument. Though the normative significance of historical practices is hardly taken seriously among law school moralists today, it has never been convincingly demonstrated that (or why) a judge's personal convictions, moral or otherwise, ought to outweigh centuries of judicial experience in the resolution of legal disputes.

In Chapter 11 it will be shown that the "reason" discussed by Saul is not Reason itself but Enlightenment Rationalism, an ideology that holds forth a truncated view of reason that effectively reduces human intellect ("mind" or psyche in its classical sense) to the purely somatic ("brain function" in the modern view). To the extent that modern ethical thought, the morality that many constitutional theorists want judges to apply, is one with modern rationality, it is necessarily based on a similarly reductive, materialist view of the mind. This instrumental, materialist, reductionist idea of reason has the little-noticed but monumental effect of eliminating the entire domain of human thought referred to by the Ancients as the "intelligible," the realm of pure ideas not rooted in sense perception.[11] Such a foreshortened idea of reason renders tenuous the causal relationship between separate events over time and undermines any notion of history that attributes meaning to the temporal complexes of related experiences that are commonly called "traditions."

Though the separate events that make up the chronicler's notion of history are amenable to sense perception, the connection between them is not and is thus accessible only as an intelligible abstraction. Since any tradition is by definition an institutional habit based on asserted causal relations underlying a particular web of experience, any worldview that eliminates or deemphasizes the intelligible also eliminates or deemphasizes tradition. Yet the normative force of a traditional practice consists entirely in this posited causal connection between discrete applications of the practice—the attribute of the tradition that causes its repetition. Therefore any attack on traditional practices based on instrumental or materialist ideas of rationality necessarily will be question-begging and should be regarded with suspicion.

Modern moral philosophy is reductive in another sense as well. Its development has not only paralleled that of enlightenment rationalism but also that of political liberalism. Thus the course of its subsequent development has been so largely devoted to the analysis and evaluation of individual moral behavior as to call its procedures into serious question when these are applied to institutions. It is well established that the behavior of collectivities cannot be explained or evaluated solely in terms of the behavior of the individuals who constitute them.[12] Thus any simplistic application of moral theory to judicial decisionmaking risks falling into reductionism. This danger is exacerbated, not mitigated, when constitutional adjudication is involved because constitutions are examples of collective decisionmaking, par excellence, in both implementation and effect.[13]

Modern constitutional moralists are generally legal "rationalists" who want the courts to decide constitutional cases on the basis of currently fashionable moral theories rather than by traditional legal principles. They are devotees of Voltaire's brand of enlightenment rationalism, the truncated version of reason noted previously.[14] They are also, again generally, devotees of modern (Austinian) legal positivism (see Chapter 12), itself grounded in the modern political philosophy that descends from Machiavelli and Hobbes, and thus regard Law primarily as a tool of sovereign power.[15] Since truncated reason is merely a "logic," or an "administrative method," devoid of tradition, custom, or experience, it is essential to understand the fundamental premises from which "conclusions" are drawn and upon which people and things are "administered" (i.e., the ultimate goals or purposes of the sovereign), an understanding that instrumental reason cannot provide.

Today these premises are most often supplied, as to legislation, by a variant of general utilitarianism—i.e., maximization of pleasure (or minimization of pain) is regarded as the ultimate end of Law—and, as to adjudication, by a strain of Millian Liberalism—i.e., individual liberty to choose one's own life plan is to be fiercely protected against that very sovereign power of which Law is conceived as the tool.[16] The institutional effect of the confluence of these strains of thought is to elevate the judiciary to a position of supremacy in all questions thought to involve an ever-expanding list of basic liberties (as in First Amendment absolutism supported by expansive judicial review). The legislature then is increasingly expected to confine its activity to the enactment of laws that enhance the greatest material happiness of the largest number yet without the guidance of moral convention and traditional legal practice to curb judicial excess in the enforcement of the boundaries between legislative and judicial authority.[17]

MORALITY IN CONSTITUTIONAL LAW

I do not mean to imply here any disparagement of the role of morality in constitutional (or any other branch of) law or that the results of individual moral philosophizing are necessarily opposed to those of moral convention. My argument is that such results should not be given the force of law by courts unless and until they have received the sanction of general acceptance. In an important sense, law is nothing but the application of morality to the resolution of concrete disputes. The common law, especially in its earlier phases, developed largely by infusion of morality, particularly in cases of first impression; it could hardly have developed at all, otherwise.

The kind of morality endemic to our law is that of generally observed custom, which possesses the authority of tradition, not the morality of academicians, which can hardly be said to have existed during the formative era of the common law. It is a social morality—derived, developed, and tested in the common law process of adjudication, case by case, and fully democratic in Chesterton's sense.[18]

As common law developed, and progressively more of the commonly observed customs became part of the case law, English judges developed a doctrine of stare decisis that, among other things, served to constrain judicial discretion by converting those generally recognized customs that had received the imprimatur of repeated judicial application into rules of decision for subsequent cases of relevant similarity. By the time moral philosophy had begun to harden into an academic discipline in the late eighteenth century, the English doctrine of stare decisis had itself begun to harden into the more or less rigid system of precedent that it was to become in the nineteenth century.[19]

These developments naturally carried over into those areas of American law most strongly influenced by English common law, i.e., in most areas of private law. In constitutional law, however, the common law approach to limiting judicial discretion by strict rules of precedent did not achieve as strong a foothold. This was partly because the American Constitution is a written document the interpretation of which is more easily conceived along the lines of a statute than in accordance with a largely judge-made private law, and partly because the influence of Blackstone's *Commentaries* in America ensured a virtually wholesale reception of English common law in its eighteenth-century state, one that embodied a much more flexible approach to the doctrine of binding precedent than that which English courts would later develop.[20]

In the end, the rules of self-limitation developed by American courts in this field were primarily those of statutory construction, which are less serviceable for the job of restraining judges than are those of stare decisis. They are also less serviceable for the task of ensuring the incremental development demanded by such "rule of law" values as predictability, fairness, efficiency, and equality, though that is largely their purpose.[21] The rules of statutory interpretation, of which the doctrine of constitutional originalism is a special case, are not strong enough—even when combined with the weaker version of stare decisis that prevails in constitutional law—to constrain judicial discretion. Thus they cannot prevent constitutional instability unless they are firmly anchored in the traditional common law approach restricting importation of moral values into constitutional law to those values that have attained the status of conventional morality.

Such values may be imported because in effect they have already been incorporated into the fabric of common law by general infusion or, in some instances, by specific importation from some other (probably private law) area. They can thus, to borrow a thought from Karl Llewellyn, provide for the future while accounting adequately for the past.[22] Indeed, this is how our constitutional system was explicitly designed, as is proved beyond doubt by Alexis de Tocqueville's remarks nearly a half-century after the Constitution's adoption.

Tocqueville notes the importance of the fact that, in the United States, judicial refusal to apply an unconstitutional law affects only the parties in particular disputes and must be repeated in subsequent cases in order to undermine the law completely. The political power inherent in judicial review is thus circumscribed so as to make review more palatable in a democracy. Unknowingly prophesying the ultimate result of instituting a judicialized constitutionalism, Tocqueville continues:

> If the judges had been able to attack laws in a general and theoretical way, if they could have taken the initiative and censored legislation, they would have played a prominent part on the political scene; a judge who had become the champion or the advocate of a party would have stirred all the passions dividing the country to take part in the struggle. But when a judge attacks a law in the course of an obscure argument in a particular case, he partly hides the importance of his attack from public observation. His decision is just intended to affect some private interest; only by chance does the law find itself harmed. Moreover, the law thus censured is not abol-

ished; its moral force is diminished, but its physical effect is not suspended. It is only gradually, under repeated judicial blows, that it finally succumbs.[23]

Allowing judges to impose conclusions derived from the exercise of their own processes of individual reasoning (or from that of any other individual, for that matter), whether that reasoning is about "moral reality," "fundamental values," or "human rights," is to authorize judges to "attack law in a general and theoretical way," to "censor legislation," to become "champions or advocates of parties" (indeed, to become partisan), to "stir the passions" that divide the country at any given moment, and, ultimately, to "harm the law." Therefore the recommendation of contemporary commentators such as Michael Moore and Soterios Barber, that presumptive weight be given to a judge's personal convictions when these are in conflict with the conventions of public morality, must be firmly rejected.

LEGAL AND MORAL CONVENTIONALISM

Closely related to the issues just discussed is the issue of "realism" versus "conventionalism." Put simply, moral realists believe that moral standards are not simply a matter of custom or agreement or social convention but exist independently of the rules and habits of any particular society, or even of all societies. In other words, at least some moral standards are objectively real, true, and thus universal, binding particular societies and individuals whether the standards are recognized or not. Moral conventionalists, however, do not regard moral standards as binding unless they are recognized and sanctioned by particular societies. Moral standards may indeed be universal under conventionalism, but if and when they are, it is the result of general acceptance and not because of any characteristic internal to the standards themselves.

Since this is not a treatise on moral philosophy, I do not intend to go into the realism versus conventionalism issue in a deep or comprehensive way.[24] Rather, I wish to point out and discuss briefly a particular confusion that seems to bedevil contemporary constitutional theory: that between legal and moral conventionalism, on the one hand, and that between legal and moral realism, on the other.

Before going any further, let me state, for the record, my own position on these issues. I am both a moral realist and a legal conventionalist. That is to say, I believe that there are objectively real moral standards that are binding on all human beings and human societies at all times and at all places by virtue of human nature. Moreover, I believe that these objectively real moral standards are discoverable by experience and subject to confirmation by reason as to their truth.

Yet I believe that there is an essential difference between morality and law and that this distinction is sufficiently sharp to support a purely conventional justification for some legal practices that is not available for moral standards. In other words, though some legal practices are based on moral standards that are themselves experienced as both universally compelling and rooted in moral absolutes, many legal practices are not so experienced and thus must be justified on purely conventional grounds.

At the same time, the fact that objective moral standards exist and are knowable does not entail a requirement that all such standards be directly translated into compulsory legal rules. If it did, there would have to be legal penalties attached to failure to perform supererogatory acts, failure to attain specified levels of moral virtue, and the like. It is within this category of moral standards—some of which may be "legalized" and some not—that the constitutional tension between law and morality is commonly experienced.

Immanuel Kant, a particularly perceptive commentator on the distinction in question, differentiates law and morals in accord with the incentives, or motives, of action.

> If legislation makes an action a duty and at the same time makes this duty the incentive, it is *ethical*. If it does not include the latter condition in the law and therefore admits an incentive other than the Idea of duty itself, it is *juridical*. As regards juridical legislation, it is easily seen that the incentive here, being different from the Idea of duty, must be derived from pathological grounds determining will, that is, from inclinations and disinclinations and, among these, specifically from disinclinations, since it is supposed to be the kind of legislation that constrains, not an allurement that invites. . . . The mere agreement or disagreement of an action with the law, without regard to the incentive of the action, is called *legality;* but, when the Idea of duty arising from the law is at the same time the incentive of the action, then the agreement is called the *morality* of the action.[25]

Although most people do not question the recognition of important distinctions between morality and law, some contemporary constitutional theorists appear to have ignored these distinctions when formulating their theories of constitutional adjudication. For example, Soterios Barber, submitting a "general theory of what the Constitution is and what it means," states his "principal thesis":

> If we are to make sense of what the Constitution says, we shall have to interpret and apply its provisions in light of our best understanding of an ideal state of affairs adumbrated by those provisions. At the center of this constitutionally ideal state of affairs is a typical citizen, who is governed by an attitude that places the highest social or political value on the activity of reasoning about how one ought to live. I consider this attitude a kind of liberalism because it tolerates, even as it works through government to weaken, such unconstitutional attitudes as racism, sexism, self-righteousness, zealotry, willfulness, acquisitiveness, and moral skepticism.[26]

Barber's failure to take seriously the Kantian distinction, reflected in his idea of "unconstitutional attitudes," perhaps explains why, in a review of my earlier book on judicial review, he mistakes my own legal conventionalism for moral conventionalism—which it is not.[27] Moreover, the remainder of Barber's preceding statement helps to shed light on some of the consequences of the failure to attend sufficiently to the distinction between law and morality.

Collapsing the distinction first leads directly to Barber's notion of constitutional citizenship, a notion that reflects a fundamental confusion of the "ideal" with the "typical" that is fully apparent on the face of his remarks. This confusion of the ideal with the typical leads straightforwardly to the identification of constitutional citizenship with the kind of person who has the ability and inclination to place "the highest social or political value on the activity of reasoning about how one ought to live."

But not only was the U.S. Constitution not drafted for a society thought destined to be populated by individuals who place the highest value on "reasoning about how one ought to live," it was demonstrably adopted in firm anticipation that the people to be governed by that instrument would be disposed continually to "racism, sexism, self-righteousness, zealotry, willfulness, acquisitiveness, and moral skepticism." Some of these traits may even have been encouraged by the Framers, acknowledging the Hobbesian character of modern political life. Adopting Barber's constitutionalism amounts, in effect, to infusing the historical constitution with a Marxian-style teleology bent on the transformation of human nature itself, a transformation that, if accomplished, would render that very constitution superfluous.

Thus Barber's constitutional theory is explicitly ideological, constitutionalizing the left-wing, progressivist values of what I referred to earlier as a "neo-Hegelian intellectual elite." Indeed, Barber comes close to conceding this point when he predicts that "some readers may suspect that I have constructed an illiberal and therefore self-contradictory liberalism that arbitrarily favors the elitist values of what some writers are now calling 'the reasoning class.' "[28]

Although I shall examine this progressivist value system in its relation to constitutional interpretation more fully in Chapters 13 and 14, it is worthwhile to note now that Barber, Moore, and other constitutional theorists who disparage conventionalism in constitutional adjudication appear to have collapsed the law-morals distinction in exactly the same way. As we have already seen, Moore urges judges merely to strive for "progressively better moral theory" when deciding cases, going even so far as to argue that, whenever a judge who is not a "moral leper" thinks he has got it right, he is entitled, if not obliged, to disregard "conventional morality" and decide according to his personal moral view.[29]

The two examples offered by Moore to shed light on what he thinks judges are likely to decide as a result of such striving should indicate that good intentions do not qualify either judges or commentators, moral realists or not, to impose their moral views on litigants. Moral reality is not something that can be grasped by good intentions, effort, or imagination. If it can be obtained, it will only be as a result of the widest possible understanding, both historical and theoretical, as to what in reality *is* moral and what is *not*—the latter category including that which is "merely legal." Moreover, since morality is particularly human, no idea of moral reality can be fully coherent without a thorough grounding in some idea of human nature that is fully developed in its ramifications.

Perhaps that is why Moore calls his theory of constitutional adjudication a "natural law" theory of interpretation. Yet one searches in vain for a comprehensive theory of human nature (indeed, for any idea of human nature at all) that might support his views, though this is the very ingredient that any defensible moral realism based on natural law must contain. Natural law is founded upon the experience of moral imperatives in the law and is developed from the attempt to provide that experience with a rational basis in human nature (see Chapters 12 and 13). Any ascription of moral truth to a rule or principle not developed thus is either a pretension or a fraud.

It is also instructive to contrast moral realism with legal realism, as these terms have been traditionally employed. One would, for instance, suspect a parallel usage so that if moral realism is taken to represent belief in objective moral standards, then legal realism would represent belief in objective legal rules. But exactly the reverse is true. Legal realism, at least since the 1920s, has been taken to stand for the *denial* of objective legal truth. To the limited extent that there has been an opposing view at all, it has been dismissed under such headings as "idealism" or "mechanical jurisprudence."

There is a method to this madness; for the absence of an effective terminological counterpart in law for realism in morals has served to obscure the distinction between law and morality, which is at the root of the problems in connection with the constitutional theories of Barber and Moore. The bottom line is this: in order to argue persuasively that judges should apply objectively correct moral standards in preference to conventionally accepted legal rules when deciding concrete cases, one must do a great deal more than simply to note the possible existence of such standards. I am not satisfied that many contemporary constitutional theorists have done even this much.

First, the standards in question must be derived from a comprehensive theory of human nature that is consonant with human experience, broadly conceived, not merely with the interests or predilections of a particular class or group of intellectual elites at a particular time. Second, it must be shown that the standards are fully discoverable in the sense that they proceed from a correspondence theory of truth, not merely from a coherence theory of meaning, else the standards will be "real" only in the limited sense of being present in the mind of the theorist or judge who is their "discoverer."[30] Finally, it must be demonstrated that judges have a valid claim, either by temperament or by training, to special competence in the discovery and application of moral truth and that they are both morally and legally entitled to exercise this competence in the course of performing regular judicial duties.

In other words, if one wishes to defend the idea that judges should use constitutional law to impose objectively correct moral standards or to inculcate moral virtue according to natural law (or any of its surrogates) in the American citizenry, one must begin with some such statement as the definition of moral virtue provided by Etienne Gilson, that "the essence of virtue is made up of a habit *(habitus)* of the will and of the conformity with natural law of the acts which follow from that habit."[31] One must then spell out the ontological, epistemological, and jurisprudential implications of that statement. One must say what "habits," "wills," and "acts" are; how acts follow from habits, and how acts following from habits may or may not conform to natural law; what the "nature" *is* from which the "law" is drawn, why it is an "is" and not merely a "what," and how that law of nature is related to the Constitution; how we know all of this, why we should expect judges to know it too, and why we should expect them to apply it correctly even if they do know it. To my knowledge, no contemporary constitutional theorist has come close to presenting a strong case for judicial application of objective moral standards that would satisfy these requirements.

Part Three · The Legacy of the British Constitution

American constitutionalism has been considered from several different perspectives and is found to involve a number of problematic tensions. Among these are the individual and society, law and morality, constitutional symbolism and constitutional experience, written and unwritten constitutions, flexible and rigid constitutions, and British and American constitutionalism. In Part Two, the distinctions represented by these relationships were emphasized in order to bring out, and to critique, some of the reductive features of contemporary constitutional theory.

In several of these instances, a single complex of reality, the essence of which is a polar antinomy experienced as a tension in the constitutional *metaxy*, is broken into its component parts, the parts then being treated as self-subsisting (hypostatic) entities. Law is treated as a field of activity completely distinct from morals, when, in truth, law and morality are the same kind of activity regarded from different perspectives—perspectives that are themselves often experienced as in tension with one another. Written and unwritten constitutions are treated as fundamentally different (and opposed) kinds of constitutions, when, in truth, written constitutions can never be more than representative (or unrepresentative) approximations of underlying real constitutions that are unwritten.

In Part Three, the emphasis will be different. In the chapters that follow, I shall argue that much of the "flexible," "real," foundation underlying the "rigid" written Constitution of the United States is (and has always been) the unwritten British Constitution, the legal basis for which is the English common law. It is this common law foundation that largely saves American constitutionalism from the gnosticism of modern political philosophy and contemporary constitutional theory (see Chapter 14) and that makes possible an escape from the groundlessness of legal positivism into a naturalistic constitutional jurisprudence even in our own skeptical, perhaps cynical, age (see Chapter 12).

First, however, the connection(s) between British and American constitutionalism must be made more clear, and the claims of legal history upon constitutional theory need to be evaluated. This can be done only by focusing on some of the details of Anglo-American legal history. The details are crucial for, as S. F. C. Milsom writes in *The Legal Framework of English Feudalism* (Cambridge: Cambridge University Press, 1976),

> History is difficult because people never state their assumptions or describe the framework in which their lives are led. To the extent that you do not unthinkingly supply these from your own experience, you can only guess at them from what your actors said and did. There will be no more evidence for the most important lines in your picture than that they fit with the demonstrable detail. They are either obvious or wrong. (P. 1)

In order to supply the "demonstrable detail" that confirms the continuity of Anglo-American legal history, in Chapter 8, I shall set the general historical framework, assessing the extent to which the British constitutional tradition and the common law are precursive of the Constitution of 1787. The American Constitution borrows heavily from that of Great Britain not only in particular provisions but also in general approach.

In Chapter 9, I examine the most important rules of interpretation traditionally applied to written legal instruments. These rules were universally expected to apply to the legal interpretation of written constitutional instruments during the American Founding era. I also consider the issue of original intent in constitutional jurisprudence in both its subjective and objective guises, contrasting original with remedial intent and placing intentionalism in its appropriate historical context within the rules of interpretation more generally.

In Chapter 10, I connect the most important rules of interpretation with those of precedent, which constitute the heart of adjudication under the common law. Contrary to some popular impressions, original intent and stare decisis, when properly employed, are fully compatible—even complementary—approaches in constitutional jurisprudence. Attention to the fictional character of these doctrines helps to reveal both their fundamental complementarity and their similarity to fictional doctrines in science and other fields. I also consider the importance of custom in the law, both from the standpoint of classical legal theory and from the perspective of the common law.

8 · The British Constitution and the Common Law

American constitutional law did not begin with the drafting or adoption of the U.S. Constitution. For a period prior to its drafting, which is roughly the temporal equivalent of that since its adoption, the American colonists developed a legal system that was in some ways distinct from, and in other ways very like, that of Great Britain. Most of the differences were in the area of procedure and reflected chiefly the altered circumstances of life in a sparsely populated, geographically immense colonial territory. At the same time, despite the distinctions, the substantive law applied in colonial courts was largely that of English common law, appropriately modified to suit novel American conditions.

When the colonists began to establish formal hierarchies of courts in the early eighteenth century, they followed the model provided by the English judicial system. An early example is found in the establishment of the Massachusetts Bay Superior Court of Judicature in 1701, which was empowered

> to deal with all matters as fully and amply, to all intents and purposes whatsoever, as the Courts of King's Bench, Common Pleas, and Exchequer within the kingdom of England had or ought to have.[1]

Later, after the original colonies had formed the states of the American Union, several made their "reception" of common law official by legislation; those that did not soon found their courts effectively bringing about a similar result through case-by-case adjudication. Ultimately, though there had been some initial resistance in the original colonies—due, no doubt, to revolutionary fervor and other political factors—the common law was officially received in most of the states, and Chief Justice Oliver Ellsworth could remark in a grand jury charge of 1799 that English common law, "with here and there an accommodating exception . . . was the law of every part of the union at the formation of the national compact."[2]

Much of the strength of this reception can be ascribed to the career of four books written by the first professor of English law at Oxford, who effectively summarized the common law as it stood on the eve of the American Revolution. These books were to become the bible of American jurisprudence in the nineteenth century. Alan Watson, a prominent legal historian, describes the event:

> The victory of the Common law would, I suggest, have been much more difficult and perhaps even impossible had it not been for Blackstone's *Commentaries of the Laws of England.* The authority and popularity of this four-volume work was enormous. In his lifetime it ran through eight editions in England, the ninth was ready at his death in 1780, and it made its author a small fortune. At least 21 "straight" English editions were published in America from 1771–1774; from 1803 onwards, at least 94 editions emerged with American notes; and there were at least 55 editions of abridgements for students, including the *Pennsylvania Blackstone* by J. Reed (1871), and the extremely popular *American Student's Blackstone.* The work covered all the law, and in American editions was usually printed in two volumes. Thus, it was comprehensive, cheap, and convenient for slipping into saddle bags—an ideal work in fact for sparsely populated areas.[3]

The common law, in its turn, had been developed by English courts over a period of several hundred years prior to the American colonization. To some observers, it was an "ungodly jumble" of unsystematized case law; but many on both sides of the Atlantic thought it had served the English well, especially in periods of crisis—of which there had been aplenty during the three centuries before America's revolt. According to one of England's greatest legal historians, Frederic William Maitland,

> The English common law was tough, one of the toughest things ever made. And well for England was it in the days of Tudors and Stuarts that this was so. A simpler, a more rational, a more elegant system would have been an apt instrument of despotic rule. At times the judges were subservient enough: the king could dismiss them from their offices at a moment's notice; but the clumsy, cumbrous system, though it might bend, would never break. It was ever awkwardly rebounding and confounding the statecraft which had tried to control it. The strongest king, the ablest minister, the rudest Lord Protector could make little of this.[4]

The common law confounded statecraft, bending but never breaking, not merely because of its much-vaunted flexibility; it was flexible because it represented the weight of centuries of legal experience. It was not the fabrication of a single individual or group working at a particular time or place, not a product of abstract reasoning. Rather, it was the product of countless experiences of both similar and varied kinds across vast reaches of time and space, absorbing essential continuities in a reality that can be known only historically.

Its basic structure, Anglophilia notwithstanding, was largely Roman. Its earliest practitioners and commentators, though not necessarily its later ones, were learned in Roman law; Blackstone organized his influential *Commentaries* along lines similar to those of Justinian's *Institutes*.[5] English common lawyers also inherited from the Romans a distinction that is arguably the most fundamental in Western law and upon which both British and American constitutionalism are largely based: that between the public and the private.

Since constitutional law, as we know it, is a branch of public law, it follows that there can be no constitutional law in the modern sense without a clear differentiation of public from private law. The best way, then, to go about looking for the origins of constitutional development in a legal system is to locate the point at which public and private law become fully differentiated in legal consciousness. In Anglo-American constitutional development, this point will be found during the century and a half following the Norman Conquest.[6]

From a virtually complete subordination of public to private law during the period of the ancient Kentish "dooms," there emerge early in the thirteenth century the provisions of Magna Carta (1215), several of which have direct descendants in the American Constitution.[7] The troubles that brought King John and the English barons to Runnymede also set in motion the process of modern Anglo-American constitutional development. As noted by Edward Jenks, during this period the law was made "common," "judicial," and "national."[8] And the process is paralleled centuries later in the formative period of American law.

Thus it is hardly surprising that when, on the eve of the American Revolution, such radical reformers as James Otis began looking about for precedents to support the rise against English tyranny, they found the musty old law books of that most English of all jurists, Sir Edward Coke, ready to hand. It was the "clumsy, cumbrous" common law itself that was experienced by the colonists as their most reliable source of protection against both royal and parliamentary abuse.

This is even more remarkable since it might have been expected that legal ideas would be relegated to a secondary role once existing institutions and practices were thrown into the boiling cauldron of the Revolution, but here was the exception that proves the rule. Apparently the belief of many Americans that they themselves and not merely their ancestors really were English counted for much. Perhaps our oft-noted litigiousness had been stimulated by the activity of colonial juries, or maybe we simply were reluctant revolutionaries from the beginning.

Whatever the cause of their conservatism, when the colonists began to talk of separation from Great Britain, they sought legal, not merely political, support. They found it mainly in the English common law and in its offshoot, English equity jurisprudence. In *Paxton's Case*, James Otis recalls and develops Lord Coke's admonition, in *Dr. Bonham's Case*, that the common law might control acts of parliament when such acts are contrary to reason or natural justice.[9] In the Declaration of Independence, the most famous tract of the period, Thomas Jefferson appeals to principles of equity in his justification of rebellion. Both instances represent appeals to overriding principles of justice that were experienced as already embodied in the law, if only the British rulers would apply the principles fairly on both sides of the Atlantic.

Superimposed on the legal system developed by the colonists was a governmental and political structure that likewise both differed from and reflected English institutional practices and constitutional principles. For instance, there was widespread acceptance among the colonists of the English philosopher John Locke's idea that government exists primarily for the sake of individual well-being, and a resulting perception that institutional protections against arbitrary assertions of power—whether legislative, executive, or judicial—are required in any properly constituted government.

Yet the colonists did not view judges as their main line of defense against tyranny; rather, they looked to the common law jury, which had law-finding and fact-finding powers, for protection against tyrannical judges as well as against autocratic administrators and overbearing legislatures.[10] Indeed, the colonists developed a much stronger attachment to the common law jury than the English themselves ever developed as the institutional locus of constitutional protection for individual rights, and they imparted to juries wide powers that were (and still are) unheard-of on the eastern side of the Atlantic.

Concern over the possibility of judicial tyranny is the probable explanation of why the Framers ultimately declined the invitation to establish separate courts of equity along the lines of the English model. After all, the injunction had been tamed, and English equity regularized, in the eighteenth century; and in nineteenth-century England it would be fused with common law along the lines of the American example.[11] Even so, since equity knows not the jury, introduction of such a system in effect would have been to institute a system of bench trials, reliant on the individual conscience of the judge rather than on the common wisdom of the community as represented in the jury; and overbearing judges were as much of a problem then as they are now.

These concerns are also reflected clearly in the earliest successful constitutional challenges to American state laws. In the most famous half-dozen cases in which such challenges occurred, at least four, and perhaps five, involved deprivation of the common law right of trial by jury. In other words, each case involved substitution either of a bench trial (trial by a judge alone) or of an attainder (trial by legislature) for a jury trial.[12] These early attempts to interfere with the jury system, and thereby to impair one of the most prized common law rights of the British, helped to generate wide support in the colonies for a sharper and more formal differentiation of governmental functions than the quasi-formal approach known under the British Constitution in which courts were nominally part of an executive establishment that did not operate in the same manner on both sides of the Atlantic.

These interferences constitute an important part of the experiential foundation both of separation of powers doctrine and of judicial review in the United States, shaping the context in which the separation provisions that were formally declared to be the guiding principles of several new state constitutions during the revolutionary period should be read. The most famous of these provisions is the separation article of the Massachusetts Constitution of 1780, which commands that the legislative department

> shall never exercise the executive and judicial powers, or either of them; the executive shall never exercise the legislative and judicial powers or either of them; the judicial shall never exercise the legislative and executive powers or either of them; to the end, it may be a government of laws, and not of men.[13]

It is important not to lose sight of the stated purpose, or end, of these sharp distinctions: that there may be "a government of laws, and not of men." It is equally important not to lose sight of the fact that what the colonists called the "laws" was preeminently the common law and that the authority of courts and judges (the "men") was seen largely to be a function of the authority of that English *ius gentium*. This view was no less true after the framing and adoption of written constitutions in America than it had been before.

Moreover, it is impossible fully to understand the singularly most important feature of American constitutional development subsequent to the Founding—the rise of the U.S. Supreme Court to a position of centrality in constitutional interpretation and thus of adjudication itself as the central focus of our constitutional law—without comprehending the rules and principles of common law adjudication that American judges inherited from their earlier English counterparts. Among these were the rules of statutory construction developed by English courts in the wake of the critical constitutional struggles of the seventeenth century among proponents of parliamentary supremacy, royal prerogative, and the common law, struggles that resulted in the triumph of parliamentary supremacy in 1688.

These rules continue to influence American judges, both in the interpretation of statutes and written constitutions. But more to the point here, it should be remembered that the role of the Supreme Court in constitutional interpretation undoubtedly would be a great deal smaller today were it not for the early Court's careful limitation of its constitutional role by strict application of common law rules that effectively reduced both the jurisdiction and interpretive discretion of courts generally. It was this careful husbanding of judicial resources that enabled the Marshall Court to assimilate fundamental to ordinary law, thus making the Constitution interpretable in the manner of other legal texts, indeed, making constitutional interpretation both possible and necessary.[14]

When contemporary constitutional theorists urge the Court to dispense with traditional interpretive rules because these are deemed to be less appropriate for constitutions than, say, for statutes, contracts, deeds, or wills, they are in fact urging the Court to dispense with the practice that is the very foundation of its own authority to interpret the Constitution in the first place.

CONSTITUTIONAL ANTECEDENTS

The continuity between the British and American Constitutions that resulted from the profound attachment of the colonists to the common law and its institutions is so impressive as to defy any attempt at a comprehensive elaboration. One is reminded of the classic opening paragraph of Pollock and Maitland's *History of English Law:*

> Such is the unity of all history that any one who endeavours to tell a piece of it must feel that his first sentence tears a seamless web. The oldest utterance of English law that has come down to us has Greek words in it: words such as *bishop, priest* and *deacon.* If we would search out the origins of Roman law, we must study Babylon: this at least was the opinion of the great Romanist of our own day. A statute of limitations must be set; but it must be arbitrary. The web must be rent; but, as we rend it, we may watch the whence and whither of a few of the severed and ravelling threads which have been making a pattern too large for any man's eye.[15]

Though the statute of limitations imposed on the discussion here indeed will be somewhat arbitrary, it is nonetheless worthwhile to remind readers of the vastness of the intersection of English and American constitutionalism by noting just a few of the threads that tie these domains together.

To begin, much of the U.S. Constitution consists of fairly straightforward and unoriginal borrowings from British constitutional documents or conventions. Our bicameral national legislature with general legislative authority (Article 1, Section 1), with its "most numerous" lower house possessing power to choose its own leaders and to impeach judges and other officials (Article 1, Section 2; English Bill of Rights), and with both upper and lower chambers constitutionally committed to regular sessions (Article 1, Section 4; English Bill of Rights) and in possession of full power to govern their own internal procedures (Article 1, Section 5; English Bill of Rights) is in these respects and more modeled after the English parliament.[16]

Moreover, the Article 1, Section 7 principle requiring initiation of revenue bills in the House of Representatives and its corollary that there may be taxation "only by legislation"[17] find their origin in the English convention that "the House of Lords does not originate any money bill."[18] The practice of multiple readings of proposed laws in both houses of Congress copies another English convention that "a bill must be read a certain number of times before passing through the House of Commons."[19] The idea that "what touches all shall be decided in parliament"[20] is the basis for the principle underlying the Tenth Amendment, perhaps best expressed in John Marshall's opinions on the division of national and state authority conditioned by the logic of "part and whole."[21]

In addition to various limitations on presidential power that stem from the English Bill of Rights,[22] the commander-in-chief and executive pardoning powers of Article 2, Section 2 have deep roots in the British Constitution as do the importance of oaths[23] and the limitations implied in the Article 1, Section 8 commission to Congress of the power to raise armies and navies.[24] There is also the Article 1, Section 3 subjection of impeached and convicted public officials to "indictment, trial, judgment and punishment, according to law," which finds its origin in the deeply rooted English principle of ministerial responsibility that is a major component in the British Constitution's idea of the Rule of Law.[25]

The Article 1, Section 9 restriction on suspension of the habeas corpus privilege is rooted in the English Act of 1679 (31 Chas. 2, c. 2, 27) and in a restatement of Magna Carta (31 Car. 11, 6.7, 8).[26] The prohibitions on bills of attainder and on ex post facto laws found in Article 1, Sections 9 and 10, as well as the concept of the "privileges and immunities" of citizenship found in Article 4 and the Fourteenth Amendment, may also be found in proposals by British statesmen generations before the adoption of the American Constitution.[27] The Statute of Mortmain (1279), which provided, among other things, that no corporation could hold land in England except under certain conditions, one of which was by a grant made prior to the statute,[28] is the basis for the Marshall Court's reading of the contract clause (Article 1, Section 10), allowing no interference with grants made previously.

From Edward III's Statute of Treasons (1352), protecting subjects against political prosecutions,[29] comes the definition of treason found in Article 3, Section 3. The judicial independence guaranteed in Article 3, Section 1 owes much to the antecedent hard-fought struggles of the English judiciary centuries before the framing of the U.S. Constitution. The institution of local juries in federal criminal trials, guaranteed in Article 3, Section 2, is likewise an outgrowth of several centuries of developing common law on the other side of the Atlantic.

In summary, of the twenty-one sections making up the first four articles of the U.S. Constitution, at least sixteen contain one or more provisions that are directly traceable to English sources. Similarly, at least seventeen of twenty-eight provisions in the first eight amendments of the U.S. Constitution find their ancestry in the common law of England. In the English Bill of Rights alone may be found early versions of provisions contained in the First, Second, Fifth, Sixth, and Eighth Amendments,[30] for instance, as in the "proportionality" requirement embodied in the "cruel and unusual punishments" clause of the Eighth Amendment.[31]

From the Petition of Right (3 Chas. 1, c.1, 7, June 1628) come additional provisions in the First and Third Amendments.[32] From the original text of Magna Carta come the right of petition for redress of grievances,[33] the right of public assembly,[34] and the right not to be amerced except by the judgment of peers, according to the law of the land, "by the due course and processe of Law" (chapter 39, Coke's paraphrase in the *Institutes*).[35]

The last provision is the forerunner of due process clauses in both the Fifth and Fourteenth Amendments, as well as in most of our state constitutions, and is the basis of much of our criminal jurisprudence. Finally, in the famous cry of Thomas Becket in reaction to Article 3 of the Constitutions of Clarendon (1164), *"Nec enim Deus iudicat bis in idipsum"* ("Even God does not judge twice in the same matter"), may be found the origin of the double jeopardy provision of the Fifth Amendment.[36]

THE COMMON LAW FOUNDATION

The influence of British on American constitutionalism is apparent not only in particular constitutional provisions but even more in the general approaches and orientations without which the particulars would be of little significance. The claim of Americans to individual rights based upon and under the protection of the common law would hardly have been intelligible had not the English long regarded such common law rights as incorporated, in effect, in their own traditional constitution. Likewise, the American habit of entrusting courts (especially federal courts) with primary responsibility for safeguarding these rights is not fully comprehensible without prior acknowledgment of a bevy of English rules safeguarding them against particular, special, or local infringement, for example, the rule requiring that special customs in derogation of the common law be strictly construed.[37]

Closely related to the last-mentioned rule, Blackstone's Tenth Rule of statutory construction, based on Lord Coke's dictum in *Dr. Bonham's Case*,[38] holds that legislative acts "impossible to be performed" are invalid and that absurd or unreasonable legal consequences arising from such acts are void.[39] This rule, when joined with Article 3's extension of federal judicial power to cases and controversies arising under the Constitution, provides the foundation for the early American doctrine of judicial review, conceived as a defensive power of courts to resist encroachment of other agencies of government on the performance of the primary judicial function: that of protecting legal rights through peaceful resolution of disputes between parties showing concrete adversity.[40]

Without this history, the constitutional liberty under law that is the great distinction of Anglo-American jurisprudence would be unknown. Our constitutional liberty is firm because it is historical; it is historical not merely because it has historic antecedents but also because it is largely customary—i.e., its institutional forms and practices are so widely disseminated as to be fully democratic in the Chestertonian sense.[41] Blackstone observes that a law's tendency to heighten liberty by itself constitutes good evidence that the law is founded on "general assent and immemorial use"; and, citing the Roman jurist Julianus, he concludes that "those laws which the people hath approved without writing ought also to bind every body."[42]

Only one reared in the traditions of that singular country in the world in which the extension of liberty, defined as the power to do what the laws permit, is generally regarded as the "very end and scope of the constitution" could make such a statement.[43] It is the Law itself that is here conceived as the wellspring of liberty, the "ordered liberty" of Justice Cardozo's famous *Palko* opinion,[44] not the abstract *liberté* of the French Revolution, which turns liberty to license by allowing, if not requiring, a virtually complete destruction of existing social institutions and practices to bring about its realization.[45] It is this idea of Law, grounded in reason, experience, and common sense, that is the most important feature of the common law constitutionalism handed down to us by the English jurists.

The idea of Law conceived as a mixture of reason and experience has a long and venerable history, much more so than the enlightenment rationalism that is characteristic of so much contemporary constitutional theorizing. The reason of the common law is classical, taking its cues from Aristotle and Aquinas, not from Hobbes and Voltaire. Indeed, English common law is arguably the main conduit through which ancient ideas of law and politics have been transmitted to an age otherwise almost completely under the sway of logical and legal positivism, scientistic reductionism, and truncated rationalism.

The profound opposition between the "reason of the common law" and the reason of the philosophes can be seen clearly in Lord Chief Justice Hale's response to Thomas Hobbes's theory of law. Objecting to the application of the Hobbesian doctrine of sovereignty to English law, to the resulting arbitrariness of the command theory of law implicit in that doctrine, and to the purely analytical and instrumental notion of reason on which all such doctrines and theories are based, Hale counters with a straightforward appeal to classical and scholastic ideas of reason and law. Against the nominalism and positivism of Hobbes, Hale offers realism and naturalism, asserting the real existence of an intelligible world that fully comprises the objects of both scientific and legal thought. For Hale, Reason

> may be found in thinges that are destitute of the faculty of Reason and is or may be antecedent to any Exercise of any humane Reasonable facultie: thus the Connexion of Effects to their Causes, the Consequences of Propertyes to their Formes or Essences, the Exertions of Acts by their Powers, the ordination and disposition of Naturall thinges in their severall places, and Orders: the Connaturall tendencyes and motions of thinges in Nature to their Preservation and Conveniences have a reasonableness that is a Decorum, Congruitie, and Conseqution though they were noe man in the world to take notice of itt. . . . And in Moralls though the objects thereof are more obscure, and not soe open to a distinct and Cleare Discoverie, yett there is a Certaine Reasonableness and Congruitie, and Intrinsick Connexion and Consequence of one thing from an other antecedent to any Artificiall Systeme of Moralls or Institution of Laws.[46]

Neither the reason of Hale, nor the law and rights that follow from it, can be circumscribed by definitions or axioms; rather, "The rights of men are in a sort of middle, incapable of definition, but not impossible to be discerned."[47] Yet discernment, unlike definition, requires experience conditioned by practice and habit. Employing Plato's favorite method of arguing to form from function, Hale strongly suggests the affinity of the common law with Aristotelian practical reason,[48] noting that Reason

> is taken complexedly when the reasonable facultie is in Conjunction with the reasonable Subject, and habituated to it by Use and Exercise, and it is this kind of reason or reason thus taken that Denominates a Man a Mathematician, a Philosopher, a Politician, a Phisician, a Lawyer; yea that renders men excellent in their particular Acts as a good Engineer, a good Watchmaker, a good Smith, a good Surgeon.[49]

This idea of law, conditioned by habit, use, and exercise, "the Production of long and Iterated Experience which . . . discovers those defects and Supplys which no witt of Man coud either at once foresee or aptly remedye,"[50] is comprised as well in the three definitions of law handed down by Lord Coke and discussed thoroughly by James Stoner.[51] According to Stoner, Coke defines Law as "the perfection of reason, which commands what is useful and necessary, and forbids the contrary",[52] "a just sanction, commanding what is right, and prohibiting the contrary";[53] and, simply, "the highest reason."[54] Elsewhere, Coke states his well-known view that "legal rules are many but legal reason is one."[55]

The most important aspect to note about these conceptions is that they resemble those of Cicero and Aquinas more than they resemble those of Hobbes or Austin.[56] Their affinity is with classical rather than modern rationalism. Coke subordinates politics to law in the manner of the ancients, not law to politics in the manner of the moderns.[57] If law commands what is "useful and necessary," it does so only because what is useful and necessary is also "just" and "right." But what is useful and necessary is just and right only if the law is a unity, only if the legal rules that are "many" are fully subordinate to, and fully explicable in terms of, the legal reason that is "one."

Blackstone too adopts this conception of the law's unity, holding that *lex non scripta*, the unwritten substance of the common law, is knowable by the application of reason to legal experience as recorded in prior judicial decisions and that precedents found to be "absurd" or "unjust" are not merely "bad law," they were never "law" at all.[58] Blackstone also clearly distinguishes between laws "declaratory of natural rights and duties" and laws "determinative of things indifferent," adding that for acts *mala in se* ("wrong in themselves"), the municipal or positive law adds nothing to the obligation stemming from natural or divine law.[59]

These examples suggest that the common law is an important vehicle by which the ideas of classical legal thought have been imported into Anglo-American constitutionalism. They are reminiscent of Socrates' effort in *Minos* to answer the question, "What is law, for us?"[60] Denying that law can be merely "the things that are lawfully accepted"[61] (because bad things can be accepted) or "the official opinion of the city"[62] (because official opinions can be false), Socrates argues that law is (or tends to be) "the discovery of what is."[63] Though the expression is perhaps curious, its import is clear enough. The things that may be "lawfully accepted" and the ideas that may become "official opinions" are, like Coke's manifold of legal rules, so "many" *appearances*. The law that embodies Coke's legal reason, thus pointing to the discovery of "what is," is both "one" and *real*. Any rule, however useful or seemingly necessary, that is at loggerheads with either the law's unity or its reality is not merely bad law; it is, as with Blackstone, no law at all.

By presupposing the intelligible reality of the *objects* of legal experience—the ideas that constitute the law's substance—the "reason of the common law" renders legal experience fully normative. Without this objectivity, which defines the sense in which judges "discover" or "find" the law rather than simply making it, the common law loses its focus and indeed becomes the "ungodly jumble" that those commentators who fail to acknowledge the presupposition have always thought it was. But the common law inherited by the American Founders was the law of Coke, Hale, and Blackstone, not that of the ungodly jumble. Stoner cogently describes the way in which this common law constitutionalism helped to determine the shape of the American Constitution and the Bill of Rights by tempering the abstract reason of the Founders in accord with their experience of a living legal tradition.[64]

The conception of law that I am propounding here may be further clarified by making use of Gerald Postema's discussion of the "two conceptions of reason in Common Law theory."[65] The first of these Postema calls "particularist":

> The reason ["in"] the law is entirely concrete and particular, inseparable from the particular situations brought to the law and resolved by it. It is the reason not of rules and principles, but of cases.[66]

The second conception, not so clearly labeled, has to do with "the nature of the reason, or reasonability, *of* the law," and

> gives reflective reason a much wider scope in the law and portrays the Common Law as a *rational science* based on first principles, or at least potentially transformable into such a science. This conception links reason with general justifying *principles* which are instanced in, and illustrated by, particular decisions and settled rules.[67]

Postema finds these strands of thought running through most of the writings of prominent common law theorists, though he finds more of the former in the works of Coke and Hale and more of the latter in those of Blackstone.[68] I think this is entirely correct; but I think Postema is mistaken to regard the admixture of these two kinds of reason as an "ambiguity."[69] There is nothing ambiguous or uncertain about a legal order exhibiting the two most important features that any viable legal order will have to exhibit in order to be viable. In the terms of my earlier discussion, "reasonability," the reason of the law, may be interpreted as the required presumption of the law's unity and reality; the reason in the law, the "particularity," is merely the reflection of that unity and reality in everyday legal experience. The "ambiguity" becomes visible only from the perspective of legal positivism, which, motivated by an irrational desire for certainty, misreads the relation between the "of" and the "in" of common law reason as somehow a defect of legal order generally.

But Americans of the Founding era were not legal positivists any more than had been their English counterparts in earlier times. Strong evidence of this argument may be found in the attitudes of eighteenth-century Anglo-American lawyers toward the relationship between common law and natural law. As William R. Casto observes, in an excellent recent account of the Supreme Court under the chief justiceships of John Jay and Oliver Ellsworth,

> Today virtually all American attorneys are more or less legal positivists, but eighteenth-century Americans were natural lawyers. . . . The most influential written example of natural-law thinking in the Founding Era was Blackstone's *Commentaries*, published in 1765. . . . Blackstone, Ellsworth, and late eighteenth-century common lawyers believed the common law existed independently from the state. Neither kings nor legislators nor even judges were necessary to create the common law. Instead, it was part of the law of nature. But by "nature" they did not mean a godless system organized by Darwinian striving. Nietzsche's announcement of God's death was more than a century into the future. In eighteenth-century America, virtually everyone still believed that nature was God's creation and was ordered by him. This vision was especially strong in the case of Calvinists like Ellsworth who believed that God had absolutely and minutely predestined human existence. Consistent with this vision of God's nature, Blackstone wrote that God had ordained a system of "external immutable laws of good and evil." Human laws—especially the common law—"derive all their force, and all their authority" from this universal natural law and are invalid if they are contrary to it. Turning specifically to England, Blackstone defined the common law as a body of unwritten customs that receive "their binding power, and the force of laws, by long and immemorial usage, and by their universal reception throughout the kingdom." Under this theory, judges do not make laws. They are not legislators. They are, to use Blackstone's phrase, "the living oracles" of a common law that preexists in nature. Reasoning in humans was a process bestowed by God that enabled them to detect the subtleties of the preexisting natural law; judges, through their talent, experience, and wisdom, were supposed to use their reasoning to discern the law in the cases that came before them. . . . Under this almost Platonic vision of the common law, a particular judicial determination was proper only to the extent that it approximated natural law that had an existence outside and independent of the court.[70]

The blend of nature, custom, and reason in the common law jurisprudence of men like Blackstone and Ellsworth, which now seems curious in the wake of nineteenth-century developments, is nonetheless firmly rooted in the legal thought of the medieval era in which English common law was born (see Chapter 12). In fact, its idea of reason is an inheritance from the scholastic jurisprudence that receives its most articulate exposition in the *Summa Theologica* of Thomas Aquinas.[71] Before reaching any further into the domains of political and legal theory, however, two additional aspects of the common law heritage should be explored: the rules of legal interpretation and the doctrine of stare decisis.

9 · Intentionalism and the Rules of Interpretation in English and American Practice

INTENTIONALISM IN CONSTITUTIONAL LAW

The "reason of the common law," which presupposes a uniform, discoverable, substantive legal reality underlying the manifold of legal rules and principles, confronts legal theory with one of the most ancient and intractable philosophical problems: that of unity and plurality, or "one versus many." It is closely related to, if not often identical with, the problems of identity and difference and of whole versus part.

Consideration of the philosophical dimensions of these problems will be postponed until Chapter 16. From the standpoint of legal theory, the problem reduces to that of the interpretation and application of law. Legal interpretation is, in the widest sense, the activity of traveling back and forth between the whole and the parts, between the law's underlying unity and its superficial diversity. In the narrow sense, the use of the term "interpretation" is generally confined to those situations in which the point of departure in this movement is a written instrument with determinable meaning. When the interpretation is being done by a court, interpretation is joined with application.

The common law's presupposition of an underlying legal order that is discoverable by the use of reason aided by experience necessitates the development of methods and procedures for use in the ongoing effort to discover the essentials of that order so that they may be applied, through mediating rules and principles, to the diverse panoply of disorders confronted by the law. Since the legal order, as experienced, is a historical reality, these methods and procedures must themselves be fully attuned to the historical dimensions of legal experience.

Just as the constitutional order adumbrated in Part Two cannot be fully encompassed by any written constitutional document and so must be elaborated by reference to its underlying historical dimensions, so legal order more generally is not fully encompassed by contracts, deeds, or statutes and must be understood historically. The problem, as Matthew Hale recognized, is that of reconciling the underlying uniformity of law with particular differences in its application, necessitating the development and use of legal conventions.

> In Moralls and Especially with relation to Lawes for a Comunitie, tho the Comon Notion of Just and fitt are comon to all men of reason, yett when Persons come to particular application of those Comon Notions to particular Instances and occasions wee shall rarely find a Comon Consent or agreement between men tho' of greate reason, and that reason Improved by greate Study and Learning, wittness the greate disagreement between Plato and Aristotle Men of greate reason in the frameing of their Laws and Comonwealth, the greate difference in most of the States and King-domes in the world in their Laws administrations and measures of right and wrong, when they come to particulars. . . . By agreeing upon "Some certaine Laws and rules and methods of administration of Comon Justice" the following advantages are gained: (1) avoidance of "the greate Instabilitie of the judgements and reasons of Judges"; (2) avoidance of "that greate oppertunitie that Judges had, when they had noe other rule for their Judgement but their own reason, to be Corrupt and partiall"; (3) avoidance of "that jangling and Contradiction that would happen uppon the un-stable reason of Men when they once came to particular Decisions."[1]

The most important conventions for legal interpretation developed by the common lawyers embody various mixtures of text, tradition, and logic. Before exploring these, however, it will be helpful to examine briefly the most controversial variation on the common law approach in modern constitutional theory: the requirement that a written constitution be interpreted in accordance with the intentions of its makers, sometimes known as the doctrine of constitutional originalism.

For whatever reason, argument between traditionalists and nontraditionalists in contemporary constitutional theory often has centered on the extent to which the ideas and perspectives of the Framers (defined sometimes broadly, sometimes narrowly) should control the decision of constitutional cases in the courts. Full coverage of this debate is beyond the scope of this book; for the details, readers are referred to the excellent book on the subject by Earl M. Maltz and the references it contains.[2]

SUBJECTIVE AND OBJECTIVE INTENT

The idea of interpretation of a written constitution in accordance with the intentions of its makers is an outgrowth of analogous forms of interpretation with respect to other written legal instruments. From that development, at least two different notions of intent have emerged, neither of which by itself adequately exhausts the idea of intentionality in the field of constitutional interpretation. The first of these notions, the idea of subjective intent, for reasons that I can hardly imagine, has been the focus of most of the contemporary debates, though it is, in the field of constitutional interpretation, by far the less appropriate and less useful of the two. Proponents of subjective intent jurisprudence insist that the proper way to understand the meaning of a legal text is in terms of what the makers of that text actually "had in mind."

The idea appears to have been derived from analogy with the interpretation of such private legal documents as wills, contracts, and the like and indeed is most useful when applied in these contexts. If we take the case where I declare in a valid will my intention to give my farm to A, my house to B, my piano to C, my horse to D, and everything else to E, it is difficult to imagine any other notion of intent that would be workable. Surely if a court set itself to discovering any other notion, we would smell a rat. One of the main purposes of drawing a will (or a contract) is precisely that of documenting someone's subjective intentions; at most, this is only a minor purpose in the writing of a constitution.

When applied to constitutional interpretation, the idea of subjective intent becomes less compelling, though not entirely useless, as some contemporary constitutional theorists would have it. Even among nontraditionalists, only the most extreme have gone so far as to suggest that knowing the subjective intentions of a constitution's makers (whether defined as the "framers" or "ratifiers" or some combination of these), if they can be known with tolerable certainty in a particular instance, would be entirely irrelevant to determining the constitution's meaning in that instance.

If this much is conceded, then it must also be conceded that there are some points upon which the historical record is sufficiently clear, and unanimity so apparent, as to put beyond all question what the subjective intention was. To be sure, this approach will always be more useful when applied negatively (i.e., when we—or judges—are trying to determine what the framers or ratifiers did *not* "have in mind"), since the number of things that the makers of any constitution positively had in mind necessarily will have been far fewer than the number of things they did not have in mind. It is perfectly clear, for example, that the makers of the Fourth Amendment did not mean to require, by institution of that provision, the exclusion of tainted evidence in criminal prosecutions. Unless one is prepared to adopt an extreme deconstructionist position in constitutional interpretation, such considerations cannot be ignored.

Yet it is often quite difficult, and sometimes impossible, to determine the subjective intentions of a collective body in a positive sense with any degree of precision. Excepting the kind of instance just noted, it even becomes unclear exactly what is meant by the ascription of a subjective intention to a collective. If we mean a majority of its members (as we usually do), and especially if the majority is a narrow one, then issues of preference-intensity and salience arise. And there is always the problem of reductionism, a problem that shadows any attempt simplistically to reduce collective to individual behavior. Such problems arise from the obvious fact that collectivities do not have subjective intentions in the way that individuals do because collectivities are not "subjects" in the way that individuals are. Any impression to the contrary is saved from complete absurdity only by an appropriate recognition of its essentially fictional character.

In light of these considerations, it is difficult to understand why traditionalists have relied so heavily on the idea of subjective intent in constitutional law, thereby offering their opponents a large target that may easily become a straw man. Perhaps it is because so many modern judicial departures from original intent in constitutional cases have occurred in situations where even the subjective intentions of the makers were palpably clear.[3] However that may be, an additional difficulty with the notion of subjective intent should give pause to conservatives. To rely upon subjective intent, even if all the problems are solved, actually weakens the more general case for originalism. After all, there is much less reason to follow the makers' intent if, by doing so, we are merely following what they "had in mind" at the moment since that was very little compared to what they did not have in mind.

A much-touted (though perhaps not altogether justifiably) illustration of this approach is sometimes said to have been provided in Chief Justice Taft's opinion for the Court in the famous *Olmstead* case, holding that electronic eavesdropping was not covered by the Fourth Amendment allegedly because the subject had not been contemplated by the Framers.[4] To argue in this manner is not necessarily wrong in all instances, but it is surely the most difficult approach to take in defense of constitutional originalism. For such an argument to succeed, it must place maximum stress on the logic of Article 5, as John Marshall seems to have done in *Marbury v. Madison:*

> That the people have an original right to establish, for their future government, such principles as, in their opinion, shall most conduce to their own happiness, is the basis on which the whole American fabric has been erected. *The exercise of this original right is a very great exertion; nor can it nor ought it to be frequently repeated.* The principles, therefore, so established, are deemed fundamental. And as the authority from which they proceed is supreme, and can seldom act, they are designed to be permanent.[5]

A useful contextual framework for understanding the italicized portion of Marshall's remarks, and for understanding why originalist interpretive methodology is so compelling, may be found in Keith Whittington's idea of "potential sovereignty."[6] According to Whittington, popular sovereignty is the political theory that lies at the foundation of American constitutional order. The American Founders, by casting the fundamental law in the terms of a written constitutional text, divorced the sovereign from the government by instituting "the people" as sovereign makers of the written constitution who delegate political authority to governmental agents. Delegated authority is to be exercised by those agents in accord with the sovereign will during the extended periods in which the sovereign is "dormant," or "potentially sovereign," thus making it unnecessary that the sovereign be always "active."

Since the will of the active sovereign to which all government agents who exercise constitutionally delegated authority (including the courts) must always be faithful is expressed only in the written constitutional text, application of the sovereign will requires an originalist interpretive approach. Any other approach would effectively substitute the will of the sovereign's agents for the will of the sovereign itself. In other words, in order for "the people" to be truly sovereign, either they will need to be always "active" (continually amending the Constitution by the procedures of Article 5), or their agents will need continually to "enact" their will *as expressed on the last occasion of its activity.* Since it is impracticable (and unhealthy) to amend the Constitution continually, it follows that sole (or even heavy) reliance upon Article 5 must be ruled out. That leaves some form of constitutional originalism as the only interpretive option that will leave sovereignty in the hands of the people.

But if the will to be enacted is a *subjective* will, then the weight will be put back on Article 5; since the subjective will is largely an inexpressed, inarticulate will. Therefore it would be inappropriate to read "in their opinion" in Marshall's above-quoted *Marbury* language as referring to the subjective intentions of "the people." An approach that puts subsequent generations to the Hobson's choice of conforming public policy to the subjective opinions of the Constitution's makers or, alternatively, amending the Constitution by the procedures of Article 5 lays a burden on those procedures that they will not bear and implies an excessively literal reading of that article as well. Thus it is better for traditionalists to rely on alternative notions of intent that are more fruitful in constitutional law.

The second general notion of intentionality is objective intent. This category includes several distinct approaches that nonetheless show common ground in their emphasis upon the objects (rather than the subjects) of the makers' intentions. An example of this approach is given by Justice Story, in a discussion of the scope of the constitutional prohibition on impairment of contractual obligations by the states:

> It is applicable to all contracts, and not confined to the forms then most known, and most divided. Although a rare or peculiar case may not of itself be of sufficient magnitude to induce the establishment of a constitutional rule; yet it must be governed by that rule, when established, unless some plain and strong reason for excluding it can be given. It is not sufficient to show, that it may not have been foreseen, or intentionally provided for. To exclude it, it is necessary to go further, and show, that if the case had been suggested, the language of the convention would have been varied so, as to exclude and except it.[7]

In other words, to determine the true intentions of the makers with respect to a constitutional provision the language of which is sufficiently general, one must attend not merely to what the makers "had in mind" but even more to what they *must reasonably be presumed to have had in mind* in light of the objects or purposes to be accomplished by the provision at issue. Illustrating this approach, Guido Calabresi reports that H. Hart and A. Sacks define the task of interpretation as deciding "what meaning ought to be given" to the directions of a statute in the respects relevant to a given case. Interpretation should not be ascertainment of the "intention of the legislature with respect to the matter at issue," for in many cases there was no such intention. . . . Nor is interpretation wise which literally applies statutory language to fringe cases, Hart and Sacks say, since in passing a bill the legislative majority, like the draftsman, fix their minds only "on the propriety of the *general policy* expressed in the bill, as tested by a few representative *examples* of application and non-application".[8]

This approach, conceived by an analogy with the interpretation of statutes rather than with private legal instruments, is more fruitful in constitutional adjudication for several reasons. First, it is more in line with the nature of a constitution, which, unlike a will or a contract, requires "that only its great outlines should be marked, its important objects designated, and the minor ingredients which compose those objects be deduced from the nature of the objects themselves."[9] Second, it more closely resembles the way the Framers themselves (if not the ratifiers too) probably intended their own intentions to be regarded, because it is more in accord with the prevailing rules for interpretation of public legal documents that were generally acknowledged in the late eighteenth century, both in England and in America.[10] Third, it is more reflective of the prevailing idea of intentionality among common lawyers at the time: that intent in the law was essentially "remedial," not "original."

ORIGINAL AND REMEDIAL INTENT

One of the most pervasive linguistic distortions involved in disputes over constitutional originalism concerns the very application of the label "originalist" to judicial conservatives who oppose wholesale adaptation of the Constitution to present-day social, economic, or political agendas. The label suggests that, once upon a time, a group of persons collectively referred to as "the Framers" got together and created a "constitution" *ex nihilo* (and thus a priori) pursuant to "intentions" that plausibly may be regarded as "original."

Thus it is made to appear that, when modern courts are asked to interpret the text of the document created by the Framers in accordance with their "intentions," the courts are really being asked to impose newly minted, untested (and thereby tenuous) preferences, attitudes, and above all, "values" concocted by the a priori rational speculations of persons (however creative) who lived long ago and in a society characterized by different "needs" from the one we live in now. Moreover, such designs as these could hardly be knowable since they are the original product and property of persons who cannot tell us what they actually "had in mind."

But treating the Constitution in this manner, as if it were essentially unprecedented, without historical antecedents, as if it had no history of its own, deflects attention from the very characteristic that, for conservatives, ought to be regarded as the Constitution's most salient feature: its firm rootedness in the Anglo-American legal tradition and the British Constitution. There is precious little in the constitutional text or in its traditions that is truly "original" in the sense usually meant in the phrase "original intent."

Blackstone, for example, unarguably the English jurist who exerted the largest influence upon antebellum jurisprudence in the United States, holds that *lex scriptae* (written laws) are either "declaratory" of the common law or "remedial" of defects in the common law. Laws in the remedial category are further subdivided into two categories, one "enlarging" and the other "restraining" the common law.[11] From these categories arises Blackstone's First Rule of Statutory Construction, the "mischief" rule, that encompasses the common law's main version of what I have referred to as "objective intent."[12] Application of this rule involves the consideration of mischiefs meant to be addressed but left intact (or addressed unsuccessfully) under the old law that may be remedied either by enlargement or restriction under a new interpretation. According to James R. Stoner, Jr., discovering legislative intent means

> to distinguish what is declaratory from what is remedial, and then to recall in regard to the latter the circumstances that occasioned the writing of the law and the attitude toward those circumstances (i.e., the definition of the mischief) among the authors.[13]

"Intentionalism," conceived in this way, is an almost universally irresistible principle of interpretation. Even Thomas Aquinas, disputing the proposition that those who are subject to the law (including judges) have "no right to interpret the intention of the lawgiver, but should always act according to the letter of the law,"[14] develops his own version of the rule:

> He who follows the intention of the lawgiver, does not interpret the law simply; but in a case in which it is evident, by reason of the manifest harm, that the lawgiver intended otherwise.[15]

This discussion demonstrates the pressing need to refine the language of our constitutional discourse by referring to remedial rather than to original intent when speaking of the Framers' designs. The Constitution was not the result of a priori invention or artifice but of long (and tested) experience, with the ever-present backdrop of the British Constitution as it stood in 1688 and beyond. Thus the question is not what the Framers had in mind with regard to the most pressing policy issues of their own day but what mischiefs in existing constitutional arrangements they meant to address by the particular remedies they advanced.

Though what they had in mind is not, and can never be, fully knowable, the mischiefs and the remedies are. That is why the mischief rule of English statutory construction figured so largely in the early landmark cases interpreting the Constitution. For example, in *Gibbons v. Ogden*, the Supreme Court rejected New York's argument that the Article 1, Section 8 phrase "commerce among the states" was "intended" to exclude navigation, holding instead that the Founders, by vesting the commerce power in the national legislature, "meant" to empower Congress to "suppress the mischief" of interstate commercial warfare more generally.[16]

These considerations suggest at least a partial explanation as to why recent debates on constitutional originalism, dominated mostly by proponents and opponents of subjective intent jurisprudence, have been largely unproductive. Such arguments often turn on assertions and denials of what the Framers (or some significant portion of them) actually had in mind (or, alternatively, of the possibility or impossibility of knowing what they had in mind) on some substantive issue of policy, with the intentions in question being treated essentially as subjective preferences.

Yet it makes little difference, in the last analysis, whether a court decides according to the Framers', or somebody else's, merely *subjective* policy preferences, for they are almost always diverse and reflective of period-bound, contingent exigencies of the Founding (or some other) environment. Such preferences cannot command the high degree of assent usually associated with full-blown constitutional principles (except perhaps in the case of first-order procedural decision rules themselves, yet to be discussed). In other words, the preferences have more to do with politics than with law in the strictly "constitutional" sense.

Since judges are constrained primarily by law, it follows that a jurisprudence of subjective intent generally will leave judges unconstrained in the choice of which competing subset of any larger set of substantive policy preferences is to govern a particular decision. Intentions can operate as real constraints only if they are *objectively* grounded either in fact or in law. Since a preference is always subjective in fact, it is only by an operation of law that it may be rendered objective. To perform such an operation is to create a legal fiction; such a fiction, if employed for long, becomes in turn a legal convention. A complete understanding of intentionalist jurisprudence therefore cannot be attained without a corresponding understanding of the role of fictions in the law, a subject I shall address more fully in connection with the discussion of stare decisis in Chapter 10.

THE RULES OF INTERPRETATION

The most important of the English rules of interpretation are, like the mischief rule, rules of statutory construction designed to assist courts in the ascertainment of legislative will, thus combining features of both subjective and objective intent but stressing heavily the latter. As attested by Madison and others, these rules were, in the Founding era, readily applicable to constitutional interpretation.[17] According to Christopher Wolfe, the rules were premised on the belief that the "best way to interpret law is to explore the intention of the lawgiver at the time the law was made," and in the words of Blackstone, "by signs the most natural and probable."[18] Three rules of interpretation are the most important.

First is the "plain meaning" or "literal" rule, according to which the best indication of what the makers intended consists in what they wrote, i.e., the words themselves, to be understood, according to Blackstone, "in their most usual and most known signification . . . their general and popular use."[19] Effective use of this rule presumes that the meaning of the words to be interpreted is tolerably clear.

The second rule is the "mischief" or "social purpose" rule, which authorizes reliance upon the "evils" that the law was designed to remedy (i.e., its "purpose" or "object" or "end"), or in Blackstone's phrase, "the cause which moved the legislator to enact it."[20] In most of its formulations, this rule is to be employed only when the words of the law are not sufficiently clear to allow exclusive reliance on the plain meaning rule. The mischief rule is also sometimes referred to as Heydon's Rule, from its classic formulation by the Barons of the Exchequer in *Heydon's Case*, decided in 1584. The barons there resolved

> that for the sure and true interpretation of all statutes in general (be they penal or beneficial, restrictive or enlarging of the common law), four things are to be discerned and considered:
>
> 1st.   What was the common law before the making of the Act,
> 2nd.   What was the mischief and defect for which the common law did not provide,
> 3rd.   What remedy the Parliament hath resolved and appointed to cure the disease of the Commonwealth, and
> 4th.   The true reason of the remedy;
>
> and then the office of all the judges is always to make such construction as shall suppress the mischief, and advance the remedy, and to suppress subtle inventions and evasions for continuance of the mischief, and *pro privato commodo*, and to add force and life to the cure and remedy, according to the true intent of the makers of the Act, *pro bono publico*. 3 Co. Rep. 7a, at 7b (1584).[21]

The third rule is the "golden rule," a rule of consistency, which authorizes departure from literal interpretation even when the language is unambiguous, where, in Blackstone's phrase, "the words bear either none, or a very absurd signification, if literally understood."[22] Proper application of this rule requires that the "absurdity" involved be a matter of logic, not merely one of policy. A particularly clear formulation of rules one and two addressed to an English audience, of which Story's statement is a plausible American example (see p. 108), is provided in an excerpt from a well-known nineteenth-century English case:

> The only rule for the construction of Acts of Parliament is that they should be construed according to the intent of the Parliament which passed the Act. If the words of the statute are in themselves precise and unambiguous, then no more can be nec-

essary than to expound those words in that natural and ordinary sense. The words themselves alone do, in such case, best declare the intention of the lawgiver. But if any doubt arises from the terms employed by the legislature, it has always been held a safe means of collecting the intention, to call in aid the ground and cause of making the statute, and to have recourse to the preamble, which . . . is "a key to open the minds of the makers of the Act, and the mischiefs which they intend to redress."[23]

This formulation expresses the fundamental idea that all rules of construction are geared to discernment of intent, and that the usual relationship between the literal and mischief rules gives priority to the former. Story's approach, laying upon those individuals who recommend a departure from the plain meaning of general words the burden of showing that such a departure would have been agreed to by the makers had they had it in mind, expresses the same idea. What the makers would have had in mind, had they had everything relevant in mind, would doubtless have been the mischiefs to be redressed by the words being construed.

The approach is useful in constitutional adjudication because its application allows the judge to get beyond the inertia that would result from a subjective intent reading of the law. It thus allows the law to maintain continuity with the past while keeping abreast of scientific and technological advance. A classic example is found in the Supreme Court's 1878 decision of *Pensacola v. Western Union,* which held interstate telegraph communications to be within the scope of the commerce clause.[24]

It is important to note that, unlike the mischief rule, the plain meaning rule contains both a subjective and an objective component. The subjective component is most apparent when a court relies on the words themselves to indicate what the makers had in mind. This approach has led to criticism of the English judiciary for its habit of giving virtually absolute priority to the literal (over the mischief) rule whenever statutory language is tolerably clear.

But such criticism is often misplaced, since English judges rarely try to justify literal interpretation solely by reference to what the makers of the law subjectively had in mind. Rather, they stress the point that unambiguous statutory language binds a court to literal interpretation because of the clarity with which such language speaks to those people who will ultimately experience the legal effects of the law.

This notion comes very close to the idea of objective intent articulated by Story. The approach is often raised to the level of constitutional principle, as in the following explanation of the traditional English refusal to rely on legislative history in the construction of acts of parliament:

The constitutional function performed by courts of justice as interpreters of the written law laid down in Acts of Parliament is often described as ascertaining "the intention of Parliament"; but what this metaphor, though convenient, omits to take into account is that the court, when acting in its interpretative role . . . is doing so as mediator between the state in the exercise of its legislative power and the private citizen for whom the law made by Parliament constitutes a rule binding upon him and enforceable by the executive power of the state. Elementary justice or, to use the concept often cited by the European Court, the need for legal certainty demands that the rules by which the citizen is to be bound should be ascertainable by him (or, more realistically, by a competent lawyer advising him) by reference to identifiable sources that are publicly accessible. The source to which Parliament must have intended the citizen to refer is the language of the Act itself. These are the words which Parliament has itself approved as accurately expressing its intentions. If the meaning of those words is clear and unambiguous and does not lead to a result that is manifestly absurd or unreasonable, it would be a confidence trick by Parliament and destructive of all legal certainty if the private citizen could not rely upon that meaning but was required to search through all that had happened before and in the course of the legislative process in order to see whether there was anything to be found from which it could be inferred that Parliament's real intention had not been accurately expressed by the actual words that Parliament had adopted to communicate it to those affected by the legislation.[25]

A strict approach is also evident in the English judiciary's use of the third rule, the golden rule, which allows departure from plain meaning when literal interpretation would produce absurdity, repugnance, or inconsistency. According to Sir Rupert Cross, the following statement in a case decided by the House of Lords in 1857 is probably the most commonly cited version of the golden rule by modern English courts:

I have been long and deeply impressed with the wisdom of the rule now, I believe, universally adopted, at least in the courts of law in Westminster Hall, that in construing wills and indeed statutes, and all written instruments, the grammatical and ordinary sense of the words is to be adhered to, unless that would lead to some absurdity, or some repugnance or inconsistency with the rest of the instrument, in which case the grammatical and ordinary sense of the words may be modified, so as to avoid the absurdity and inconsistency, *but no farther.*[26]

The final phrase underscores the strictness of the English approach and suggests that English judges do not usually regard themselves entitled either to read in words not in the law or to disregard words that are in the law, even to advance the purpose of the law in a general sense, when the statutory language is itself unambiguous. The approach thus restricts the effect of the rule to contradictions or inconsistencies of logic (such as colliding provisions in the same statute) but does not extend to contradictions or inconsistencies with the goals or purposes of the statute. The approach would not justify calling in the mischief rule based on an invocation of the golden rule.

By contrast, American judges generally have used a more flexible approach when deciding upon the relative priority of the rules, as is indicated by the follow-ing passage from Justice Reed's opinion for the U.S. Supreme Court in *United States v. American Trucking Association*. It is particularly handy for our purposes because it draws together the three rules:

> There is, of course, no more persuasive evidence of the purpose of a statute than the words by which the legislature undertook to give expression to its wishes. Often these words are sufficient in and of themselves to determine the purpose of the legislation. In such cases we have followed their plain meaning. When that meaning has led to absurd or futile results, however, this court has looked beyond the words to the pur-pose of the Act. Frequently, however, even when the plain meaning did not produce absurd results but merely an unreasonable one "plainly at variance with the policy of the legislation as a whole" this court has followed that purpose, rather than the literal words. When aid to the construction of the meaning of words, as used in the statute, is available, there can certainly be no "rule of law" which forbids its use, however clear the words may be on superficial investigation.[27]

Hart and Sacks, in their formulation of the rules of statutory interpretation, go a step farther than Justice Reed by asserting that the primary goal of a court in this field consists in the attribution of a "statutory purpose" (rule two) to the original legislature, subject to the constraints that the attributed purpose should not be applied if doing so "would violate any established policy of clear state-ment" (rule one) or would impart to the words "a meaning they will not bear" (rule three).[28] In other words, American judicial practice and legal scholarship places much heavier reliance on rule two than does English practice, even to the point of allowing general purpose to override plain meaning whether literal inter-pretation produces logical absurdity (Hart and Sacks) or not (Justice Reed). No doubt this difference between English and American practice has been caused by many factors, most of which are well beyond the scope of our present topic. Yet one factor is of particular relevance: American judges must interpret a written constitution that, at least since the decision of *Marbury v. Madison* in 1803, has been accorded the status of law.

Since the American Constitution's most controversial provisions (i.e., those that would generate the most litigation) are pitched at a much higher level of generality than most statutory language, American judges have been forced to deploy the rules of interpretation at correspondingly more general levels than are considered appropriate by their English counterparts. This difference is indeed one of the main reasons why the rules have not always effectively prevented intrusion of the private moral convictions of judges upon our constitutional law. Moreover, the approach has not been confined to constitutional adjudication but has spilled over into the field of statutory litigation as well. There are some recent indications that English judges are presently being influenced by the American approach. The whole matter illustrates nicely the ultimate futility of legal compartmentalization, whether by geography (e.g., English versus American law) or by subject matter (e.g., constitutional versus statutory law).

THE FOUNDERS AND THE RULES OF INTERPRETATION

The crucial point is this: the three rules of interpretation, when combined with a few of somewhat lesser importance, carefully developed over a period of several centuries by English courts and subsequently adapted to American conditions well before the adoption of the Constitution, were plainly rules that the Framers, the ratifiers, the people generally, and early American judges expected would be applied in the process of constitutional adjudication. Early American courts established these rules as an important part of our constitutional law, and subsequent courts have applied them almost invariably (if sometimes questionably) ever since. They are no longer grounded merely on our system of constitutional and statutory interpretation but also on the doctrine of stare decisis and the rules of precedent (see Chapter 10).

James Madison regarded this approach as beyond question at least as early as 1830, as is shown clearly in a letter to M. L. Hurlbert, in which Madison combined a version of the mischief rule with original intent and the idea of precedent:

> That in a Constitution, so new, and so complicated, there should be occasional difficulties & differences in the practical expositions of it, can surprise no one; and this must continue to be the case, as happens to new laws on complex subjects, until a course of practice of sufficient uniformity and duration to carry with it the public sanction shall settle doubtful or contested meanings. . . . As there are legal rules for interpreting laws, there must be analogous rules for interpreting constitutions and among the obvious and just guides to the Constitution of the U.S. may be mentioned—1. The evils & defects for curing which the Constitution was called for & introduced. 2. The comments prevailing at the time it was adopted. 3. The early, deliberate & continued practice under the Constitution, as preferable to constructions adopted on the spur of occasions, and subject to the vicissitudes of party or personal ascendencies.[29]

As for "early, deliberate & continued practice under the Constitution," virtually all of the Marshall Court's leading constitutional decisions had been straightforwardly based on one or more of the traditional rules of interpretation. The Court's crucial holding in *Marbury v. Madison,* that Congress could not enlarge its original jurisdiction, was based on a literal reading of both Article 3 of the Constitution and Section 13 of the Judiciary Act of 1789,[30] just as the famous rulings in *Fletcher v. Peck*[31] and *Dartmouth College v. Woodward,*[32] that public contracts fell within the ambit of the contract clause, were based on Story's version of the plain meaning and mischief rules.[33] The holding in *Cohens v. Virginia,*[34] that Congress could enlarge the Court's appellate jurisdiction, as it had allegedly done in Section 25 of the Judiciary Act, was based partly on the mischief rule and partly on the golden rule.[35] And the landmark decisions in *McCulloch v. Maryland*,[36] that a state may not levy destructive taxes upon federal instrumentalities, and in *Gibbons v. Ogden*,[37] that "commerce" extended to any commercial activity that affected more than one state, were classic applications of the mischief rule.[38] As a cursory glance at any American government or constitutional law text will show, the impact of this "early, deliberate & continued practice" still is felt mightily.

In place of the traditional practice of interpreting the Constitution in accordance with the objective intentions of the Framers, ratifiers, or people of the Founding generation, with special attention to the constitutional language itself supplemented by historical sources, informal logic, and "early, deliberate and continued practice" in the courts, contemporary nontraditionalist constitutional theorists would substitute judicial discretion to reinterpret the original constitutional language. By so doing, they seek to accommodate values and interests recently deemed constitutionally significant but that have no discernible (or only a tenuous) relationship to the Constitution when read according to any combination of the rules of interpretation discussed in this chapter. It should be clear by now that they are asking a lot.

10· The Rules of Interpretation, Stare Decisis, and Legal Fiction in Constitutional Law

Madison's formulation of the rules of statutory interpretation as applied to the field of constitutional law, by joining the mischief rule with "early, deliberate & continued practice," suggests a strong relationship between original objective intent and the doctrine of stare decisis. That is no accident, for the interpretation of a constitutional or statutory provision in accordance with original intent, broadly conceived (i.e., as objective rather than subjective intent), is directly analogous to the common law procedure of deciding cases in accord with precedent.

That these notions are essentially complementary, not conflictual, has been somewhat obscured in contemporary debates on constitutional interpretation, due to the failure of traditionalists and nontraditionalists alike to understand the basically fictitious character, and thus the primary function, of both doctrines. Guido Calabresi has provided a good description of the role of precedent in accommodating stability and change within a framework conditioned by the values of legal equality and political democracy:

> The most powerful engine of change in the common law was, strangely enough, the great "principle" that like cases should be treated alike. Courts acting on that principle could change law, indeed make law, without arrogating to themselves undue power because they always seemed to apply past precedents or principles in new ways to situations *made* new by the world around them. Sometimes, of course, this was in fact the case—because of technological or social change an old rule would begin to treat some litigants unlike other similar litigants. The courts responded, in one way or another, to treat both classes of litigants alike. At other times, however, the change was self-imposed. What is a like case always involves a judgment as to the level of generality to use in assessing similarity. By moving to treat cases alike on successively different levels of generality, common law courts could slowly adjust the law to fit new social policies, and could still claim that all they were doing was treating like cases alike. . . . Since such changes usually required the concurrence of many judges over a

long time, and since the legislatures could reverse such judicial decisions when the courts' policy judgments were wrong, such an allocation of accretional law-making authority could not ultimately be criticized as undemocratic.[1]

The practice of reading previous case holdings at differing levels of generality in order to fulfill the demand of the common law that litigants be treated equally—not just contemporaneously but also over time—finds its counterpart in the reading of statutory and constitutional language in accordance with the objective intent of the makers. In this approach, courts are held to the original purposes of statutory and constitutional provisions without being forced to treat litigants unequally from one era to the next by application of a frozen subjective intent. The constraining features of the approach are noted by J. W. Hurst:

> Of course we use a fiction if we speak of the legislature as if it were a being of one mind. But so durable a fiction endures because it has a use validated by experience. This formula reminds all who deal with a statute that they are operating in a field of law in which they are not free to define public policy simply according to their own judgment.[2]

Yet as Cross has pointed out, "The notion of the intention of Parliament identifies a perspective or orientation within which judicial decision-making takes place, rather than a rigid set of instructions whose execution requires little originality or discretion."[3]

Viewed from these perspectives, the prevailing belief that original intent and stare decisis are reactionary devices designed to retard social progress by allowing the past to govern the present appears to be unfounded. Indeed the rules of interpretation and the rules of precedent are the two most important doctrinal methods of the common law for incorporating legal change into the framework of standing (preexisting) law. The ideas of original intent and precedent thus accommodate the future while accounting for the past, constraining the tendency of legal principles to expand to the limits of logic by confining those principles within the limits of history. They assure us not that we will be ruled by the dead from their graves, as Jefferson apparently thought; rather, they assure us, as Chesterton thought, that we "will have the dead at our councils."[4]

Their function is that of producing a balance, or preserving a constructive tension, between the emergent reality that defines the future and the web of experience that defines the past, a tension that has ever been the fundamental requirement, and the defining feature, of an orderly present. They symbolize, then, our experience of the normative force of the past, of tradition, the experience of an order in which the present can become truly future only by giving the past its due. Because this experience is essentially mysterious, its symbolization in literature requires resort to metaphor (recalling again Chesterton's "democracy of the dead"); in Law its symbolization requires the fiction.

This is not the place to go into the important questions regarding the nature and different types of legal fiction. Here it is necessary only to make use of Lon L. Fuller's definition that a fiction is either "a statement propounded with a complete or partial consciousness of its falsity" or "a false statement recognized as having utility."[5] Apparently recognizing the overly positivistic tone of the definition, Fuller continues:

> This definition seems on the face of things to embrace two entirely discordant elements. In the first alternative the criterion is "consciousness of falsity," in the second "utility." Yet current usage probably permits of this alternative definition. What is the explanation for this apparently unreasonable linguistic development? There is often underlying the seemingly illogical usages of language a penetrating comprehension which does not find expression in any other way. That is the case here. In practice, it is precisely those false statements that are realized as being false that have utility. A fiction taken seriously, i.e., "believed," becomes dangerous and loses its utility. It ceases to be a fiction under either alternative of the definition given above.[6]

So as to leave no doubt that the notions of original intent and precedent should be removed from the category of "dangerous fictions" (since they seem to have been so frequently "believed," both by traditionalists and nontraditionalists in contemporary debates), it is advisable at this point to state clearly just what it is about these two doctrines that is false. Strictly speaking, a case cannot be decided in full accord with the "intention" of a collective body because *collective bodies do not have "intentions."* Likewise, a case cannot be decided in accordance with the decision of any previous case, again strictly speaking, because *no two cases are exactly alike.* In the latter instance, if they were exactly alike (in other words, if the parties and the cause of action were the same), the suit would be barred by the doctrines of *res judicata* in private law or double jeopardy in criminal law.

It is crucial to note that, in these two situations, the "falsity" is contained entirely within the second part of each statement, or more accurately, within the implied statement that is negated in the italicized portion of each statement. The fiction proper consists in the *connection* between the two portions of each statement. It is false to say that collective bodies have intentions, but it is not false to say that courts can decide cases *as if* they did have such intentions. It is likewise false to say that any two cases are exactly alike, but it is not false to say that courts may treat two cases *as if* they were exactly alike. The "as if" component of legal fictions brings into focus their similarity with fictional assumptions in science and suggests that one of the primary functions of each is to allow the use of deductive procedures in the application of law (whether legal or scientific) to individual cases or events. Thus it is nonsensical to evaluate a fiction in terms of its degree of falsity; it must be evaluated in terms of its utility.

The conclusion that must be drawn from these observations is that, whatever the degree of falsity ascribed to the false component of a fictional statement, its character cannot be wholly a function of its falsity. We might thus, by reformulating slightly Fuller's definition, come up with a working definition of a "good" or "useful" fiction, one that will account for the aspect of a fiction that expresses, in Fuller's words, "a penetrating comprehension which does not find expression in any other way." Defined in this manner, a fiction is a false statement that, because of its recognized utility and because its character is not fully circumscribed by its falsity, is nonetheless propounded with either a complete or partial consciousness of its falsity. Perhaps this is just another way of saying that a fiction is a useful statement with a "true" and a "false" component that, because of the difficulty or impossibility of distinguishing these components effectively in practice, is propounded with either a complete or partial awareness of its false component. Maitland expressed the idea with his usual "penetrating comprehension" when he said that a fiction "we needs must feign is somehow or another very like the simple truth."[7]

What is the "simple truth" that is symbolized by the fictions of original intent and precedent? I submit that the answer will be found by recalling the discussion regarding the difficulty of constructing a purely rational defense of tradition (see Chapter 7). Any such defense, however well drawn, will necessarily fall short of conveying the full force of the normative weight of a tradition because that force is the product of a cumulative experience that is not reducible to the constraints of a syllogism. This is not only to say, with Holmes, that "a page of history is worth a volume of logic";[8] it is also to say that logic is the creature (and servant) of history and not the other way around. We use reason to formulate theories that may help us to understand our experience; we do not fabricate that experience in order to understand reason. Experience is a given; lawyers, no less than scientists, must submit the product of their reasoned reflections to the test of experience, which ultimately will determine the true character of those reflections.

When the capacity of reasoned reflection to symbolize fully and effectively the content and character of experience fails, as it must, sooner or later, the fiction emerges to supply the defect. The fiction is thus the homage that reason, in virtue of its defect, pays to experience. In the terms of our earlier discussion of tradition, the fiction is the expression that symbolizes the intellectual gap between the experienced force of the tradition, on the one hand, and its purely rational basis, on the other. The fiction, to borrow a well-worn phrase from economics, "makes good the difference."

LAW AND CUSTOM

There is a tendency, "observable everywhere in human society, for the habitual behavior of a community to become normative." So reports Michael Gagarin in a recent excellent account of archaic Greek law.[9] This tendency suggests that custom, the wellspring of the conventional morality that constitutes so much of the common law's substance, is also the experiential foundation of normative ethics. Even Kant, arguably the greatest of the analytical moral philosophers, self-consciously regarded his system as a formal account of the commonsensical, everyday notion of a "morally good" person.[10]

This tendency helps to explain why some kind of common law is found in every known legal system, even those modern ones that take their cues from the Roman model. More than a century ago, Sir Henry Maine pointed out the similarity between the Roman *Responsa Prudentum* and English case law.[11] J. W. Jones has noted the use of precedent in the courts of classical Greece.[12] It has even been persuasively argued that the origin of the idea of precedent is coterminous with the origin of written law itself. Among the earliest known written laws were judgments handed down in previous decisions of courts that the people demanded be recorded so as not to be susceptible to distortion in future cases.[13] It is also known that the ancient Athenians employed *mnemones* ("rememberers"), who were officials charged with remembering previous decisions as a service for judges.[14]

The tendency of habitual behavior to become normative also explains why the most characteristic features of any legal system are those that adjust the ever-present tension between continuity and change.[15] Constitutional originalism, stare decisis, and other legal fictions stand at the intersection of analytical and historical jurisprudence (and therefore at the center of law) because they are intelligible abstractions by which, in the words of Maine, "Law is brought into harmony with society" through simultaneous accommodation of change and maintenance of continuity with the past.[16]

Indeed, a legal system may appropriately be defined as an institutional framework the main purpose of which is to resolve disputes by applying rules and principles that provide for the future while accounting for the past. A reductio ad absurdum is immediately available to counter any assumption to the contrary, for any purported legal system that resolved disputes by applying rules or principles that did not account for the past would lose any initial semblance of law-likeness and come to be viewed as entirely arbitrary. Karl Llewellyn, one of the leading lights of modern legal realism, captures the point with characteristic clarity and ease:

> It takes time and effort to solve problems. Once you have solved one it seems foolish to reopen it. . . . Both inertia and convenience speak for building further on what you have already built; for incorporating the decision once made, the solution once worked out, into your operating technique without reexamination of what earlier went into reaching your solution. From this side you will observe that the urge to precedent will be present in the action of any official, irrespective of whether he wants it, or not; irrespective likewise of whether he thinks it is there, or not. From this angle precedent is but a somewhat dignified name for the practice of the officer or of the office. And it should be clear that unless there were such practices it would be hard to know there was an office or an officer. . . . To continue past practices is to provide a

new official in his inexperience with the accumulated experience of his predecessors. If he is ignorant, he can learn from them and profit by the knowledge of those who have gone before him. If he is idle he can have their action brought to his attention and profit by their industry. If he is foolish he can profit by their wisdom. If he is biased or corrupt the existence of past practices to compare his action with gives a public check upon his biases and his corruption, limits the frame in which he can indulge them unchallenged. . . . Hence it is readily understandable that in our system there has grown up first the habit of following precedent, and then the legal norm that precedent is to be followed. The main form that this principle takes we have seen. It is essentially the canon that each case must be decided as one instance under a general rule. This much is common to almost all systems of law.[17]

The canon prescribing that each case, so far as is possible, should be decided under a general rule points to the form of analogical reasoning that is at the heart of case-by-case adjudication under the common law.[18] As a matter of English doctrine, it was in the process of development at least as early as 1268, when Henry de Bracton's *De legibus et consuetudinibus Angliae,* containing references to about 500 cases decided in the royal courts, first appeared.[19] In his treatise, Bracton announced the rule,

> If any new and unwonted circumstances shall arise, then, if anything analogous has happened before, let the case be adjudged in like manner, proceeding *a similibus ad similia* ("from like to like").[20]

Though Bracton and his medieval contemporaries, to be sure, regarded the *ad similia* rule somewhat more loosely than would their modern counterparts, this is probably due more to the general unavailability of reported judicial decisions in the Middle Ages than to any logic underlying the rule itself.[21] In any case, clearly this early form of law reporting, which continued virtually unabated for three centuries, ultimately encouraged lawyers and judges to think of written judicial decisions as declarations of preexisting law that should be binding on subsequent courts deciding similar cases. This attitude would later harden into the rigid rules of precedent employed in modern times by English judges and soften into the more flexible rules used by contemporary American judges.

Such a development was, I think, inevitable, given the declaratory theory of law that has been both logically and historically complementary to the *ad similia* rule. One of the best statements of the declaratory theory is found in Sir Matthew Hale's *History of the Common Law of England.* According to Hale, courts cannot

> make a law properly so called, for that only the King and Parliament can do; yet they have a great weight and authority in expounding, declaring, and publishing what the law of this Kingdom is, especially when such decisions hold a consonancy and congruity with resolutions and decisions of former times, and though such decisions are

less than a law, yet they are a greater evidence thereof than the opinion of any private persons, as such whatsoever.[22]

Though the declaratory theory was the prevailing view in common law juris-dictions, at least until the early twentieth century,[23] the regnant positivism of our time has led most commentators to the position that it is historically but not ana-lytically compelling. For instance, Sir Rupert Cross, otherwise a thorough and perceptive authority on English law, nevertheless dismisses the declaratory theory with an unsubstantiated and, in truth, somewhat self-contradictory assertion:

> If a previous decision is only evidence of what the law is, no judge could ever be absolutely bound to follow it, and it could never be effectively overruled because a subsequent judge might always treat it as having some evidential value.[24]

Cross's positivism has got the better of him here, for his argument is entirely question-begging; his assertion can be true only if one first denies the common law's presumption of its own underlying essence. One must deny Coke's premise that there is a "reason of the law," Blackstone's supposition that there is a law "common" to all, and, for that matter, the idea that there is any law at all aside from an "ungodly jumble" of particular judicial decisions. The assumption of a legal reality behind the manifold of disparate legal phenomena is the very founda-tion of the declaratory theory; without such an assumption, the theory is utterly unintelligible.

Cross purports to defeat the declaratory theory by tacitly (i.e., without argu-ment) negating its most important theoretical presumption, or, in other words, by tacitly assuming (again, without argument) some version of the "command" the-ory of law. Cross apparently has in mind an idea that precedents must bind judges "absolutely" and that the only way a precedent can bind a judge absolutely is if the binding quality of the precedent is solely the result of its having been prom-ulgated as a "command." But the binding quality of precedent is not experienced in this simplistic way.

Recall briefly one of the Greek examples, that of the *mnemones* (rememberers), which suggests that one of the main reasons that a gap exists between the experi-enced force, or normative weight, of a legal tradition and its purely rational basis, thus producing the need for fictional representations, is that the historical origin of many of our most authoritative norms is beyond legal memory. Blackstone, for example, defines *lex non scripta*, the original institution of and authority for which is not set down in writing, as a collection of maxims and customs "of higher an-tiquity than memory or history can reach," maxims and customs used "time out of mind . . . whereof the memory of man runneth not to the contrary."[25]

Regardless of how deeply such maxims and customs are rooted in antiquity, they are not to be regarded as legally authoritative solely on the basis of their habitual observance. Rather, they must satisfy the "reason of the common law" both in their discovery and in their application, keeping in mind that the reason of the common law includes the presumption of an underlying legal order that is not only conventional but also uniform, discoverable, and real.

Though the existence of a general legal custom can be known only by experience (i.e., by the study of respected authorities, prior judicial decisions or precedents, by observing the mischiefs that result from statutory revision of rules, and so on), such a custom may receive judicial application only if it is not absurd, unreasonable, unjust, or impossible to be performed.[26] At the same time, a particular custom is legally good only if it is ancient and immemorial, commonly and continuously observed, and neither self-contradictory nor at loggerheads with any other legally good custom.[27]

The rules for the recognition and application of customary legal maxims, together with the common law's presumption of an underlying uniform legal reality, fully imply that judicial decisions may be regarded as good evidence of the common law but cannot plausibly be regarded as the law itself.[28] It is this feature of common law reasoning, more than any other, that explains the enormous historical influence of the doctrine of stare decisis in Anglo-American jurisprudence. It imparts to that doctrine the flexibility required to make possible the authoritative judicial application of a Law that is both a seamless web and yet susceptible to transformation in its everyday application to particular events.

Yet if judicial decisions were law in the full, strict, sense (i.e., if the declaratory theory is not true), then Cross is right in suggesting that judges would be bound absolutely by previous judicial decisions but wrong to suggest that such decisions could be effectively overruled. If every prior judicial decision is "law itself" in the fullest sense, then such a decision cannot be overruled without rendering the law incoherent when taken as a whole, without tearing the seamless web. The only way out of this dilemma is to adopt some form of legal positivism, which destroys the common law by undermining custom as a viable source of law.

Yet any view that undermines custom as a source of law is questionable from a jurisprudential standpoint. Any view that deemphasizes the intelligible also deemphasizes tradition because tradition is an "intelligible species," and custom is an intelligible species in exactly the same sense. Even Thomas Aquinas, himself immersed in a Roman-based legal order known for its heavy emphasis on *lex scriptae*, argues:

> All law proceeds from the reason and will of the lawgiver; the Divine and natural laws from the reasonable will of God; the human law from the will of man, regulated by reason. Now just as human reason and will, in practical matters, may be made manifest by speech, so may they be made known by deeds: since seemingly a man chooses as good that which he carries into execution. But it is evident that by human speech, law can be both changed and expounded, in so far as it manifests the interior movement and thought of human reason. Wherefore by actions also, especially if they be repeated, so as to make a custom, law can be changed and expounded; and also

something can be established which obtains force of law, in so far as by repeated external actions, the inward movement of the will, and concepts of reason are most effectually declared; for when a thing is done again and again, it seems to proceed from a deliberate judgment of reason. Accordingly, custom has the force of a law, abolishes law, and is the interpreter of law.[29]

It is the normative force of custom, noted by Aquinas, that renders the idea of precedent legally compelling. Though the doctrine of stare decisis, technically speaking, may be peculiarly English, the idea that underlies it is not. Legal history is virtually permeated with examples of the appeal of, and to, precedent; I shall close this chapter with two of these examples, one medieval and the other modern. Though they are distant in time, they are similar enough in spirit to constitute a sufficient demonstration of my proposition.

PSEUDO-ISIDORE AND THE *MARBURY* MYTH

The medieval example comes from the ninth century and concerns the ecclesiastical law that took shape in the age of the Holy Roman Empire, an age in which local populations throughout Western Europe fell under the temporal dominion of the Frankish kings and the concomitant spiritual dominion of the popes in Rome. As early as the seventh century, a large collection of canons and decretals known as the *Hispana,* or *Isidoriana* (due to its early attribution to Saint Isidore of Seville), had taken shape in Spain.[30] In the early ninth century, by which time the *Hispana* had made its way into France, a collection of capitularies, laws declared by Frankish kings, was compiled into four books by Ansegis, abbot of St. Wandrille.[31] The events that followed, here told by F. Pollock and F. Maitland, constitute one of the most colorful tales in Western legal history:

Then out of the depth of the ninth century emerged a book which was to give law to mankind for a long time to come. Its core was the *Hispana;* but into it there had been foisted besides other forgeries, some sixty decretals professing to come from the very earliest successors of St. Peter. The compiler called himself Isidorus Mercator; he seems to have tried to personate Isidore of Seville. Many guesses have been made as to his name and time and home. It seems certain that he did his work in Frankland, and near the middle of the ninth century. He has been sought as far west as le Mans, but suspicion hangs thickest over the church of Reims. The false decretals are elaborate mosaics made up out of phrases from the bible, the fathers, genuine canons, genuine decretals, the West Goth's Roman lawbook; but all these materials, wherever collected, are so arranged as to establish a few great principles: the grandeur and superhuman origin of ecclesiastical power, the sacrosanctity of the persons and the property of bishops, and, though this is not so prominent, the supremacy of the bishop of Rome. Episcopal rights are to be maintained against the *chorepiscopi,* against the metropolitans, and against the secular power. Above all (and this is the burden of the song), no accusation can be brought against a bishop so long as he is despoiled of his see. . . . Closely connected with this fraud was another. Some one who called himself a deacon of the church of Mainz and gave his name as Benedict, added to the four books of capitularies, which Ansegis had published, three other books containing would-be, but false capitularies, which had the same bent as the decretals concocted by the Pseudo-Isidore. These are not the only, but they are the most famous manifestations of the lying spirit which had seized the Frankish clergy. The Isidorian forgeries were soon accepted at Rome. The popes profited by documents which taught that ever since the apostolic age the bishops of Rome had been declaring, or even making, law for the universal church. On this rock or on this sand a lofty edifice was reared.[32]

The modern example arises from the pages of our own legal and constitutional history, and thus its background is much more familiar. At the time the U.S. Constitution was adopted, the concept of judicial function most widely held by American colonists was derived from the British model, with the single difference that on this side of the Atlantic courts would be forced to apply English rules of interpretation to written constitutional documents as well as to statutes, contracts, and other written legal instruments. This view implied a narrow form of constitutional judicial review under Article 3's "case-controversy" provision, with courts having the power to disregard unconstitutional legislative or executive actions when they interfered with the capacity of the judiciary to perform its functions properly.[33]

The doctrine that supports this approach was first laid down by the Supreme Court in 1803 and was to remain the guiding principle of judicial review throughout the antebellum period,[34] as is revealed both in the Court's actual exercise(s) of review, and in its use of the *Marbury* precedent during that period.[35] But during the early postbellum period, as important business interests began to assert the need for more aggressive judicial protection of property rights, the *Marbury* doctrine came to be viewed as too limited in its scope. At the same time, for obvious reasons, those interests clamoring for greater protection were loathe to seek support in the discredited *Dred Scott* decision,[36] the only other antebellum case in which the Court actually exercised its power to invalidate an act of Congress.

Thus the proponents of a more aggressive, or activist, judicial review found themselves in the position of having no precedent to bolster the controversial conception of judicial power they were advocating. Some authority on the order of a Gilded Age Pseudo-Isidore was needed, and it was found in several leading lights of the American bar's conservative wing, two or three Supreme Court justices, and commentators such as Thomas M. Cooley and Christopher Tiedeman. Throughout the last quarter of the nineteenth century and the first two decades of the twentieth, these and other individuals propounded the idea that *Marbury* had actually advanced a much broader conception of judicial power than formerly had been thought and that the Court had really been "making law," not just "deciding cases," from the beginning.[37]

Remarkably, even though expansive judicial review suffered important setbacks in the New Deal era, the idea regained prominence beginning in the 1950s, as commentators joined an ever-expanding judicial effort to justify broad-gauged judicial activism in civil liberties cases.[38] The result of this long development has been wide acceptance of the *Marbury* Myth. Much like Pseudo-Isidore's teaching that "ever since the apostolic age the bishops of Rome had been . . . making . . . law for the universal church,"[39] this myth has taught that ever since the Founding era, the justices of the Supreme Court have been making law for the American Republic. Just as Pseudo-Isidore aggrandized the papacy and the clerical establishment in the Middle Ages, so has the *Marbury* Myth aggrandized the Supreme Court and the American judicial establishment in modern times.

The examples constitute a graphic illustration of the overpowering force of precedent in the law, an indispensable reliance upon historical practices even when, ironically, the history of those very practices is being misconstrued. They demonstrate that even in an age of supposed rationalism, one cannot escape the truth embedded in J. S. Mill's understated characterization of Coleridge's philosophy of history: "The long or extensive prevalence of any opinion was a presumption that it was not altogether a fallacy."[40]

Part Four · The Normative Force of Tradition

In Part Three, the common law foundation of American constitutionalism was explored in depth, with close attention paid to traditional rules of legal interpretation and the role of precedent in constitutional law. Although the common law provides the most important background material for understanding the American Founding from the standpoint of legal history, it must be remembered that legal development does not occur in a vacuum but within the wider context of legal and political theory.

As I suggested in Part Three, the "reason of the common law" has its roots in a classical idea of reason. Yet the common law's later development was accomplished alongside the rise of modern liberal political and legal thought, and the truncated rationalism that complements it. Professor James Stoner has demonstrated that the relationship between liberalism and the common law has sometimes been accommodating (as in the American Founding). But it has just as often been a tense struggle (as in the attacks of Hobbes and Bentham).

It is my contention that the tension between liberalism and the common law is real and is rooted in the incompatibility of some ancient perspectives smuggled into modernity via common law tradition with the modern impulse to scuttle tradition altogether.

In the next three chapters, these ancient perspectives will be contrasted with the modern perspectives that have arguably supplanted them. In Chapter 11, the Hobbesian perspective will be explored through application of a game-theoretic approach, and the empiricist epistemological foundations that support Hobbesianism and its derivatives will be contrasted to those that support classical political thought. The differences between the classical and modern perspectives are rooted not only in their different ways of conceiving the relationship between the individual and society but also in their fundamentally different ideas of reason. The philosophical and epistemological background covered in Chapter 11 is crucial for understanding the distinction between legal naturalism and legal positivism, the main subject of Chapter 12, and the place of natural law in the American constitutional order, the main subject of Chapter 13.

In Chapter 12, the naturalistic and positivistic legal traditions are contrasted, with special attention given to the jurisprudence of Thomas Aquinas and John Austin. Modern legal positivism is self-contradictory and contrary to experience. Legal naturalism is fully concordant with our everyday experience of legal reality and points with clarity to a transcendently ordered legal cosmos. A convenient illustration of both approaches may be found in the modern constitutional jurisprudence of the Supreme Court regarding the application of certain provisions in the Bill of Rights against the states through the Fourteenth Amendment.

In Chapter 13, the place of natural law in American constitutional jurisprudence is reexamined by means of a contrast between Lockean natural law and the Millian progressivism that appears to be its main modern substitute. Contrary to popular wisdom, the Supreme Court never applied natural law in the decision of constitutional cases, nor could it have done so successfully even if it had tried. The popular impression is a myth that appears to have been used by modern commentators and judges to lend precedential support to judicial supremacy in constitutional law. Some of the constitutionally relevant portions of J. S. Mill's thought are then considered and critiqued. Contemporary adoption of Mill's constitutional perspective(s) has served to undermine several of the most important ideas in the Western legal tradition, ideas that if properly conceived are indispensable to the healthy survival not only of that tradition but also of our constitutionalism.

11 · Political Philosophy

According to Plato, human reality is experienced as a tensional struggle in a *metaxy*, an "in-between" of existence: between matter and spirit, between the individual and society, between animality and humanity, between passion and reason, between immanence and transcendence, between the phenomenal and the noumenal.[1] Ancient political philosophy, in its descent from Socrates, Plato, and Aristotle to Cicero, Augustine, and Aquinas, and whether Platonic, Neoplatonic, Aristotelian, Stoic, Patristic, or Scholastic, is distinctive both in its clear awareness of these tensional forces in the *metaxy* and in its ongoing effort to hold them in an intelligible balance.

In Plato's thought, for example, the tension between the claims to preeminence of the individual (most prominently articulated in the *Apology*) and those of society (most prominently articulated in the *Crito*) is held in balance, if sometimes precariously, by an "anthropological" principle with a double meaning, which takes the individual to be a microcosm of society and society to be a macrocosm of the individual.[2]

In this view, the order of the psyche is necessarily a function of the order of the polis, and the order of the polis a function of the order of the psyche. If a society's fundamental, first-order, constitution, its underlying set of predispositions with regard to decisionmaking, is such that the passional elements in that society are allowed a large measure of influence on public policy and law, then individuals will be governed largely by passion as well. The character of the state will in turn reciprocally assume the character suggested by the particular passions emergent in the individual souls that are prototypical for that society. Since individual passions are by nature both manifold and unruly, such societies will be fundamentally disorderly. Because of the reciprocity governing the relationship between individuals and social institutions, the resulting social and political disorder will generate more disordered souls, which in turn will produce an even more disordered society, and so on.

Against this unending cycle of disorder, Plato and his philosophic descendants in the ancient and medieval world pose the alternative of a society governed by reason. Here the inherently disorderly passional elements in the psyche are denied a primary role in the development of the individual, except as they are harnessed and made to serve the governing interest of the rational faculty, which is itself constituted by its attunement to a transcendent source of cosmic order. The type of society brought into being by the predominance of this kind of individual results in a polis in which the rational element has pride of place and for which its government and laws are allowed, if not required, continually to reinforce and reaffirm, by custom and tradition, those intellectual (and other) virtues that constitute the character of its prototypical individuals. It is this vision, incomplete and missing some essential ingredients in Plato, that is brought to fulfillment, with the help of numerous permutations and refinements along the way, in the social and political thought of Thomas Aquinas.

In marked contrast to this approach, modern political thought is distinctive in its effort to abolish the tensions in the metaxy. Taking as its starting point the denial of Plato's anthropomorphic equation, the individual is no longer *zoon politikon*, sharing a common nature with all other social beings. Rather, the individual is conceived as divorced from society, the legal embodiment of which becomes the abstracted, artificial unity known as the modern state.

It will be noticed that I said "conceived as." That is because Plato's insight into the relationship between individual and social order holds true for modern societies as much as for ancient ones. It is simply denied or ignored by most modern political thinkers, who have become apologists for the arbitrariness and alleged artificiality of the modern state through construction of competing abstract, comprehensive, architectonic "systems" rather than seekers after political wisdom grounded in experience in the manner of the ancients.

If philosophy is a search for wisdom, political philosophy is a search for wisdom about right order in the polis. Classical political thought is characterized by a foundational principle regarding the relationship between polities and their individual members: the order of the psyche both constitutes and is constituted by the order of the polis. For the ancients, this parallelism holds whether the respective characters of psyche and polis are dominated by reason or by passion. Modern political thought denies this parallelism with respect to the rational element but not with respect to the passional element. Hence the famous Hobbesian "state of nature" is produced, a condition of primeval social disorder, a "war of all against all" that arises inevitably from the presumed fundamental passion of human nature: the fear of violent death.[3]

In a Hobbesian world, the defining characteristic of human beings is the same feature that characterizes other animals in nature; humans can hope to escape the resulting condition only because they possess larger brains capable of projecting and comparing the hypothetical long-term consequences of anarchy versus society. They are able to decide that abandoning their natural condition will provide more security against violent death (and thus more opportunity to pursue the desires, drives, and interests dictated by their other passions) than will their remaining in that condition.

The result of this decision is the Hobbesian social covenant.[4] Yet since the natural end of passion is disorder, as much for Hobbes as for Plato, and since for Hobbes, unlike for Plato, reason is not a faculty that governs passion in accordance with a knowable and transcendent source of cosmic order, thereby producing a natural order both in the psyche and in the polis, the continuing stability of the decision to live collectively rather than individually becomes problematic in a Hobbesian world.

THE PRISONER'S DILEMMA

The problem of social order in a Hobbesian world is structural, even mathematical, and can be addressed most fruitfully by resorting to some ideas that have been developed in public choice and game theory.[5] In this view, the situation described by Hobbes in *Leviathan* is a "problem of cooperation," in which self-interested individuals in a condition of virtual anarchy have to decide whether to establish a government.

It is also a classic "prisoner's dilemma," where A and B are two individuals (in a two-person society, yielding a "two-person game"), or where A is any individual and B all other individuals taken as a whole (in an n-person society, yielding an "n-person game").[6] The "payoffs" in the matrix (illustrated in Table 11.1) represent values for A and B (3 = best, 2 = second best, 1 = second worst, 0 = worst) for outcomes in each cell. A's values are depicted by the number appearing before, and B's after, the comma.

Table 11.1. Prisoner's Dilemma

		B	
		Cooperate	Don't Cooperate
	Cooperate	2, 2	0, 3
A			
	Don't Cooperate	3, 0	1, 1

Clearly there is a "dominant strategy" for both A and B: noncooperative. No matter what B does, A is better off not cooperating; no matter what A does, B is better off not cooperating. For example, suppose that A cooperates (choosing the top row); B will get a higher payoff by not cooperating (choosing the right column). On the other hand, if A does not cooperate (choosing the bottom row), B will still get a higher payoff by not cooperating (choosing the right column). Since the game is symmetrical, the payoff matrix for each player mirrors that for the other, so the strategy for A is the same as for B. This result is paradoxical, since both A and B will receive larger individual payoffs if each cooperates than either will receive if neither cooperates.

This paradox necessitates closer examination of the cooperative strategy. Perhaps cooperation might be conceived as involving A and B trading support across the issue of cooperation itself, in a manner analogous to "vote trading" or "logrolling" in a legislative body. Specifically, A might agree to support B on the issue of A's cooperation if B agrees to support A on the issue of B's cooperation. Clearly, each prefers that the other cooperate, no matter what. If we symbolize the alternative that A cooperate by "a," the alternative that B cooperate by "b," and the negations of these alternatives by "–a" and "–b," then the preference profiles for A and B may be constructed in descending order (see Table 11.2).

Table 11.2. Cooperative Strategy

Matrix Values	A	B
3	–a, b	a, –b
2	a, b	a, b
1	–a, –b	–a, –b
0	a, –b	–a, b

The situation can also be diagrammed, which shows that there is now no stable outcome, assuming that both A and B have the ability to exchange support on the issue of cooperation, unless there is some way of enforcing an agreement between them (see Table 11.3). If we start from the noncooperative position (–a, –b), A and B, collectively, have the ability and incentive to move to (a, b), since they both prefer (a, b) to (–a, –b). However, in the absence of enforcement, A has the ability and incentive to move from (a, b) to (–a, b), since that move depends on his action alone, and he prefers (–a, b) to (a, b). But from (–a, b), B has the ability and incentive to move from (–a, b) to (–a, –b), since this move depends only on his initiative, and he prefers (–a, –b) to (–a, b).

Likewise, starting again from (a, b) and going the other way, B has the ability and incentive to move from (a, b) to (a, –b), since the move depends only on his initiative and he prefers (a, –b) to (a, b). Finally, A has the ability and incentive to move from (a, –b) to (–a, –b), since this move depends only on his initiative and he prefers (–a, –b) to (a, –b). But then, as before, A and B together have the ability and incentive to move from (–a, –b) to (a, b), and so on.

Table 11.3. Unstable Outcomes

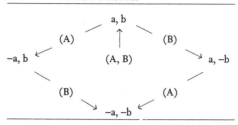

We can now understand more clearly why Hobbes ultimately arrived at externally imposed enforcement (coercion) as the only practicable method for stabilizing the social contract. Under egoistic assumptions, with no preexisting conventional morality, social custom, or legal tradition, enforcement of agreements must be externally imposed (hence, Leviathan). This is the heart of the cooperation dilemma and thus the essence of the modern political problem: reconciliation of individuality with collectivity. The problem is ongoing, for the situation of A and B is easily generalizable to such problems as inflation, pollution control, population control, or nuclear disarmament, to name only a few. To make matters worse, it can be (and has been) proved that any outcome that depends on trading of support across issues is per se unstable in the manner just demonstrated.[7]

It comes to this: the Hobbesian agreement is inherently untenable because, in Hobbesian thought, the problem of social order is resolved only at the level of the collectivity and thus by an intellectual abstraction. Hobbesian individuals remain, even after an initial agreement, as they were in the state of nature, like the prisoners in Plato's cave, chained to the very same material aversions and desires that had rendered that state intolerable in the first place.[8]

Hobbesian reason, restricted to immanent calculation of individual advantage (i.e., to maximization of desired objects and minimization of feared ones), will thus discover itself to be in the "prisoner's dilemma," from which the only escape is defection and a return to the state of nature, followed by another agreement, and so on in an infinite regress. Analysis of the Hobbesian contract thus confirms the truth of Plato's maxim, illustrated in the famous allegory of the *Republic*, that disordered souls necessarily produce disordered societies that in turn can produce only more disordered souls.[9]

MODERN POLITICAL SCIENCE

Plato's anthropology was the means for holding in balance a real polarity of tensional forces in the *metaxy* that cannot be resolved by mere verbal formulas. These forces must be recognized and embraced as fundamental constituents of social and political reality. Thus it is hardly surprising that the modern destruction of that balance has produced forms of thought that appear to be defined in terms of the effort to escape the forces embodied in such tensions. As in the prisoner's dilemma, the results of these efforts have been paradoxical.

For instance, in the thought of Hobbes, who has often been regarded as the founder of modern political philosophy, we find a defense of monarchical absolutism resting upon the unlikely foundation of radical individualism. In Locke, we discover parliamentary absolutism springing from an original agreement to preserve individual rights of property. In Marx, we have a nearly complete abolition of individuality rooted in Lockean economic theory. In Hegel, we have an attempted reunification of society and the individual at the highest possible level of abstraction, in the person of an "absolute state" conceived as the ultimate fulfillment of the underlying principles of the French Revolution. In Mill, we find libertarian individualism resting upon a principle of social utility. And in Bentham, Mill's mentor, there is a near-complete denial of the relevance of individuals, save as abstract units of analysis forming the basis for calculations of the "greatest good for the greatest number."

The paradoxical quality in these examples arises from a general denial of the natural, though tension-filled, relationship between psyche and polis and from a corresponding denial of the rootedness of this relationship in a transcendent source of order that is accessible to reason. As I have suggested, the "in-between" of existence that comprises the world of human experience is characterized by a number of antinomies that figure largely in the thought of the ancients, all of which are circumvented by hypostatic means in one way or another by most modern thinkers. Any attempt to do away with one of the poles of such an antinomy invariably results in a denial of some important feature of reality by a concealment of the experiential basis through which the other pole is brought to light. Again, as Heraclitus warned more than two millennia ago, "One of a pair of opposites cannot exist without the other."[10]

Arguably the most important of the antinomies from the standpoint of modern political thought is that between matter and spirit. Materialism is the metaphysical basis of Hobbesian political philosophy and thus is an important piece of groundwork underlying the development of the contract theory of the state. Materialism, which denies the reality of spiritual experience by doing away with the spiritual pole of the matter-spirit antinomy, is an intellectual distortion from which many other prominent features of modern political and legal thought are derived.

From the assumption that all reality is physical (material), we may derive the now-familiar assortment of reductionist maxims that characterize modern political science: the study of social and political institutions is reducible to a study of "phenomena," or "data"; "epistemology" is reducible to "scientific method"; "societies" are reducible to collections of "individuals" ("social atoms"); "individuals" are reducible to "particles of matter"; and human intellect ("mind") is reducible to brain functioning ("body").

Closely related to these reductive maxims are the ideas that human nature is radically egoistic; the natural condition of man without government is anarchy; societies are (and must be) created by human artifice in the form of an essentially unstable "social contract," the underlying logic of which, by implication, extends even to such institutions as the Church—which, by tradition, is regarded as divinely ordained; the purpose of organized society and government is solely the advancement of the material well-being of its members (i.e., the goal of the state is devoid of any spiritual aspect); and the very definition of politics can be fully comprised in such statements as "who gets what, when, where, how much," and so on.

Jurisprudentially, we find Machiavelli's maxim that law is merely a tool of some territorial sovereign; that law, morality, and religion are fully subservient to "politics"; and that the theoretical foundation of commercial society and its law is "enlightened self-interest." Further, we discover Austin's definition of law as "a direct or circuitous command of a monarch or sovereign number to a person or persons in a state of subjection to its author," and Bentham's subjugation of right and wrong to the category of pleasure and pain and the consequent subjugation of law to the principle of utility.

Finally, there is a close relationship between the materialist foundation of modern political thought and contemporary constitutional rights conceived as Millian entitlements to relatively unrestricted pursuit of physical pleasure and material well-being. If the character of a desired object defines the consciousness of the desiring subject,[11] such "rights," when construed in accordance with a Benthamite utilitarian foundation under a Hegelian theory of interpretation, presuppose the materialism of Hobbes (see Chapter 14). Modern liberalism is thus thoroughly materialist at its core and is fully subject to the antimaterialist critique in Chapter 16.

These principles and maxims, traceable in one way or another to the dominance of metaphysical or scientific materialism in the modern age, deny the centrality of divinity and spirituality in the organization of public affairs. Yet the materialism on which they are founded is, at best, irrelevant to any question concerning the existence of the divine presence they deny; and, at worst, it argues the other way. Before treating these issues, however, the contrasting ideas of reason in ancient and modern times that were introduced in Chapter 7 should be examined more closely, for the preceding complex of maxims, when viewed as a whole, presumes a peculiarly truncated notion of reason that has little in common with the reason of the ancients.

CLASSICAL AND MODERN RATIONALISM

The denial of the classical parallelism between psyche and polis at the level of rationality suggests a sharp epistemological divergence between ancients and moderns on the scope and function of reason. Since the end, or telos, of Hobbesian reason is fulfillment of the individual desire for material security (as a means to avoid violent death), and since its method is the calculation of individual advantage, its substantive scope is limited to synthetic observations concerning the material world, conceived as data of sense perception, and its procedural scope to such purely analytical functions as logical derivations and mathematical tautologies. Individual reason is not conceived as the source of order in the psyche, the source from which the unruly passions of animal nature may be regulated.

For the ancients, the end, or telos, the pursuit of which necessitates the presence of regulative reason in the psyche, is the transcendent Good, conceived in different ways by Greeks, Hellenes, early Romans, late Romans, early Christians, barbarians, and Scholastics, but always as a nonmaterial, hence a spiritual, Good. Reason, for the ancients, is not a calculating function designed to serve ends that are purely immanent; it is a faculty providing access to the intelligible world, answering to the experience of a reality that lies behind things as they appear when given as objects of sense perception.

Reason thus can be regulative for individuals in such a way as to generate order in society according to the terms of Plato's anthropomorphic equation. The reality made accessible by the use of reason is simply rational order itself, considered in relation to its transcendent source, which necessarily subordinates all distinctions between and among individuals and societies.

For Cicero and for Aquinas (see Chapter 12), this rational order is the natural law, conceived by the former as the mind and reason of an intelligent being and for the latter as the imprint of eternal law on a rational creature. Thus classical naturalism and classical rationalism are complementary worldviews, neither of which is fully comprehensible without reference to the other. To explore this complementarity further, it will be useful to examine the epistemological foundations of the classical idea of reason more closely by a comparison with those that undergird its modern counterpart.

It is agreed that human beings possess, along with other animals, the faculty of sense perception. By its use, we gain access to the material world insofar as it is manifested in particular embodiments, or phenomena. The representations or images in the mind that are produced by the interaction of our senses of sight, smell, sound, taste, and touch with phenomena may be called "percepts."

Though perception enables us to explain our experience of the external world as a succession of sensations, and as such is a necessary condition of all corporeal experience, it is not sufficient to explain how human beings can form mental images that subsume aggregates of such experiences and then treat these aggregates as particular objects of thought. Explanation of human mental activity thus requires positing a faculty of conception, in which the aggregates of experience are termed "concepts." Broadly interpreted, conception would include such activities as remembering, imagining, classifying, and the like.[12]

Within the category of conception, unlike that of perception, there appear to be activities that plausibly might be regarded as different in kind, not merely in degree. For example, I can remember (or imagine) a simple succession of particular perceptions without resorting to anything more general than the concept of that particular succession; but I cannot classify that succession without relating it to another succession (and thus to another concept), the comparison with which provides the basis for a conceptual distinction. The formulation of conceptual distinctions therefore appears to involve a qualitatively higher type of mental activity than does the formulation of simple concepts based solely on perception.

Then there is the problem of causal inference. As David Hume demonstrated, perception is limited in the sense that we cannot perceive causal relations; rather, we perceive only successions of perceived objects as they are presented to the mind as objects of thought by percepts. We then, by a leap of faith turned into psychological habit, add the idea of causation to that of succession, a habit that cannot be externally validated, however, because what we really observe, when we are perceiving, are not the objects of perception themselves but the percepts in which the objects are represented. According to Hume,

> The mind never has anything present to it but the perceptions, and cannot possibly reach any experience of their connexion with objects. The supposition of such a connexion is, therefore, without any foundation in reasoning.[13]

In other words, when a thinking subject perceives, it perceives nothing but the contents of its own mind; and since concepts are simply aggregates of percepts, the same argument holds for conception as for perception. Indeed, it holds even more strongly because, though Hume takes for granted the real existence of objects of perception since these can be directly experienced, pure concepts or abstract ideas cannot be experienced directly and thus there is no warrant for presuming their existence at all. So even though we can safely assume the existence of perceived objects based on direct experience, since causality is an abstract idea, it is inadmissible, in Hume's view, to infer a causal relationship between such objects and the percepts that constitute our mental representations of them (i.e., to infer that the objects "caused" the perceptions).

If we deny that objects of thought (whether perceptual or conceptual) cause the ideas that represent those objects in our minds, then we are, in effect, denying the existence of an external reality whose structure is capable of determining or orienting the internal structure of human mental activity (i.e., of thought). Particularly, we are denying the existence of an intellect whose function is to apprehend or conceive such purely intelligible objects as causation—a denial of the intelligible world from which the ancients derived the source of order in both psyche and polis.

The implications of Hume's radical subjectivism were not lost on Immanuel Kant. According to Kant, Hume's epistemology undermined not only the idea of a transcendent source of order but also the foundations of modern science. Kant's response was the *Critique of Pure Reason*, in which he attempted to save human understanding and scientific knowledge from Humean skepticism by attributing to the mind an innate structure that enables it to "determine the structure and features of all possible experience."[14] At the center of this structure are a number of a priori concepts (including that of causation), which predetermine the mind's receptivity to empirical intuitions (i.e., sense impressions, broadly defined) in such a way as to organize its cognitive processes and thereby render experience comprehensible as a whole.

> The effect of an object upon the faculty of representation, so far as we are affected by the said object, is sensation. That sort of intuition which relates to an object by means of sensation, is called an empirical intuition. The undetermined object of an empirical intuition, is called phenomenon. That which in the phenomenon corresponds to the sensation, I term its matter; but that which effects that the content of the phenomenon can be arranged under certain relations, I call its form. But that in which our sensations are merely arranged, and that by which they are susceptible assuming a certain form, cannot be itself sensation. It is, then, the matter of all phenomena that is given to us *a posteriori;* the form must lie ready *a priori* for them in the mind, and consequently can be regarded separately from all sensation.[15]

Kant's aprioristic theory of the understanding allowed him both to give an adequate account of existing scientific knowledge and to lay groundwork for a model of the scientific enterprise that has remained influential. Commenting upon the nature of scientific inquiry, Kant says that

> reason only perceives that which it produces after its own design; . . . it must not be content to follow, as it were, in the leading-strings of nature, but must proceed in advance with principles of judgment according to unvarying laws, and compel nature to reply to its questions. For accidental observations, made according to no preconceived plan, cannot be united under a necessary law. But it is this that reason seeks for and requires. It is only the principles of reason which can give to concordant phenomena the validity of laws, and it is only when experiment is directed by these rational principles that it can have any real utility. Reason must approach nature with the view, indeed, of receiving information from it, not, however, in the character of a pupil, who listens to all that his master chooses to tell him, but in that of a judge, who compels the witnesses to reply to those questions which he himself thinks fit to propose.[16]

Though Kant was able, through his account of speculative reason, to explain the possibility of scientific knowledge and thereby to lay a plausible groundwork for the attribution of real existence to objects of empirical cognition, this attribution of reality was limited to "undetermined" objects of empirical intuition, or "phenomena." Since the reality of such objects is comprised, for Kant, solely in their "effect upon the faculty of representation," it follows that the reality in question is one of mere appearance, not of things as such. Moreover, it also follows from this position that objects of thought not connected to empirical cognition are not knowable, since such objects have no purely phenomenal aspects. Summarizing Kant's views on these issues, Etienne Gilson observes:

> If it is so, where nothing is given, there is no knowledge; yet that which is given is an *x* that is not even existence, but is that to which existence is ascribed by the assertive modality of judgment. Of that *x*, taken in itself, we know nothing, save only that it is. And how could we know it? Inasmuch as it is known, or even simply perceived, what is either perceived or known is its phenomenon, that is, its appearance through the *a priori* conditions that are required for both its intellectual knowledge and its sensory perception. In short "all those properties which constitute the intuition of a material thing belong solely to its appearance.... For the existence of the thing which appears is not thereby suppressed, ... but it is thereby only shown that, through sense, we absolutely cannot know that thing such as it is in itself."[17]

I shall have more to say about the metaphysical aspects of Kant's denial of the knowability of nonphenomenal, or noumenal, reality in Chapter 16 as well as its crucial importance for the ideas of history, tradition, and custom as viable normative sources of law in Chapter 17. Here it is only necessary to note that though such a denial does not require a corresponding denial of the existence of noumena, it does require a denial of the classical idea of reason conceived as an immaterial intellectual faculty whose function is to provide access to, and render knowable, a realm of purely intelligible objects of thought. Though it does not require the absolute denial of transcendence, it does require the denial of a transcendent source of order that is accessible to regulative reason as a means of controlling passion and of the classical symbiosis of psyche and polis.

TOOLS AND OBJECTS OF THOUGHT

In accordance with the logic of reductio ad absurdum, any position that generates consequences so manifestly at war with common experience should have been rejected at the moment of its inception. Sadly, it was not, and thus the accumulated wisdom of two millennia was scuttled in favor of a truncated view of reason that is, oddly enough, alleged to be empirical.

Kant was driven to this position by his presumption, shared with Locke, Berkeley, and Hume, that the contents of the understanding, its "ideas," are the things *which* the mind thinks, not the things *by which* it thinks. According to this view, the objects of human thought are our percepts, concepts, images, memories, sensations, emotions, and feelings, not their external referents. In other words, when I look at a painting, I am not really aware of the painting itself but only of a percept, an "idea" of the painting that has somehow been impressed upon my mind. As has been cogently argued by Mortimer J. Adler, this presumption is erroneous and has led to absurd results in modern philosophy.[18]

The presumption is false because if, when we think, we are aware only of the contents of our own individual minds, then it would be impossible to distinguish between, say, my stomachache, which is a private bodily feeling that cannot be experienced by anyone else, and the painting on my wall, which can be made an object of common experience and thus is intersubjectively verifiable or falsifiable as a matter of knowledge. Intersubjectively verifiable experience is possible, not only with regard to material objects but also with regard to abstract ideas without immediate physical embodiments, such as memories of past events, the concept of infinity, predictions of future states, or the idea of God.[19]

Anticipating Kant's Humean problem by five centuries, Thomas Aquinas addressed the issue squarely in the *Summa Theologica* while responding to the arguments of Protagoras and Heraclitus that the intellect knows only the impressions made on it, "that sense is cognizant only of the impression made on its own organ."

> This is, however, manifestly false for two reasons. First, because the things we understand and the objects of science are the same. Therefore if what we understand is merely the intelligible species in the soul, it would follow that every science would not be concerned with things outside the soul, but only with the intelligible species within the soul; thus, according to the teaching of the Platonists all science is about ideas, which they held to be actually understood. Secondly, it is untrue because it would lead to the opinion of the philosophers of antiquity who maintained that "whatever seems, is true," and that consequently contradictories are true simultaneously. For if the power knows its own impression only, it can judge of that only. Now a thing seems according to the impression made on the knowing power. Consequently the knowing power will always judge of its own impression as such, and so every judgment will be true; for instance, if taste perceived only its own impression, when anyone with a healthy taste judges that honey is sweet, he would judge truly; and likewise if anyone with a corrupt taste judges that honey is bitter, this would be true, for each would judge according to the impression on his taste. Thus every opinion would be equally true; in fact, every sort of apprehension.[20]

For Aquinas, to hold that the mind understands only its own contents is to collapse the commonsensical distinction between appearance and reality and thereby to destroy the basis of scientific knowledge. The absurdity of such a result thus compels adoption of the position that our ideas are *that by which* we understand, not *that which* we understand. Adoption of the presumption that the objects of our thoughts are merely our own ideas, by denying the full reality and knowability of the external world, throws into doubt the normativity of common, publicly validated experience, severs the classical connection between psyche and polis, and leads ultimately to the denial of an objective reality that lies beneath, behind, within, and beyond the manifold of phenomenal representations.

Epistemologically, it has taken the form of a denial of an immaterial, regulative intellect conceived as a kind of sixth sense whose function is the apprehension of purely intelligible objects (objects of thought) in a realm of pure ideas—that which the ancients referred to as the "intelligible world." Ontologically, it has taken the form of a denial of spirituality as an essential feature of the human psyche and a corresponding materialism that has dominated the modern age for at least a century. Mortimer J. Adler has noted the profound consequences of a view that treats ideas as the only things with which we are directly aware:

> We are compelled to live in two worlds without any bridge between them. One is the world of physical reality, in which our own bodies occupy space, move about, and interact with other bodies. Our belief in the existence of this world is [in this view] a blind and irrational faith. The other is the completely private world in which each of us is enclosed—the world in which our only experience is the experience constituted by consciousness of our own ideas. The assumption that individuals other than ourselves also and similarly live in the private worlds of their own conscious experience is as blind a faith as the belief that we all live together in the one world of external physical reality.[21]

It is in this modern truncation of reason, and its consequent denial of the knowability of an external reality, that we may discover the origins of the coherence epistemologies that now seem to dominate constitutional scholarship. Such a model leads to a kind of constitutional solipsism in which a constitution, and the judicially created law that follows from it, is evaluated according to its internal consistency rather than its correspondence with external reality. We shall see in Chapter 12 how the truncation of reason has generated a correspondingly truncated jurisprudence that is as contrary to experience as its epistemological counterpart.

12 · Law and Jurisprudence

Understanding the distinctions drawn in Chapter 11 between classical and modern political thought and between classical and modern rationalism is essential for understanding the most important jurisprudential debate of modern times, which involves the well-known but not always well-understood ideas of natural law and legal positivism. The subject is nowadays almost always characterized as a fundamental opposition between proponents of naturalism or positivism, but this characterization is misleading.

The classical jurists, including the classical common lawyers, not being cognizant of any distinction between ideas as tools of thought and ideas as things thought, and so believing that they were directly conscious of and in full contact with external reality *as they experienced it*, developed a naturalistic jurisprudence based on the idea of a common human nature. For the classical jurists and the early common lawyers, a concept of human nature was possible only by virtue of a corresponding idea of a common reason, which, for each individual, allowed the encounter with other individuals to be experienced directly and therefore as real.

Modern acceptance of the notion that we can be directly aware only of the contents of our individual minds means, among other things, that there can be no direct experience of other individuals or of the contents of their minds. There can be no common reason and no rational basis for assuming even the existence of a common humanity. This view leads straightforwardly to an extreme variant of legal positivism, in which the laws of nature either are fully secularized, as in the political philosophy of Thomas Hobbes, or operationally defined as nonexistent, as in the jurisprudential thought of John Austin.

Here the views of Coke, Hale, and Blackstone become clearer in their assumption of a singular reality underlying the multiplicity of legal phenomena, a reality accessible to the "reason of the common law," the natural affinity of which is with classical (Aristotelian practical) reason rather than with modern (enlightenment) rationalism. The assumption of that reality also explains why Hobbes and Bentham opposed Coke, Hale, and Blackstone with such vehemence.

Classical naturalism arose from ancient and medieval political thought. It was based on the twin assumptions that human intellect (psyche) was an incorporeal substance capable of accessing the realm of ideas or concepts (intelligible species) and that those ideas, concepts, or objects of thought were *real* in the sense that they corresponded to things having a real existence in the external world. These assumptions were not merely empty abstractions but were formulated on the basis of an experienced tension arising from having been drawn or pulled toward the intelligible objects from beyond the world of sense perception, i.e., from an experience of transcendence.

It is important to remember that the classical naturalists did not disregard or deny the existence or significance of purely positive law, conceived as a set of commands emanating from a legitimately (or, perhaps, illegitimately) empowered sovereign. In this sense, the analyses of constitutional forms in Plato's *Republic,* Aristotle's *Politeia,* Cicero's *De Legibus,* or Augustine's *Civitas Dei* are, in part, exercises in legal or constitutional positivism.[1]

Thomas Aquinas also devotes a large segment of his *Treatise on Law* to a discussion of positive law.[2] In the interest of earthly peace, he even goes so far as to concede something like a duty of obedience even to unjust positive laws, especially if these represent commands of a legitimate sovereign. Augustine had carried this principle even further in defense of the Christian principle counseling rendition of earthly things to Caesar and divine things to God.[3]

Nor can it be said that the classical naturalists were unfamiliar with legal positivism in its more modern guise, as an ideology propounded largely for the purpose of defeating arguments resting on the presumed existence of a human nature distinct from other animal natures. From this point of view, one may plausibly regard the entirety of Plato's *Republic* as a response to the argument of Thrasymachus that "justice is the interest of the stronger," or of the second half of Plato's *Gorgias* as a response to the argument of Callicles that "nature" requires the "rule of the strong over the weak."[4] In both these instances, the ideological positivist arguments were defeated, not by exercises in propositional logic but by careful exegeses of philosophical experience stemming from the erotic attunement of human nature to sources of cosmic order through the love of wisdom.

The brand of positivism exemplified by Thrasymachus and Callicles and defeated by Plato and others in ancient times reemerged triumphant two millennia later in the thought of Niccolo Machiavelli and Thomas Hobbes. Machiavelli's complete subordination of morality and religion to political necessity led naturally to an idea of law as the mere tool of a territorial sovereign.[5] Hobbes's rejection of custom as the basis of law in *The Elements of Law,*[6] his concomitant founding of the modern state upon the necessity of maintaining an inherently unstable social compact in *Leviathan*,[7] and, above all, his adoption of an atomistic psychology grounded in a nominalist epistemology and a materialist ontology effectively circumvented or denied the reality of the whole realm of intelligible objects (objects of thought) from which the ancients saw human nature as an experience of being drawn or pulled away from preoccupation with the purely phenomenal or immanent toward a noumenal or transcendent reality.

The overthrow of these two cardinal assumptions of classical philosophy, that the psyche is a sensorium of transcendence and that the objects sensed here are real, led Hobbes and subsequent contractarian political thinkers to adopt a severely truncated version of natural law that is best described as a law of the jungle, based on the necessity of self-preservation. It also led straightforwardly to the modern, ideologized version of legal positivism that, at least in its more radical forms, has nothing whatever to do with positive law but is solely concerned with denying the name of Law to any rule, principle, or practice that might plausibly be thought to have a nonimmanent origin.

To deny legal status to such rules is to deny the reality of human experience from the cradle to the grave. It has long been noted that even toddlers occasionally display a marvelously well-tuned sense of justice, however partisan particular demonstrations of the characteristic may appear to be. Certainly most adults live their lives in a fairly constant state of tension between "seen" and "unseen" measures, between material drives and other inclinations that seem to beckon from beyond. And when, in the face of such thankfully rare events as the Nazi Holocaust, the clarity of the unseen measure is revealed with resplendent force, it becomes all but unthinkable, at least for a time, to regard Law as man's work alone.

In sum, the peculiar world that is described by the legal positivist, a world in which laws are arbitrary commands, in which human beings have nothing in common save their animality, in which the pulls, tugs, and tensions that cannot be traced to a purely phenomenal source are regarded as mere illusions, is an empty abstraction. The world of human experience, on the other hand, is a world richly permeated by things unseen, by noumena as well as phenomena, by justice and injustice, by good laws and bad laws. Above all, it is a world peopled by characters who stubbornly persist in responding to entreaties that are experienced as transcendent callings.

Natural law should thus be understood as the result of a series of attempts to transform reactions to such experiences of transcendence, of unseen measures, of defective laws that lead to injustice in concrete instances "into a body of fundamental, substantive rules that claim authority as expressing the true nature of man and society."[8] Thus natural law is not a product of speculative, abstract reason; rather, much like the common law, it is the result of practical reason applied to human experience. William T. Tete explains that it was so understood even by the Romans who first developed it as a theory prior to Justinian's codification:

Classical Roman law had been largely developed by magistrates and jurists in concrete cases applying traditional Roman legal and moral concepts, such as the importance of good faith. Magistrates tried to make sense out of the situation at hand, making free use of their broad authority to adopt new remedies for novel situations. Roman jurists, in turn, both advised the magistrates and tried to make sense out of what magistrates incorporated into their edicts. Later jurists tried to explain the sense of the traditional Roman morality underlying the law to the layman, or law school freshman, in terms of natural law. However, with a few important exceptions (such as the presumption of liberty) Roman emperors, lawyers, magistrates and jurists did not derive their rules of law by speculative reason from abstract idealistic principles of natural law. . . . For the Romans, natural law in practice was not very idealistic. It was mostly the pattern of ordinary transactions that were intelligible to all nations and enforceable by the Roman magistrate. Subsequent Christian jurists borrowed freely from Roman practical experience. That the starting point was ordinary concrete human experience is a crucial point. What the Romans considered natural law—natural and normal as a matter of the daily life of any civilized society—included most ordinary contracts, particularly the contract of buying and selling. These rules were natural in contradistinction to the technical legal rules peculiar to particular societies.[9]

This view of natural law, taken to be the culmination of a historical development and not merely as a bundle of rules and principles made up by some philosopher, brings the continuity of the Western legal tradition into clearer focus. The much-vaunted disjunction between Roman and English law that has been propagated by Anglophilic legal scholars for several centuries is a half-truth at best. Natural law first arose as the edictal, common law developed by the peregrine praetors who were responsible for declaring the law to be applied in cases involving non-Romans.[10]

Since jurisdiction was personal, not territorial, this law had to be common to Romans and non-Romans alike; and it was to become the *ius gentium,* or "common law," of Western Europe after the collapse of Rome. Whether early English jurists knew it or not, the fact that the *gentic* law was general and natural, not particular or technical, meant that it would play a large role in the early development of English common law.

In light of the real, common experiences upon which all theoretizations must be founded and against which all theories must be tested, any alleged fundamental opposition between natural law and positive law, properly conceived, disappears. Natural law is seen to be as well-grounded in human experience as positive law. Some laws, by virtue of their generally recognized universality, are clearly experienced as being of such a nature as to bind whether "posited" or not; others, just as clearly, bind only because they are posited, as in the rules of the road. Ideological positivism collapses this distinction, rolling all laws of the former type into the latter category, thereby crippling legal analysis by denying the existence of a representative class of legally relevant experiences.

CARDOZO'S NATURALISM

One of the consequences of this truncation in the twentieth century is amply illustrated by an example from the Supreme Court's constitutional law of criminal procedure. In *Palko v. Connecticut*,[11] Justice Benjamin Cardozo, a jurist thought by many observers to have been a legal positivist, nonetheless captured the essence of the naturalistic approach when deciding whether the state's appeal of a murder conviction on a writ of error should be held to contravene the Fifth Amendment's double jeopardy provision, and thus whether that portion of the Federal Constitution should be held applicable to the states by the Fourteenth Amendment's due process clause.

Cardozo resolved the issue by dividing the procedural protections of the Bill of Rights into two classes. In one category he placed those protections that could plausibly be regarded as applicable in all civilized legal orders (i.e., those that are obviously fundamental to any common, reasonable, intersubjectively verifiable concept of due process). In the other, he placed those provisions that clearly have a more limited scope (i.e., those for which the relation to due process is more tenuous, arguable, or not intersubjectively verifiable). The former category, for example, includes such protections as "notice and opportunity to be heard" (recognized as fundamental at least since the Draconian homicide statute of ancient Athenian law),[12] "confrontation of hostile witnesses," and "compulsory process." The latter category takes in the right to a jury trial, the right of a defendant not to testify (both of which are recognized as fundamental only in common law jurisdictions), and state appeals of felony convictions (as in Palko's case).

The Court as a whole, however, never quite seemed to understand fully the significance of Cardozo's analysis, the point being to conserve truly fundamental rights without completely disregarding state autonomy. The *Palko* standard began to break down in the 1940s and 1950s, the process culminating in the explicit overthrow of the universality principle in *Duncan v. Louisiana*.[13] In *Duncan*, the Court adopted a straightforwardly positivistic approach in overturning Louisiana's refusal to provide jury trials in certain nonfelony criminal cases. After conceding that "few would be so narrow or provincial as to maintain that a fair and enlightened system of justice would be impossible without [jury trials]" and that a "criminal process which was fair and equitable but used no juries is easy to imagine," the Court, in fundamental disregard of the state's civil law traditions, abolished the narrowly circumscribed set of nonjury cases anyway. The justices concluded that the question was not whether "a civilized system could be imagined that would not accord the particular protection" but was whether "a particular procedure is fundamental . . . to an Anglo-American regime of ordered liberty."[14]

Finding Louisiana's legal parochialism intolerable, the Court ironically employed a much stronger form of jurisprudential parochialism to eliminate it. Finding *Palko*'s naturalistic universalism too restrictive, the Court resorted to a positivistic particularism that effectively denies recognition to the class of rules, practices, and principles that are experienced as originating from beyond the realm of the merely posited.

A word of caution should be added here: by avowing and applauding the naturalistic basis of Justice Cardozo's *Palko* opinion, it might seem that I am arguing for a judicial carte blanche to read natural law into the Constitution, but exactly the reverse is true. Naturalism, properly understood, because of its reliance upon universalizable, intersubjectively verifiable constitutional and legal norms, which are the product of "experience, not logic," always counsels a healthy judicial *restraint*.

Positivism, on the other hand, because of its deliberate truncation of experience, its corresponding denial of universalizable norms, and its consequent particularism, tends to encourage arbitrary, even unprincipled judicial *activism*.[15] The imagined connection between natural law and judicial activism in constitutional law has resulted largely from the modern response to some Supreme Court decisions of the late nineteenth and early twentieth centuries, in which the Court appears to have confused the tenets of a particular socioeconomic ideology (Social Darwinism) with one version of the laws of nature (Lockean property rights).

In order first to justify, and later to excoriate, these decisions, more than a few commentators have tried to link them with earlier decisions of the antebellum Supreme Court. They have alleged, in effect, that the controversial turn-of-the-century decisions protecting business interests against government regulation were really based on precedential foundations laid by the Marshall or Taney Courts protecting property rights.[16] But the natural law widely presumed in the late eighteenth century was worlds removed from the social philosophy confused with it a century later, and the early Supreme Court never employed natural law in the decision of constitutional cases. Even if it had, the effort could not possibly have been successful.

It is important to stress that these distinctions are not matters of opinion. They are statements of fact subject to verification (or falsification) by experience. As was Justice Cardozo's appeal to universalism in *Palko*, so all legitimate appeals to natural law are appeals to experience based on a faith that the things experienced are real. Unfortunately, modern positivism, founded on nominalism and coherence epistemologies that raise the absolute denial of that faith to the status of a central tenet, has obscured the experiential basis of the naturalistic approach. This response is largely a result of the empiricist tendency to view ideas as objects of thought rather than as perceptual and conceptual tools by which we think.

This misconception, in turn, has led to a habit of thinking about natural law and positive law, which together are experienced as a complex of tensions in a *metaxy* of spirit and matter, as if they were "things" with "properties" that might be made subject to human manipulation according to the rules of predicate logic (i.e., as if they were "subjects" of which "objects" could be "predicated"). This kind of thinking has resulted in the familiar natural law–positive law dichotomy, in which the two headings are conceived as standing for mutually exclusive categories for legal analysis and according to which each category is held to comprise all laws of the particular type denoted by its term.

Thus, instead of a single category of Law encompassing a wide spectrum of legal activities and experiences, one of which is the experience of legal rules apparently founded on universally regarded constants leading to efforts to capture such constants in a valid theory of human nature, and another of which is the experience of rules apparently founded on considerations more parochial or conventional (though the line distinguishing these two kinds of experience is not always bright), we have two mutually exclusive and exhaustive categories. One of them is made to comprise all man-made laws and the other to comprise all laws made by God (or otherwise "implanted in nature").

But we do not directly experience God-made or nature-made laws; we experience man-made or man-discovered laws that are plausibly regarded as having a universalizable, natural, or divine character. The dichotomous categorization is therefore contrary to experience. Its adoption, by analytically isolating the class of experiences covered by the term "natural law" and by treating the members of that class as if they were "objects" or "things," has the ultimate effect of rendering credible the denial of the very existence of natural law as an empty set of nonexistent entities.

Adoption of the dichotomy also has the primary effect of creating "analytical jurisprudence," conceived by John Austin, its founder, as the science of positive law.[17] I shall contrast Austin's thought to that of Thomas Aquinas, his most worthy rival across the centuries, in an effort to provide an understanding of the real alternatives presented by naturalism and positivism when they are given their clearest, fullest, and most pristine expressions.

AQUINAS AND AUSTIN

Natural law and positive law, conceived as mutually exclusive, exhaustive categories comprising distinct entities, do not exist. There is only Law, a term representing a continuum of experiences that are generally recognized as possessing the character of law-likeness.

Some of these experiences are marked by a quality of arbitrariness, in which the rules involved appear to have resulted from considerations peculiar to localities, groups, or societies: social conveniences; particular interests, habits or customs; convention and agreement; or even the imposition of brute force—all seem to play a role. The distinctive feature of this class of experiences is their particularity, such that, were it not for the fact that the rules in question had been posited, very different rules might have done just as well. The lawlike character of the experience is purely contingent, sometimes even appearing to be the result of fiat.

A second class of experiences is marked by a very different quality: that of universality, which appears to have resulted from some natural necessity in such a way that the rules involved could not have been otherwise without completely undermining the lawlike character of the experience. We would expect to find these rules anywhere, any time, in any society that was civilized in even the most minimal sense. They are not experienced as contingent or relative to place and time but point to a transcendent source of legal order, whose compulsion is felt to be irresistible yet nonarbitrary in its nature.

Historically, this distinction has passed under several terminological rubrics: the "convention/nature" *(nomos/physis)* rubric of Greek philosophy, the "civil law/law of nations" *(ius civile/ius gentium)* rubric of Roman law, the "common law/natural law" *(ius commune/ius naturale)* rubric of medieval law, and the "positive law/natural law" rubric of modern law. In each of these denotations, the line distinguishing the two categories has been drawn in fundamentally different ways, so that, for example, much of what was thought *ius gentium* in ancient times would have been regarded *ius commune* in later times. But though the characterization has been subject to change, the character of the experience has not. Again, as Eric Voegelin has noted, all "natural law" should be understood as resulting from attempts to transform "a reaction toward injustice experienced in the concrete case into a body of fundamental, substantive rules that claim authority as expressing the true nature of man and society."[18]

This transformative potential for universalization is the quality that most clearly distinguishes the type of experience that generates natural law from that which produces the merely posited. But it must be cautioned that few experiences of concrete injustice in the world actually lead to an attempt to naturalize legal experience in this way. The *successful* formulation of authoritative rules expressive of human nature has been an extremely rare event.

In Questions 90–97 of *Summa Theologica*, Thomas Aquinas provides one of the most successful historical examples of legal naturalization and thus may serve as a prototypical natural law thinker. He presents a comprehensive theory of the structure of Law and its relation to human nature that is implied by two observations. The first is that people experience legal obligation not merely extrinsically (as imposition of force or command) but also intrinsically (as a moral bond). The second is that the intrinsic, or moral, bond of Law is not experienced as fully autonomous but as proceeding both from within and from beyond the individual who experiences the bond. Indeed, the word "law" itself derives from this bond, as *lex* is rooted in the Latin *ligare*, which means "to bind."[19]

Law in its very essence, as a component in the structure of Being, points beyond itself to a transcendent source, which for Aquinas is the *lex aeterna*.[20] It is man's participation in the eternal law that in turn constitutes the foundation of Thomistic natural law. Aquinas defines Law, in general, as "an ordinance of reason for the common good, promulgated by him who has the care of the community," the purpose of which is the inculcation of "peace and virtue."[21] The six crucial elements in this definition are Reason, Will (made by the sovereign, or "him who has the care of the community"), Publicity (promulgation), Generality (common good), Peace (security), and Virtue. Though deceptively simple, the definition, taken as a whole, can be interpreted to cover all laws, including those that moderns would refer to as "purely positive." The definition also comprises the primary objectives of both classical (virtue) and modern (peace or security) political philosophy as the foundation, or end (telos) of Law.

After defining law in general, Aquinas makes a fourfold division of the field. "Eternal law" is defined as "God's government of the universe via divine providence" (pro-video, or foresight). This kind of law is not subject to time and is thus "eternal," an ordinance of "divine reason" inherent in things created. It is the lex aeterna to which legal experience points as the transcendent source of all Law.[22]

"Natural law" is then defined as the "special government of rational creatures by divine providence," the "imprint of eternal law on rational creatures directing natural inclination to its proper end" (telos). It is an "irruption of the eternal in time," the end of which is "happiness" or "beatitude," a mode of "participation in divine reality."[23] It is "natural" because God "instilled it into man's mind so as to be known by him naturally," the sense in which human nature is conceived in God's image. In Voegelin's words, "Thomas understands natural law as the insights into right order that are possible to man by virtue of his participation in the lex aeterna. These insights are imperfect and must be aided by the revealed lex divina."[24]

"Divine law" (lex divina) is the "ordinance of grace due to sin, since man's ability to reach his natural end is beyond his power." The foundation of this "revealed" law, which includes the law of punishment, is the pervasive experience of human inability to conceptualize the natural law fully and adequately in an effort to establish positive law in accordance with it.[25]

"Human law" is derived from natural law (which is, in its turn, derived from eternal law) but only if it is "legislative," not if it is "judicial" (i.e., not if it is mere application of law). This fourth division is the law that moderns call "positive."[26] Aquinas adds that if human laws are not just, then they are not "law" at all, except in a "perverse" sense; to be "just" requires an orientation to the common good, not merely to particular goods. His notion of positive law includes both the attempt to translate natural law into positive commands and the promulgation of the familiar (and arbitrary) rules of the road.

The Thomistic view of Law is distinctive in its consistency and its completeness. It accounts for the entire manifold of legal experience, including that of custom, which is regarded by Aquinas as an appropriate source of law because of its relation to habit. For him, the "law of our mind" is a "habit containing the precepts of the natural law, which are the first principles of human action," so that the "natural law is held habitually," though sometimes "a man is unable to make use of that which is in him habitually, on account of some impediment" and so again requires the aid of the lex divina.[27]

Since the natural law is for Aquinas, as it had been for Cicero, the "mind and reason of the intelligent man,"[28] and since "reason" is not merely a logical method but is a faculty providing access, however imperfectly, to the intelligible world and thus to the eternal law, it follows that actions that manifest the "interior movement and thought of human reason . . . especially if they be repeated, so as to make a custom," obtain the force of law.[29] "By repeated external actions, the inward movement of the will, and concepts of reason are most effectually declared; for when a thing is done again and again, it seems to proceed from a deliberate judgment of reason. Accordingly, custom has the force of a law, abolishes law, and is the interpreter of law."[30] Joining nature and custom, Aquinas quotes Tully:

> Justice has its source in nature; thence certain things came into custom by reason of their utility; afterwards these things which emanated from nature and were approved by custom, were sanctioned by fear and reverence for the law.[31]

In marked contrast to Thomistic jurisprudence, John Austin claims in his famous first lecture that the proper subject, or "province," of jurisprudence is "positive law," described as proceeding from the "positional" relationship between political "superiors" and "inferiors." Austin's category of positive law is roughly equivalent to Aquinas's category of "human law," an "aggregate of rules" set "by men to men" in "independent political societies."[32]

For Austin, the key element in positive law is the superior's ability to enforce his commands upon the inferior by visitation of some "pain" or "evil." When the element of enforceability is present, the law "obliges" or creates a "duty of obedience" in the inferior that is directly correlative with the "command" (i.e., not with the "right") of the superior (the "sovereign").[33] By assimilating obligation to enforceability in this manner, Austin is able to subordinate fully the intrinsic to the extrinsic legal bond and therewith morality and law to political power.

It is important to note that Austin does not deny the existence or significance of eternal or divine law. In his second lecture, he redefines the Thomistic categories. First, eternal and divine law are collapsed into a single category termed "divine law," or the "laws of God." This category has two components: "revealed law" (roughly, the Thomistic "divine law") and "unrevealed law" (roughly, the Thomistic "eternal law").[34] The unrevealed law is then assimilated to the principle of general utility, which is referred to as the "only index or guide to [God's] unrevealed law."[35] Utility thus becomes a surrogate for the natural law that had been, for Aquinas, an image of eternity imprinted on the psyches of rational creatures and thus the preeminent mode of participation by human beings in divine reality.

God, who wills the greatest happiness for all, is, for Austin, a utilitarian and a rule-utilitarian at that, since he "wills" only those acts for which the effect of their probable consequences (and those of all similar acts) is to increase the general happiness. Dismissing, as principles on which a legal system can be adequately grounded, not only Thomistic natural law but also the "moral sense" of Hume, the "common sense" of Paine, and the "practical reason" of Kant, Austin grounds positive law squarely on the principle of utility previously adumbrated by Bentham. The effect of Austin's approach is to immanentize Thomistic natural law, substituting an administrative method, or social calculus, for an experience of transcendence.

In his fifth lecture, Austin structures further the definition of positive law, asserting that "law" is "a direct or circuitous command of a monarch or sovereign number to a person or persons in a state of subjection to its author."[36] Distinguishing "positive laws" from "rules of positive morality" by reference to this definition, Austin then divides the "rules of positive morality" into two classes. The first is termed "laws proper," consisting of rules that are imperative but not set by political superiors, so that there is no legal sanction attached to their violation. The best examples are found in the so-called "conventions" of the British Constitution.[37] The second is termed "laws improper" and consists of rules, set by the "general opinion" of some class of persons, that are neither imperative nor set by political superiors. Examples are the "law of nations," "rules of honour," "laws of fashion," and "rules of professional behavior."[38]

In the sixth lecture, an analysis of the concept of sovereignty, Austin (following Hobbes and Bentham) defines an "independent political society" in terms of habitual obedience to a sovereign and then declares that the true sovereign "is he, not by whose authority the law was first made, but by whose authority it continues to be a law."[39] Austin is thus able to divorce the essence of law from its origin, completing the separation of positive law from divine, eternal, and natural law. Dismissal of the Thomistic categories effectively dethrones God from rulership of the legal cosmos. It is this move that allows Austin to establish the modern preoccupation with "human law" and legal positivism as the epistemology of this "province of jurisprudence determined."

Austin's substitution of utility for natural law is contrary to experience. People experience law as a manifold of tensions, codified and uncodified customs, concrete injustices that point to "higher" laws, habitual regularities, more or less arbitrary rules, and a veritable host of other things, including utility. But they emphatically do *not* experience law, either in its source or in its justification, and either explicitly or implicitly, as proceeding exclusively from directives aimed at maximizing "utility" or "general happiness," however defined.

Substituting utility for natural law also confuses "that by which the intellect understands" with "that which is understood."[40] Thomistic natural law comprises a series of fully justified theoretical inferences about human nature resulting from concrete experiences of a particular type. It is a perspective from which the understanding may be brought into accord with experience or a method by which the reality of experience may be affirmed, even in the presence of apparent contradiction.

It is a mode of participation in divine reality, the *lex aeterna*, by imprint of that law on human reason. It is reason itself, the window that God has provided so that rational creatures may access eternity. Since rational creatures do experience law as partly immanent and partly transcendent, such creatures have no reason (or right) to assume that the inferred access to eternity in natural law is illusory. Above all, natural law is not a class of "thing-like" rules or principles that are susceptible to analysis or evaluation in terms of a social calculus; for, as we have seen, no such class of things has ever been determined to exist.

Utility, on the other hand, is neither a perspective nor a method; it is rather a teleological principle with definite content and thus is a "thing to be understood," not "that by which things are understood." Moreover, as Austin understands the principle, it is nothing less than the definite content of the mind of God; and it is the function of moralists and jurisprudents to bring "sentiment" on this point into full accord with "calculation."[41] According to Austin, "If . . . the principle of utility were the presiding principle of our conduct, our conduct would be determined immediately by Divine rules, or rather by moral sentiments associated with those rules."[42]

If utility is a "thing to be understood," Austin cannot tell us "that by which it is to be understood" because, dispensing with naturalism, he has denied his theory an epistemological basis that is adequately grounded in experience. He cannot therefore explain how it is he knows that rule-utilitarianism is constitutive of the divine mind.

Nor can he articulate the basis on which the "moral sentiments associated with those rules" are to be made effective in the human psyche. Since, for Austin, these sentiments do not arise from common experience, it would appear that they can be imposed only externally (i.e., by force). Such a result would be fully consistent with Austin's complete subordination of the intrinsic to the extrinsic legal bond that is itself contrary to experience.

Divorcing the essence from the origin of Law by defining the "true" lawgiver as he who perpetuates, rather than he who makes, the law, effectively undermines the Law's historical character and thus is contrary to experience (see Chapter 14). The most obvious and immediate consequence of this turn of thought is to rule out custom as a viable source of law.

Commenting more than a century ago on analytical jurisprudence, Henry Sumner Maine observed that to rule out custom as a predominant source of legal authority amounts to ruling out most of legal history as well.[43] In particular, it degrades anything outside the framework of post–Roman Western legal history to the status of irrelevancy. And, as Eric Voegelin has persuasively argued, a large portion of the historical material that is most useful in contributing to an understanding of the nature of law is found in the civilizations of Asia and the ancient Near East.[44]

Austin's view of law is suffocatingly narrow. Throughout most of recorded history, law has been characterized not only by a heavy reliance upon custom but also by the very interconnections between and among law, morality, and religion that he tries to sever. Maine's critique, however, was not strong enough, for Austin's jurisprudence disregards the significance of English legal history as well as that of ancient and non-Western law. Distinguishing "positive laws" from "rules of positive morality" as Austin does, especially with regard to the category of "laws proper," effectively dismisses the all-important conventions of the British Constitution as nonlaw.

In his classic work on British constitutionalism, Albert Venn Dicey demonstrated convincingly that, absent such Austinian "nonlaws" as dissolution of parliament, royal convocation of legislative sessions, and the like, the entire structure of technically enforceable laws supporting the rights of the English would most likely fall to the ground.[45] This aspect of Austin's jurisprudence is indeed so counterintuitive that Austin himself appears to be somewhat uncomfortable with it, hence the ascription of the name "laws proper" to this branch of the "rules of positive morality"—a category of rules that Austin elsewhere claims not to be part of the subject of jurisprudence, "properly so-called."[46]

Austin's summary dismissal of such a large portion of common legal experience once again brings us face to face with the problems of written and unwritten constitutions, symbols and experience, essences and existence. Ruling out custom as a viable source of law effectively dismisses the common law by allowing its underlying reality to be treated as nonexistent. Ruling out convention and the rules of positive morality effectively dismisses much of the legal experience that informs and undergirds the British, and by indirection, the American, Constitutions.

Most important, excluding natural law from the province of jurisprudence, a move that allows the "merely posited" to be treated as the self-subsistent whole of Law and that accordingly allows that which is experienced as universally compelling to be treated as nonexistent, throws out (without argument) the divine source of order in the legal cosmos. Yet Austin knows that he cannot really get rid of God, so he simply defines him away. "Bracketing" the one Being that cannot be turned into an object of abstract representation and made subject to "analytical jurisprudence"—that very Being whose essence and existence are identical and who thus truly Is—Austin commits an error that has been made by many philosophers, which Etienne Gilson describes:

> When confronted with an element of reality for which no conceptual representation is available, human understanding feels bound, if not always to reduce it into nothingness, at least to bracket it, so that everything may proceed as though that element did not exist. It is unpleasant for philosophy to admit that it flows from a source which, *qua* source, will never become an object of abstract representation. Hence the ceaselessly renewed attempts of philosophers to pretend that there is no such source or that, if there is one, we need not worry about it.[47]

13 · Natural Law and the Constitution

THE JUDICIALIZATION OF NATURAL LAW

In the Thomistic view of law, natural law is a window providing rational creatures access to the *lex aeterna*. Legal naturalism is a perspective, a way of thinking, a set of ideas that are themselves instruments of cognition. It is not a body of substantive legal rules sufficiently precise to allow enforcement by courts, and that is why Thomas Aquinas asserted that judicial interpretation and application of natural law did not itself constitute Law.[1] Judicial enforcement would require turning ideas, which are essentially *instruments* of cognition, into *objects* of cognition, which amounts to thinking of them as "things," not "thoughts." It also amounts to filling the mind of God with human things, much as John Austin did by positing utility as the fundamental principle of his teleological jurisprudence.[2]

Yet some contemporary commentators persist in arguing that the courts should enforce principles of natural law, often grounding their argument on the supposition that judges have always done exactly that.[3] This supposition is mistaken. Whatever some individual judges may have thought they were doing in the past when employing natural law rhetoric, they were not deciding cases on the basis of rules derived from natural law. Natural law, in its most viable (classical) form, does not lend itself to such application in any case. Even in its more truncated modern forms, translating general principles of the so-called "law and rights of nature" into concrete legal rules is a notoriously difficult task, as revealed in the tortured examples that some modern commentators have trotted out to buttress an allegation that the early Supreme Court used natural law as a ground of decision in constitutional cases.

Unquestionably, among the most influential versions of natural law in the American Founding era was that propounded by John Locke. Locke followed Thomas Hobbes in positing a state of nature in which the laws and rights of nature are fully operative and out of which the social compact is designed largely as a means of escape.[4] For both Hobbes and Locke, the fundamental right of nature is that of self-preservation. For Hobbes, it is surrendered to the state in the agreement that forms the commonwealth; for Locke, it is brought into civil society in the guise of preexisting property rights that are regarded as anterior to the formation of government. For Locke, the protection of the rights of property becomes the very purpose of civil society and its government, and failure adequately to perform this function justifies rebellion.[5]

Under Lockeanism, individual property is treated as part of the natural order of things, and the rights arising from possession and use of such property tend to be viewed as sacred, ordained by God. This view is contrary to experience. Though individuals often regard acquisitions, especially when value is added by the admixture of their own labor, along the lines of "staking a valid claim," it is simply not the case that they always do so. "Public goods" are merely the most obvious of many examples in which the things of the world are experienced as being "held in common."[6]

The predominant view in earlier times is shown by another example from the disputations of Thomas Aquinas. Responding to the argument that holds it to be unnatural for an individual to possess external things, he answers that

> external things can be considered in two ways. First, as regards their nature, and this is not subject to the power of man but only to the power of God, Whose mere will all things obey. Secondly, as regards their use, and in this way man has a natural dominion over external things because, by his reason and will, he is able to use them for his own profit, as they were made on his account, for the imperfect is always for the sake of the perfect. . . . It is by this argument that the Philosopher [Aristotle] proves that the possession of external things is natural to man.[7]

After having thus justified private possession, Aquinas then turns to the argument that private ownership is "contrary to the natural law," because "according to the natural law, all things are common property." His answer defeats the argument as to private ownership but without accepting the contrary assumption that natural law requires common ownership:

> Community of goods is ascribed to the natural law, not because the natural law dictates that all things should be possessed in common, and that nothing should be possessed as one's own, but because there is division of possessions, not according to the natural law, but rather according to human agreement, which belongs to positive law. . . . Hence, the ownership of possessions is not contrary to the natural law but an addition thereto devised by human reason.[8]

Aquinas's explicit refusal to ascribe a naturalistic basis to either legal proprietarianism or legal communitarianism is founded on the same considerations as was his implicit refusal to provide such a basis for legal utilitarianism: all are human, not divine, creations and are thus creatures of positive, not natural, law. In fact, the relationship among these three principles is even more intimate than this statement would suggest, for particular social orderings of individual property claims find their most potent justification in considerations of social utility, and such considerations are almost infinitely variable and therefore contingent.

Property arrangements must ultimately be judged according to whether or not they promote the general good, and since a principle can be no more compelling than the more general principle that justifies it, it follows that private (or any other) property can have no closer relationship to natural law than can utility itself. Locke's attempt to ground property rights in the law of nature therefore should be viewed in the same light as Austin's attempt to ascribe utilitarianism to God.

NATURAL LAW IN THE SUPREME COURT

I do not mean to deny the importance of property as a central feature of legal development, either conceptually or historically. Property has proved an especially resilient category for subsumption and explication of diverse legal phenomena both in English legal history and in Roman-based jurisprudence. Clearly property rights were widely regarded by Americans during the Founding era as making up an important part of the natural law foundation of American constitutionalism, a concern that found expression in the Declaration of Independence, the Articles of Confederation, and the Constitution of 1787.

Yet some commentators have gone further, claiming that the early Supreme Court actually decided constitutional cases according to natural law and urging that the modern Court employ a similar approach based on a surrogate "fundamental values," in order to infuse a largely procedural eighteenth-century constitutional instrument with substantive law. There are several variations on this approach, one of which is the progressive view, which relies on the idea that the early Supreme Court, through application of a form of Lockean natural law, insulated property rights, conceived as "vested interests," from assault by would-be government regulators. In its fullest development, this application is said to have led to the jurisprudence of the laissez-faire era.[9]

The early Court is often criticized for protecting property rights by application of the "old" natural law, but the modern Court is just as often applauded for protecting personal rights by application of a "new" set of fundamental rights and interests. Yet any attempt to distinguish between rights of persons and rights of property according to such a scheme is purely artificial and thus inappropriate. Similarly, the so-called natural law jurisprudence of the laissez-faire era had little in common with its Lockean counterpart of the previous century.

Although most of the commentators who espouse the centrality of property in U.S. constitutional history are opponents of the laissez-faire/Social Darwinian/property-rights jurisprudence of the late nineteenth and early twentieth centuries, they are usually proponents of the contemporary Court's efforts to protect personal rights. Jurists of the Chicago School of Law and Economics, however, recently have been arguing for a return to laissez-faire jurisprudence.[10]

According to representatives of this school of thought, property and such particular constitutional provisions as the contract, commerce, and takings clauses that provide for its security make up the central features of the U.S. Constitution. The turn-of-the-century Court's extension of other constitutional provisions such as the due process and equal protection clauses to protect it was merely a natural development of the Constitution's underlying spirit.

Like the Progressive School, the Chicago School subordinates the Constitution to property rights, though the progressives do so from a critical standpoint and the legal economists from a promotional one. Richard Epstein, for instance, believes that the Constitution incorporates Locke's theory of property and views the primary judicial role to be an aggressive protection of Lockean property rights under those constitutional provisions best fitted to that employment.[11] Arguably, Epstein's theory counsels a particularly activist form of judicial review that goes beyond even the approach exercised at the turn of the century. If I am right in my conclusions about natural law, then the Chicago School, like the Progressive School that is its complement on the Left, is wrong. Natural law can never be reduced to a bundle of substantive rules and principles in such a way as to allow their straightforward application by courts.

As Lane Sunderland has demonstrated, Epstein's approach is mistaken also because the Constitution incorporates Lockeanism only as background and because judicialization of natural law actually violates Lockean principles. According to Sunderland, the fundamental premise of Locke's political thought consists in the principle of protection of natural rights by majority rule (not by courts). Since Locke posits no substantive limits on legislative (parliamentary) supremacy, the idea of judicial review must be regarded as completely foreign to his thought.[12]

Sunderland's discussion is useful not only for understanding the judicial role in the early American republic but also for understanding the more general relationship between natural law thinking and constitutional thought during the Founding period. According to Sunderland, the Declaration of Independence established the primary end (telos) of government for Americans: to secure individual liberty under natural law. The Constitution's makers determined that this end would be best achieved by a transfer of sovereignty from local majorities (the people of the states) to a national majority (the people of the United States), by giving the national majority full power to govern, and thus to repress, local sects or factions inimical to private rights and to the public good. From the first line of the *Federalist*, which refers to the importance of union and a strong national government to replace the "inefficiency of the subsisting" government under the Articles of Confederation, the transfer of sovereignty effected by the Constitution is shown to be fundamentally *democratic*.[13]

Joined with the commerce clause and related provisions, this transfer of authority entails the creation and maintenance of a "large commercial republic" as a barrier against "domestic faction and insurrection." Faction must be controlled because it is adverse to the common interest and because it tends to destroy the individual liberty that, according to the Declaration, it is the main purpose of government to protect. In order to accomplish this on a national scale, the central government had to have sufficient (or plenary) power in each of the areas to which its competence extends.

The primary limitations on national authority thus were conceived to be internal (enumerated and separated powers) and really were not designed to diminish national authority at all. They were devised instead to enable a powerful central government to control itself. So after the national majority was given full power to "control the governed," that same majority was then "obliged to control itself" by the institution of an elaborate system of internal checks and balances and by deliberate circumscription of its powers to those enumerated in the Constitution.[14]

The role of property in the American Founding now comes more fully into focus. The Framers' interest in protecting property rights was grounded in the desire to forestall domestic insurrection, not to install in perpetuity abstract ideas of ownership or possession that were thought to be sanctioned by the laws of nature. The Founders' preoccupation with promoting stability and consolidating the advance of democracy had more to do with the design of the Constitution than did any desire to safeguard the interests of wealth, per se. As Michael Lienesch has suggested, the tyranny of the majority was only a penultimate concern of the Founders—their main concern being the *authoritarian* tyranny they thought more likely to arise from the ashes of democratic oppression: "On the eve of the Philadelphia convention, observers could agree that the most serious danger to the new republic arose not from popular protest, but from authoritarian response."[15]

As with the role of property, the role of natural law in the Founding comes more fully into focus. Natural rights (including Lockean rights of property) were preeminently individual rights and were regarded as "ends of government" in the sense that national majorities were empowered (and expected) to enforce them "by appropriate legislation." At the same time, "minority" or "group" interests were regarded as the primary cause of faction and thus of disorder. Minority rights were not regarded as rights at all and certainly not such as to be in need of protection against majority rule, as tends to be thought in modern times. Rather, minority interests were to be suppressed as an even larger danger to individual rights than were overbearing national majorities.[16]

The constitutional role of the judiciary in this scheme at most was limited to that of enforcing the specified (enumerated) limits to legislative authority, including those in the Bill of Rights, in the manner in which those limits were understood by the Framers and ratifiers. That is to say, the rights subject to enforcement were purely individual (not group) rights. Though it was certainly expected that courts would apply the law in a manner consistent with (though not on the basis of) the natural law/natural rights background of the Constitution as manifested most prominently in the Declaration of Independence, the Declaration itself was not regarded to be a justiciable legal instrument. The courts were granted no general authority to decide cases according to natural law, the "spirit of the Constitution," or any other idiosyncratic mode of interpretation that would tend to impair the fundamental right of the majority to govern effectively. In that day, the right of a majority to govern effectively meant, among other things, the power to protect the rights of individuals against minority (i.e., factional) oppression. At the same time, judicial decisions were expected to be compatible with the natural law basis of American constitutionalism, insofar as this foundation secures individual rights (though not group interests) against overreaching majorities.[17]

If this discussion is close to the mark, it would indeed be surprising to discover that the early Supreme Court had applied (or even tried to apply) natural law in constitutional cases, as some commentators have urged. Matthew J. Franck, in a painstakingly thorough exegesis of the culprit cases, confirms unsurprisingly that the Court did not do so, thus fortifying my conclusions concerning the impossibility and impropriety of a justiciable law of nature.[18] Franck demonstrates that the legal arguments commentators have taken to represent natural law or natural rights applications in these early cases are almost always based on other considerations.

In *Van Horne's Lessee v. Dorrance*, for instance, what commentators have mistaken for an extratextual application of natural rights by Justice William Paterson is really a literal application of a state constitutional provision declaring that property is "natural, inherent, and inalienable."[19] In *Calder v. Bull*[20] and *Wilkinson v. Leland*,[21] commentators have found natural law in the *obiter dicta* of Justices Samuel Chase and Joseph Story stating that courts have no right to *presume* that a legislature has enacted laws that contravene the "great first principles of the social compact."[22] In *Terrett v. Taylor*,[23] a straightforward application of traditional equity jurisprudence by Justice Story, which supplies a " 'correction of the law' whenever the strict law is defective by reason of its universality," is mistaken for an application of natural law. In *Ogden v. Saunders*,[24] Chief Justice John Marshall's literal reading of the contract clause as related to the distinction between rights and remedies is misread as a foray into natural rights. In *Fletcher v. Peck*,[25] another literal reading of the contract clause by Marshall, accompanied by a concessionary remark about "general principles" made in order to forge a unanimous decision, is used to show that Marshall was willing to "go beyond the text" of the Constitution. Finally, in the only really plausible example of explicit extratextual constitutional interpretation according to natural law, Justice William Johnson's famous remark in *Fletcher* concerning "a principle which will impose laws even on the Deity,"[26] to which Marshall's "concession" had been directed, the justice himself all but explicitly rescinded the position seventeen years later.[27]

In sum, there is not a single, nonrescinded instance of explicit extratextual judicial application of natural law or natural rights during the entire antebellum period, and we are talking about individual judicial opinions, not collective decisions of the Court. Franck shows that the present prominence of these examples of the use of natural law by the early Supreme Court resulted from postbellum efforts by a small group of lawyers, judges, and politicians in the era of the greenback controversy to enlist the opinions in support of the oncoming laissez-faire jurisprudence of the Gilded Age.[28] The whole matter reveals poignantly the consequences of the modern failure to take seriously the historical traditions I have outlined and defended and, for that matter, our failure to take seriously history at all.

MILLIAN PROGRESSIVISM AND THE
CONSTITUTIONAL TRADITION

I have suggested that classical natural law, in substance, could never be applied by a court; the Supreme Court of the United States has never applied Lockean natural law in the decision of concrete cases; the "natural law" applied by the Supreme Court in the late nineteenth century was natural law in neither its classical nor its Lockean variant; and application of natural law should not be attempted by courts even if it were possible for judges to apply it. But if natural law cannot be, has not been, and should not be applied by courts, what then is the "real" basis of the "fundamental rights and values" jurisprudence that seems to characterize the modern era?

Though a complete answer to this question must await discussion of the theological dimensions of modern constitutionalism in Part Five, some of the answer has already been suggested. For example, one of the dominant strands in modern jurisprudential thought might best be described as a variant of Austinian or Benthamite legal positivism existing in an easy alliance with rule-utilitarianism and in an uneasy alliance with Hobbesian or Lockean contract theories. Yet Austinian positivism and rule-utilitarianism either exclude or reject all forms of natural law, and contract theory rejects classical natural law in favor of a truncated version based on personal security and property rights. None of these theories will support the recommendations of contemporary commentators who advocate the judiciary's imposition of "fundamental values" in constitutional cases.

Examination of the thought of John Stuart Mill will bring us a step closer to full understanding of the evolution of modern liberal constitutional thought. More than any other thinker, Mill came nearest to articulating the ostensible (though not necessarily the real) basis of modern constitutional jurisprudence. Upon apparently utilitarian and egalitarian foundations, Mill grafted a libertarian progressivism that is, in some respects, complementary to, and in other respects, incompatible with, those very foundations. It is indeed a strange and bitter irony that the security of individual rights in the modern era appears to be founded largely on the philosophy of a thinker who, rather than "naturalizing" rights through the development of a law firmly rooted in human nature, sought instead to abolish or destroy that nature.

I shall summarize Mill's constitutional philosophy as simply and straightforwardly as I can, bearing in mind that his thought has often been regarded as multidimensional, complex, and even contradictory. A good place to start is with the best known of Mill's fundamental principles, the so-called "harm principle" from his famous tract *On Liberty*. Put simply, this principle holds that social or legal coercion is never justified except to prevent harm to others.[29]

James Fitzjames Stephen, Mill's most acute nineteenth-century critic, pointed out that two corollaries result from adoption of the harm principle. The first implies another famous and fundamental Millian principle, the "principle of liberty," a portion of which includes the Lifestyle Liberalism mentioned in Chapter 6. Insofar as this principle is read to extend to the individual formulation of alternative social states, it engenders an extreme version of Arrow's condition of "unrestricted domain." According to Mill, the principle

> comprises, first, the inward domain of consciousness; demanding liberty of conscience in the most comprehensive sense, liberty of thought and feeling; absolute freedom of opinion and sentiment on all subjects practical or speculative, scientific, moral, or theological. The liberty of expressing and publishing opinions may seem to fall under a different principle, since it belongs to that part of the conduct of an individual which concerns other people, but being almost of as much importance as the liberty of thought itself, and resting in great part on the same reasons, is practically inseparable from it. Secondly, the principle requires liberty of tastes and pursuits, of framing our plan of life to suit our own character, of doing as we like, subject to such consequences as may follow, without impediment from our fellow-creatures, so long as what we do does not harm them—even though they should think our conduct foolish, perverse, or wrong. Thirdly, from this liberty of each individual follows the liberty within the same limits of combination among individuals.[30]

The second corollary of the harm principal holds that coercion must be entirely eliminated where used for establishing and maintaining religions, for establishing and practically maintaining morality, or for making alterations in existing forms of government.[31] The first part of the corollary implies a third fundamental Millian principle, that a sharp distinction must be taken between the "spiritual" and the "temporal" spheres of life, or more familiarly, the absolute separation of church and state.[32]

This principle follows from the fact that the spiritual sphere is defined as the province of "persuasion" whereas the temporal sphere is defined as the province of "force."[33] Since the principle of liberty requires absolute freedom of opinion, discussion, and publication on religious subjects and since that principle is, in turn, implied by the prohibition of coercion (force) derived from the harm principle, it follows that no spiritual or religious matter can ever give rise to a justifiable use of force.

Mill's views on religion may seem benign at first blush, but closer examination reveals that such is hardly the case. That it is not religious freedom, traditionally understood, that Mill is zealous to defend is made clear upon careful reading of a little-known volume, *Three Essays on Religion,* published in 1874, a year after the author's death.[34] The last of these essays was also the author's final work and thus contains his most fully developed ideas on religion.[35] Together, the essays show that religion is central, not peripheral, to Mill's project and that its thrust is to divide the spiritual from the temporal, not, as is so often thought, to free religion from the fetters of secular control. Rather, its thrust is to make possible a transformation of religious sentiment in such a way as to get rid of God.

We can begin this phase of the discussion with a fourth fundamental Millian principle, taken from the second of these three essays. This principle holds that, since traditional religious doctrine is not true—a thesis that Mill attempts (and fails) to prove in the third essay[36]—the value of religion must be calculated in terms of its utility.[37] But since utility, in this context, simply means "usefulness," one is entitled to ask, "usefulness for what?"

Mill's answer, the fifth fundamental Millian precept, is given in the final pages of the essay "Theism," where it is made abundantly clear that the "religious" sentiment to be fostered is Rousseau's generalized, altruistic "love of mankind," nurtured and developed, Comtean style, into a full-fledged "Religion of Humanity."[38] After concluding that the evidence supporting supernatural religion is insufficient, Mill concedes that religious "feeling" can be an inducement "for cultivating a religious devotion to the welfare of our fellow-creatures as an obligatory limit to every selfish aim, and an end for the direct promotion of which no sacrifice can be too great."[39] Large doses of egalitarianism, Manichaeism, progressivism, and utilitarianism are present in the final flourish that brings the essay to its close:

> The conditions of human existence are highly favourable to the growth of such a feeling inasmuch as a battle is constantly going on, in which the humblest human creature is not incapable of taking some part, between the powers of good and those of evil, and in which every even the smallest help to the right side has its value in promoting the very slow and often almost insensible progress by which good is gradually gaining ground from evil, yet gaining it so visibly at considerable intervals as to promise the very distant but not uncertain final victory of Good. To do something during life, on even the humblest scale if nothing more is within reach, towards bringing this consummation ever so little nearer, is the most animating and invigorating thought which can inspire a human creature; and that it is destined, with or without supernatural sanctions, to be the religion of the Future I cannot entertain a doubt. But it appears to me that supernatural hopes, in the degree and kind in which

what I have called rational scepticism does not refuse to sanction them, may still contribute not a little to give to this religion its due ascendancy over the human mind.[40]

Mill knows that the victory of good over evil, the triumph of altruism over selfishness, will require nothing less than a transformation of human nature itself, and probably a transformation of nature as well. That is why nothing less than a new religion is demanded, for nothing short of the power of a spiritual force is sufficient to accomplish such a transformation. The old religion will not do, for it teaches that gratitude is the proper attitude toward what is given and that freedom, not nature, is the cause of evil in the world.

Mill confirms this observation, while articulating the sixth and final fundamental precept, in a passage taken from the essay, "Nature." After a "brief survey" of phenomena that are supposed to indicate the relationship(s) between man and nature, a survey that, interestingly, includes the assertion that law and justice are entirely "artificial," not "natural,"[41] Mill states that "this brief survey is amply sufficient to prove that the duty of man is the same in respect to his own nature as in respect to the nature of all other things, namely not to follow but to amend it."[42] This final precept I shall call the principle of "gnosticism," and will be, as viewed from the perspective of constitutional theory, the main subject of Chapter 14. It is this feature, more than any other, that has defeated the prospect of a naturalistic constitutional jurisprudence in our time.

With Mill's agenda now clear, we are in a position to see just how right he was in predicting the triumph of his humanistic religion in the twentieth century. Three of the constitutional principles held most dear by modern constitutional commentators are the religious establishment principle of the First Amendment, as interpreted antitheistically by the modern Supreme Court; the expressive freedom principle embodied in that same amendment's speech and press clauses, in the "preferred position" given it by the modern Court; and the principle of equality embodied in the equal protection clause of the Fourteenth Amendment, in the modern Court's "fundamental rights and interests/discrete and insular minorities" interpretation of the post-1938 period.[43] Each of these principles derives, in one way or another, from Mill's liberal manifestos. And each, interestingly if not too surprisingly, undermines one of the central tenets of traditional jurisprudence as understood from the beginning of recorded legal history.

The first of these tenets is that of the essentially religious character of law. This character is evident in such ancient legal documents as the *Code of Hammurabi*.[44] It is no less apparent in the hypothetical legal system adumbrated by Plato in the *Laws*. Moreover, it is strongly evident in the law of republican and late imperial Rome, in the barbarian codes of the early Middle Ages, and in the formative period of English common law.[45]

The second tenet concerns the central role of the state in the guardianship of public morality. In classical jurisprudence, it is generally acknowledged that one of the primary purposes of law is the inculcation of virtue in the citizenry, or at least the maintenance of constitutional conditions under which the pursuit of virtue is possible. This is true no matter what the form of government. Examples are found most prominently in several of the codes of the ancient Greek poleis, and in Plato's *Laws* as well—which is known to have been modeled to an extent upon an agglomeration of such poleis. This tenet is also evident in virtually all definitions of law from Cicero to Aquinas.[46]

The third tenet is the importance of social status, the most significant feature of which, in traditional jurisprudence, is the ascription of certain public responsibilities to members of different social orders. This feature is found most prominently in the Roman law of persons.[47] Its influence is also prominent in the development of the English law of property, though, during more recent times, modern law has tended more toward thinking of property as a bundle of "rights" rather than "duties."

The significance of these three reversals is perhaps best understood by noting their impact at the highest level of generality. Collectively and respectively, their effect is to remove from the province of constitutional jurisprudence God, the Good, and Being.

Beginning in 1947, with the U.S. Supreme Court's decision of *Everson v. Board of Education*, the Court has stressed Thomas Jefferson's famous "wall of separation" doctrine as a controlling metaphor in establishment clause cases.[48] The result has been to convert a provision designed to protect particular forms of belief and worship against governmental suppression into a provision that suppresses public displays of belief and worship in the interest of nonbelievers.[49] The situation has led to a wild assortment of cases, in which contradiction rather than consistency seems to have been the rule. Even the constitutionality of the Court's own historic "God save this honorable court" invocation has been questioned; and, by now, the situation has inspired such antireligious paranoia that the constitutionality even of a suggested "moment of silence" in public schools has been questioned.[50] An articulate foundation for the prevailing attitude may be easily discovered in the secularist professions and projections of Mill and his modern disciples.

Beginning in the early 1940s, the Supreme Court began to widen the scope of the First Amendment's speech and press clauses to protect forms of expression previously regarded as "action," not "speech."[51] In the 1950s and 1960s, this effort continued in other "symbolic speech" cases,[52] subversion and sedition cases,[53] and obscenity and pornography cases,[54] culminating in *Stanley v. Georgia*, which established a constitutional right to use pornography.[55] These lines of case law dovetail with another line of cases establishing a constitutional "zone of privacy"[56] in matters related to sexual mores and choice of "lifestyle."[57] The cumulative effect of these decisions has been seriously to impair the exercise of public authority in the areas affected, an effect that has not been confined only to the domains of personal thought and belief or even to purely private behavior. It extends also to public behavior and to private behavior "affected with a public interest."[58] The whole approach seems to be grounded on the idea that government must be absolutely neutral with respect to competing conceptions of the good life—an idea that arguably finds its origin in Mill.

In 1938, the Court suggested a broader reading of the Fourteenth Amendment's equal protection clause than theretofore it had ever applied, extending an essentially race-based provision to cover any "discrete and insular minority" or any group rights deemed by the Court to be "fundamental."[59] Beginning in the early 1960s with the reapportionment cases[60] and later extending the categories to cover such "previously disadvantaged" groups as females,[61] aliens,[62] and illegitimate children,[63] the Court began to apply "strict scrutiny" analysis to those classifications that appeared to the Court not to be justified by "compelling state interests." Since all governmental classifications (to the extent that they are meaningful) work to the disadvantage of somebody and since many, if not most, classifications are merely "rational" (in Marshall's sense of "convenient"), not "compelling," the effect of this approach has been seriously to impair the regulatory functions of government. At a deeper level, the effect has been to defeat the idea that legally recognized distinctions between and among social groups are appropriate and necessary tools of regulation and that it is proper for governments to impose duties upon (not merely to recognize rights of) members of particular groups in society, by virtue of their membership in that group. Modern government's inability to recognize such distinctions is the result of an ideological egalitarianism that can be traced, in large measure, to Mill and his disciples.

The Millian principles, especially as interpreted by modern courts and commentators, are contrary to experience. The near-absolute separation of church and state suggested by Justice Hugo Black in *Everson v. Board of Education* is a classic instance of trying to define away reality by words alone (see Chapter 14).[64] People really do experience political authority as infused with religious overtones and undertones. People do not experience political authority as completely separate from religious authority. Political and religious authority, as Augustine once taught, are "mixed up" in the world and are experienced as a complex of institutional forces.[65] Attempting to separate the two complexes conceptually, treating each as a self-subsisting essence, will always turn out to be a futile exercise in abstraction.

If the Millian project is to get rid of God, the Court's modern establishment clause jurisprudence appears to have taken long strides toward fulfillment of that objective.[66] But it must be remembered that appearance is not necessarily reality. Indeed, no single essence is given by itself and as self-subsistent in concrete reality; rather, essences are given "in actual complexes of mutual determinations."[67] As Gilson has remarked,

Each concrete essence is a sharing in several different essences, and it is not from looking at them in particular that we can see how they can fit together. Existence is the catalyser of essences. Because it itself is act in a higher order than that of essences, it can melt them together in the unity of a single being.[68]

Attempting to avoid "legislating morality" leads to similar results. The distinction between the kind of experience that generates the effort to formulate theories of natural law and the kind of legal experience that does not is relevant here. People experience law, at least in part, as an imposition of moral standards on themselves and on others. Notwithstanding the popular cliché, it is simply a truism that law "legislates morality." The question is always *what* (not whether) morality gets legislated. Millian liberalism advocates a position of neutrality between competing conceptions of the Good. But this supposed neutrality often is really a pretension masking a deeper skepticism, if not outright nihilism, about the existence or knowability of the Good. One is put in mind of a statement by G. K. Chesterton on skepticism:

I suppose it is true in a sense that a man can be a fundamental sceptic, but he cannot be anything else; certainly not even a defender of fundamental scepticism. If a man feels that all the movements of his own mind are meaningless, then his mind is meaningless, and he is meaningless; and it does not mean anything to attempt to discover his meaning. Most fundamental sceptics appear to survive, because they are not consistently sceptical and not at all fundamental. They will first deny everything and then admit something, if for the sake of argument—or often rather of attack without argument. I saw an almost startling example of this essential frivolity in the professor of final scepticism, in a paper the other day. A man wrote to say that he accepted nothing but Solipsism, and added that he had often wondered it was not a more common philosophy. Now Solipsism simply means that a man believes in his own existence, but not in anybody or anything else. And it never struck this simple sophist, that if his philosophy was true, there obviously were no other philosophers to profess it.[69]

Thus the Millian liberal, like Chesterton's fundamental skeptic, first denies everything and then admits something—namely, the particular conception of the Good that is embodied in (or is the result of) a process of "free thought" and unrestricted discussion (and perhaps, in the end, of free or unrestricted living). Now, this may turn out to be a worthy notion of the Good, but it is not so as a matter of logic or reason and thus can only be held as an article of faith.

Perhaps the Millian system is prototypical for an academic community or a debating society, but it is hopelessly inadequate as a principle of organization for a whole society.[70] The modern academic community's acceptance of it seems at least as much a matter of self-interest as of principled commitment. Professors, after all, make their living exercising freedom of thought and discussion, speech and press; thus it is hardly surprising that academics would be among Mill's strongest defenders.

People experience the phenomena of class and status as politically relevant. British diplomacy is widely respected in international affairs because there is a "diplomatic class" in Britain. American diplomacy is not as highly regarded (and often is viewed as a contradiction in terms) because there is no comparable diplomatic class in the United States. Status differentials are crucial to the healthy functioning of any society. To say otherwise is essentially to deny Being itself, and to say that there is only "flux," or "becoming." But this is both contradictory as a matter of logic and contrary to experience as a matter of fact; for if nothing exists in itself, there is nothing to become, and people do experience many things as more or less permanent, or static, not merely as a continual flux.

Ultimately, a constitutionalism of any really viable sort presupposes Being and thus presupposes God. A plausible and valid argument is available to show that God is the efficient cause of everything in continuous, identifiable existence (see Chapters 15 and 16)[71] and that the set of continuous, identifiable features of any polity is its "constitution" (see Chapters 14 and 17).

In sum, adoption of Mill's principles destroys American constitutionalism as a natural growth by digging up the Constitution at its roots. Adoption of Millian libertarianism destroys the foundations of constitutional consensus by individualizing the procedure by which the range of allowable social alternatives is determined.[72] Adoption of Mill's absolute division of the spiritual and the temporal erodes the foundation upon which a constitutional polity can be plausibly described as having a continuous existence over time. Adoption of Millian sentimentalism compromises the rational element in constitutionalism, allowing reason to be eclipsed by passion. Adoption of Millian gnosticism undermines the naturalistic basis of the Constitution, setting in motion a process of constitutional self-destruction.

Part Five · Constitutional Gnosticism and Constitutional Theism

In preceding chapters, several of the most important underpinnings of modern constitutional theory have been examined. Since the varied strands of thought that, taken together, make up today's dominant constitutional outlook are multiple and complex, it might be advantageous, before going any further, to catch a breath by way of summarizing some of the ideas that have already been introduced.

First, modern thought holds fast to a restrictive view of reason that effectively eliminates the idea of the mind as an organ providing direct access to an intelligible reality. This perspective has led to a conception of the mind as an organ whose task is merely to process sense data by the application of logical or mathematical functions. Commensurate with the empiricist assumption that ideas are the very things we think and not merely the vehicles of our thoughts, modern reason is denied access to things in themselves ("things as such," or "things as they are") through its denial of any necessary connection between thought and its objects. We are led to the position described by Bertrand Russell in *The Principles of Pure Mathematics:*

> When actual objects are counted, or when geometry or dynamics are applied to actual space or actual matter, or when, in any other way, mathematical reasoning is applied to what exists, the reasoning employed has a form not dependent upon the objects to which it is applied being just those objects that they are, but only upon their having certain general properties. . . . Thus when space or motion is spoken of in pure mathematics, it is not actual space or actual motion, as we know them in experience, that are spoken of, but any entity possessing those abstract general properties of space or motion that are employed in the reasonings of geometry or dynamics. The question whether these properties belong, as a matter of fact, to actual space or actual motion, is irrelevant to pure mathematics, and therefore to the present work, being, in my opinion, a purely empirical question, to be investigated in the laboratory or the observatory. (Quoted in Robin Farquharson, *Theory of Voting* [New Haven: Yale University Press, 1969], p. 1.)

The divorce of objects "just as they are" (and just as they are experienced) from their "abstract general properties" leads straightforwardly to an epistemological skepticism that denies the possibility of discovering objective truth in the cosmos and ultimately to a metaphysical nihilism that denies the very existence of any external reality apart from that which is accessible through sense perception.

Closely related to (and in part stemming from) this truncated idea of reason comes a willingness to isolate the symbols that represent experiences of reality and to use them without regard to the contextual features of the particular realities that generated the symbols in the first place. This disregard effectively denies the fundamental connection between words and things, which is the hallmark of the commonsensical way of experiencing reality in the world. One of the consequences of this tendency in constitutional decisionmaking has been an overreliance on abstractions, prophylactic rules, and wooden legal formulas in derogation from the historical constitutional experiences that have generated those very abstractions, rules, and principles.

Truncated modern reason has also led to a denial of natural law as conceived in earlier times as a doctrine derived from the experience of an unchanging and distinctive human nature that stresses reason in the classical sense as the foundation of this distinctive humanity. In place of the human nature that grounds classical natural law, modernity has substituted narrow versions of natural law that employ such principles as property rights, social utility, tolerance, or even unrestrained choice as the fundamental principle of sociopolitical organization. Closely allied with these developments has been the recent prevalence of a positivistic approach to law, in which "laws" are viewed as more or less arbitrarily imposed commands of a territorial sovereign, and a contractarianism that "denatures" the state and regards all social and political institutions to be the result of human artifice.

Finally, a pervasive secularism that denies God as creator and sustainer of the cosmos and denies spirituality to be an essential characteristic of public man has been reinforced to an uncomfortably large extent by the First and Fourteenth Amendment jurisprudence of the modern Supreme Court. Modern secularism, in its turn, has been a natural complement to the beliefs of individuals who assert that all is matter (metaphysical materialism), a subject that will be treated in Chapter 16.

In the remaining chapters of this book, the complex of ideas just summarized will be given a theological interpretation. In Chapter 14, the secularist framework of modern constitutional theory is examined with respect to its implications for constitutional interpretation. These implications have been most graphically and most coherently laid out in the constitutional theory of William Harris. Harris's theory explicitly rules out constitutional interpretation based on history as indicative of a divine source of legal order.

In Chapters 15 and 16, Harris's approach is challenged by the provision of a theistic foundation for constitutional order. In Chapter 15, it is argued that belief in a supreme being who is creator and sustainer of the cosmos as a whole is warranted both by experience and by logic, given the current state of knowledge in theology, philosophy, and science. In Chapter 16, it is argued further that, given again this current state of knowledge, our experience of the world justifies belief in a supreme being whose action in history is reflected in the institutional practices of human societies.

In Chapter 17, the implications of such a divinely constituted order are explored from the perspective of historical jurisprudence. It is argued that the continuity of the Western legal tradition, which embraces not only Roman and English jurisprudence but also classical (Greek) political and legal philosophy, is so profound as to become normative for constitutional order in the United States. Thus the historical interpretive practices that have been generated by that tradition should be regarded as normative by courts engaged in the application of the law founded upon it, at least where the decisions of such courts are thought to be "final," or conclusive upon all other interpreters. Put another way, judicial supremacy is incompatible with the Western legal tradition because judicial supremacy includes judicial freedom to employ interpretive approaches that are incompatible with those sanctioned by historical practice in Western jurisprudence.

14 · The Gnostic Alternative

The strands of thought listed in the introduction to Part Five, including the truncation of reason, the severing of any connection between thought and its objects, epistemological skepticism, metaphysical nihilism, logical and legal positivism, overreliance upon abstraction, denial of the experience of a knowable human nature, materialism and secularism, when combined with two additional strands—ingratitude for the cosmos as given and knowledge about how it came to be something to be ungrateful for—entail a perspective that may be fairly described as "gnostic." The term derives from the Greek *gnosis* (knowledge) and was applied by the church fathers to a collection of heretical doctrines that challenged orthodox Christianity.[1]

Though theological gnosticism, comprising the classical heresies of early Christianity and some modern derivatives, is probably the oldest variant of the genre, a second variant, which I shall term philosophical gnosticism, stems from the efforts of secular modern thinkers such as Hegel, Marx, Nietzsche, and Heidegger to redefine and reinterpret reality in accordance with the internal logic of a closed "philosophical system."[2] Closely related to the second variant is a third, which I call political gnosticism. It includes the progressivist fantasy world of modern social engineering, a world inhabited by many contemporary constitutional commentators who want to reform society in accordance with some secular "value" deemed "fundamental" but that is not to be found in the Constitution as given—at least not in the proper dosage.

In modern times, the term has been applied by Eric Voegelin and others to ideological mass movements that attempt to transform the given order of being (e.g., human nature) through collective political action.[3] This transformative project invariably is directed toward the destruction of existing social institutions and the creation of new patterns of social interaction and, as such, is essentially revolutionary. For Voegelin and his followers, the chief motivational source for the project is the desire to "immanentize the Christian *eschaton*," by replacing the hope of personal salvation after death with a salvational utopia, concocted in the mind of the gnostic thinker, on earth.[4] The gnostic thus becomes the "prophet" or "savior" of a new age of mankind, an age that is to be devoid of the defective character of God's original creation. Since God's original creation, as most people understand it, developed in and through history, it follows that a gnostic thinker must either get rid of history altogether or create an alternative version. Thus the second of the additional strands noted is the claim of gnostics to be in possession of knowledge that, if true, would abolish history as we know it and justify the desired transformation of human nature and society. Unfortunately, this knowledge is most often hidden from the rest of humankind (those outside the gnostic sect).

The first strand, a presupposition of the second, is ingratitude for the cosmos as given, including one's own nature as nurtured by one's own society. This explains why orthodox Christianity has always been at war with gnosticism; for, as Augustine taught, gratitude is the quintessential Christian virtue, the complement of divine grace. It is also the basis of human freedom, conceived by Augustine as a disposition to respond either in gratitude or ingratitude to the call of grace.[5] Any disparagement of the world as it actually is, coupled with an assertion of hidden knowledge about how it can be "saved from itself," presupposes ingratitude in the most fundamental sense.

In part, gnosticism represents a hypersensitive yet hardened response to humankind's seemingly intractable problems: e.g., poverty, disease, famine, homelessness, war, crime, racism, injustice, environmental disaster, death—to name only a few. Such problems have traditionally been experienced by most people, at least in large measure, as beyond human control. The world's great religions have developed elaborate responses to these experiences that attempt, in one way or another, to place them in a context sufficiently broad to provide hope for the sufferer without denying the reality of the experience itself. By contrast, the terrorized gnostic, sensing a void, denies the given reality and fills the void with a fantasized, substitute "reality" that is more appealing to his sense of indignation about the inadequacies of the cosmos as given.

This helps to explain the gnostic element in the thought of J. S. Mill, who, hypersensitive to the suffering he witnessed and experienced in the world, concluded that no all-powerful deity could allow such suffering and that, if a god exists at all, then that god is either limited in power or malevolent.[6] Eugene August vividly describes Mill's "outrage" at "Nature's appalling atrocities," likening them to the "terrifying images . . . that sweep across the canvases of J. M. W. Turner." Nature, and Nature's God if he is omnipotent, is described as "that most hated of Millian villains—a despot who delights in inflicting pain . . . a murderer slaying everyone, sometimes with the most horrifying torments." Continuing, August quotes from Mill's essay, "Nature":

> Nature impales men, breaks them as if on the wheel, casts them to be devoured by wild beasts, burns them to death, crushes them with stones like the first christian martyr, starves them with hunger, freezes them with cold, poisons them by the quick or slow venom of her exhalation, and has hundreds of other hideous deaths in reserve, such as the ingenious cruelty of a Nabis or a Domitian never surpassed.[7]

Recall that Mill's solution was to "amend," to whatever extent possible, both nature in general and human nature in particular. The natural human inclination to belief is to be placed in the service of a progressivist "religion of humanity" that may have its origins in the ideas of Auguste Comte.[8] Unlike Comte, Mill is equivocal as to the details concerning how this vision is to be realized—i.e., how the required transformation of human nature is to be accomplished. But the central point is perfectly clear: man, not God, is to be the object of worship; and the created human nature of Christianity, the sense of man having been made in God's image, is to give way to a transformed nature created in the imaginings of gnostic intellectuals who share Mill's heightened "sensitivity."

Mill's approach, and the outlook that underlies it, has since become prototypical in modern constitutional thought, providing critical support for much of the "fundamental values" jurisprudence that has become familiar in the last forty years. Mill's humanistic progressivism, which incorporates large doses of utilitarianism and libertarianism, also is complemented by other intellectual distortions in modern times. For instance, modern jurisprudence is gnostic to the extent that it substitutes positivism for naturalism and fills the mind of God with such human ideas as utility, property rights, socialism, and the like. The process may be observed, early on and perhaps most prominently, as we have seen, in the jurisprudence of John Austin, who unflinchingly ascribes utilitarianism to God.[9] Moving on, however, I shall now examine the structure of the gnostic interpretive enterprise in contemporary constitutional theory.

THE PRESUMPTUOUS CONSTITUTIONALISM
OF WILLIAM HARRIS

The most successful recent attempt to provide an adequate theoretical framework for modern constitutional interpretation has been made by William F. Harris II. In the adumbration of his theory, Harris has also furnished an illuminating description and analysis of the direction in which constitutional theory has been moving during the past forty years. In *The Interpretable Constitution*,[10] Harris claims that "interpretability" is the essence of a written constitution, providing the standard against which all such instruments must be measured and laying out the boundaries of the constitutional enterprise beyond which no written constitution can be a "constitution" at all.[11]

According to Harris, constitutionalism is an independent, free-standing legal-political philosophy occupying a middle ground between (and thus competing with) natural law jurisprudence and legal positivism.[12] The progenitor of a constitutionalism conceived in this manner is Thomas Hobbes, whose radical project of justifying modern government by reference to a social contract, arising by consensus from a state of nature, provides the model for the American Founders' effort to render explicit (i.e., to commit to writing) the terms of the Hobbesian covenant.[13]

According to Harris, an American-style written constitution is an audacious attempt to bind the future by mere words *(logoi)*, the audacity of which is comprised both in the "mere" status of the words and in the creativity of the act. Its effect is to achieve a heretofore unknown (perhaps even unimagined) bonding of word and polity.[14] It is also an act of creation, since the polity established is, quite literally, brought into being (given life, or at least the possibility of life) by the mere "speaking" of the *logos*. This creative act is essentially *ex nihilo*, since the conceptual novelty of the establishment depends on the previous existence of something like the primordial chaos of a Hobbesian state of nature.[15]

In Harris's conceptual world, constitutional interpretation becomes the preeminent mode of constitutional preservation, the main goal of which is to cement, by continual "re-creation" or "ongoing ratification," the bond of word and polity established in the original creative act.[16] Constitutional interpretation thus must be conceived as a continuous, twofold process. First, the polity created by the *logos* is reexamined, readjusted, and conformed to the language of the constitutional text, the implications of which are to be regarded in the fullness of interpretive possibility. Second, the constitutional text is continually reexamined and reinterpreted according to the various transformations of the polity, which have previously evolved from the implications and outworkings of that very text.

In Harris's language, the Constitution must be "readable" both linguistically (the text must be understandable in terms of the institutions that have evolved from it) and politically (the polity must be comprehensible in terms of the documentary bases from which it is derived).[17] Since readability in this sense presupposes a special kind of "literacy," constitutional interpretation should be understood as a response to an invitation to government by "rational discourse," the aim of which is to maintain the underlying conditions of the social compact upon which the whole constitutional enterprise is founded.[18]

The elaboration of Harris's system leads to a fourfold, two-dimensional theory of constitutional interpretation, which, it is claimed, comprises the whole range of interpretive possibilities required by the demand that the Constitution be fully "interpretable" as "text."[19] The first of the two dimensions that are crossed to yield the four possibilities includes *immanence*—roughly, "staying within the text" either literally or in consideration of clear implications—and *transcendence*— roughly, "going beyond the text" in consideration of more remote inferences or implications to which the text "points." The second dimension includes *positivism*—roughly, "clause-bound" in the phrase-specific sense—and *structuralism*— roughly, "non-clause-bound" in a sense that recognizes coherent general features of the Constitution not fully transparent in any single provision.

Four combinations result. First, there is *immanent positivism*—most apparent when courts rely on the "plain meaning" rule of statutory interpretation in constitutional cases, exemplified for Harris by Justice Hugo Black's insistence "on the conclusiveness and sufficiency of plain words in the Constitution."[20] Second is *immanent structuralism*—as in text-oriented process-based theories like those of Charles Black and John Hart Ely, where an interpreter seeks an "exposition which best harmonizes with [the Constitution's] design, its objects and its general structure."[21] The third combination is *transcendent positivism*—the annexation of implications "beyond the document" to "self-contained parts of the document,"[22] as when constitutional rights are found to be "dependent on interests not mentioned in the Constitution."[23] The fourth is *transcendent structuralism*—as when constitutional values are held to "emanate from the totality of the constitutional scheme under which we live."[24]

Harris's theory thus embraces and legitimizes the entire spectrum of textualist approaches, even supplying textual grounds to support decisions regarded by many commentators as well beyond acceptable constitutional bounds (e.g., *Griswold v. Connecticut*). At the same time, it does rule out what Harris thinks are some of the more egregious varieties of noninterpretivist extratextualism in American judicial history. These would include, for example, "popular consensus" (e.g., some of the opinions in *Furman v. Georgia*), certain applications of "natural law" (e.g., Justice Johnson's concurring opinion in *Fletcher v. Peck*), and "free-form political theory" (e.g., the abstract theory of representation in *Reynolds v. Sims*).[25]

The most controversial, and least well-founded, feature of Harris's textualism is its denial of any role for intentionalist approaches, even when these are tied closely to textual considerations. Blackstone, for example, followed closely by Marshall and other early American jurists, regarded textual literalism to be the best point of departure in the judicial interpretation of written legal instruments, but only because the words of an enactment are often the best guide to the "will of the lawgiver."[26]

Indeed, Harris goes so far as to place the Framers' intent in the same category as such supposedly extraconstitutional sources as "consensus, reason, and natural law,"[27] all of which appear to be conceived in the narrow manner characteristic of modern ways of thinking about such notions. Assimilating, at least momentarily, constitutional interpretation to deconstructive interpretive strategies developed in relation to other kinds of text, Harris states that once written, a work leaves the control of its drafter. The words of the Constitution, once they began their work of bringing a polity into force, lost their bond with the thoughts of the framers and established a bond with the political order. Because the polity develops as a fulfillment of its form, in accordance with the logic incorporated in it, the regulative link with the framers' thoughts about specific constitutional contents could not plausibly endure. More important, the maintenance of such a bond— as well as judicial autopsies on the framers' minds—would militate against the rule of law itself. The homage paid to intent, moreover, obscures the fundamental dynamics of the constitutional enterprise: the continuing ratification that occurs in the process of mutually adjusting the linguistic and political texts, assuring their evolving readability with respect to each other, as an appeal to the Constitution's normative author, the lively People of the United States.[28]

Harris's facile dismissal of the "homage paid to intent" effectively subordinates constitutional substance to constitutional form, leaving in its wake a trail of linguistic artifacts designed to take the place of a richly textured instrument that was the product of generations of constitutional experience. If the words of the Constitution are symbols representing the conscious (and unconscious) experience of its constitutionally relevant antecedents, Harris's constitutionalism converts the symbols into unrepresentative abstractions. In Voegelin's words, "The symbols expressing the experiences become subjects in sentences with predicates as if they were 'things' with properties."[29] Harris's procedure virtually ensures the loss of "the consciousness of the experiences that have engendered the symbols" in the first place, consequently committing his theory to a radical ahistoricity.[30]

It is worth noting that Harris's identification of intentionalism with a "regulative link" between the constitutional text and "the framers' thoughts about specific constitutional contents"—thus requiring "judicial autopsies on the framers' minds" to render their thoughts accessible to interpreters—suggests the straw man of subjective intent that was raised and discussed in Chapter 9. But this suggestion does not implicate objective intent, which neither demands nor seeks knowledge of the Framers' psyches but rather requires reasoned (if sometimes difficult) legal-historical analysis based on the Framers' *words* and the *purposes* that may be legitimately inferred from those words when they are read with full understanding of their historical and jurisprudential context. That context extends both backward and forward in time, comprising, first, the traditional practices already taken for granted by the Founders and their contemporaries, and second, those that were destined to become traditional as a result of early, considered, deliberate practice in the courts and other agencies of government.

Despite these and other problems, there is much to be admired in Harris's constitutional interpretivism. He takes more seriously than most contemporary commentators the distinction between the Constitution itself and the constitutional law developed by subordinate governmental institutions like the Supreme Court. He recognizes the paradox of judicial finality and judicial freedom, asserting the duty of all government agencies, officials, and even citizens bound by the Constitution to engage in the enterprise of interpreting the fundamental law. His crucial distinction between text and polity seems to embody a recognition that American constitutionalism cannot be fully comprised in a literal rendering of the written text. He realizes that a viable constitutionalism cannot be a matter of the ephemeral wants and needs of the citizenry. He recognizes the critical importance of keeping alive the constitutional antinomies underlying the system while holding "their dissonance in intelligible bounds."[31]

Most important, Harris travels further than anyone else has in the direction of "setting out a coherent picture of what makes sense of the enterprise" at the heart of much of the constitutional theorizing of the past four decades, especially of exposing its "astounding presumption" that "people can design a non-existent public order in words and then project themselves into it, tentatively at first by discussing how this verbally contrived order would operate in practice, then by ratifying the words into institutional existence, and thereafter by interpreting their accomplished political world through the initial model."[32] This clarification is of inestimable value for one who wishes to question this presumption.

THE CONSTITUTIONALISM OF HARRIS, HOBBES, AND HEGEL

To initiate the questioning, one need go no further than the opening lines of Harris's book:

> American constitutional interpretation takes for granted the elemental preposterousness of its subject—the presumption that a political world can be constructed and controlled with words. For the document that is the Constitution of the United States did not describe a political "constitution" that already existed: it generated and animated a republic, wresting the three-dimensional contours of a new public order from the two-dimensional realm of thought and theory.[33]

The passage suggests the interpretive dilemma posed by Harris's theory: either the written constitutional text did "describe a political 'constitution' that already existed" or it presumptuously constructed a political world to be controlled by words alone. It also suggests the counterintuitive nature of any constitutional textualism that is regarded as independent of all historical foundations. Harris frankly admits that the human creation, and subsequent continual re-creation *via interpretatio,* of such a constitutional world *ex nihilo* merely by giving names to things is "preposterous." It is so both in the sense of its being "contrary to nature, reason, or common sense" and in the sense of its being "inverted in time, the 'later' [re-creation, or "interpretation"] coming before [because the entire range of re-creative or "interpretive" possibilities must be understood as compactly present in the original creative act], and the 'before' [the original creation, or "founding"] coming later" [because the ultimate fulfillment of the Founders' design can be achieved only by re-creation or "interpretation"].[34]

If these words are understood to be indicative of the "awesome presumptions" of contemporary constitutional theory, laying bare the roots of the "hegemonic paradigm"[35] that has dominated constitutional theorizing for the past four decades, they are certainly apt. Such a conception of the American Founding is flatly contrary to nature, reason, and common sense in a variety of ways. First, everything that human beings know is known in some historical context; that is to say, all our experiences of things in the world that give rise to acts of knowing about those things manifest an irreducibly temporal character. It does not seem to matter whether the things known are other human beings, societies, institutions, animals, vegetables, inanimate material objects, or such animate immaterial objects of thought as morality, reason, common sense, or experience. Even our self-knowledge is essentially historical; otherwise amnesia could hardly be considered much of a problem.

Second, all human creative activity takes place within some historical tradition, the strength of which vitally circumscribes and ultimately determines the provenance of the individual creative acts that modify, develop, or extend such traditions. Even the most revolutionary composers, painters, or writers must have something to revolt against and contexts to revolt within. Generations beyond will invariably assess the contributions of artistic revolutionaries as developments or extensions of the very traditions that were the object of their revolt in the first place.

Third, no instance of exnihilation (creation from nothing) has ever been observed in nature. As Mortimer Adler puts it: "In all our experience of the world and in all our scientific knowledge of nature, we have no evidence or indication of anything ever having been . . . exnihilated. The natural process of generation . . . of coming to be . . . does not involve . . . exnihilation."[36]

Fourth, a preponderance of provisions in the written U.S. Constitution and the interpretive practices traditionally associated with it have direct historical antecedents in the British Constitution and the common law. If, in the face of this evidence, one is forced to choose either to regard the Constitution as entirely preexistent or to regard it as utterly unprecedented, with no middle ground allowed, then common sense surely would suggest the former rather than the latter alternative, for obvious reasons. Just as nature abhors a vacuum, common sense abhors a void. If common sense abhors a void even when a void really exists, how much more so when the void is merely "posited" in the manner of a theoretical fiction?

The conception of American constitutionalism implied by the presumptions of contemporary constitutional theory is contrary not only to nature, common sense, and experience but also to reason, because it is based on epistemological assumptions that are questionable. Remember that Harris conceives the constitutionalism exemplified by the American Founders' effort to construct and control a political world with words alone as an alternative (a "third option") to the extremes of naturalism and positivism. He also believes that these options parallel John Locke's three epistemological alternatives: "the correspondence theory of knowledge [naturalism], nominalism [positivism], and things with names whose corresponding essences can be known because they are the constructions of linguistically ordered human intelligence [constitutionalism]."[37] For Harris, "The constitutionalist position is that one can be objectivist within an artifactual world," the constitutional commitments of which "need not be validated by a transcendental reality whose features are not the product of [human] choice."[38]

Though it may be conceded that it is possible to infer a theory of this kind from Locke's linguistic constructivism,[39] it should be noted that such an inference raises serious difficulties that Harris does not seem to notice. First, Locke makes a sharp distinction between "real" and "nominal" essences. Real essences are defined as the "internal . . . but . . . unknown constitution of things," the "very being" of a thing, that "whereby it is what it is."[40] Nominal essences, conversely, are defined as abstract ideas represented by the "general, or sortal" names that we give them.[41] The important point is that, for Locke, only nominal essences are knowable; and this makes it difficult to see how Harris can regard a constitutional theory based on Lockean epistemology as a viable means of escape from nominalism (and thereby positivism).

Second, the abstract ideas constitutive of nominal essences are just that— "ideas" and nothing more. Recall from Chapter 11 that Locke—along with Berkeley and Hume—believed that all that human beings are really aware of when we think are the contents of our own minds. In empiricist epistemology, "ideas" are not "tools of thought" by which we gain access to external reality; they are our very "objects of thought." Thus we are left with no direct link between our minds and the external world. Locke tries to bridge this gulf by constructing a complex theory of language, but then he appears to undermine the whole effort by denying any necessary connection between external reality and the words we use to represent our ideas in language:

> Words are often secretly referred, first to the ideas supposed to be in other men's minds. But . . . words, as they are used by men, can properly and immediately signify nothing but the ideas that are in the mind of the speaker. . . . Secondly . . . they often suppose the words to stand also for the reality of things . . . though . . . it is a perverting the use of words, and brings unavoidable obscurity and confusion into their signification, whenever we make them stand for anything but these ideas we have in our own minds.[42]

Perhaps we are here facing again what Etienne Gilson referred to as "the irrepressible essentialism of the human mind," which, once it starts thinking about things in terms of abstract essences, forgets that real being is a composite of essence and *existence* and that existence adds to essence a radical "givenness" that is irreducible to any combination of essential attributes. Recall from the discussion in Chapter 6 that essences, whether real or nominal, denote the formal qualities of a being, those attributes that render its actual existence possible or impossible. The ideas of "round square" and "liberal totalitarianism" are essences just as the idea of "equilateral triangle" is an essence. But essence does not imply existence, though existence does imply essence. For any actually existing being, we can be assured that such a being possesses some required minima of essential self-identity and absence of inner contradiction among its primary constituents, else its actual existence would have been impossible. But the same cannot be said of essences, which, however self-consistent and internally coherent, cannot guarantee the actual existence of even a single existing thing.

Finally, if essence does not imply existence, and if existence must therefore be regarded as radically "given," from whence comes the gift? Of course theories of language or of constitutional interpretation must be "coherent," as must be the nominal essences that are their primary constituents. But where is the assurance that a coherence epistemology drawn from the empiricism just described will bear any relation whatever to external reality (i.e., will not be merely a fantasy world in which intellectuals may amuse themselves)? Or, to use Harris's language, how can one be "objectivist within an artifactual world?" For Locke himself, objectivity is guaranteed by the identity of the artificer:

> God, having designed man for a sociable creature, made him not only with an inclination, and under a necessity to have fellowship with those of his own kind, but furnished him also with language, which was to be the great instrument and common tie of society. Man, therefore, had by nature his organs so fashioned, as to be fit to frame articulate sounds, which we call words. . . . Besides articulate sounds . . . it was further necessary that he should be able to use these sounds as signs of internal conceptions; and to make them stand as marks for the ideas within his own mind, whereby they might be made known to others. . . . It may also lead us a little towards the original of all our notions and knowledge, if we remark how great a dependence our words have on common sensible ideas; and how those which are made use of to stand for actions and notions quite removed from sense, have their rise from thence, and from obvious sensible ideas are transferred to more abstruse significations.[43]

But the constitutional enterprise, as conceived by Harris, knowing not a transcendent source of order to validate the external objects of constitutional experience, can offer no rational assurance that the objects of a constitutional discourse based on Lockean coherence epistemology will represent anything having real existence in the world. To be sure, Harris recognizes the problem, though dismissing it as quickly as it is acknowledged:

> As I have said, this enterprise is a preposterous undertaking. To explain and justify it may in itself be participating in a grand ruse, a historic bluff, a big lie, or an engine of systematic public deception. Or more likely, as I believe, such explanation may

justify the kind of hegemonic paradigm that merely makes sense of the experience within its bounds—even as we tremble at the question of the ultimate solidity of the presumptuous constitutional model itself, and as we doubt further whether it is grounded in anything besides, at best, its own intricate coherence, constantly threatened as it is by the model's insistence that it can make constitutive sense of such contrary substantive political qualities as individualism and collectivity, reason and will. Whatever may be the ultimate "truth" of the constitutional model from the external perspective, I am not concerned about it. The theory of constitutionalism that I advance here is predicated on the idea that "truth" is an inapposite category in political theory, which is itself the prime example of the value of workable fiction that finds its validity in a structured coherence between human thought and political power.[44]

Something is amiss here. The fact that political theory contains workable fictions hardly implies that the conformity of the objects of political thought with external reality is unimportant. On the contrary, scientific fictions are the measure of the lengths to which human beings will go in order to obtain fuller understanding of objects of experience that are not themselves fictitious. Human thought and political power are not fictions; they are existing realities with determinate essences and momentous observable consequences. If theorizing about the relation between such essences exhibits "structured coherence," it is not by virtue of any fictionalized account of their relations, but because the essences are understood in their relation to that by which they are determined.

The most fundamental question of constitutional theory must therefore be: What is that by which the essential attributes of constitutional order are determined? And not far away lurks this question: What is the context from which such determinants are derived? Now, either the essential attributes of constitutional order are determined "externally" (i.e., outside the mind of the constitutional theorist) or they are not. Likewise, the context from which the determinants of constitutional order are drawn either is "historical" or it is not. Harris may be unconcerned, but his theory gives negative answers to both questions by default. The answers drive Harris's theory toward a position aptly described as "constitutional gnosticism," according to which man—the measure of all things—usurps the place of God as ruler and originator of the constitutional order, claiming to be that by which the essential attributes of that order have been derived from an antecedent constitutional nothingness.

Harris's constitution, emptied of all historical meaning, becomes the springboard for an interpretive process characterized by rational discourse under coherence epistemology—the ultimate aim of which is the institutionalizing of a reflexive, self-conscious constitutional order wherein the polity is realized as a fulfillment of its form through attainment of full coherence in the relation between constitutional polity and constitutional text. Disavowing both a divine source of order toward which a constitutional polity might naturally be drawn and an authoritative history from which knowledge of such an order might be gained,

Harris substitutes a telos and a teleology that bears striking resemblance to a Hegelian process of dialectical movement to a predetermined end. Since, for Hegel, self-conscious coherence is wisdom (and perfectly self-conscious coherence is absolute wisdom), and since, for Harris, such coherence must be the product of human choice, not transcendental reality, it follows that, for Harris, as for Hegel, wisdom (even absolute wisdom) must be regarded as attainable (in principle) by man in the world and susceptible of institutionalization in the state. A brief comparison of Harris's ideas with some Hegelian ones advanced by Alexandre Kojeve, one of Hegel's most eminent twentieth-century interpreters, will illustrate the point more fully.

According to Kojeve, Hegelian "wisdom" *(sophia)* is perfect self-consciousness in the sense that a perfectly wise man would be capable of answering, comprehensibly, all questions that can be asked him concerning his actions, so that his answers, in toto, form a coherent discourse.[45] Since philosophy demands directing oneself toward the ideal of wisdom, three possibilities, called "existential attitudes" by Kojeve,[46] result, each of which has led to one or more "schools of thought" in philosophy.[47]

The first possibility is that wisdom cannot be realized at all, a view that implies that the philosopher wants to be what he knows to be impossible and so is mad.[48] Under the influence of this view, one is led naturally to some variant of skepticism, cynicism, or nihilism.

The second possibility is that wisdom cannot be realized by man in time because such wisdom is a kind of "omniscience," but it may be realized by a being other than man outside of time (i.e., God).[49] In this view, absolute knowledge (wisdom) necessarily becomes knowledge of God, and philosophy necessarily becomes theology,[50] as in the progression of Plato's thought from the earlier dialogues to the *Timaeus*.

The third possibility is Hegel's own solution: that the ideal of wisdom is attainable, can be realized by man in the world, and, indeed, is personified and realized in Hegel himself, who is "potentially omniscient."[51] To deny the possibility of realizing wisdom in the here and now is to transform philosophy into theology, and to deny God is necessarily to assert the possibility of man's realizing wisdom on earth.

The presumptuous constitutional enterprise described by Harris, fully extended and applied by him to the whole of American constitutional history and thought, summarily dismisses God, Nature, and History from the constitutional arena (and therewith Kojeve's "second possibility"). It substitutes for these a self-contained, self-propelled, self-fulfilling dialectical interpretive process through which constitutional meaning is created and re-created, at ever-ascending levels of abstraction, until polity and text unite in ultimate fulfillment of that which was once only form—the fully realized Concept (of a Constitution) *as such* (Kojeve's "third possibility").

The cogency of the enterprise thus depends largely upon the truth of the Hegelian worldview and its consequent substitution of man for God as the primary creative and preservative force in the social cosmos. Remember that, for Harris, "interpretation" is "re-creation." The act of creation *ex nihilo* that is imputed to the Founders by Harris, since it rests (by definition) on no preexisting determinations of reason or will (i.e., it has no "history"), is a godlike act. Likewise, creation by utterance of the *logos* is the preeminent godlike act, described in the opening words of the Gospel of John: "In the beginning was the Word, and the Word was with the God, and God was the Word."[52] Finally, to create by setting in motion out of nothing a chain of causes the ultimate effects of which are in some sense predetermined by a logic implicit in the original motion (so that what is "later" comes before and what is "before" comes later) is to "predestine" in the manner of a god who predetermines the will in foreknowledge.

It is difficult not to conclude that, to the extent that Harris's depiction is accurate, modern constitutionalism is profoundly a gnostic enterprise, revealing ingratitude for the cosmos as given (hence the need for a *novus ordo seclorum*) while concealing knowledge about how it came to be as it is. What are the unstated assumptions about the meaning of history that lead to Harris's summary dismissal of the only conventional and widely accepted approach to constitutional interpretation that is entirely excluded by his theory—historical intentionalism? What is the basis for Harris's apparent insistence that a theory of interpretation attached to a written constitution must be completely abstracted from that constitution's historical foundation? Why neglect so completely the historically given?

History is only recognizable because it has a "double aspect," which is experienced as a tension between the immanent events that become objects of thought in space and time and the transcendent reality that imparts significance to those events and objects by rendering them intelligible. It follows that history, as an object of thought or conceptualization, ordering sequences of events in space and time, is fully comprehensible (has real meaning) only in relation to the possibility of an equally real constituting of such objects and events beyond space and time— i.e., constitution by the very "transcendental reality" that is denied by Harris.[53] History's "transcendental texture," linking the "configuration of history" with "experiences of transcendence," has been widely acknowledged by historiographers and philosophers of history.[54]

Reflection upon the intimate connection between gnosticism and ahistoricity raises another major question concerning Harris's theory. The idea of a founding *ex nihilo* is not only profoundly ahistorical in the sense that it grossly overstates the novelty in the Framers' enterprise, but it also distorts the Hobbesian "state of nature" on which the whole constitutional enterprise, as conceived by Harris, depends. Hobbes's state of nature is a theoretical abstraction from which conclusions about forms of government may be drawn, a set of unrealistic assumptions, akin to other fictional assumptions in science, about human nature, which nonetheless may lead to useful (because, in a certain sense, testable) hypotheses. For example, the assumption of radical individualism or social atomism, as in Hobbes, yields an absolute monarchy; in Locke, a relaxed individualism may yield a constitutional monarchy tempering parliamentary absolutism.

In both instances, the derived form follows from the assumptions as a matter of positive law based on the passions and interests (e.g., to escape the fear of violent death in Hobbes), not on the rights and duties, of the contracting parties. Therefore a constitutionalism derived from Hobbes and Locke cannot bridge the gulf between natural law and legal positivism. For the modern contractarians, the laws and rights of nature are fully operative only in the passional state of nature and are to be circumvented or superseded, not conserved, by institution of the social contract. This approach effectively assimilates human nature to animal nature and thus renders the "natural law–legal positivism" dichotomy senseless. Put simply, there is no gulf left to bridge. As Leo Strauss has remarked, "Modern natural law as originated by Hobbes did not start as traditional natural law did from the hierarchic order of man's natural ends but from the lowest of those ends (self-preservation) which could be thought to be more effective than the higher ends."[55]

Moreover, the truncated human nature of modern contractarian political thought, as distinguished from the human nature of classical natural law, was a proximate cause of the emergence of modern legal positivism in the first place. Arguably, it is even now its main supporting ground. This remains true even though the most influential early legal positivists (e.g., Austin) made no claim that the law of nature was being supplanted by their "science." They claimed only that their science was not naturalistic in its scope.[56] Faced with this history, attempting to harmonize the circumvented natural law of modern political thought with that very legal positivism which is arguably its own offspring is to entrust the henhouse to the fox.

Some remarks of Eric Voegelin on the "specific kind of natural law that attempts to construct the order of a society out of contractual relations between the members" are apropos in this context:

> The origin of this type of contract theory was analyzed by Plato in the *Republic*. It originates in the conception of man as a being that is motivated by passions alone. The order among human beings that exists by virtue of *homonoia*, that is, by virtue of their common participation in transcendent reality, is not recognized as existent. The withdrawal of man from participation in the common *nous* into the shell of his passions was characterized by Heraclitus as the creation of a private dream-world in opposition to the public world of participation in the *koinon*, the common *nous*. Plato resumes the Heraclitian idea of the dream-worlds of individual passion. Out of such individual dream-worlds no common order can be constructed because the agreement lacks the obligatory force that stems from participation in the common transcendent reality. The contracts would be empty formulae. This analysis is valid for all later constructions of a similar type.[57]

If Madison's Americans of 1787 were not Heraclitian sleepwalkers, and if the American Founders were not Hobbesian contractors, then what were they? This question has largely been answered in Chapter 8, where it was observed, *contra* Harris, that the Framers were indeed "describing a political constitution that already existed," using the underlying principles and practices of that constitution to strengthen an already existing polity against very real internal and external threats. To be sure, the constitutional political world inhabited by the Founders was increasingly a Hobbesian world; but against that background, the Framers imported a large measure of classical legal thought into the American Constitution by their assumption of a common law foundation for the fundamental law and a natural law foundation for the common law. It is largely the Aristotelian practical reason of this common law foundation, the prominence of which was noted previously in the writings of Sir Matthew Hale, that saves the Founders themselves from the charge of gnosticism.[58]

James R. Stoner, Jr., has advanced several good examples of the way in which the traditional practice-oriented approach of common law constitutionalism in the American Founding, personified in Roger Sherman, tempered the "scientific reason" of institution-building political theorists such as James Madison during the Philadelphia Convention and subsequent ratification struggles. According to Stoner, the restraining force of the common lawyers throughout the Founding era helped to prevent the Framers from becoming "builders of Babel," designing our institutions without sufficient regard for the way in which those institutions would map themselves into the inherited traditions already in process of development in the underlying constitutional order of the American polity.[59]

To demand, with Harris, that a constitution conceived in such circumstances be interpreted (and be "interpretable") as if it had no history, as if it had been "erected in the midst of the metaphorical Hobbesian-like chaos,"[60] instigating a "new order of creation" so as to cordon off "a secure area . . . from the rest of an incoherent universe,"[61] the fundamental character of which is "insignificance," "disorder," and "cacophony,"[62] is to charge the Founders with constitutional solipsism. It is also to charge them with supreme ingratitude, with violation of the First Commandment in the most extreme form possible, and with conspiracy for having committed the violation in secret, since they did not publicize their dissatisfaction with God's rulership of the cosmos or their intention to overthrow it.

Worse still, in the constitutional order described by Harris, all Americans who presume to be constitutional interpreters—aspiration to which, as in Soterios Barber's constitutional order, is required for full citizenship in the Founders' republic—are implicated in the violation. As Harris says, "This constitutive story is authoritatively invoked and reaffirmed, by reference, with each subsequent exercise of constitutional review."[63]

That said, I close this chapter with the observation that Harris's elaboration of the roots of the enterprise of constitutional interpretation has gone a long way toward clarification of the underlying terms of debate, starkly revealing what is really at stake. Ultimately, it comes to this: either there is a God who creates and orders the human legal cosmos by the infusion of a natural law, which is the imprint of eternal law in the human psyche and which thus cannot but be reflected in the common historical practices of humanly devised legal institutions, or there is not and we are abandoned to our own devices.

15 · The God of the Cosmos as a Whole

RATIONAL THEOLOGY AND MODERN SCIENCE

The considerations advanced and discussed in Chapter 14 suggest that such issues as whether the Constitution should be interpreted according to textualism, clause-bound or non–clause-bound interpretivism, structuralism, proceduralism, aspirationalism, moralism, or some other theory of meaning should be regarded as secondary. Indeed, all such theories presuppose an answer to a more fundamental question about the nature and source of constitutional order.

If the nature of order is transcendent, and its source is a supreme being who creates and preserves it, then the history of order—the cumulative record of experiences of order symbolized and institutionalized—must be accorded pride of place in the determination of the right way to interpret the Constitution. As Graham Walker observes with a large measure of understatement, while admonishing constitutional moralists who would disregard tradition in judicial decision-making, "The historical record of past human experience might furnish some substantially accurate information about the content of moral reality—thanks to the real discoveries of earlier generations."[1]

Merely stating the issue does not, of course, resolve it. The normative weight of the historical record depends largely on the extent to which there are reasonable grounds for believing in the existence of a transcendent source of order in history. It is my purpose in this chapter and the two that follow to demonstrate that there are such grounds and that their existence creates a rational obligation to interpret the Constitution in accordance with traditional legal practices.

I shall begin by stressing the point that belief in a supreme being, as such, violates no established facts or theories, scientific or otherwise. The contrary impression has been created largely by the successful influence of modern gnosticism, in which the natural order is conceived as deficient in ways that are susceptible of correction by human action. Gnosticism, in its turn, has influenced political movements as widely diverse as progressivism—which views human society as capable of evolution toward a state of perfection—socialism—which views society as evolving (or revolving) toward an egalitarian utopia—and Nazism—which proclaims the necessity of replacing traditional order with one characterized by racial purity.

Gnosticism also is closely related to such modern philosophical movements as scientific materialism, logical (and legal) positivism, behaviorism, enlightenment rationalism, and nihilistic existentialism. Yet in none of the vast literature stemming from any of these movements can be found a plausible and valid argument that would support a denial of the central claim of rational theology: that belief in a supreme being who is conceived as the constitutive, transcendent source of cosmic order is warranted both by experience and by logic. Nor can any such argument be found in modern science, the very success of which has sometimes been thought to have undermined not only religious faith but also belief in the possibility of moral truth.[2]

Ungrounded in reason or experience, the denial of religious or moral truth in particular, and philosophical truth more generally, appears to rest on an inchoate "feeling," according to Mortimer Adler. He addresses the question of why Bertrand Russell's theory of descriptions is widely regarded to be an "advance" over the Aristotelian and Thomistic theory of signs:

> Why is this so? My only answer is that it must be believed that, because Aristotle and Aquinas did their thinking so long ago, they cannot reasonably be supposed to have been right in matters about which those who came later were wrong. Much must have happened in the realm of philosophical thought during the last three or four hundred years that requires an open-minded person to abandon their teachings for something more recent and, therefore, supposedly better.[3]

As I have suggested, for the case of moral philosophy it is implausible to regard the ethics of Hume or Kant as representing a significant advance over those of Aristotle or Aquinas. I would add that it is just as implausible to regard the theologies of Niebuhr or Tillich as a large improvement on those of Augustine or Molina. The reason for the latter observation is similar to the twofold explanation that Adler offers in the case of moral philosophy.

First, in contrast to science, which is investigative and thus reliant on the accumulation of observational data and the development of ever more refined technologies for the measurement of that data, philosophy—of religion as well as of morals—is an elaboration of reflections on common experience, the core of which has remained relatively constant over time. Thus one may reasonably expect remarkable advances in science during later phases of scientific development, consequent upon technological advances that are possible only in the wake of previous advances of a similar type. Since philosophical or theological advances do not depend on such cumulative technological developments, philosophy and theology can be expected to develop early and advance slowly beyond the point of their early development.[4]

Second, since rational philosophic inquiry—which includes rational theology—"is a persistent effort to explain what needs to be explained and cannot be explained by scientific investigation," coming to a halt "only when there is nothing left to be explained," more recent developments in philosophy or theology may be credited as advances in knowledge only to the extent that such developments are the result of incorporating recent scientific discoveries into the existing body of knowledge.[5]

Since the question of the existence or nonexistence of a supreme being has not been answered—let alone "explained"—by scientific investigation, philosophic or theologic inquiry on the subject can come to a halt only if it is concluded that God's existence or nonexistence does not need to be explained. Adler has aptly noted that one's position on the question of whether an explanation is needed boils down to whether one thinks that the cosmos is "necessary" or merely "contingent."[6] Explanation of these alternatives will take us to the heart of the problem concerning the plausibility of belief.

NATURAL AND LOGICAL CONTINGENCY

In a famous BBC broadcast of 1948, the following exchange took place between F. S. Copleston and Bertrand Russell.

RUSSELL: You ask whether I consider that the universe is unintelligible. I shouldn't say unintelligible—I think it is without explanation. Intelligible, to my mind, is a different thing. Intelligible has to do with the thing itself and not with its relations.

COPLESTON: Well, my point is that what we call the world is intrinsically unintelligible, apart from the existence of God. You see, I don't believe that the infinity of the series of events—I mean a horizontal series, so to speak—if such an infinity could be proved, would be in the slightest degree relevant to the situation. . . . If you add up contingent beings to infinity, you still get contingent beings, not a necessary being. An infinite series of contingent beings will be, to my way of thinking, as unable to cause itself as one contingent being. However, you say, I think, that it is illegitimate to raise the question of what will explain the existence of any particular object?

RUSSELL: It's quite all right if you mean by explaining it, simply finding a cause for it.

COPLESTON: Well, why stop at one particular object? Why shouldn't one raise the question of the cause of the existence of all particular objects?

RUSSELL: Because I see no reason to think there is any. The whole concept of cause is one we derive from our observation of particular things; I see no reason whatsoever to suppose that the total has any cause. . . .

COPLESTON: Well, to say that there isn't any cause is not the same thing as saying that we shouldn't look for a cause. The statement that there isn't any cause should come, if it comes at all, at the end of the enquiry, not the beginning. In any case, if the total has no cause, then to my way of thinking it must be its own cause, which seems to me impossible. Moreover, the statement that the world is simply there if in answer to a question, presupposes that the question has meaning.

RUSSELL: No, it doesn't need to be its own cause, what I'm saying is that the concept of cause is not applicable to the total.

COPLESTON: Then you would agree with Sartre that the universe is what he calls "gratuitous"?

RUSSELL: Well, the word "gratuitous" suggests that it might be something else; I should say that the universe is just there, and that's all.

COPLESTON: Well, I can't see how you can rule out the legitimacy of asking the question how the total, or anything at all come to be there. Why something rather than nothing, that is the question? The fact that we gain our knowledge of causality empirically, from particular causes, does not rule out the possibility of asking what the cause of the series is.[7]

Russell's position here is rooted in the familiar logical positivist assumption that metaphysical or theological statements are inherently senseless because such statements are neither analytic (tautological) propositions nor synthetic (empirical) hypotheses subject to verification.[8] But this position is refutable even on its own terms, since the statement "God exists" plausibly may be viewed as synthetic in at least two senses.

First, if God really does exist, then it is safe to assume that his existence may be amply and graphically demonstrated any time he chooses to demonstrate it; hence, the proposition is a prediction.[9] Second, positing God's existence may turn out to account for observed phenomena better than the alternative hypothesis; hence, the proposition is a theoretical assumption. The well-known "argument from design" may be viewed as an inverted form of this hypothetical version.[10]

Copleston's position is a form of the third version of the "cosmological" argument for God's existence given by Thomas Aquinas in the *Summa Theologica:*

> The third way is taken from possibility and necessity, and runs thus. We find in nature things that are possible to be and not to be, since they are found to be generated, and to be corrupted, and consequently they are possible to be and not to be. But it is impossible for these always to exist, for that which is possible not to be at some time is not. Therefore, if everything is possible not to be, then at one time there could have been nothing in existence. Now if this were true, even now there would be nothing in existence, because that which does not exist only begins to exist by something already existing. Therefore, if at one time nothing was in existence, it would have been impossible for anything to have begun to exist; and thus even now nothing would be in existence—which is clearly false. Therefore, not all beings are merely possible, but there must exist something the existence of which is necessary. But every necessary thing either has its necessity caused by another, or not. Now it is impossible to go on to infinity in necessary things which have their necessity caused by another, as has been already proved in regard to efficient causes. Therefore we must admit the exis-

tence of some being having of itself its own necessity, and not receiving it from another, but rather causing in others their necessity. This all men speak of as God.[11]

One of the main criticisms of the cosmological argument has come from utilitarian positivists such as J. J. C. Smart, who interpret the argument as resting on the idea of a "logically necessary being."[12] To a positivist, "necessity" is a concept that can be applied only to propositions, not to things. Thus "logically necessary being" is like "round square"—an absurdity. But this response is a misreading when applied to Aquinas's third version of the cosmological argument. The notion of "possibility" in the passage is akin to Kant's idea of "contingency," not to the empiricist idea of "logical possibility." Thus the concept of "necessity" that is contrasted with that of "possibility" represents an idea of self-sufficiency or independence of natural contingencies—an empirical, not a logical, property. In other words, Aquinas does not mean that God's existence is logically necessary or that "God exists" is a logically necessary truth.[13] Rather, he means that God's existence is not dependent on anything outside itself, is not "transient," is not finite in the sense of having a beginning or an end within time. In the terms of Plato or Kant, God's existence is a noumenal, not a phenomenal, reality.

The remaining alternative open to the positivist is to fall back on the dogmatic supposition that Aquinas and others who advance the cosmological argument are simply talking nonsense when they refer to God as a "necessary being" in an ontological rather than a logical sense, because "necessary" has no meaning outside the domain of propositional logic. But this argument begs the question by assuming the very point that needs to be proved. Supporting the conclusion that necessity is a purely analytical construct requires an argument containing the premise that meaningful reality is fully representable by mathematical tautologies and observational statements. Since such a premise is equivalent to the denial of a meaningful noumenal reality, it is not open to the positivist to then argue, in reverse, against the noumenal realm on the basis of the assertion that necessity is wholly an attribute of propositions.

Presumably, it is the evident circularity of such arguments that led Kant, while fully accepting the empirical grounds of scientific method, to assert the existence of nonphenomenal reality as a necessary precondition of all efforts to render phenomenal reality fully intelligible according to the postulates of speculative (scientific) reason.[14] It is true that Kant denied the knowability of the contents of the noumenal realm and that his denial resulted largely from his acceptance of the empiricists' supposition that "ideas" are "that which is thought" rather than "that by which we think." In consequence of this view, Kant was driven to think that we can only really "know" the contents of our own minds, a position that implies rejection of an immaterial intellectual faculty whose function is to provide access to noumenal reality.

Yet Kant's adoption of these views did not lead him to the absurd position, held by the positivists, that all reality is phenomenal. Indeed, Kant exposed that absurdity by demonstrating that any theoretically justified phenomenalism presupposes the existence of noumenal reality in quite the same way as figure presupposes ground. Kant's denial of the knowability of the noumenal is thus a world removed from the positivists' denial of the meaningfulness of any statement about nonphenomenal reality because in Kant's system, all knowledge has the transcendent structure that is the ground of meaning for any statement about the attributes of noumenal objects.

If we dispense with Kant's subjectivism, his system is otherwise epistemologically sound, and his insistence on the meaningfulness of the nonphenomenal becomes the ground for asserting its knowability. One such nonphenomenal object, an "intelligible" object, or an "object of pure thought," is the idea of God. And Aquinas's "attributes of God" in the cosmological proof describe commonsensical aspects of any fully coherent idea of divine being.[15]

THE COSMOLOGICAL ARGUMENT

Mortimer Adler has provided a useful survey of arguments for and against the existence of a supreme being in *How to Think About God: A Guide for the 20th-Century Pagan*.[16] He addresses his book explicitly to "open-minded pagans," persons who, like himself,[17] do not "worship the God of Christians, Jews, or Muslims" but who are not among those "who have also closed their minds on the subject."[18] After some fairly extensive preliminaries, Adler asks, "IF God, or IF the supreme being, really exists, what is the existence of God, or of the supreme being, like?"[19]

Following the lead of Saint Anselm, who thought of God as "a being than which no greater can be thought of" and who must therefore be thought of as "supreme,"[20] Adler formulates a "definite description of God" that conforms to most commonly accepted notions about what God "is" as an object of thought: "(1) immaterial, incorporeal, non-physical, non-temporal, immutable, and also (2) necessary, (3) independent, unconditioned, uncaused, and (4) infinite."[21] The question is this: are there reasonable grounds for believing that such a being really "exists" (in whatever modes of "existence" are appropriate for a being with the ascribed attributes)? In response to this query, Adler contrasts two arguments. One he labels the "best traditional" argument, which usually travels under the label "cosmological." The other he calls a "truly cosmological" argument.

Making use of two of Aquinas's versions of the cosmological argument, the Kantian distinction between necessity and contingency, and an Aristotelian distinction between causes "of being or existence" and causes "of becoming, change, or motion,"[22] Adler provides a reconstruction of the premises in the "best traditional" cosmological argument supporting God's existence.

1. The existence of an effect that requires the operation of a co-existent cause implies the co-existence of that cause.
2. Whatever exists either does or does not need a cause of its existence at every moment of its existence; that is, during the time in which it endures, from the moment of its coming to be to the moment of its passing away.
3. A contingent being is one that needs a cause of its continuing existence at every moment of its endurance in existence.
4. No contingent being causes the continuing existence of any other contingent being.
5. Contingent beings exist in this world and endure, or continue in existence, from the moment of their coming to be to the moment of their passing away.
6. Any object the existence of which we can think of must be thought of as having its real existence either (1) necessarily or (2) contingently. It must be thought of as a being that has its existence either (1) *a se* or (2) *ab alio*, either (1) from, through, and in itself or (2) from, through, and in another.[23]

Since the argument is formally valid, it follows that either a supreme being with these attributes exists or at least one of the six premises of the argument is false. Premise one is a fundamental postulate of science, premise two is true by the "law of excluded middle," premise four is confirmed by our experience of nature, premise five simply asserts our existence, and premise six is Kant's distinction. All of these are true either self-evidently or by definition of the terms.

That leaves premise three as the only questionable one. According to Adler, premise three is false; thus the "best traditional" argument fails. The premise is false, in Adler's view, essentially for two closely related reasons.

First, it is untenable because "the modern discovery of the principle of inertia requires us to reject as false Aristotle's view that the continuing motion of a body set in motion needs a continuing efficient cause."[24] In other words, an analogy borrowed from modern physics holds also in metaphysics, so that everything that exists possesses a natural inclination to persevere in existence by inertia until countervailing forces coalesce in such a way as to overpower that existence.[25] Though a contingent being needs an efficient external cause of its "coming to be," the principle of inertia, conceived as purely internal, is sufficient to explain the perseverance in existence of such a being at every moment of its existence.

Second, the "contingency" of individual things in nature must be understood as "superficial," not "radical." Radical contingency is signified by "exnihilation" and "annihilation"; superficial contingency is signified by "transformation." For example, when physical organisms are born and later die, they are neither exnihilated (born "out of nothing") nor annihilated (pass into nothingness). Rather, they undergo material transformation. According to Adler,

> In all our experience of the world and in all our scientific knowledge of nature, we have no evidence or indication of anything ever having been annihilated—or, for that

matter, ever having been exnihilated. The natural process of generation and corruption, of coming to be and passing away, does not involve either exnihilation or annihilation.[26]

These observations lead Adler to conclude that, since the perseverance in existence of all contingent beings can be adequately explained by natural forces, we are not entitled (because we do not need) to posit the existence of supernatural forces in order to account for such perseverance. Thus the "best traditional" argument for God's existence fails.

One might wonder why Adler focused so heavily on the perseverance, rather than on the creation, of contingent beings. The reason is that to assume a creation is to presuppose God's existence—the very thing that needs to be proved—and thus begs the question. To avoid this circularity, Adler, following Aquinas, begins by assuming that the cosmos has always existed and thus is "uncreated."[27]

After thus disposing of the "traditional" cosmological argument, Adler offers his own "truly cosmological" argument, in which the "effect to be explained" is not the continuing existence of contingent individual things but "the existence of the cosmos as a whole."

> Stated in the briefest possible fashion, a truly cosmological argument runs as follows: IF the existence of the cosmos as a whole needs to be explained, and IF it cannot be explained by natural causes, THEN we must look to the existence and action of a supernatural cause for its explanation.[28]

Adler then provides a longer version of the argument:

1. The existence of an effect requiring the concurrent existence and action of an efficient cause implies the existence and action of that cause.
2. The cosmos as a whole exists.
3. The existence of the cosmos as a whole is radically contingent, which is to say that, while not needing an efficient cause of its coming to be, since it is everlasting [by assumption], it nevertheless does need an efficient cause of its continuing existence, to preserve it in being and prevent it from being replaced by nothingness.
4. If the cosmos needs an efficient cause of its continuing existence to prevent its annihilation, then that cause must be a supernatural being, supernatural in its action, and one the existence of which is uncaused; in other words, the supreme being, or God.[29]

As before, the argument is formally valid, so the only question concerns the truth of the premises. Premise one, identical to the first premise in the "best traditional" argument, is self-evidently true. Premise two is also self-evidently true. Premise four is true by definition, since "natural" and "supernatural" are mutually exclusive alternatives, and no natural cause can be itself uncaused. Premise three, according to Adler, is true "beyond a reasonable doubt," thereby establishing

God's existence and preservative action to maintain the cosmos as a whole at each moment of its existence.[30]

Adler's main reason for accepting premise three is found in the distinction between "superficial" and "radical" contingency. As we have seen, premise three in the traditional cosmological argument was defective because the contingency of individual things in the cosmos, as parts of a larger whole that are dependent for their continuing existence on the continued existence of that whole, must be regarded as superficial since, when these individual things pass into and out of existence, they are neither exnihilated or annihilated but are merely transformed. The efficient causes of the generation and destruction of such things, as well as their perseverance in being while they exist (by inertia), are fully contained within nature.

However, to apply this logic to the cosmos taken as a whole, conceived "as the totality of everything that exists physically," is inadmissible.[31] To do so would be to commit the "fallacy of composition," using a characteristic of the parts of a given whole to characterize the whole itself.[32] Individual things in the cosmos remain parts of the same whole when they are transformed either by generation or corruption, but the cosmos itself cannot be thought of in this manner.

Whenever the cosmos is thought of as "coming to be," it must be thought of as "created" or "exnihilated"; when it is thought of as "ceasing to exist," it must be thought of as "exterminated" or "annihilated." If the cosmos were to be thought of as something that could be "transformed" into anything other than itself, it could not be thought of as the totality of all existing things and thus would not be a "cosmos." In other words, if the cosmos is contingent, then its contingency must be "radical," not "superficial."[33]

Since it is the superficial contingency of the individual parts of the cosmos that makes possible an explanation of their continuing existence by reference to inertia (and thus makes it unnecessary to posit God as the efficient cause of their perseverance), that explanation is not available as to the continuing existence of the cosmos as a whole. Because the principle of inertia applies only to the continuation of a particular state once a change of state either to rest or to motion has been brought about, inertia of being in time can explain the perseverance of a radically contingent cosmos only if that cosmos has been caused to exist at some point in time. But a radically contingent cosmos can be brought into being only by exnihilation, as we have seen. To suppose this is to presuppose a creation, and thereby God—the very presumption that Adler persistently refuses to allow.[34]

If inertia cannot be used to account for the continuing existence of the cosmos under conditions of radical contingency without presupposing God, then either God must be presupposed or the cosmos must not be contingent. The question, then, is whether the cosmos is contingent, a "merely possible" cosmos rather than an "absolutely necessary" one. According to Adler, that the present cosmos is only "one of many possibilities that might exist" rather than "the only one that can ever exist" can be inferred

> from the fact that the arrangement and disarray—the order and disorder—of the present cosmos might have been otherwise, might have been different from what it is. There is no compelling reason to think that the natural laws which govern the present cosmos are the only possible natural laws. The cosmos as we know it manifests chance and random happenings, as well as lawful behavior. Even the electrons and protons, which are thought to be imperishable once they exist as the building blocks of the present cosmos, might not be the building blocks of a different cosmos.[35]

That which necessarily exists cannot be other than it is; conversely, that which might be other than it is does not necessarily exist and so might not exist at all. But that which might not exist at all cannot be uncaused; and if natural causes (e.g., inertia) do not suffice to account for the perseverance in being of something that might not exist at all, then we must look to supernatural causes. According to Adler,

> The cosmological argument, carried out in this way, appears to establish the existence of the supreme being that acts as the exnihilating cause of this merely possible cosmos, and so explains why it continues to exist. The reasoning conforms to Ockham's rule. We have found it necessary to posit the existence of God, the supreme being, in order to explain what needs to be explained—the actual existence here and now of a merely possible cosmos.[36]

Adler's "truly cosmological" argument thus answers the most fundamental question: "Why is there anything rather than nothing?" It does not, however, answer the less fundamental, but perhaps no less important, question as to why there is any particular thing rather than something else. Adler's God, as he candidly admits, stands in a remote relationship to individual things in the cosmos, being only the preserver (and perhaps creator) of the cosmos as totality. It is not a supreme being whose existence or activity imparts significance to the historical events, beliefs, and practices of human institutions or who provides a transcendent source of order for human societies. I shall attempt to show in Chapter 16 that there are reasonable grounds for faith in such a being.

16 · The God of the Cosmos and Its Parts

I have attempted to show how and why belief in a supreme being is plausible in the sense that such belief raises no contradiction to any existing body of knowledge, scientific or otherwise, when such knowledge is properly understood. The best reasoning about God always presupposes available scientific knowledge about the natural world, and as we saw with regard to the cosmological argument(s), it often incorporates or uses such knowledge explicitly.

We have seen that a valid and plausible argument can be made in support of the conclusion that a supreme being exists who is the exnihilating preservative cause of the continuing existence of the cosmos as a whole. This argument, however, provides no basis for concluding that such a being bears any direct relationship to human beings or human societies, considered as superficially contingent parts of the whole.[1]

This conception of God is unnecessarily restrictive and follows from a mistake in the reasoning that generates Mortimer Adler's "truly cosmological" argument. Following Adler's own oft-repeated injunction against building upon previous errors in thinking,[2] I propose to set right Adler's mistake and put forward a "corrected" proof of God's existence that will generate a concept of a supreme being who is related directly to individual parts of the cosmos, including human beings, societies, and their institutional practices. Making this correction will have the effect of restoring the "best traditional" argument for God's existence that Adler rejected in *How to Think About God*.[3]

We need only to review another of Adler's works, published a decade after his treatise on God. The differences between ancient and modern notions of reason already have been elaborated against the background of classical and modern political thought. The most important of these differences, from my point of view, was that the ancients viewed the mind, or psyche, as an immaterial intellectual faculty providing access to a realm of pure ideas, an "intelligible world"; the moderns, under the influence of materialistic monism, regard the mind as purely physical, reducible to brain function.

Adler's book, *Intellect: Mind over Matter*, stood fast with the ancients on this question, and he held forth as one of his central theses "the defense of the immateriality of the intellect against the metaphysical materialism that is currently rampant in accounts of man's constitution and human behavior."[4] Adler argued convincingly that "the brain is only a necessary, but not a sufficient, condition for conceptual thought; that an immaterial intellect is also requisite as a condition; and that the difference between human and animal behavior is a radical difference in kind."[5]

Let us first reexamine briefly the "best traditional" argument for God's existence, rejected by Adler in *How to Think About God*. Adler's rejection was founded on his dismissal of the third premise, which asserts that "a contingent being is one that needs a cause of its continuing existence at every moment of its endurance in existence."[6] It was concluded that this assertion was false because the principle of inertia, unknown in the time of Aristotle or Aquinas, sufficed to explain the perseverance in being of the individual things that constitute parts of the cosmos and thus compels rejection of "the mediaeval view that the continuing existence of individual things needs the continuing action of an efficient cause."[7]

Adler also defined the cosmos as "the totality of everything that exists physically."[8] Yet ten years later, Adler argued forcefully that the human intellect is immaterial, or "non-physical."[9] Moreover, just two years after the publication of *How to Think About God*, Adler defended just as forcefully the possibility (though not the actuality) that angels, defined simply as "minds without bodies," have real existence, exposing as highly questionable the materialistic dogma that constitutes the main ground for asserting the impossibility of such beings.[10] This dogma holds "that nothing really exists except corporeal substances or bodies."[11] Adler supplies a number of cogent reasons for disavowing this dogma, among which is the apparent correctness of the view affirmed by Aristotle and Aquinas that "intellection—understanding and thinking—is . . . the act of an incorporeal power that man possesses."[12]

Though Adler embraced the idea of an immaterial intellectual faculty in human beings at least as early as 1982,[13] if not before, apparently he did not think it necessary to consider the possible bearing of this idea on his earlier analysis of the cosmological argument in *How to Think About God*. Perhaps the reason he did not may be found in a sharp distinction he draws near the end of his treatise on angels, between that which is "immaterial in its operation" and that which is "immaterial in its mode of being."[14]

The distinction is rooted in Aristotle's belief that the brain (i.e., matter) is a necessary, though not a sufficient, condition for human thought.[15] According to Etienne Gilson, "In any genuinely Aristotelian metaphysics, the form of corporeal individuals does not subsist apart from the matter to which it owes its individuation."[16] Although this view affirms the presence of a human intellectual faculty that is immaterial "in its operation," it denies that such a faculty can be immaterial "in its mode of being." In other words, the human intellect, albeit immaterial, is nonetheless inextricably entwined with body and brain and thus is inseparable from its material foundation.

Even if one accepts this distinction, it remains true that Adler's failure to reexamine his theological position in the light of his views on the intellect exposes his own argument to the charge of materialism. It may even be that Adler has not been entirely faithful to Aristotle on this point; for if that philosopher held that the form of a corporeal substance cannot *subsist* apart from its material foundation, he also held that the form (not the matter) by which such a being is a substance "is what truly *is* in that which actually is."[17]

For Aristotle, incorporeal substances *exist* in even a larger sense than do purely corporeal ones. Yet as we have seen, Adler defines "cosmos" restrictively as "the totality of everything that exists *physically*" (emphasis added). But if incorporeal substances exist (and Adler appears to think that holding otherwise is unwarrantably to presuppose materialism), it is arbitrary and unreasonable to exclude, without argument, such substances (or anything else that truly exists) from the definition of a cosmos.

PLATO AND PARMENIDES

The question about the status of the intellect is closely related to—if not derived from—problems concerning the universal and the particular, the one and the many, the whole and its parts. Some of these problems were raised and discussed in connection with the "reason of the common law" and again in connection with natural law and positive law. Plato's *Parmenides* addresses these problems in a somewhat surprising manner. Plato is often thought to have held a view that has been called "immoderate immaterialism,"[18] asserting a radical independence of the intelligible from the sensible worlds and attributing the fullness of being only to purely intelligible objects of thought—the "forms" or "ideas." Yet such a judgment may be overly harsh, at least when applied to Plato's later works. We have already seen that, even for Aristotle, whose views are usually distinguished sharply from those of Plato on this account, the forms of things constitute definitive attributes of reality.

In *Parmenides*, Plato raises Aristotle's contention (later defended by Aquinas, though with a different interpretation)[19] that the forms cannot subsist independently of the things in which they are embodied. In the dialogue, Parmenides criticizes Socrates for wanting to talk about the forms and the world of physical reality as two completely separate worlds, to which he has been led by the view that the forms have independent existence.[20]

The problem is this: if Being is a "form" or an "essence" that somehow imparts being to the things it is embodied in, then Being must be a unity (i.e., "one"). But for Being to be embodied in such a way as to impart being to individual, particular things, it must be dispersed (i.e., "many"). There must be a bridge between the world of the forms and the world of physical reality. Being must be susceptible to differentiation. But for Parmenides, since there can be no self-subsisting forms, Being must contain within itself Non-being as possibility; indeed, in the ultimate, Being and Non-being must be One, the unity of which is "Becoming." Hence the long speech of Parmenides in Plato's dialogue is devoted to explicating the paradoxical implications of this idea.[21] According to Eric Voegelin, the Parmenidean insight was an attack on Homeric-Hesiodian symbolism regarding the plurality of particular things, and it arose from an essentially religious experience:

> If the experience of the Beyond was to be adequately expressed, it could not be classified as one of the "things," of *ta eonta*, in which it was revealed as a formative presence. In Parmenides [the man] we have to note, therefore, the transition from the plural *ta eonta* to the singular *to eon*. The "being" that is compactly predicated of all being "things" becomes for him the "Being" that is none of the "things."[22]

In *Timaeus*, Plato again takes up the problem of the conceptual and existential tension produced by the Parmenidean insight:

> First then, in my judgment, we must make a distinction and ask, What is that which always is and has no becoming; and what is that which is always becoming and never is? That which is apprehended by intelligence and reason is always in the same state; but that which is conceived by opinion with the help of sensation and without reason, is always in a process of becoming and perishing and never really is.[23]

Without going into the details of Timaeus's creation myth, Plato's answer must be considered faithful in all relevant respects to his experience of the world. And his experience was that of a Greek philosopher living in the pagan Mediterranean world four centuries before the incarnation of Christ as *logos* and the Christian philosophy that followed upon that event.

The simultaneous presence of being and non-being (becoming) demands a "third presence" in which the tension between being and non-being is somehow contained and preserved. This third presence is a created Cosmos, or an All *(to pan)*, that comprises and comprehends the whole of existence—material and immaterial, particular and universal, temporal and eternal—in the fullness of its paradoxical, tensional character but that does not strive to overcome its irreducibly mysterious nature.[24]

It will be noted that I did not say the tension is "resolved," because the tensional character of the experience that produces the Parmenidean insight (the simultaneous presence of actual being and possible non-being) is inescapably paradoxical.

Resolution of the problem, in the intellectual context of Plato's time, would have risked the consequences of attempting to abolish the very tension that brought the insight to consciousness in the first place. Had Plato attempted a resolution, he might have been led in the direction of the attempted solution of Hegel, who, according to Voegelin, "tried to master the problem by inventing a language that would out-comprehend the comprehending paradox."[25] Rather than moving in that direction, Plato rightly chooses to leave the matter as he finds it, allowing the spectacular linguistic ambiguities that characterize his *Parmenides* to remain fully ambiguous.

Conceptual resolution of the tension would have required defining being not as an essence but as the composite of essence and existence later suggested by Thomas Aquinas and developed by Etienne Gilson. Remember that essences are the formal attributes of things, their defining or essential features, and, as such, characterize merely possible, as well as actually existing, beings. Though one cannot really "think" at all without thinking of essences, essences alone cannot account for the actual existence of any actually existing being. Existence imparts to being, or adds to essence, a radical "givenness" that is not reducible to the formal attributes of anything.

Plato was forced to leave the Parmenidean problem unresolved because he conceived Being simply as an essence or a form, not complexedly as a composite of essence and existence. Yet it is the composite nature of being that gives rise to the conceptual possibility of not being, for non-being is only conceivable by, to, and for an actually existing being. The situation is not very different in biology, where death is possible only for one who is alive. Death is characterized not by annihilation, but by the reduction of a composite substance to its constituent parts, as "any composition entails the possibility of its own decomposition."[26] That is also why souls, which are simple, not composite, substances, are necessarily immortal.[27]

But let us not be too hard on Plato, Parmenides, and other thinkers in antiquity for not "solving" this problem. As I have suggested, full existential resolution of the tension can be obtained only by a joinder of essence and existence in concrete reality: a *logos* incarnate. At the same time, existence is prior to essence in the sense that, though an essence is what makes a being to be such a being as it is, existence is what makes it to be any kind of actually existing being at all. According to Gilson,

> This is to say that "to be," or to exist, is the supreme act of all that is. And the reason for it is clear, since, before being anything else, that is, this or that substance, any substance *is*, or is a "being." The form of a horse makes it "to be a horse"; it does not make it to be, nor, consequently, does it make it to be a being. And so, if being comes first in reality, then the existential act which causes it should come first among the constituent acts of concrete reality.[28]

Since the incarnate word had not yet appeared in Plato's time, thus effecting the existential resolution that would lay a foundation for the subsequent conceptual resolution of Aquinas and others, it seems unfair to blame the thinkers of antiquity for an overreaching essentialism, as Adler, Gilson, and many others are prone to do.

In any event, the idea of being as joinder of essence and existence in a composite from which existence has priority resolves (or supersedes) the problem that led to Aristotle's distinction between the modus operandi and modus essendi of the intellect. Remember that the distinction followed from the need to bridge the gulf between the forms of things and their actual existence, a gulf that itself was occasioned by the formalist metaphysics of the age—the restriction of being to essences, to their "whatness." That even Aristotle failed to escape this metaphysics is confirmed by Gilson in his description of the radical transformation of Aristotelian metaphysics wrought in the Christian philosophy of Thomas Aquinas:

> True enough, Aristotle's metaphysics was already a thorough dynamism, but it was a dynamism of the form. The form of the being-still-to-be was there, acting as both the formal law of its development and as the end to be reached by that development. Aristotelian beings were self-realizing formal types, and the only cause for their individual variations rested with the accidental failures of various matters completely to imbibe the forms. Individuals then were little more than abortive attempts to be their own forms; none of them could add anything to its species; rather, there was infinitely more in the species than there was in the whole collection of its individuals. Because Aristotelianism had been a dynamism, Thomas Aquinas has seen his way to including it within his own metaphysics of being, but, because it had been a dynamism of the form, he has had to deepen it into a dynamism of *esse* (to be). When he did it, the whole philosophical outlook on reality at once became different. Each and every individual, even among corporeal beings, was hence forward to enjoy its own *to be,* that is, a to be of its own; and this is why, in such a doctrine, to be is not univocal, but analogical in its own right. True enough, corporeal individuals still remain individuated by matter, but if they owe matter their individuation, they are indebted to their to be for their individuality. For indeed, "all that which is has its to be," . . . and "that to be is its own. . . ." It is also true that such individuals still are determined by their forms, but they no longer are the automatic self-realizations of forms merely hampered by the natural indocility of matter; they are individualities in the making, each of which is being actively built up by its own *esse.* And this, of course, is eminently true in the case of man, whose soul is itself an intellectual substance. There still is formal causality in such a doctrine, and it remains whole, but it has been metamorphosed by its subordination to efficient existential causality.[29]

If the intellect's mode of being is both essential and existential, then any distinction between the intellect's mode of being and its modus operandi seems beside the point. To be, no less than to operate, is to act; and active operation fully presupposes active being. If beings *are* by virtue of their existence, they are *what they are* by virtue of their essence or nature. If the nature of an intellectual being is to operate so as to render accessible a realm of purely intelligible, immaterial objects of thought, then the existence of that being is defined and constituted by the immaterial nature of its operation and its object. While discussing the incorruptibility of intellectual substances, Thomas Aquinas observes:

> A sign of this incorruptibility can be gathered from its intellectual operation, for since everything acts according as it is in act, the operation of a thing indicates its mode of being. Now the species and nature of the operation is understood from the object. But an intelligible object, being above time, is everlasting. Hence every intellectual substance is incorruptible of its own nature.[30]

THE BEST TRADITIONAL ARGUMENT REVISITED

Adler's distinction between the being and operation of the intellect, based largely on Aristotle, should be rejected. Indeed, Plato's conception of a cosmos is better than Adler's because it comprehends more of existence and is more in accord with experience. We do *not* experience reality as purely physical any more than we experience things in the world as merely particular. (See Chapter 12 for a discussion of the experience of laws as particular.)

The main argument Adler advances for the existence of an immaterial intellectual faculty, and thus for a radical ("in kind") rather than a superficial ("in degree") distinction between humans and animals, is the impossibility of otherwise explaining our use of general nouns that represent "classes" or "kinds" (i.e., "universals") even though our sensory experience of things in the world seems always to be of "individuals" or "particulars."[31] Yet the facts that nothing purely physical has ever been experienced as universal or that no universal concept can be fully contained in matter remain facts no matter how the cosmos is defined. The paradox of particulars and universals, the tension between the material and the immaterial, or that between the temporal and the eternal, cannot be put aside merely by making a distinction between the intellect's being "immaterial as to mode of operation" and its being "immaterial as to mode of being."

The cryptic final words of Voegelin's *In Search of Order* are apropos: "The paradoxic tension in the revelation of formative reality is experienced as ultimate in the sense that intelligibly it cannot be out-experienced or out-symbolized by further experiences of reality. This experienced ultimacy of the tension becomes luminous in the symbol 'divine.' "[32]

It is therefore appropriate to revise Adler's earlier definition in accord with the findings in his more recent volume(s). "Cosmos" must then be defined as "the totality of everything that exists physically or non-physically." When we read this definition back into the rejected third premise of the "best traditional" cosmological argument, that premise appears in an altogether different light. It was initially rejected on the basis of the principle of inertia applied by analogy to the realm of material existence, an analogy justified because the principle of inertia is itself derived from our experience of the material world. But there is no parallel justification for extending the analogy to things that exist nonmaterially, even if such things are inextricably entwined with material substances. It would thus appear that immaterial intellects, like angels, are in need of an efficient exnihilating preservative cause in order to maintain their continuing existence from moment to moment. To assume otherwise is equivalent to presupposing materialism.

Revising the third premise in accord with this reasoning yields a new version: "A contingent being distinctively defined in terms of its possession of an immaterial intellect (a psyche, or "soul," or "mind") is one that needs a cause of its continuing existence at every moment of its endurance in existence." Since this version of the third premise is not exposed to the objections that defeated the initial version, and since all the other premises in the "best traditional" argument are true, it follows that the cosmological argument, so interpreted, establishes the existence of a supreme being that is the exnihilating preservative cause of the continuing existence of contingent beings who are characterized by their possession of an immaterial intellectual faculty (i.e., whose "minds" are "over" their "matter").

It also follows that this argument, unlike Adler's "truly cosmological" argument, establishes the existence of a God who stands in a direct relationship to the individual parts of the cosmos, including human beings and human societies. The presence of such a God provides a fully sufficient, transcendent ground of individual order in the psyche and social order in the polis; and thus a fully sufficient ground for the attribution of normative significance to the historical events, beliefs, and institutional practices that make up the complex of relationships between psyche and polis that are constitutive for any polity representable in historical time—its underlying "real" constitution.

A qualification is now in order. Neither Adler's truly cosmological argument nor my version of the best traditional cosmological argument establishes the existence of a supreme being with certainty; that requires a leap of faith beyond reason. Adler's argument rests on the assertion that the cosmos as a whole is radically contingent, a merely possible cosmos. It is an assertion founded on a reasonable assessment of the structure of the cosmos insofar as we presently understand it. My argument rests on the assertion that the intellect is an immaterial or incorporeal substance. It is also a reasonable assertion because it best accords with present understanding, despite the efforts of scientists working in the field of artificial intelligence to refute it.[33]

Assertions of this kind may be regarded as true only because, negatively speaking, science has not proved them to be false, and because, positively speaking, the weight of experience at this point in the development of knowledge appears to confirm them. In other words, they can only be regarded as true "beyond a reasonable doubt." Continuing for a moment longer with lawyer's talk: why "beyond a reasonable doubt" rather than by "preponderance of the evidence"? Because "reasonable doubt" is necessarily circumscribed by the requirements of rational argument and enquiry, not merely by the strictures normally placed on the evaluation of observational data.

If rational philosophic enquiry is a persistent, uncompromising effort to explain what needs to be explained and cannot (at least at present) be explained by scientific investigation, coming to a halt only when there is nothing left to explain,[34] then there exists a rational obligation to exhaust all avenues of enquiry (including that of reasoning about the character of unobservable entities) so as to ensure the subordination of doubt to reason. The alternative is to elevate doubt into dogma.

MATTER, SPIRIT, AND A PROOF OF GOD'S EXISTENCE

The strength of the theological arguments just outlined may perhaps be seen more clearly by contrasting them to their most pervasive competitor in modern times, that of materialism. The best place to start is with the cardinal presupposition of Hobbes, presupposed because never argued for but simply presumed: that fundamental reality is composed of matter—the principle of "metaphysical materialism," or "materialistic monism." Conceived as an outgrowth of scientific method, or, put differently, as an epistemological assertion that all that is "really" known is known by virtue of the logic inherent in material investigations, the idea is known as "scientific materialism."

It is hardly new, having been asserted by the Ionian thinkers of ancient Greece, in opposition to which Western philosophy was founded by Socrates and his disciples.[35] As Stanley Jaki has recently argued, some of the origins of modern science may be found in the rejection of the Ionian view.[36] Indeed, it is otherwise inconceivable, since "science," conceived in modern terms, as a particular reality made accessible by the application of a particular method, comes to light only in relationship to that which is not understandable in terms of that method.

As was demonstrated brilliantly by Kant in *Critique of Pure Reason*, the particular reality that is not understandable in terms of modern scientific method is supraphenomenal, or noumenal reality: "things in themselves," which lie beyond the province of "sensuous cognition."

> The conception of a *noumenon*, that is, of a thing which must be cogitated not as an object of sense, but as a thing in itself (solely through the pure understanding), is not self-contradictory, for we are not entitled to maintain that sensibility is the only possible mode of intuition. Nay, further, this conception is necessary to restrain sensuous intuition within the bounds of phenomena, and thus to limit the objective validity of

sensuous cognition; for things in themselves, which lie beyond its province, are called *noumena* for the very purpose of indicating that this cognition does not extend its application to all that the understanding thinks.[37]

In his preface to the second edition of the *Critique,* Kant is emphatic about the centrality of this point to the entire project, saying that "The estimate of our rational cognition *a priori* at which we arrive is that it has only to do with phenomena, and that things in themselves, while possessing a real existence, lie beyond its sphere."[38]

According to A.D. Lindsay, the ultimate effect of these distinctions, consistent with the fundamental purpose of Kant's thought in general, is to clarify the distinction between science and morality: to preserve "the integrity and independence of science without prejudice to the integrity of the principles of conduct" through limitation of the scope of rational scientific thinking (speculative reason) to its proper objects.[39] Without such a limitation, the domain of moral thought (practical reason) would be unduly circumscribed and the "principles of conduct" severely compromised:

> Kant has shown the validity of the assumptions of the sciences by showing that they are principles of the possibility of objective experience. They are implied in any judgment which claims to be true. For without them the distinction between subjective and objective has no meaning. But if we can assume the validity of principles which we can show to be implied in the distinction between truth and falsehood, we can equally assume the validity of principles which can be shown to be implied in the distinction between right and wrong. As Kant has shown in the "Analytic" to this *Critique* that there could be no meaning in the distinction between true and false if we denied the validity of the categories, so he shows in his discussion of conduct that there can be no meaning in the distinction between right and wrong unless we assume the freedom of the will and the transcendency of moral purposes. The principles implied in conduct have a metaphysical status, for, unlike the principles of the sciences, they are assumptions about the nature of reality or they are nothing. If Kant's negative doctrine sets severe limits to the speculative reason, his positive doctrine makes high claims for practical reason. His criticism of the metaphysical status of the principles of science leaves room for the metaphysical status of the principles of conduct.[40]

From an epistemological point of view, the embrace of materialism by modern thinkers is more aptly termed "scientistic" than scientific, since it rests upon an unwarranted extension of methods appropriate to one mode of reality to fields wholly unreachable by those methods. It thereby renders incoherent the scientific enterprise itself by destroying the boundaries that mark out its limits.

This unwarranted methodological extension has taken several forms since the time of Kant. One of the most prominent of these is an overreaching—yet stunted and hardened—empiricism that has sometimes traveled under the denotation "logical positivism," a term once made fashionable by A. J. Ayer and his followers. Though positivistic empiricism is hardly the dominant paradigm in the natural sciences today, it has retained a large influence in the social sciences. According to Ayer, all human utterances are either factual reports based on observation, mathematical tautologies, or metaphysical/theological statements—which Ayer terms "senseless."[41] The logical positivists thus cope with science's failure to access noumenal reality by denying the very existence (or at least the meaningfulness) of any nonphenomenal reality. Kant's discussion of the "cosmological antinomies" in the *Critique of Pure Reason* both anticipates and answers Ayer's manifesto. In the midst of an argument defending empiricism against dogmatism, Kant remarks that

> if—as often happens—empiricism, in relation to ideas, becomes itself dogmatic, and boldly denies that which is above the sphere of its phenomenal cognition, it falls itself into the error of intemperance—an error which is here all the more reprehensible, as thereby the practical interest of reason [its interest in principles of conduct] receives an irreparable injury.[42]

This "boundary error" is a species of a more general mistake noted by Eric Voegelin involving "the improper transfer of categories fashioned for things of the external [phenomenal] world to problems of transcendence."[43] The modern scientistic thinker, stumbling over these unrecognized boundaries, falls into a void, the various reactions to which have generated such prominent enterprises in modern thought as behavioralism, progressivism, nihilism, and gnosticism. For present purposes, I wish to suggest only that the success of these enterprises is predicated in no small measure upon the truth of Hobbesian materialism and its epistemological corollary: that the human mind, or psyche, is fully reducible to the physical functions of the brain.[44] Moreover, even if these enterprises turn out to be successful in the long run, materialism has little, if any, bearing on the reasonableness of traditional beliefs in a supreme being.

In order to demonstrate the truth of this proposition, I need only make a single assumption. Admittedly, the assumption is controversial and was denied by Kant with respect to knowability.[45] My supposition is that the phenomena of nature are (or are reflections of) "things in themselves" that exist independently of human cognition and that are knowable as such. As G. K. Chesterton noted in his biography of Thomas Aquinas, the denial of the supposition that things in the external world are real, which amounts to saying that "a thing can 'be' intelligible and not as yet 'be' at all," constitutes the major "stumbling block" of modern philosophy.[46]

In view of the discussion in Chapter 14 of contractarianism, nominalism, and coherence epistemology in the artifactual constitutional world of William Harris, it is perhaps not too much to say that such a denial is a major problem for contemporary constitutional theory as well. As elsewhere, Chesterton's views are worth extensive quotation on this point.

> Since the modern world began in the sixteenth century, nobody's system of philosophy has really corresponded to everybody's sense of reality; to what, if left to them-

selves, common men would call common sense. Each started with a paradox; a peculiar point of view demanding the sacrifice of what they would call a sane point of view. This is the one thing common to Hobbes and Hegel, to Kant and Bergson, to Berkeley and William James. A man had to believe something that no normal man would believe, if it were suddenly propounded to his simplicity; as that law is above right, or right is outside reason, or things are only as we think them, or everything is relative to a reality that is not there. The modern philosopher claims, like a sort of confidence man, that if once we will grant him this, the rest will be easy; he will straighten out the world, if once he is allowed to give this one twist to the mind.[47]

The supposition, following Chesterton and Aquinas, that "the primary act of recognition of any reality [including the reality of the material world] is real"[48] renders admissible the following kind of argument: "Matter" is extended in space and time and is therefore "finite." "Finite," in its most general sense, means "characterized by limits," and so something not characterized by limits must be nonfinite, or "infinite." The "excluded middle" between finitude and infinity follows from the presumption regarding the reality and knowability of the external world.

Now, if the cosmos is infinite, it has no beginning or end (either in space or in time). Thus it could not have been created, since "creation" (in this cosmological sense) requires bringing something into existence out of nothing ("exnihilation"—see Adler, *How To Think About God*) and thereby implies a "beginning."

If the only way a thing can be brought into existence *ex nihilo* is by an act of creation, it follows that either the cosmos was created or it has no beginning or end. But since all matter is finite, the following propositions are necessarily true: (1) if the cosmos is wholly material, it is finite, has a beginning or end, and is therefore created; (2) if the cosmos is infinite, it has no beginning or end, and thus cannot be material. Further, by double negation (3) if the cosmos is *not* nonmaterial (i.e., if it is material) it has *not* no beginning or end (i.e., it has a beginning or end), and is therefore not infinite (i.e., it is finite). In other words, propositions two and three are rigorously equivalent propositions.

Since we can assume that the cosmos is either material in toto or it is not (i.e., either it is fully material or it contains immaterial elements), we are now in a position to evaluate fully the materialistic assumption of modern political philosophy. Assuming first that the cosmos is material it follows that the cosmos is finite, has a beginning or end, and is created (by proposition one). Since matter cannot have been exnihilated by matter (else it would have been created "out of something" and thus not exnihilated), the cosmos must have been created by something nonmaterial. But things that are nonmaterial and, at the same time, are alive in the sense that they could create, are necessarily "spiritual"; and such beings that do, in fact, create, are what we denote by the term "gods." It follows that, if the cosmos is truly material, it must have been created by a god (or by gods); and since anything that creates must also exist, it follows that at least one god exists.

Assuming, alternatively, that the cosmos is immaterial (not material in toto), whatever is immaterial is spiritual, and creative spiritual beings are "gods" (uncreative spiritual beings might, for example, be referred to as "angels"). It follows that, since the cosmos is immaterial (by assumption), it must have been constituted by a god (or by gods). But for gods to constitute a cosmos, they must exist. Therefore at least one god exists.

Whether or not one accepts this sort of demonstration as conclusive with respect to the existence of a supreme being (or of supreme beings), it does show clearly that rational belief in such a being cannot be undermined merely by presupposing materialism. Yet materialism is the fundamental presupposition of modern atheism.

That metaphysical, monistic, scientistic materialism—and thereby atheism—is incoherent at its core should not be surprising, in view of the point I have made repeatedly: that human reality is experienced as a tensional struggle in the Platonic *metaxy*, or an "in-between" of existence, between matter and spirit.[49] Any attempt to do away completely with one of these polarities will inevitably result in concealment of the experiential basis through which the other is brought to light. That is why materialism and atheism are fundamentally contrary to human experience and have been so regarded throughout the larger and better part of human history.

Though, as Chesterton noted, dogmatic materialism began its rise in the sixteenth century, its ascendancy was not complete until the nineteenth century, when a succession of such prominent thinkers as Laplace in physics, Lyell in geology, Darwin in biology, Marx in economics, and Freud in psychology offered purportedly "scientific" theories explaining the origins of the solar system, the earth's topography, new forms of life, social structures, and human behavior solely in terms of material determinants or physical processes.[50] By the onset of the twentieth century, the rupture between science and religion had become so complete that, according to Stephen C. Meyer,

> For many intellectuals a scientifically-informed world view was a materialistic world view in which the mere mention of entities such as God, free will, mind, soul, or purpose seemed inherently disreputable. Materialism denied evidence of any intelligent design in nature and any ultimate purpose to human existence.[51]

During the present century, this worldview hardened into what George Gilder recently has termed the "materialist superstition."[52] Noting the "continued prevalence" of the superstitious belief that everything in existence is reducible to "mundane, wholly physical processes," Gilder quotes the dictum of a leading medical school neuroscientist cited in a 1995 *Time* magazine cover story. In a manner reminiscent of Chesterton's "fundamental skeptic–modern philosopher–confidence man," the neuroscientist blandly declares that " 'being awake or being conscious is nothing but a dreamlike state' that has 'no objective reality' because we can 'never actually touch or measure it.' "[53]

Yet, as Meyer has pointed out, twentieth-century scientists are well behind twentieth-century science; for it is science itself, especially quantum physics, molecular biology, and information theory, that has undermined ideological materialism more thoroughly than any book of theology or philosophy could have done.[54] For example, while reviewing the recent literature in origin-of-life biology, Meyer considers "the probabilistic hurdles that must be overcome to construct even one short protein molecule of about one hundred amino acids in length."[55] Such a molecule is simpler than most protein molecules and considerably simpler than DNA or RNA.

After describing these hurdles at length, which include chemical bonding, mirror imaging, and sequential arrangement, Meyer concludes that "the probability of achieving a functional sequence of amino acids in several functioning proteins at random" (a minimal requisite for the origination of life by chance rather than by design) is roughly $1/10^{65}$—a fraction the denominator of which happens to be the number of atoms in our galaxy.[56] Meyer embellishes the example:

> In light of these results, biochemist Michael Behe has compared the odds of attaining proper sequencing in a 100 amino acid length proteins to the odds of a blindfolded man finding a single marked grain of sand hidden in the Sahara Desert, not once, but three times. Moreover, if one also factors in the probability of attaining proper bonding and optical isomers, the probability of constructing a rather short, functional protein at random becomes so small as to be effectively zero (1 chance in 10^{135}) even given our multi-billion-year-old universe.[57]

Findings like these suggest that it is time to reexamine such past theological efforts as the "argument from design" in light of recent developments in modern science. They suggest the virtual impossibility of life in an ordered cosmos having originated or persevered by accident. They suggest the ultimate futility of continuing efforts to account for ourselves, our societies, our world, or our universe by resort to physical factors alone. They confirm the high plausibility of regarding the cosmos, life itself, and, for humans, such institutional outworkings of life as the law, to be the production of an ordering intelligence. Jacques Maritain explains modern science's failure to access the whole of reality while pointing a ray of light to the future:

> The modern image of the atom—each day more complicated, more mysterious and more fecund in practical applications—is a mathematical image or ideal entity founded on reality, which gives us an invaluable symbolical or phenomenological knowledge of *how matter behaves*, but cannot instruct us philosophically or ontologically about *what matter is*. Yet the fact remains that the conceptions of modern science and the extraordinary progress of microphysics provide the human intellect with a scientific imagery, an imaginable or supra-imaginable picture of nature which is incomparably more favorable to the edification of a philosophy of nature and more open to the deepening labor of metaphysical reason than the old Newtonian physics.

The opportunity is now given for that reconciliation between science and wisdom for which the human mind thirsts.[58]

Though it may take the scientific community a generation or two to catch up with its science—and the social science community perhaps three or four generations—if Gilder, Meyer, Behe, and others with similar views are right, materialism is already dead. I am convinced that, when its demise has been generally acknowledged, the secularized, judicialized constitutionalism of present times will be seen to have collapsed with it.

17 · The Implications of Belief and the Continuity of the Western Legal Tradition

Dogmatic atheism is contrary to human experience not only because it is fundamentally and necessarily grounded in a self-refuting materialism, and is therefore contrary to reason, but also because people, from time immemorial, have experienced human reality as constituted by a divine or transcendent appeal that demands acceptance or rejection. This kind of experience is by no means confined to such prototypical examples of acceptance as the famous conversion scene in Augustine's *Confessions*.[1] It is also present in Kant's call for adoption of a moral point of view consisting of a "kingdom of ends" that necessarily transcends any preoccupation with things in the merely contingent or "sensible" world.[2] And it is in the Jewish experience of "chosenness," first described in the Book of Exodus and reinforced throughout more than three millennia of historical existence, most recently in the reaffirmation of the Kantian imperative in response to the Holocaust of the mid-twentieth century.

Acceptance is present in the calls of such men as Mohandas Gandhi and Martin Luther King to participation in a theistically driven morality that is experienced as superseding that which is in effect in the given society of the time. And it is in countless other examples, in which perceived injustices lead to efforts to transform human law in accord with precepts regarded as "higher."

On the other hand, rejection, too, is apparent. It is found in the ancient heresies against which Augustine so forcibly and effectively inveighed.[3] It is also seen in the negative utopias of such gnostic political reformers as Comte and Marx, in the systems of such thinkers as Hegel and Heidegger, and in the actual attempts of such men as Stalin and Hitler to establish godless societies in the world by force of arms.

Eric Voegelin remarks that the earliest known usage of the term "theology" in the history of philosophy occurs in Plato's *Republic*, in which Plato refers to a particular set of propositions, invoked during his time to deny God's existence, concern for human affairs, or both, as *typoi peri theologias* (types of theology).[4] According to Voegelin, these negative propositions express, in Greek society, "the potentiality of responding to the divine appeal by rejecting it."[5] Plato offers the propositions in the *Republic* and the *Laws:*

1a. It seems that no gods exist;
2a. Even if they do exist, they do not care about men;
3a. Even if they care, they can be propitiated by gifts.[6]

Voegelin ascribes this triad to the Sophistic School, since its structure is identical to another found in the essay "On Being," by Gorgias, the famous teacher of rhetoric whose name gives the title to another Platonic dialogue:

1b. Nothing exists;
2b. If anything exists, it is incomprehensible;
3b. If it is comprehensible, it is incommunicable.[7]

The triads clearly express more than mere skepticism. They suggest a profound contempt for the gods and a corresponding truncation of experience directly analogous to that found in radical empiricism, logical and legal positivism, and nihilistic existentialism. According to Voegelin, they show a "general loss of experiential contact with cosmic-divine reality," that is, "a radical denial of divine reality experienced as present in either the order of the cosmos or the soul of man."[8]

Plato's response, prefaced by a lengthy apology deploring the embarrassing fact that such a response is called for in the society of his time, is an early form of the argument from motion based on the idea of a first cause and may be found in Book 10 of the *Laws*, in which Plato attacks the underlying metaphysical materialism of the Sophistic constructions. Particularly, he attacks the assumption that "all reality originates in the movement of material elements."[9]

Against this view Plato argues convincingly that the immaterial psyche, not the material element, is the only reality commonly experienced as self-moving. The very commonality of the experience points to the divine Psyche as the source of "the self-movement in which all ordered movement in the world originates."[10] Thus, "Not the existence of God is at stake, but the existence of man."[11] Plato shows that the two sets of negative propositions are intimately related so that, if those in the first set are true, then so must be their counterparts in the second. The very existence of a human psyche is experienced as radically dependent upon the corresponding existence and operation of a divine Psyche.

For Plato, the negative propositions are not "a philosopher's statement concerning a structure in reality" but are "the syndrome of a disease that affects man's humanity and destroys the order of society."[12] Thus the need to respond to them by constructing a proof that the gods exist is both deplorable and embarrassing to Plato.

> [Plato's] argument sounds quite modern in its recourse to the reality of the psyche, and of its experiences, against constructions that express the loss of reality and the contraction of the self. . . . But it is neither modern nor ancient; it rather is the argument that will recur whenever the quest of divine reality has to be resumed in a situation in which the "rationalization" of contracted existence, the existence of the fool, has become a mass phenomenon. The argument, of course, is not a "proof" in the sense of a logical demonstration . . . , but only in the sense of . . . a pointing to an area of reality that the constructor of the negative propositions has chosen to overlook, or to ignore, or refuses to perceive. One cannot prove reality by a syllogism; one can only point to it and invite the doubter to look. The more or less deliberate confusion of the two meanings of the word "proof" is still a standard trick employed by the negators in the contemporary ideological debates; and it plays an important role in the genesis of the "proofs" for the existence of God ever since the time of Anselm.[13]

Modern constitutional theory denies the relevance of divinity and spirituality for the conduct of public affairs, yet the fundamental presuppositions underlying that very theory compel no such denial. Therefore the denial itself is a matter of choice, and the expectations based on this choice are articles of faith, not reason.

Since faith implies lack of certainty, it may be concluded that the proponents of modern constitutional secularism have *chosen* to assert, *without proof*, at least one of the following propositions: (1) that there is no God; or (2) that, if there is, he is unconcerned with the public affairs of humans; or (3) that, even if there is a God who is concerned with human affairs, this concern is not accessible to human reason. It will be recognized that these three propositions are functionally equivalent to the Sophistic triads, with the Gorgian version of the third proposition substituted for Plato's version (i.e., substituting 3b for 3a). It should also be noted that 3b, when read together with the second half of 2b, amounts to a denial of the classical notion of reason, conceived as a faculty providing access to an intelligible realm, a realm of pure objects of thought, or of things as such.

Since all (other than merely wishful) thinking about God presupposes the existence, comprehensibility, and communicability of such a realm (or of such objects), it follows that an assertion of proposition 3b entails the central tenet of modern constitutional faith: the gnostic replacement of God with man as ruler of the legal cosmos. This ideology nowadays travels under the term "humanism," a name laced with irony since there is hardly anything humanistic about the worldview that is represented by the label. Rather, modern constitutional thought tends to view the human being as just another kind of animal, and many (if not most) modern constitutional "rights" look toward fulfillment of drives and desires stemming largely from animal natures.

Thus have such principles as equality of opportunity degenerated into the notion of equality of material conditions, or the right of marital privacy into that of a right to pursue uninhibited sexual gratification through sodomy or pornography, or the right of subsistence into that of a right to consumer credit, or the right of personal autonomy in procreative matters into that of a right to eliminate the fruits of such activity by unrestricted access to abortion on demand, or the right of believers to be let alone while worshiping peacefully into that of a right of unbelievers not to be confronted with the artifacts of belief in public places. The wrong-headedness of each of these extensions is self-evident to anyone with a just measure of common sense. They are all examples of the paradox stated by Oliver Wendell Holmes, Sr.: "Give us the luxuries of life and we will dispense with the necessities."[14] Carried sufficiently far, equality of material conditions will invariably cancel equality of opportunity. Carried sufficiently far, a right to sexual gratification through sodomy or pornography will invariably impair the right of a married couple to raise their own children as they see fit. Carried sufficiently far, a right of unbelievers not to be confronted with the artifacts of belief will invariably impair the right of believers to worship, and so on.

These examples are paradoxical only in appearance. The paradoxical effect in each instance is the result of the self-contradictory character arising from the material or physical essence of what is protected in each bundle of "rights." As Plato taught, all physical substances have in common a capacity for exhaustion by overextension. A familiar example is the "scratching an itch" analogy of the *Gorgias*.[15] The issue is also treated in the *Phaedo*, where Plato distinguishes between things that can have (or be) opposites and things that cannot.[16]

Materialism, with its complement of truncations and reductions, leads to a debased view of human nature and a corresponding vulgarization of the human sciences, including that of jurisprudence. Much as the Ionian philosophers of old, mistakenly assuming that all was matter, embarked on a futile search for its fundamental constituent, modern political and legal philosophers, though ostensibly eschewing or denying the actual existence of any fundamental *reality* at all, have nevertheless been positing substitute "realities" for the past 350 years.

From Hobbes's security against violent death to Locke's private property to Bentham's general utility to Mill's liberty of expression to the Rawlsian-Dworkinian equal concern and respect and beyond, modern constitutional theorists, following modern political philosophers, have searched for the basic principle that will somehow fill the void created by the largely unexamined philosophical presuppositions of their own theories. Uncritically accepting a debased and debauched human nature, these theorists then try to "elevate" that nature by persuading policymakers—especially judges, in recent times—to impose their favored "values" on everyone else.[17]

Like Chesterton's fundamental skeptic, who first denies everything and then admits something, today's court-watching, values-oriented constitutional theorists begin by denying God, human nature, the intelligible world, the objectivity of values, the normativity of history, the authority of reason, sometimes even the real existence of the objects of sense perception—in short, just about everything on which any truly adequate constitutional theory would have to be based (so they are not really "fundamental"). They then end up admitting some conjured-up "value" such as "equal concern and respect" or "tolerance of diversity" or "liberty of contract" or "personal autonomy," none of which has any foundation without the support of one or more of the very principles previously denied (so they are not really "skeptical").

Penultimately, unsatisfied with the prospect that their highly partial, ungrounded, favored "value" might indeed be regarded as only partially constitutive for the polity, the theorists assert its general applicability, sometimes even going so far as to claim that all other constitutional principles are derivative from or subordinate to it. Such is the case, for example, with Dworkin's version of "equal concern and respect."[18]

The theorists then almost always conclude with the call for judicial imposition of the favored fundamental value(s) by the exercise of constitutional judicial review. That this final, crucial step is virtually invariable is shown clearly by the fact that few contemporary constitutional theorists are in the business of persuading the public, or its elected representatives, to accept their favored constitutional values. Rather, virtually all contemporary commentators attempt primarily to persuade judges, lawyers, and professors.

It can hardly be otherwise, since the prescriptions of many commentators, at least in their recommended applications, are at war with experience and common sense to such an extent that few normal persons would give them a moment's consideration.[19] Prescriptions thus arbitrarily conceived can be imposed only arbitrarily (as an act of will or power, not of reason) and in the contemporary American constitutional context—i.e., under a judicialized constitutionalism, this means by the courts.

The point is that to select such principles ("immersed in matter") as worthy of constitutional protection is fundamentally arbitrary. This arbitrariness is matched perfectly by the arbitrariness of their necessitated judicial application. Arbitrary principles, in a principled constitutional system, can be applied only arbitrarily (i.e., as a matter of will or power, not of law).

THE OBLIGATIONS OF REASON AND THE AUTHORITY OF TRADITION

According to Ockham's rule we are not entitled to affirm the real existence of unobserved phenomena unless such an affirmation is required in order to explain observed phenomena.[20] As Kant conclusively demonstrated in the *Critique of Pure Reason*, and as has been repeatedly confirmed by subsequent developments, modern science is based largely upon such affirmations.[21] As Mortimer Adler has demonstrated in *How to Think About God*, and as I have argued, so is rational, or natural, theology and naturalistic jurisprudence.[22]

As Adler has shown, we cannot adequately explain the continuing existence of the cosmos, conceived as a whole, without positing the real existence of a supreme being "as the supernatural—and uncaused—cause that explains the preservation of the cosmos if its existence is everlasting, or its creation if it came into being out of nothing."[23] And as I have shown, we cannot adequately account for our experience of the cosmos without positing a supreme being who is related to human institutions and traditional practices. Moreover, since "rational philosophical inquiry is a persistent effort to explain what needs to be explained and cannot be explained by scientific investigation, or any other form of inquiry that employs as its means perceptual observations and reflective or analytical thought," and since such an inquiry ceases "only when there is nothing left to be explained,"[24] positing the real existence of God is a rational obligation.

A similar obligation exists in the field of epistemology. Since the depth and variety of human knowledge and understanding cannot adequately be explained by reference to a purely material mental faculty in which Mind is reduced to "brain," we are obligated to posit the real existence of a purely immaterial intellectual faculty to which necessarily corresponds a realm of purely intelligible objects of thought. Since logical positivism, scientific materialism, and all forms of empiricism that rest on the presumption that our purely subjective ideas are the sole objects of human thought lead to absurd conclusions contradictory to common sense and common experience, rejection of such theories is a rational obligation for thinking beings.

The same kind of argument holds in jurisprudence. Since no form of legal positivism can adequately account for our common experience and our consistent enactment, throughout the entirety of recorded legal history, of universalizable legal norms, we are obligated to posit the real existence of a natural law derived from human nature and discoverable by reason in a transcendent source of order. Constitutions should be regarded as attempts to discover and capture, insofar as it is given to particular societies to do so, essential features of this order. And written constitutions are best viewed as symbolic forms developed for the representation of such societies in historical time.[25]

Natural law is thus a background against which all constitutions must, in the last analysis, be measured,[26] even though the "laws and rights of nature" can never be transformed into ordinary law applicable directly by courts.[27] At the same time, the universalizability of naturalistic legal norms requires that constitutions, in this sense, be regarded as thoroughly consensual in the manner described in Chapter 5. Since all truly consensual constitutional practices develop only over long periods of time, constitutional law must be conceived largely as a development of constitutional history.

The primacy of history implies that all forms of constitutional gnosticism must be rejected because they represent the efforts of a part of society to overcome the whole by subverting or circumventing the common experience that is the foundation of all truly consensual constitutional rules. These efforts include the enterprise of constitutional theory as articulated in the constitutional artifactualism of William Harris, as well as the purely textualist, extratextualist, and noninterpretive approaches in constitutional theory.

Judicial supremacy in all its forms (i.e., the joinder of judicial finality and judicial freedom) must also be rejected. I do not mean that textualism (or even extratextualism, for that matter) must be completely discarded; indeed, as we have seen, textualism, when related properly to intentionalism, is a time-honored mode of interpretation. Textualism divorced from intentionalism, however, the tendency of most contemporary constitutional theory as exemplified in Harris's constitutional thought, must be ruled out.

Most important, historical practice must be taken seriously; for, as I have suggested, faithfulness to experience demands recognition and acknowledgment of history's "double aspect." The meaningfulness of historical events and beliefs thus is experienced as arising from a tension between the immanent happenings themselves and the conceptual orderings from which the events and beliefs derive their significance. Although on rare occasions this tension appears to rise to the level of sharp contradiction, more often it is the pattern and regularity of the historical process itself, comprised in the well-known cliché about history repeating itself, that provide the impetus for the conceptualization and reconceptualization that make historiography both possible and necessary.

Tradition and reason are therefore complementary. Without historical recurrence, there is no raw material from which traditional practice may be drawn. Without the traditional practices that constitute (literally, "make up") institutional life, there is no way to reason about human social activity.

Recently, it has become fashionable to assert (or, more often, simply to assume) that human activity can be analyzed or evaluated in isolation from its historical foundations. Soterios Barber, for example, opposes the activity of "fresh moral argumentation" to that of following historical conventions in the law.[28] And behavioralistic social scientists at times attempt to quantify "snapshots" of human activity divorced from historical time.

But moral argumentation, not to mention the quantification of human behavior, especially when carried out without regard to the historical conventions that have determined in the past the manner in which authoritative moral decisions are made, is itself an institutional practice that serves particular interests and has important social consequences. To attempt analysis of any human activity without regard to its historicity is to risk a lapse into subjectivity and solipsism. History is objective because its patterns of recurrence simply are "there." Moreover, its continuities may be represented to the mind as pure objects of thought (intelligible abstractions) and subjected to reasoned analysis.

Eric Voegelin distinguishes the serious study of the "configuration of history" from the extremes of gnostic speculation about its meaning, on the one hand, and cynical disregard of its materials, on the other:

> The intelligible configuration is strictly a subject matter for empirical exploration. Our knowledge of it, at any given time, will depend on the state of science, which in its turn is determined by a) our knowledge of materials and b) the penetration of theoretical issues. This warning . . . disposes of the much debated question whether history is "subjective" or "objective," for all propositions concerning the configuration can be verified and falsified by the ordinary methods of science. Empirically, the propositions must take into account all the materials available. . . . If the range of subjectivity is nevertheless assumed to be quite large, the apparent largeness can be traced to certain conventions regarding the treatment of history that have come to be accepted as legitimate: from the empirical side it is considered legitimate, under the pretext of specialization, to ignore large bodies of well-known materials, though they would pertain to the configurative problem under discussion; from the theoretical side, it is considered legitimate to replace philosophical analysis by ideological speculation, by Weltanschauungen, by political opinions, or even by what just goes through somebody's head, as the principles for selecting historical phenomena and constructing a meaning of history.[29]

History is not only objective, it is also normative because its traditions constitute the institutional record of those continuities nurtured by particular societies as representative for them in historical time. At the same time, certain historical patterns, along with some traditional practices that appear to flow from them, transcend particular societies, places, and times, attaining a degree of historical constancy that dominates the historiographical landscape. The most prominent of these patterns may be found in the experiences of transcendence that gave rise to the earliest known historiographical writing in the ancient societies of Hellas, Israel, and China.[30]

HISTORICAL JURISPRUDENCE AND TRADITIONAL PRACTICE IN CONSTITUTIONAL LAW

The transcendent character of history, in which events, beliefs, and practices attain historical significance only as the result of reflective experiences that go beyond the merely immanent happenings themselves to their pattern and meaning, imparts to law a similarly transcendent character. Western legal history, from its "awakening" in Greek philosophy to the present time,[31] shows remarkable continuity both in its stages of development and in the constancy of its fundamental precepts.

Much as Eric Voegelin has argued for the rejection of a theory of "axial time" in favor of a theory of "dominant constants" in historiography,[32] I would argue against the prevailing theory of sharp divergence between different legal cultures in Western civilization in support of a theory of essential continuity in the Western legal tradition. Indeed, the constants that dominate the history of law and jurisprudence are even more pervasive than those that dominate history more generally. This observation should not be surprising, since law, beginning with historical materials that simply are "given," adds an element of artifice to nature, instituting regularities of behavior that are at once experienced as both descriptive and prescriptive.

For example, in Chapter 12 I discussed the distinction between universalizable legal norms and "rules of the road" in terms of the constantly recurring tension between legal naturalism and legal positivism. This tension, profoundly articulated in the dialogues of Plato, is discoverable in different guises throughout the entirety of Western jurisprudence. Within the naturalistic tradition, at least two variants of natural law have appeared in recurrent fashion at different times: a "revolutionary" brand, which stresses opposition to existing order and thus endangers the existence of society, and a "conservative" brand, which stresses preservation of a historically grown order.[33]

Closely related to the revolutionary brand of natural law is the social contract theory of the state, first analyzed by Plato in the *Republic*, which arises in "periods of spiritual and moral crisis" and "attempts to construct the order of a society out of the contractual relations between the members."[34] The inherent instability of the contractual approach, together with the truncated view of human nature that almost always accompanies it, has been discussed. As Eric Voegelin has suggested, contractualism historically has gone hand in hand with the idea of man as "motivated by passions alone" in situations where common participation in transcendent reality *(homonoia)* "is not recognized as existent":

> The withdrawal of man from participation in the common nous into the shell of his passions was characterized by Heraclitus as the creation of a private dream-world in opposition to the public world of participation in the koinon, the common nous. Plato resumes the Heraclitian idea of the dream-worlds of individual passion. Out of such individual dream-worlds no common order can be constructed because the agreement lacks the obligatory force that stems from participation in the common transcendent reality. The contracts would be empty formulae. This analysis is valid for all later constructions of a similar type.[35]

In addition to these patterns of recurrence in the history of law-relevant theoretical constructions, we observe a nearly absolute primacy of procedure over substance in the early development of legal institutions, fully documented for early Greek law by Michael Gagarin.[36] This primacy is just as evident in the *leges actiones* of early Roman law[37] and in the later "forms of action" during the formative era of English common law.[38]

Focusing more closely on the often alleged divergence of English common law from Roman-based civil law, we may observe instead the previously discussed ubiquity of precedent (see Chapter 10 on the *thesmothetai* and *mnemones*) in the development of both substantive law and judicial procedure, as in the historical parallelism of the Roman *Responsa Prudentum* and the English *ad similibus* doctrine.[39] Nor should Blackstone's following of Justinian's institutional scheme in the *Commentaries* be forgotten.[40]

Finally, there is the puzzling "convergence" of judicial procedure in common law and civil law systems, observed by Martin Shapiro and others.[41] In this process, common law systems over time tend to take on aspects of civil law systems via "statutorification,"[42] and civil law systems take on aspects of the common law by incremental "judicialization" in the form of increased reliance on precedent, establishment of judicial review, and other related innovations.

The tendency of such differently rooted legal orders to become more and more alike cannot be attributed solely to the diffusion effects of enhanced communication technology in modern times. There is much evidence to indicate, for example, that the statutorification process in England was well under way by the early fourteenth century, when the statutes of Edward I (the English Justinian) codified much of the common law.[43] The tendency rather suggests that by far the largest part of all law is truly "common" and that efforts to innovate very distinctive legal orders, in the long run, are destined to fail.

Consider once more, by way of example, the U.S. Constitution, arguably the most blatant attempt in legal history to establish (some would say *ex nihilo,* as we have seen) an essentially *novus ordo seclorum.* Though the most striking continuities in the relationship between the British and American Constitutions have been previously examined, it may be surprising to some readers to discover the jurisprudential foundations of many important constitutional provisions in the poleis of ancient Greece. Yet the origin of the Sixth Amendment's notice requirement can be found in Draco's ancient homicide law.[44] The habeas corpus provision and several modern rules of evidence may be recognized in the ancient Gortynian Code.[45] And concepts somewhat resembling the modern ideas of fair hearing, double jeopardy, ex post facto laws, cruel and unusual punishment, and illegal search and seizure are apparent in other ancient Greek constitutions.[46]

Plato's *Apology* and *Crito* alone include ideas on the need to confront and cross-examine accusers in order to prevent conviction on hearsay; the concept of adversarial procedure in criminal trials; retribution and rehabilitation as competing goals of punishment; civil disobedience in connection with just and unjust laws; the "public-private," "law-fact," and "law-discretion," "tort-contract," and "tort-crime" distinctions; the distinction between intentional and negligent torts; and the distinction between Law itself and the application of laws.[47] And in the procedural law of the Greeks may be found motions for summary judgment, the concept of *demurrer,* the right of arraignment *(antikrisis),* and the principle of *res judicata.*[48] Most of these ideas are inconceivable without the assumption of a transcendent source of order that can be knowable only through an immaterial intellectual faculty capable of accessing directly a realm of intelligible objects (abstract ideas) and that can be given justifiable legal effect only if a symmetrical relationship between psyche and polis also is presumed.

The nonmaterial basis of the Western law of property, laid down by the Roman jurist Gaius and later by the emperor Justinian and confirmed throughout the entirety of Western legal history to the present day, is the distinction between *corporeal* (tangible) and *incorporeal* (intangible) property. Without it, for instance, the modern law of intellectual property, constitutionalized by the American Founders, is rendered inconceivable.[49]

Yet another instance of the immaterial basis of modern law is found in the Anglo-American conception of judicial interpretation with respect to written legal instruments, which are notably conceived as resting upon intangibles. The modern law of testamentary succession is founded upon the idea that a will is merely evidence of the intangible intentions of the testator. The modern law of contract is founded upon the idea that a written contract is merely evidence of the commensurable intentions of the contracting parties, a fact that makes oral contracts as legally binding as written ones.

The rules of statutory interpretation in English and American law (extended to constitutional decisionmaking in the United States) are based largely upon the idea that the will of the lawgiver controls the law and that the words of a statute on occasion may fail adequately to reflect the legislative will. This fact makes both possible and necessary the frequent nonliteral application of statutory provisions by English and American courts. It also made necessary frequent nonliteral application of law by the courts in ancient Greece, whose judges were well acquainted with the idea of "legislative intent."[50] Lysias mentions a rule of interpretation resembling later ones construing statutes not literally but by "meaning and spirit"; and both Lysias and Demosthenes discuss an early form of the mischief *(Heydon's)* rule.[51]

Like these rules of interpretation, most of the rules, principles, and maxims noted are not confined to one or two legal orders but exist in some form in all civilized legal systems and are fully traceable through the major ones. One example is Aristotle's maxim that criminal intent may exist with or without premeditation.[52] Another is his rule basing liability in tort on whether the harmful consequences of an injurious act were, or were not, to be "reasonably anticipated."[53] The latter rule is arguably the origin of the *bonus paterfamilias* of Roman law and the "reasonable man" of English law and is unarguably the origin of the rule applied by Justice Cardozo and the New York Court of Appeals in the famous *Macpherson* case.[54]

The Law, in its most essential aspects, is a seamless web transcending times, places, societies, and cultures. Its essentials are not negotiable, and neither are the traditional practices that form the bridge across which pass the intelligible essentials into experience. Western legal history thus confirms the transcendent basis of all law as revealed in the theoretical analyses of the most acute legal thinkers in the Western philosophical tradition and also in the most enduring institutions of actual legal systems.

The continuity of the legal tradition stands as a virtually unbroken testament to (and the most reliable verification of) the existence of an immaterial, knowable, transcendent source of legal order. The transcendent basis confirms the historic truths that constitute the Law, traditionally understood as a fountain of legal practices and principles honored time out of mind.

The contents of the legal order, thus understood, do not, however, reveal themselves in snapshot fashion to individual interpreters engaged in "peeking" at them. Indeed, the particular contents of the order are not, strictly speaking, directly accessible to individuals at all. Rather, the order is accessible only indirectly through repeated experiences that follow from its presumed truth.

It is the tradition as a whole with which judges are confronted and to which they owe homage and fealty down to every jot and tittle. The situation is not altogether unlike the supposition of noumena required, in Kant's thought, for rendering phenomena comprehensible. We must respect the legal tradition because—as a seamless web—it is the noumenal reality that must be presupposed in order to render the phenomenal material of the Law comprehensible.

If, as Eric Voegelin once suggested, "the existence of man in society is historical existence,"[55] and if the law in historical development is a society's best self-interpretation, then it follows that renunciation of traditional legal practice in the name of *any* theory of constitutional "interpretation" raises a profound contradiction through the substitution of an interpreter's fantasy for a society's own self-interpretation. This leads to an unhealthy constitutional solipsism and ultimately amounts to nothing less than a denial of man as *zoon politikon*.

To be *zoon politikon* is, preeminently, to "be," to have a "nature" that is common to all "beings" of the given character. The source of that nature necessarily transcends its particular embodiments and cannot be individually interpreted or bargained away by the plausible sophistries of modern reason.

The judicialized constitutionalism described and denounced in this book bargains away God and the Law, thereby immersing man in the anarchy of matter; but it does so in vain. In the Old Testament, the Book of Judges tells the story in a way that seems remarkably compelling today. The story is of idol-worshiping peoples with ineffectual gods confounded by the presence of a people whose God was invisible yet effectual. It is also a story of the almost irresistible temptations and terrible consequences of material idolatry, as shown in the repeated lapses of God's people and their consequent deliverance into the hands of their enemies. In the end, it was the judge who emerged to show the people the error of their immersion in visible matter and to deliver them back to the invisible God from the hands of their oppressors. The method was, and is, always the same: the judges accomplish their task not by calling the people to follow them into a hypothetical, abstract future but by calling them to reclaim the traditions of a real and concrete past.

Notes

1. INTRODUCTION

1. Justinian, *Justinian's Institutes,* trans. Peter Birks and Grant McLeod (Ithaca, N.Y.: Cornell University Press, 1987), p. 37.

2. Thomas Aquinas, *Summa Theologica,* trans. Fathers of the English Dominican Province, rev. Daniel J. Sullivan, in *Great Books of the Western World,* vols. 19–20, ed. Robert Maynard Hutchins (Chicago: Encyclopaedia Britannica, 1952).

3. Thomas Hobbes, *Leviathan,* ed. C. B. Macpherson (London: Penguin Books, 1968).

4. I am indebted to Prof. Soterios A. Barber for the wording of the phrase in quotation marks. See Barber, "Review," *American Political Science Review* 85 (1991): 635.

5. Soterios A. Barber, "Michael Perry and the Future of Constitutional Theory," *Tulane Law Review* 63 (1989): 1294.

2. PROBLEMS IN CONTEMPORARY CONSTITUTIONAL THEORY

1. Robert Lowry Clinton, *Marbury v. Madison and Judicial Review* (Lawrence: University Press of Kansas, 1989); hereafter cited as Clinton, *Marbury and Review.*

2. Robert Nagel, *Constitutional Cultures: The Mentality and Consequences of Judicial Review* (Berkeley: University of California Press, 1989), pp. 1–2.

3. Ibid., p. 2. Jeremy Rabkin, in an excellent book on the judicialization of administrative law in the United States, employs the term "compulsion" to symbolize the way in which contemporary federal courts have "legalized" the terms of debate on policy questions before administrative agencies, leading to a situation in which essentially political decisions allocating the benefits and burdens of public regulations routinely are regarded (often unjustifiably) as decisions about the legal rights of private persons and interest groups claiming (again, often unjustifiably) to speak for the public interest. See Rabkin, *Judicial Compulsions: How Public Law Distorts Public Policy* (New York: Basic Books, 1989).

4. Nagel, *Constitutional Cultures,* p. 3.

5. Ibid., p. 1. It should be stressed here that questioning the intellectual habits and

training of lawyers and judges is hardly a critique confined to commentators with conservative tendencies. Arthur S. Miller, for instance, rejecting the idea that the "writtenness" of the Constitution operates (or has ever operated) as a meaningful constraint on judges, has proposed that we stop appointing lawyers to the Supreme Court and appoint people "renowned for ethical wisdom" instead. See Leslie Friedman Goldstein, *In Defense of the Text: Democracy and Constitutional Theory* (Savage, Md.: Rowman and Littlefield, 1991), p. 101.

6. Soterios A. Barber, "Michael Perry and the Future of Constitutional Theory," *Tulane Law Review* 63 (1989): 1298.

7. Ibid., p. 1290.

8. Michael Perry, *Morality, Politics, and Law: A Bicentennial Essay* (New York: Oxford University Press, 1988).

9. Soterios A. Barber, *On What the Constitution Means* (Baltimore: Johns Hopkins University Press, 1984).

10. Michael Perry, "Review," *Ethics* (October 1985): 203.

11. Mark Tushnet, "Judicial Review," *Harvard Journal of Law and Public Policy* 7 (1984): 77.

12. See *Cooper v. Aaron*, 358 U.S. 1, at 18 (1958); see also Clinton, *Marbury and Review*, pp. 14–15.

13. See Clinton, *Marbury and Review*, pp. 190–91.

14. Ibid., p. 121, notes 46–48 and accompanying text.

15. Ibid., p. 113.

16. See, e.g., ibid., pp. 72–77.

17. Ibid., chaps. 10–11.

18. Soterios A. Barber, "Review," *American Political Science Review* 85 (1991): 634–35.

19. Ibid., p. 635.

20. Ibid.

21. Gilbert K. Chesterton, *Orthodoxy* (New York: John Lane Company, 1908), pp. 84–86. For an explicitly Christian application of a concept of tradition to American constitutional law, see H. Jefferson Powell, *The Moral Tradition of American Constitutionalism: A Theological Interpretation* (Durham and London: Duke University Press, 1993).

22. Michael S. Moore, "A Natural Law Theory of Interpretation," *Southern California Law Review* 58 (1985): 394.

23. Eric Voegelin, *The Nature of the Law and Related Legal Writings*, in *The Collected Works of Eric Voegelin*, ed. Robert A. Pascal, James L. Babin, and John W. Corrington (Baton Rouge: Louisiana State University Press, 1991), 27:43.

24. Ibid., 27:36–37.

25. Plato, *Minos; or, On Law*, trans. Thomas L. Pangle, in *The Roots of Political Philosophy: Ten Forgotten Socratic Dialogues* (Ithaca, N.Y.: Cornell University Press, 1987), p. 53.

26. See Henry Sumner Maine, "The Limits of the Analytical System," in *The Nature of Law: Readings in Legal Philosophy*, ed. M. P. Golding (New York: Random House, 1966), pp. 98–103.

27. See Clinton, *Marbury and Review*, p. 185; see also Edward S. Corwin, "The Supreme Court and Unconstitutional Acts of Congress," *Michigan Law Review* 4 (1906): 617–23, 632–34.

3. CONSTITUTIONAL INTERPRETATION AND JUDICIAL REVIEW

1. Keith E. Whittington, *Constitutional Constructions*, 2 vols. (typescript, Department of Politics, Catholic University of America, Washington, D.C., 1996).

2. Ibid., *Interpretation and Original Intent*, vol. 1, chap. 1.

3. Ibid., *Divided Powers and Constitutional Meaning*, vol. 2, esp. chap. 1.

4. Ibid., vol. 2, chaps. 2–4.

5. 4 Wheaton 316 (1819).

6. On dual federalism, see Robert Lowry Clinton, "Judicial Review, Nationalism, and the Commerce Clause: Contrasting Antebellum and Postbellum Supreme Court Decision Making," *Political Research Quarterly* 47 (1994): 857–76. On substantive due process, see Clinton, *Marbury and Review*, chap. 12.

7. See Wallace Mendelson, "The Influence of James Bradley Thayer upon the Work of Holmes, Brandeis, and Frankfurter," *Vanderbilt Law Review* 31 (1978): 71–87. On the Roosevelt Court's restraint, see Clinton, *Marbury and Review*, pp. 208–9 nn. 94–97 and accompanying text.

8. See, e.g., Wallace Mendelson, "Was Chief Justice Marshall an Activist?" in *Supreme Court Activism and Restraint*, ed. Morton Halpern and Charles Lamb (Lexington, Mass.: Lexington Books, 1982); Christopher Wolfe, *The Rise of Modern Judicial Review: From Constitutional Interpretation to Judge-Made Law* (New York: Basic Books, 1986); Lino A. Graglia, *Disaster by Decree: The Supreme Court Decisions on Race and the Schools* (Ithaca, N.Y.: Cornell University Press, 1976).

9. For a classic statement, see the materials cited in *Ashwander v. TVA*, 297 U.S. 288, at 236–348 (1936)(Brandeis, J., concurring).

10. See Clinton, *Marbury and Review*, chap. 12, and "Historical Constitutionalism and Judicial Review in America," *Policy Studies Journal* 19 (1990): 173–91. Sylvia Snowiss, in *Judicial Review and the Law of the Constitution* (New Haven: Yale University Press, 1990), has suggested that judicial overreaching through constitutional interpretation could not have been a concern for the Framers because judicial interpretation of constitutional language was not part of the original constitutional design. According to Snowiss, judicial interpretation of the Constitution, in the modern sense of determining the "meaning" of otherwise "vague" provisions, was largely a nineteenth-century development.

11. See, e.g., Raoul Berger, *Government by Judiciary: The Transformation of the Fourteenth Amendment* (Cambridge: Harvard University Press, 1977); John Hart Ely, *Democracy and Distrust: Theory of Judicial Review* (Cambridge: Harvard University Press, 1980); Thomas Grey, "Do We Have an Unwritten Constitution?" *Stanford Law Review* 27 (1975): 703–18; Michael J. Perry, *The Constitution, the Courts, and Human Rights: An Inquiry into the Legitimacy of Policymaking by the Judiciary* (New Haven: Yale University Press, 1982); Gary J. Jacobsohn, *The Supreme Court and the Decline of Constitutional Aspiration* (Totowa, N.J.: Rowman and Littlefield, 1986); Jesse H. Choper, *Judicial Review and the National Political Process: A Functional Reconsideration of the Role of the Supreme Court* (Chicago: University of Chicago Press, 1980); Leslie Friedman Goldstein, *In Defense of the Text: Democracy and Constitutional Theory* (Savage, Md.: Rowman and Littlefield, 1991); Earl M. Maltz, *Rethinking Constitutional Law: Originalism, Interventionism, and the Politics of Judicial Review* (Lawrence: University Press of Kansas, 1994). This list is by no means exhaustive.

12. See Clinton, *Marbury and Review*, pp. 72–77.

13. Ibid., p. 113.

14. Ibid., chap. 5.

15. On the "Letters of Brutus," probably penned by prominent Antifederalist Robert Yates, and Alexander Hamilton's (Publius's) response to them, see ibid., pp. 69–71. Brutus clearly saw vast potential for expansive judicial development in the 1787 Constitution, but his worst fears did not materialize until a century later. The relevant letters of Brutus may be found in Cecelia Kenyon, ed., *The Antifederalists* (Indianapolis: Bobbs-Merrill, 1966), pp. 334–57. Alexis de Tocqueville's best discussion of the level of judicial power being exercised roughly a half-century after the Constitution's adoption may be found in his *Democracy in America*, 2 vols., trans. George Lawrence, ed. J. P. Mayer and Max Lerner (New York: Harper and Row, 1966), pp. 89–93.

16. See Clinton, *Marbury and Review*, chap. 6.

17. Ibid., chap. 11.

18. *Cooper v. Aaron*, 358 U.S. 1 (1958); see also Clinton, *Marbury and Review*, pp. 14–15, 207–11.

19. *Cooper v. Aaron*, at p. 18. The Court there declared that "the federal judiciary is supreme in the exposition of the law of the Constitution."

20. See Clinton, *Marbury and Review*, chap. 12.

21. Ibid., p. 225.

22. 112 S.Ct. 2791 (1992).

23. Ibid., at 2800–2801.

24. Perry, *Constitution, Courts, and Rights*, esp. pp. 1–3.

25. See ibid., p. 2, where Perry runs through a short list of "human rights" cases since 1954, all of which were decided "without reference to any value judgment constitutionalized by the framers," and suggests that if any of these cases were wrongly decided, then so was *Brown*—since *Brown* was not "the outcome of interpretation or application of any value judgment constitutionalized by the framers" either. But see Robert Nagel, *Constitutional Cultures: The Mentality and Consequences of Judicial Review* (Berkeley: University of California Press, 1989), pp. 4–5, for the suggestion that *Brown* can be justified on the basis of consensus and tradition, and Maltz, *Rethinking Constitutional Law*, p. 87, for the view that *Brown* can be justified on originalist grounds.

26. *Dred Scott v. Sanford*, 19 Howard 393 (1857); *Plessy v. Ferguson*, 163 U.S. 537 (1896); *United States v. E. C. Knight Company*, 156 U.S. 1 (1895); *Pollock v. Farmer's Loan & Trust Company*, 157 U.S. 429 (1895); *Lochner v. New York*, 198 U.S. 45 (1905); *Adkins v. Children's Hospital*, 261 U.S. 525 (1923); and *Hammer v. Dagenhart*, 247 U.S. 251 (1918).

27. E.g., *Dred Scott*, via the Fourteenth Amendment, and *Pollock* via the Sixteenth Amendment (see note 26).

28. E.g., *Plessy*, via the Court's holding in *Brown v. Board of Education*, 347 U.S. 483 (1954); *Knight*, via *Wickard v. Filburn*, 317 U.S. 111 (1942); *Hammer*, via *United States v. Darby Lumber Co.*, 312 U.S. 100 (1941); *Adkins*, via *West Coast Hotel Co. v. Parrish*, 300 U.S. 379 (1937); and *Lochner*, via *Ferguson v. Skrupa*, 372 U.S. 726 (1963) (see note 22). See also *National Labor Relations Board v. Jones & Laughlin Steel Corporation*, 301 U.S. 1 (1937), and *Steward Machine Co. v. Davis*, 301 U.S. 548 (1937).

29. NLRB, Darby, and *Wickard*, for example (see note 28), returned the Court to Marshall's understanding of the commerce clause.

30. *Brown v. Board of Education*, 347 U.S. 483 (1954) (establishing constitutional right to attend desegregated public school); *Griswold v. Connecticut*, 381 U.S. 479 (1965) (establishing constitutional right to distribute contraceptives); *Roe v. Wade*, 410 U.S. 113 (1973) (establishing constitutional right to abortion on demand during first trimester of pregnancy).

31. See Barry Nicholas, *An Introduction to Roman Law* (Oxford: Clarendon Press, 1962), pp. 60–64, 98–107.

32. See William Blackstone, *Commentaries on the Laws of England*, 4 vols. (1765; Chicago: University of Chicago Press, 1979), 1:117–41.

33. See Arthur R. Hogue, *Origins of the Common Law* (Indianapolis: Liberty Fund, 1985), Part 2.

34. See Martin Shapiro, "The Supreme Court's 'Return' to Economic Regulation," in *Studies in American Political Development: An Annual*, ed. Karen Orren and Stephen Skowronek, vol. 1 (New Haven: Yale University Press, 1986), pp. 91–141.

35. See Thomas Sowell, *Civil Rights: Rhetoric or Reality?* (New York: William Morrow and Company, 1984), esp. chap. 3.

36. See, e.g., Graglia, *Disaster by Decree*.

37. See generally Sowell, *Civil Rights;* see also Thomas Sowell, *Black Education: Myths and Tragedies* (New York: David McKay Company, 1972), and Sowell, *Inside American Education: The Decline, the Deception, the Dogmas* (New York: Free Press, 1993). See also Glen C. Loury, *One by One from the Inside Out: Essays and Reviews on Race and Responsibility in America* (New York: Free Press, 1995).

38. See Loury, *One by One*, esp. pp. 117–32.

39. The "joint opinion" in *Planned Parenthood of Southeastern Pennsylvania v. Casey*, 112 S.Ct. 1791 (1992), at 2808–16, devotes considerable space to a discussion of stare decisis as a ground of justification for its decision.

40. Indeed, the entirety of Clinton, *Marbury and Review*, was premised on this notion.

4. JUDICIAL SUPREMACY AND JUDICIAL REVIEW

1. Alexander Bickel, *The Least Dangerous Branch: The Supreme Court at the Bar of Politics* (Indianapolis: Bobbs-Merrill, 1962); Bickel, *The Morality of Consent* (New Haven: Yale University Press, 1975); Bickel, *The Supreme Court and the Idea of Progress* (New York: Harper and Row, 1970); Herbert Wechsler, "Toward Neutral Principles of Constitutional Law," *Harvard Law Review* 73 (1959): 1–35; Charles Black, *The People and the Court* (New York: Macmillan, 1960); Black, *Structure and Relationship in Constitutional Law* (Baton Rouge: Louisiana State University Press, 1969); John Hart Ely, *Democracy and Distrust: A Theory of Judicial Review* (Cambridge: Harvard University Press, 1980); Jesse Choper, *Judicial Review and the National Political Process: A Functional Reconsideration of the Role of the Supreme Court* (Chicago: University of Chicago Press, 1980). See Leslie Friedman Goldstein, *In Defense of the Text* (Savage, Md.: Rowman and Littlefield, 1991), pp. 95–98, for a good discussion of how these commentators proceed from an essentially "interpretivist" paradigm.

2. See, e.g., Paul Brest, "The Fundamental Rights Controversy: The Essential Contradictions of Normative Constitutional Scholarship," *Yale Law Journal* 90 (1981): 1063–1109; Brest, "The Misconceived Quest for the Original Understanding," *Boston University Law*

Review 60 (1980): 204–38; Lief H. Carter, *Contemporary Constitutional Lawmaking: The Supreme Court and the Art of Politics* (New York: Pergamon, 1985); Sanford Levinson, *Constitutional Faith* (Princeton, N.J.: Princeton University Press, 1988); Mark Tushnet, "Following the Rules Laid Down: A Critique of Interpretivism and Neutral Principles," *Harvard Law Review* 96 (1983): 781–827; Tushnet, *Red, White, and Blue* (Cambridge: Harvard University Press, 1988). See Goldstein, *Defense of Text,* chap. 6, for a useful discussion of some of the works listed in this note.

3. 1 Cranch (5 U.S.) 137 (1803).

4. See, e.g., Leonard Levy, ed., *Judicial Review and the Supreme Court* (New York: Harper and Row, 1967).

5. Ibid.; see also Edward S. Corwin, "The Basic Doctrine of American Constitutional Law," *Michigan Law Review* 12 (1914): 247–76.

6. See, e.g., R. Kent Newmyer, *The Supreme Court Under Marshall and Taney* (Chicago: Harlan Davidson, 1968), p. 81; Melvin I. Urofsky, *A March of Liberty: A Constitutional History of the United States* (New York: Knopf, 1988), p. 242; Leonard W. Levy, *Original Intent and the Framers' Constitution* (New York: Collier Macmillan, 1988), p. 136.

7. See Gordon Wood, *The Creation of the American Republic, 1776–1787* (New York: Norton, 1972), p. 513; Jennifer Nedelsky, *Private Property and the Limits of American Constitutionalism: The Madisonian Framework and its Legacy* (Chicago: University of Chicago Press, 1990); Corwin, "Basic Doctrine of American Constitutional Law," p. 255.

8. See generally Albert P. Melone and George Mace, eds., *Judicial Review and American Democracy* (Ames: Iowa State University Press, 1988). Wood, in *Creation of the American Republic,* says that "the Constitution was an intrinsically aristocratic document designed to check the democratic tendencies of the period" (p. 513).

9. See Nedelsky, *Private Property and the Limits of American Constitutionalism,* pp. 187–231.

10. See, e.g., Louis Boudin, *Government by Judiciary,* 2 vols. (New York: Godwin, 1932).

11. See, e.g., Levy, *Original Intent,* p. 136. See also Carter, *Contemporary Constitutional Lawmaking,* and Tushnet, *Red, White, and Blue.*

12. See Christopher Wolfe, *The Rise of Modern Judicial Review: From Constitutional Interpretation to Judge-Made Law* (New York: Basic Books, 1986), pp. 3–5.

13. Wolfe, *Rise of Modern Review,* esp. Part 1.

14. See Clinton, *Marbury and Review,* esp. chaps. 2 and 3.

15. See ibid., esp. Part 3; see also Robert Lowry Clinton, "Judicial Review, Nationalism, and the Commerce Clause: Contrasting Antebellum and Postbellum Supreme Court Decision Making," *Political Research Quarterly* 47 (1994): 857–76. For a response to the views expressed in this article, see Howard Gillman, "The Struggle Over Marshall and the Politics of Constitutional History," *Political Research Quarterly* 47 (1994): 877–86. See also Howard Gillman, *The Constitution Besieged: The Rise and Decline of Lochner Era Police Power Jurisprudence* (Durham, N.C.: Duke University Press), 1993.

16. Sylvia Snowiss, *Judicial Review and the Law of the Constitution* (New Haven: Yale University Press, 1990), esp. chap. 3.

17. Clinton, *Marbury and Review,* esp. chap. 5.

18. Ibid., Part 3.

19. *Dred Scott v. Sanford,* 19 Howard 393 (1857).

20. Clinton, *Marbury and Review,* chap. 7.

21. Wolfe, *Rise of Modern Review*, p. 203.

22. See generally Matthew J. Franck, *Against the Imperial Judiciary: The Supreme Court vs. the Sovereignty of the People* (Lawrence: University Press of Kansas, 1996; see also Lane V. Sunderland, *Popular Government and the Supreme Court: Securing the Public Good and Private Rights* (Lawrence: University Press of Kansas, 1995). See Chapter 13.

23. See, e.g., *Lochner v. New York*, 198 U.S. 45, at 75 (1905); see also Paul Kens, *Judicial Power and Reform Politics: The Anatomy of Lochner v. New York* (Lawrence: University Press of Kansas, 1990).

24. See Benjamin Twiss, *Lawyers and the Constitution: How Laissez-Faire Came to the Supreme Court* (Princeton, N.J.: Princeton University Press, 1942).

25. Recall that Tushnet suggested that, under prevailing constitutional theories, judicial review is "an 'all or nothing' proposition" in which "one allows judges to do whatever they want or one allows majorities to do whatever they want," resulting in a "self-contradictory" constitutionalism (Mark Tushnet, "Judicial Review," *Harvard Journal of Law and Public Policy* 7 (1984): 77).

26. See Martin Shapiro, *Who Guards the Guardians? Judicial Control of Administration* (Athens: University of Georgia Press, 1988), esp. pp. 36–41.

27. See Ernest Gellhorn and Ronald M. Levin, *Administrative Law and Process in a Nutshell*, 3d ed. (St. Paul, Minn.: West Publishing Company, 1990), pp. 75–83.

28. Shapiro, *Who Guards the Guardians?* pp. 56 ff.

29. Ibid., p. 48.

30. Ibid., chap. 1.

31. Ibid., pp. 44–54.

32. Ibid., p. 54.

33. Ibid., pp. 29 ff.

34. Ibid., chap. 5. See also John A. Rohr, *To Run a Constitution: The Legitimacy of the Administrative State* (Lawrence: University Press of Kansas, 1986).

35. Shapiro, *Who Guards the Guardians?* chap. 7, esp. pp. 167–73.

36. Ibid., p. 55.

5. CONSTITUTIONALISM IN A LIBERAL DEMOCRACY

1. Plato, *The Republic*, in *Great Dialogues of Plato*, trans. W. H. D. Rouse (New York: Penguin Books, 1984), pp. 376–78.

2. Ibid., p. 375.

3. Kenneth J. Arrow, *Social Choice and Individual Values* (New Haven: Yale University Press, 1951), p. 1.

4. Ibid.: "That is, we ask if it is formally possible to construct a procedure for passing from a set of known individual tastes to a pattern of social decision-making, the procedure in question being required to satisfy certain natural conditions." The "natural conditions" are those of "rationality": "The methods of dictatorship and convention are, or can be, rational in the sense that any individual can be rational in his choices. Can such consistency be attributed to collective modes of choice, where the wills of many people are involved?" (p. 2).

5. Ibid., pp. 48–59.

6. Ibid., pp. 9–19.

7. Ibid., p. 13.

8. Ibid., p. 23.

9. See ibid., pp. 17–19; Arrow adopts, for the most part, the "liberal" interpretation (see ibid., pp. 22–25).

10. Ibid., p. 24.

11. Ibid., p. 25.

12. Ibid., p. 24.

13. Ibid., p. 25.

14. Ibid., pp. 27–28.

15. Ibid., p. 28.

16. Ibid., p. 30.

17. Ibid., p. 31.

18. Arrow's description of the Condorcet Effect is standard and may be found in ibid., pp. 2–3. The effect is most simply described by making use of the following model. Assuming three alternatives (x, y, z) and three decisionmakers (a, b, c), these preference orderings may be obtained:

a	b	c
x	z	y
y	x	z
z	y	x

Under this scenario, using majority rule, there is a "preference cycle" for the group as a whole, since a clear majority (a and b) prefers x to y, another majority (a and c) prefers y to z, and still another majority (b and c) prefers z to x. Thus, by majority rule, x beats y, y beats z, and z beats x. As in the "prisoner's dilemma" example that will be used to elaborate Hobbes's "state of nature" in Chapter 11, any of the three "majorities" might form a "coalition of minorities" (each is a minority by itself) in order to achieve an outcome that is preferred to some other outcome. But for this to occur, cooperation must be possible, and in the absence of an enforceable bargain, the coalition will be unstable. For present purposes, the important point is that this situation is not a rarity in democratic politics, and many of our most important institutional practices (e.g., the two-party system, the electoral college, and so on) may plausibly be viewed as attempts to circumvent or suppress the paradoxical effect of having individually rational preferences translated into collectively irrational ones. The final point to note is that, assuming a wide range of admissible orderings, the larger the number of alternatives, the greater the probability that the Condorcet Effect will occur.

19. Ibid., pp. 51–59.

20. Ibid., chap. 6.

21. Ibid., p. 60.

22. Ibid., pp. 46–48.

23. Ibid., p. 81.

24. Ibid., pp. 75–80. See also Duncan Black, *Theory of Committees and Elections* (Cambridge: Cambridge University Press, 1958).

25. Arrow, *Social Choice*, pp. 81–86.

26. Ibid., p. 85.

27. Ibid., p. 30.

28. Ibid., p. 28.

29. Ibid., pp. 28–29.

30. Ibid., p. 29.

31. Donald R. Kelley, *The Human Measure: Social Thought in the Western Legal Tradition* (Cambridge: Harvard University Press, 1990), p. xi.

32. See *The Laws of Plato*, trans. Thomas Pangle (Chicago: University of Chicago Press, 1988), esp. Books 1 and 2.

33. John Locke, *Two Treatises on Civil Government*, Book 2, chap. 6. Quoted in Edgar Bodenheimer, John Bilyeu Oakley, and Jean C. Love, *An Introduction to the Anglo-American Legal System: Readings and Cases*, 2d ed. (St. Paul, Minn.: West Publishing Company, 1988), p. 2.

6. WRITTEN AND UNWRITTEN CONSTITUTIONS

1. 1 Cranch (5 U.S.) 137 (1803).

2. Ibid., at 176–77.

3. Ibid., at 177–80.

4. See Sylvia Snowiss, *Judicial Review and the Law of the Constitution* (New Haven: Yale University Press, 1990).

5. Etienne Gilson, *Being and Some Philosophers*, 2d ed. (Toronto: Pontifical Institute of Mediaeval Studies, 1952), esp. chap. 4.

6. Eric Voegelin, *The New Science of Politics* (Chicago: University of Chicago Press, 1952).

7. 4 Wheaton (17 U.S.) 316, at 407 (1819).

8. Albert Venn Dicey, *Introduction to the Study of the Law of the Constitution*, 8th ed. (1915; rpt., Indianapolis: Liberty Classics, 1982), pp. cxliv–v.

9. See John A. Rohr, *To Run a Constitution: The Legitimacy of the Administrative State* (Lawrence: University Press of Kansas, 1986), esp. chap. 7.

10. *Roe v. Wade*, 410 U.S. 113 (1973).

11. Ibid. See Wallace Mendelson, *The American Constitution and the Judicial Process* (Homewood, Ill.: Dorsey Press, 1980), p. 231.

12. See Dicey, *Law of Constitution*, Part 3.

13. The most extensive analysis of symbolism in its relation to political experience generally has been undertaken by Eric Voegelin in *Order and History*, 5 vols. (Baton Rouge: Louisiana State University Press, 1956–1987).

14. Dicey, *Law of Constitution*, p. cxl.

15. Benjamin Twiss, *Lawyers and the Constitution: How Laissez-Faire Came to the Supreme Court* (Princeton, N.J.: Princeton University Press, 1942), chap. 7.

16. 21 L.Ed. 395–96 (1873).

17. See Clinton, *Marbury and Review*, pp. 199–207.

18. See *Allgeyer v. Louisiana*, 165 U.S. 578 (1897).

19. See, for example, the "public interest" doctrine of *Munn v. Illinois*, 94 U.S. 113 (1877), or the doctrine of fraudulent misrepresentation in contract law (*Di Santo v. Pennsylvania*, 273 U.S. 34 [1927]).

20. See, e.g., *Schechter Poultry Corporation v. United States*, 295 U.S. 495 (1935); *Carter v. Carter Coal Company*, 298 U.S. 238 (1936); *United States v. Butler*, 297 U.S. 1 (1936); *Nebbia v. New York*, 291 U.S. 502 (1934).

21. See, e.g., *United States v. Darby*, 312 U.S. 100 (1941); *Wickard v. Filburn*, 317 U.S. 111 (1942); *National Labor Relations Board v. Jones & Laughlin Steel Corporation*, 301 U.S. 1 (1937); *Steward Machine Company v. Davis*, 301 U.S. 548 (1937); *West Coast Hotel v. Parrish*, 300 U.S. 379 (1937).

22. Guido Calabresi, *A Common Law for the Age of Statutes* (Cambridge: Harvard University Press, 1982), pp. 3–4.

23. Benjamin N. Cardozo, *The Nature of the Judicial Process* (New Haven: Yale University Press, 1921), p. 51.

24. Immanuel Kant, *Critique of Practical Reason*, trans. Lewis White Beck (Indianapolis: Bobbs-Merrill, 1956), p. 153.

25. *Griswold v. Connecticut*, 381 U.S. 479 (1965).

26. *Eisenstadt v. Baird*, 405 U.S. 438 (1972).

27. *Stanley v. Georgia*, 394 U.S. 561 (1969).

28. *Carey v. Population Services International*, 431 U.S. 678 (1977).

29. *Roe v. Wade*, 410 U.S. 113 (1973).

30. *Planned Parenthood Association of Kansas City v. Ashcroft*, 462 U.S. 476 (1983).

31. *Bellotti v. Baird*, 428 U.S. 132 (1976).

32. *Planned Parenthood of Central Missouri v. Danforth*, 428 U.S. 52 (1976).

33. *Doe v. Bolton*, 410 U.S. 179 (1973).

34. *Thornburg v. American College of Obstetricians & Gynecologists*, 476 U.S. 747 (1986).

35. *Colautti v. Franklin*, 439 U.S. 379 (1979).

36. *Paul v. Davis*, 424 U.S. 693 (1976).

37. See *Planned Parenthood of Southeastern Pennsylvania v. Casey*, 112 S.Ct. 2791, at 2832.

38. See Mary Ann Glendon, *Abortion and Divorce in Western Law* (Cambridge: Harvard University Press, 1988).

39. As of 1992, this was the firm view of four justices of the Supreme Court. See *Planned Parenthood of Southeastern Pennsylvania v. Casey*, 112 S.Ct. 2791, at 2855 (1992) (Rehnquist, Chief Justice, joined by Justices White, Scalia, and Thomas, dissenting).

40. Calabresi, *Common Law*, pp. 202–3 n. 46.

41. William H. McNeill and Jean W. Sedlar, eds., *The Classical Mediterranean World* (New York: Oxford University Press, 1969), p. 15 n. 8.

42. Dicey, *Law of Constitution*, pp. cxli ff.

43. Ibid., pp. 281–85.

44. See esp. *Foster v. Neilson*, 2 Peters 253 (1829), and *Martin v. Mott*, 12 Wheaton 19 (1827).

45. See, e.g., *Reynolds v. Sims*, 377 U.S. 533 (1964).

46. See Lane V. Sunderland, *Popular Government and the Supreme Court: Securing the Public Good and Private Rights* (Lawrence: University Press of Kansas, 1995).

47. Gilson, *Being and Some Philosophers*, p. 211.

48. Ibid., p. 213.

49. Ibid., p. 215.

50. Ibid., p. 210.

51. James R. Stoner, Jr., *Common Law and Liberal Theory: Coke, Hobbes, and the Origins of American Constitutionalism* (Lawrence: University Press of Kansas, 1992).

52. See ibid., pp. 1–9.

53. See ibid., esp. chap. 13.

54. See, for examples of such denial in the constitutional field, Arthur S. Miller and Ronald F. Howell, "The Myth of Neutrality in Constitutional Adjudication," *University of Chicago Law Review* 27 (1960): 61–95; see also Eugene V. Rostow, *The Sovereign Prerogative: The Supreme Court and the Quest for Law* (Westport, Conn.: Greenwood Press, 1962).

55. For the best discussion of the idea of *metaxy* in political thought, see Eric Voegelin, *Order and History*, vol. 3, *Plato and Aristotle* (Baton Rouge: Louisiana State University Press, 1957).

7. LAW AND MORALITY

1. William H. McNeill and Jean W. Sedlar, eds., *The Classical Mediterranean World* (New York: Oxford University Press, 1969), p. 15 n. 8. The best recent treatment of the tensions in the modern political *metaxy*, especially as these pertain to the crucial public-private distinction (to be discussed below), is to be found in Clarke E. Cochran, *Religion in Public and Private Life* (New York and London: Routledge, 1990).

2. William Blackstone, *Commentaries on the Laws of England*, 4 vols. (1765; Chicago: University of Chicago Press, 1979), 1:73.

3. Graham Walker, *Moral Foundations of Constitutional Thought: Current Problems, Augustinian Prospects* (Princeton, N.J.: Princeton University Press, 1990), p. 53 n. 96.

4. The overthrow of traditional practice has resulted not only in judicial activism but also in a recent proliferation of books and articles advancing theories about the best way to interpret the Constitution and in a proliferation of studies that attempt to classify this burgeoning array of literature. Among the best recent efforts in the latter genre, providing summaries and evaluations of leading contemporary constitutional theorists, are Gregory Bassham, *Original Intent and the Constitution: A Philosophical Study* (Lanham, Md.: Rowman and Littlefield, 1992); Leslie Friedman Goldstein, *In Defense of the Text* (Savage, Md.: Rowman and Littlefield, 1991); Earl Maltz, *Rethinking Constitutional Law: Originalism, Interventionism, and the Politics of Judicial Review* (Lawrence: University Press of Kansas, 1994); and Walker, *Moral Foundations of Constitutional Thought*.

Each of these scholars has a different way of conceptualizing the field of constitutional interpretation, and each represents a different school of thought on the best approach. Goldstein, a textualist, sorts contemporary theorists, first, into "intentionalist," "textualist," "extratextualist," "indeterminist," and "Dworkinist" categories (*In Defense of Text*, pp. 1–6); and later reorganizes these categories along a "constraintist-discretionist" continuum (chap. 4). Maltz, an originalist, suggests that "originalist-nonoriginalist" and "interventionist-noninterventionist" dimensions are the most salient ones (*Rethinking Constitutional Law*, esp. pp. 18–20). Walker, a constraintist moral realist, focuses more directly on the variety of underlying moral positions reflected by modern commentators, offering a "conventionalist-realist" dimension overlapping a "teleologist-deontologist" one (*Moral Foundations*, chap. 2).

Though there is much insight to be gained from the nuanced analyses provided in these works, so long as one accepts the basic presupposition of the whole enterprise—that neither the Constitution nor traditional practice gives sufficient guidance to judges in constitutional law—my concern here is not so much with the particular interpretive strategies of constitutional interpretation that might be chosen from a list of all logically possible alternatives. Rather it is with the cardinal assumption that underlies the construction of such a list in the first place and then deems selection of one of its alternatives to be the kind of decision that judges are constitutionally entitled to make.

Put bluntly, one of my main theses is that judges, when dealing with cases and controversies, have no authority whatsoever to decide whether they are going to be "textualists," "extratextualists," "interpretivists," "noninterpretivists," "indeterminists," or any other such thing. Rather, they are obligated to decide *every* case in accordance with the traditional legal practices and professional standards applicable in their respective jurisdictions, and they are absolutely unqualified and unauthorized to do anything else.

Though defining these traditional practices will require my efforts for the remainder of this book (and probably a great deal more), it is worth saying now that, in my view, their authority has nothing to do with the ruminations, recommendations, or categorizations set up by legal academicians. It is also worth noting that the field of constitutional theory, from which these ideas spring, came into being only when influential academicians and judges began to believe that constitutional law failed to operate as a constraint on constitutional decisionmaking (see Goldstein, *In Defense of Text*, pp. 161–62). That observation by itself should be enough to give one pause when considering the relative merits of different modes of constitutional interpretation.

5. See Blackstone, *Commentaries on the Laws of England*, 1:91.

6. The proponents of the primacy of moral theory over legal history thus far have demonstrated little agreement on the particular substantive principles to be employed when judges set about reconstructing the American constitutional order in accordance with their views (let alone how such principles are to be applied in particular cases). One has only to recall the recent—and yet unresolved—debates among Rawlsians, Nozickians, and utilitarians; or those between deontological moral realists, teleological moral realists, and moral conventionalists to see the problem clearly. As summarized by Goldstein (*In Defense of Text*, p. 34), Maltz (*Rethinking Constitutional Law*, p. 7), and Walker (*Moral Foundations*, pp. 42–45), the following are just a few of the "fundamental values" sought for maximization by contemporary constitutional theorists: "social justice, brotherhood, and human dignity"; "toleration"; "liberty and equality"; "equal concern and respect"; and "rational liberty."

So long as the highest possible level of generality is maintained, these notions are, of course, unexceptionable. But when one tries to imagine their application to the resolution of everyday legal disputes—which is, after all, the business of courts—it is easy enough to imagine how conflicts will arise. I realize that the progenitors of the constitutional theories based on these values are engaged in an ongoing enterprise of devising methods of ever-increasing complexity to deal with the problems arising from their application to particular cases. Yet no one has successfully answered the more fundamental question of why we should want such a ptolemaic intellectual monstrosity superimposed on our law in the first place.

7. Michael S. Moore, "A Natural Law Theory of Interpretation," *Southern California Law Review* 58 (1985): 392–93.

8. Ibid., p. 393.

9. John Ralston Saul, *Voltaire's Bastards: The Dictatorship of Reason in the West* (New York: Free Press, 1992), p. 327.

10. Ibid., pp. 14–15.

11. See generally Mortimer J. Adler, *Intellect: Mind over Matter* (New York: Macmillan, 1990).

12. See Mancur Olson, *The Logic of Collective Action* (Cambridge: Harvard University Press, 1971).

13. Indeed, reductionism is one of the most striking characteristics of the whole debate over "original intent." Nontraditionalists indulge in the practice in the manner just described; traditionalists do it by trying to reduce the "intention" of a collective body—e.g., the "Framers" or the "ratifiers"—to the intentions of the individuals who compose these bodies, but more on this later (see Chapter 10).

14. See generally Saul, *Voltaire's Bastards*.

15. See John Austin, *The Province of Jurisprudence Determined*, liberally excerpted in Lon L. Fuller, *The Problems of Jurisprudence: A Selection of Readings Supplemented by Comments Prepared by the Editor* (Brooklyn, N.Y.: Foundation Press, 1949), pp. 115–299. See also Niccolo Machiavelli, *The Prince*, trans. George Bull (New York: Penguin, 1961), and Thomas Hobbes, *Leviathan*, ed. C. B. Macpherson (London: Penguin Books, 1968).

16. See Jeremy Bentham, *Introduction to the Principles of Morals and Legislation*, excerpted in John Stuart Mill, *Utilitarianism, On Liberty, Essay on Bentham: Together with Selected Writings of Jeremy Bentham and John Austin*, ed. Mary Warnock (New York: Penguin Books, 1974); see also Mill, *On Liberty*, in Warnock, ed., *Utilitarianism*.

17. An excellent discussion about the need to impose severe restrictions on the power of magistrates to use discretion in the application of law may be found in Gerald J. Postema's discussion of David Hume's legal philosophy. See Postema, *Bentham and the Common Law Tradition* (Oxford: Clarendon Press, 1986), for a good discussion of Hume's opposition to judicial activism. As is well known, Hume was both a moral and a legal conventionalist and grounded his theory of law and government on an agreement to respect existing social customs. Postema notes that Hume's political and legal thought is a unity because the Humean "account of the origin of government exactly parallels his account of property" (p. 121), which is the foundation of law.

Indeed, in Hume's view, law and government arise from social convention in the very same sense that the common law arises from social convention. Though I dissent from Hume's moral conventionalism, which is founded upon his conception of reason as merely a faculty for processing sense data and thus incapable of directly accessing an intelligible reality, and his insistence upon a purely material basis for the organization of human society, his rejection of Hobbesian atomism in recognition (with Aristotle) of the social nature of men and his refusal to disregard experience as a basis for knowledge lead to a conception of law more closely resembling the one presented in this book than do those of most other modern thinkers.

Hume's constitutionalism destroys the basis for making a sharp distinction between written and unwritten constitutions; his insistence on inflexible application of law excludes any possibility of judicial resort to private moral judgment in the decision of cases; and his jurisprudence precludes judicial imposition of prophylactic rules, which are always based on private abstract reason rather than on common sense.

18. Gilbert K. Chesterton, *Orthodoxy* (New York: John Lane Company, 1908), pp. 84–86. See Chapter 2 n. 21 and accompanying text.

19. See Jim Evans, "Change in the Doctrine of Precedent During the Nineteenth Century," in *Precedent in Law*, ed. Lawrence Goldstein (Oxford: Clarendon Press, 1987), pp. 35–72, esp. pp. 46–63.

20. Alan Watson, *Legal Transplants: An Approach to Comparative Law* (Edinburgh: Scottish Academic Press, 1974), pp. 93–94.

21. See Michael S. Moore, "Precedent, Induction, and Ethical Generalization," in Goldstein, ed., *Precedent in Law*, p. 201.

22. Karl Llewellyn, *The Case Law System in America*, trans. Michael Ansaldi, ed. Alan Gewirth (Chicago: University of Chicago Press, 1989), p. 80.

23. Alexis de Tocqueville, *Democracy in America*, 2 vols., trans. George Lawrence, ed. J. P. Mayer and Max Lerner (New York: Harper Row, 1966), 1:92.

24. The best recent discussion of the realism-conventionalism controversy in the constitutional field is that of Walker, *Moral Foundations of Constitutional Thought*.

25. Immanuel Kant, *The Metaphysical Elements of Justice*, trans. John Ladd (Indianapolis: Bobbs-Merrill, 1965), p. 19.

26. Soterios A. Barber, *On What the Constitution Means* (Baltimore: Johns Hopkins University Press, 1984), p. vii.

27. Soterios A. Barber, "Review," *American Political Science Review* 85 (1991): 635; see Chapter 2 nn. 18–20 and accompanying text.

28. Barber, *On What the Constitution Means*, p. vii; see also Chapter 14.

29. Moore, "Natural Law Theory of Interpretation," pp. 392–93; see also Walker, *Moral Foundations*, esp. pp. 47–54.

30. On correspondence and coherence theories, see Walker, *Moral Foundations*, esp. pp. 48–52.

31. Etienne Gilson, *Being and Some Philosophers*, 2d. ed. (Toronto: Pontifical Institute of Mediaeval Studies, 1952), p. 115.

8. THE BRITISH CONSTITUTION AND THE COMMON LAW

1. J. M. Sosin, *The Aristocracy of the Long Robe: The Origins of Judicial Review in America* (New York: Greenwood Press, 1989), p. 7.

2. William R. Casto, *The Supreme Court in the Early Republic: The Chief Justiceships of John Jay and Oliver Ellsworth* (Columbia: University of South Carolina Press, 1995), pp. 151–52. See also William F. Walsh, *A History of Anglo-American Law*, 2d ed. (Indianapolis: Bobbs-Merrill, 1932), pp. 85–96; Edgar Bodenheimer, John Bilyeu Oakley, and Jean C. Love, eds., *An Introduction to the Anglo-American Legal System: Readings and Cases*, 2d ed. (St. Paul, Minn.: West Publishing Company, 1988), pp. 46–52.

3. Alan Watson, *Legal Transplants: An Approach to Comparative Law* (Edinburgh: Scottish Academic Press, 1974), p. 94.

4. Frederic William Maitland, *Selected Historical Essays of F. W. Maitland,* ed. Helen M. Cam (Cambridge: Cambridge University Press, 1957), p. 127.

5. On the relation between Justinian's *Institutes* and Blackstone's *Commentaries,* see the excellent introductory essay by Peter Birks and Grant McLeod in *Justinian's Institutes,* trans. Peter Birks and Grant McLeod (Ithaca, N.Y.: Cornell University Press, 1987), esp. pp. 23–26.

6. See Doris M. Stenton, *English Justice Between the Norman Conquest and the Great Charter, 1066–1215* (London: Allen and Unwin, 1963).

7. The Anglo-Saxon laws of King Aethelbert (A.D. 600) are reprinted in Frederic W. Maitland and Francis C. Montague, *A Sketch of English Legal History,* ed. James F. Colby (New York: G. P. Putnam's Sons), pp. 193–99; extracts from Magna Carta may be found on pp. 206–8 in the same volume.

8. Edward Jenks, "Effects of the Norman Conquest on the History of English Law and on the Development of the Common Law," in Maitland and Montague, *Sketch of English History,* pp. 200–205.

9. *Paxton's Case,* Quincy 51, at 56, excerpted in James Bradley Thayer, *Cases on Constitutional Law,* 2 vols. (Cambridge, Mass.: George H. Kent, 1895), 1:48–55. *Dr. Bonham's Case,* Hil. 7 Jac. 1, in 8 *Reports* 114a, at 118a.

10. See Shannon C. Stimson, *The American Revolution in the Law: Anglo-American Jurisprudence Before John Marshall* (Princeton, N.J.: Princeton University Press, 1990). The colonists also depended on the common law itself, especially the doctrine of precedent. According to William D. Bader, "The common law method, as adapted by the Framers' generation and rooted in Article III, emphasized Blackstonian precedent in all cases, not primarily for commercial predictability but as the principal bulwark against usurpation of the rule of law by judicial tyranny" ("Some Thoughts on Blackstone, Precedent, and Originalism," *Vermont Law Review* 19 [1994] 18).

11. See Bodenheimer et al., eds., *Anglo-American Legal System,* p. 51; also Frederic William Maitland, *The Forms of Action at Common Law,* ed. A. H. Chaytor and W. J. Whittaker (Cambridge: Cambridge University Press, 1936), p. 7.

12. See Clinton, *Marbury and Review,* pp. 48–54.

13. Massachusetts Constitution of 1780, Part 1, Article 30.

14. On the assimilation of fundamental to ordinary law, see generally Sylvia Snowiss, *Judicial Review and the Law of the Constitution* (New Haven: Yale University Press, 1990).

15. Sir Frederick Pollock and Frederic William Maitland, *The History of English Law Before the Time of Edward I,* 2 vols. (1895; rpt., Cambridge: Cambridge University Press, 1968), p. 1.

16. See M. E. Bradford, *Original Intentions: On the Making and Ratification of the Constitution* (Athens: University of Georgia Press, 1993), esp. pp. 19–21.

17. See Arthur R. Hogue, *Origins of the Common Law* (Indianapolis: Liberty Fund, 1985), p. 70.

18. See Albert Venn Dicey, *Introduction to the Study of the Law of the Constitution,* 8th ed. (1915; rpt., Indianapolis: Liberty Classics, 1982), p. cxlii; see also Bradford, *Original Intentions,* pp. 19–21.

19. Dicey, *Law of Constitution,* p. cxlii.

20. Hogue, *Origins of Common Law,* p. 80.

21. See, e.g., *McCulloch v. Maryland*, 4 Wheaton 316 (1819); *Gibbons v. Ogden*, 9 Wheaton 1 (1824).

22. See Bradford, *Original Intentions*, pp. 19–21.

23. See Sir Matthew Hale, "Reflections by the Lrd. Cheife Justice Hale on Mr. Hobbes his Dialogue of the Lawe," in Sir William Holdsworth, *A History of English Law*, 16 vols., 3d. ed. (London: Methuen and Company, Sweet and Maxwell, 1945), 5:511.

24. Ibid., 5:508.

25. See Dicey, *Law of Constitution*, pp. 210–12.

26. See Bradford, *Original Intentions*, pp. 19–21.

27. See ibid.

28. See Hogue, *Origins of Common Law*, p. 75. See also *Dartmouth College v. Woodward*, 4 Wheaton 518 (1819).

29. See Bradford, *Original Intentions*, pp. 19–21.

30. See generally ibid.

31. Versions of this requirement may also be found in the Statute of Westminster (1275) and in Magna Carta (1215). See Frank A. Schubert, *Grilliot's Introduction to Law and the Legal System*, 6th ed. (Boston: Houghton Mifflin, 1996), pp. 262–63; see also *Coker v. Georgia*, 433 U.S. 584 (1977).

32. See Bradford, *Original Intentions*, pp. 19–21.

33. See ibid.; see also Hogue, *Origins of Common Law*, p. 71.

34. See Bradford, *Original Intentions*, pp. 19–21; see also Dicey, *Law of Constitution*, pp. 169–79.

35. Bradford, *Original Intentions*, p. 20; see also Hogue, *Origins of Common Law*, p. 53.

36. See Hogue, *Origins of Common Law*, p. 42.

37. See William Blackstone, *Commentaries on the Laws of England: A Facsimile of the First Edition of 1765–1769*, 4 vols. (Chicago: University of Chicago Press, 1979), 1:78.

38. 8 Reports 114a, at 118a. See James R. Stoner, Jr., *Common Law and Liberal Theory: Coke, Hobbes, and the Origins of American Constitutionalism* (Lawrence: University Press of Kansas, 1992), p. 14.

39. Blackstone, *Commentaries*, 1:91.

40. See Clinton, *Marbury and Review*, esp. chap. 1.

41. Gilbert K. Chesterton, *Orthodoxy* (New York: John Lane Company, 1908), pp. 84–86; see Chapter 2 n. 21 and accompanying text.

42. Blackstone, *Commentaries*, 1:73.

43. Ibid., 1:6.

44. See *Palko v. Connecticut*, 302 U.S. 319 (1937).

45. See generally Edmund Burke, *Reflections on the Revolution in France*, ed. Thomas H. D. Mahoney (1790; Indianapolis: Bobbs-Merrill, 1955).

46. Hale, "Reflections," 5:500–501. For an excellent discussion of Hale's critique of Hobbes, see Stoner, *Common Law and Liberal Theory*, pp. 130–33, and for an equally good discussion of the Hobbesian theory of law that Hale was responding to, see pp. 116–30.

47. Hale, 5:502 n. 1, on *metaxy*.

48. See Stoner, *Common Law and Liberal Theory*, p. 133.

49. Hale, "Reflections," 5:501–2.

50. Ibid., 5:505.

51. See generally Stoner, *Common Law and Liberal Theory*, pp. 18 ff.

52. Ibid., p. 18.

53. Ibid.

54. Ibid., p. 23.

55. Ibid., p. 54.

56. For an extended discussion of the ideas of law held by Cicero, Aquinas, and Austin, see Chapter 12; see also Stoner, *Common Law and Liberal Theory*, p. 23.

57. See Stoner, *Common Law and Liberal Theory*, p. 28.

58. See Blackstone, *Commentaries*, 1:70.

59. See ibid., 1:54; See also Stoner, *Common Law and Liberal Theory*, p. 167, where Stoner, to an extent, discounts Blackstone's distinction between natural and positive law, apparently believing that Blackstone was essentially a legal positivist paying lip service to the natural law tradition. Admittedly Blackstone devoted his attention primarily to the discussion of positive law, as did Austin (though for very different reasons) more than a half-century later. But I think that other interpretations are more plausible. A near-exclusive focus on municipal law does not, by itself, imply any disbelief or disregard for natural or divine law. According to Blackstone, divine law is declared by God *directly* in consequence of Man's inability to discover by *unaided* Reason what natural law requires in particular circumstances. But since *lex non scripta*, consisting of maxims and customs of higher antiquity than memory or history can reach, is the foundation of the common law with which Blackstone is most concerned, his efforts are, and must be, directed to the discovery of what God has placed in nature only *indirectly* and to the *aids* that God has provided to Reason for use in the process of discovery. Since he is not a theologian, his approach is different from that of, say, Aquinas, but his conception of Law is much the same (see Chapter 12).

60. Plato, *Minos; or, On Law*, in *The Roots of Political Philosophy: Ten Forgotten Socratic Dialogues*, trans. Thomas L. Pangle (Ithaca, N.Y.: Cornell University Press, 1987), p. 53.

61. Ibid., pp. 53–54.

62. Ibid., pp. 54–55.

63. Ibid., p. 56.

64. See Stoner, *Common Law and Liberal Theory*, esp. pp. 215 ff. Striking examples are Madison and Sherman in the convention and the fact that the Bill of Rights was appended to rather than incorporated into the text. In Chapter 14 I shall return to these and other examples to show that the Framers are in fact saved from the charge of political gnosticism by their exposure to the common law.

65. Gerald J. Postema, *Bentham and the Common Law Tradition* (Oxford: Clarendon Press, 1986), pp. 30–38.

66. Ibid., pp. 30–31.

67. Ibid., p. 33.

68. Ibid.

69. Ibid., p. 30.

70. Casto, *Supreme Court in the Early Republic*, pp. 34–35. Notwithstanding this characterization of the outlook of eighteenth-century common lawyers, some of Casto's subsequent remarks show how difficult it is for even a very good twentieth-century legal scholar to escape completely from the bondage of modern legal positivism. In the following passage, Casto appears to make the same mistake that was made by Postema in his comments on the "reason of the common law"—the mistake of reading twentieth-century at-

titudes conditioned by positivist ideology back into the history of the Founding era (see notes 65–69 with accompanying text). According to Casto, "The common law in the late eighteenth century was fundamentally at war with itself. It had a natural-law foundation and was considered to be the expression of divine wisdom and the perfection of human reason. In theory, the common law was a complete, systematic, and cohesive body of principles. But in practice, common lawyers exalted shared community experience and placed immense trust in tradition and local customs. . . . Common lawyers professed to be natural lawyers, but their immense reliance upon tradition had the practical effect of leading them to define law by reference to the received customs or traditions of a particular human community. The practice of placing immense emphasis upon custom and tradition is closer to legal positivism than to natural law. . . . The key issue is the existence of the tradition, not the substantive content of the rule. . . . Under natural-law thinking, the key issue was whether a putative legal principle was the embodiment of reason" (p. 158). But this is wrong on at least two counts. First, custom contradicts nature only on the assumption that "immemorial usage" and "universal reception" are not considered to be *avenues by which nature reveals herself to man*. But such an assumption could be made only by one already under the sway of positivism. Second, "local" or "particular" customs did not make up the common law for eighteenth-century jurists; rather, the common law is "general custom," the "custom of the realm," to which local or particular customs are exceptions. It was so for the Romans, too; for it was the gentic law, not the civil law, that would become the "common law" of Western Europe in the aftermath of the Empire's collapse.

71. According to Roscoe Pound, Hugo Grotius, whose legal thought influenced both English and American law, believed that "the end for which law exists is to produce conformity to the nature of rational creatures." Thus, "at the very time that the victory of the courts in the contests between the common-law courts and the Stuart kings had established that there were fundamental common-law rights of Englishmen . . . a juristic theory of fundamental natural rights, independent of and running back of all states . . . had sprung up independently. . . . By a natural transition, the common-law limitations on royal authority became natural limitations upon all authority; the common-law rights of Englishmen became the natural rights of man." Hugo Grotius, *Prolegomena to the Law of War and Peace*, trans. Francis W. Kelsey, ed. Edward Dumbauld (Indianapolis: Bobbs-Merrill, 1957), quoted in editor's introduction, p. xiv.

9. INTENTIONALISM AND THE RULES OF INTERPRETATION IN ENGLISH AND AMERICAN PRACTICE

1. Sir Matthew Hale, "Reflections by the Lrd. Cheife Justice Hale on Mr. Hobbes his Dialogue of the Lawe," in Sir William Holdsworth, *A History of English Law*, 16 vols., 3d. ed. (London: Methuen and Company, Sweet and Maxwell, 1945), 5:502–3.

2. Earl M. Maltz, *Rethinking Constitutional Law: Originalism, Interventionism, and the Politics of Judicial Review* (Lawrence: University Press of Kansas, 1994).

3. See, on this point, Michael J. Perry, *The Constitution, the Courts, and Human Rights: An Inquiry into the Legitimacy of Policymaking by the Judiciary* (New Haven: Yale University Press, 1982), pp. 1–8.

4. *Olmstead v. United States*, 277 U.S. 438 (1928).

5. 1 Cranch (5 U.S.) 137, at 176–77 (1803) (emphasis added).

6. See Keith E. Whittington, *Constitutional Construction*, vol. 1, *Interpretation and Original Intent* (typescript, Catholic University of America, Washington, D.C.), esp. chap. 5.

7. Joseph Story, *Commentaries on the Constitution of the United States*, ed. Thomas M. Cooley, 2 vols., 4th ed. (Boston: Little, Brown and Company, 1873), 2:257–58. Story is here quoting from John Marshall's opinion in *Dartmouth College v. Woodward*, 4 Wheaton 518 (1819).

8. Guido Calabresi, *A Common Law for the Age of Statutes* (Cambridge: Harvard University Press, 1982), p. 203 n. 1. Calabresi is quoting from H. Hart and A. Sacks, *The Legal Process: Basic Problems in the Making and Application of Law* (typescript, Harvard University, 1958). This typescript, containing the highly influential lecture notes of the founders of the so-called "legal process" school of American jurisprudence, is discussed in Calabresi, *Common Law*, pp. 203–4 n. 1.

9. Chief Justice Marshall, writing for the Court in *McCulloch v. Maryland*, 4 Wheaton 316 (1819), quoted in Wallace Mendelson, *The American Constitution and the Judicial Process* (Homewood, Ill.: Dorsey Press, 1980), p. 150.

10. See, on this point, H. Jefferson Powell, "The Original Understanding of Original Intent," in *Interpreting the Constitution: The Debate over Original Intent*, ed. Jack N. Rakove (Boston: Northeastern University Press, 1990) pp. 53–116.

11. William Blackstone, *Commentaries on the Laws of England*, 4 vols. (Chicago: University of Chicago Press, 1979), 1:86–87.

12. Ibid., 1:87–88.

13. James R. Stoner, Jr., *Common Law and Liberal Theory: Coke, Hobbes, and the Origins of American Constitutionalism* (Lawrence: University Press of Kansas, 1992), p. 215.

14. Thomas Aquinas, *Treatise on Law (Summa Theologica, Questions 90–97)*, ed. Stanley Parry (Chicago: Regnery Gateway), p. 102.

15. Ibid., p. 104.

16. *Gibbons v. Ogden*, 9 Wheaton 1 (1824).

17. See, on Madison's views, Charles A. Lofgren, "The Original Understanding of Original Intent?" in Rakove, ed., *Interpreting the Constitution*, pp. 135–41.

18. Christopher Wolfe, *The Rise of Modern Judicial Review: From Constitutional Interpretation to Judge-Made Law* (New York: Basic Books, 1986), p. 18.

19. Ibid.

20. Ibid., p. 19.

21. *Heydon's Case*, 3 *Coke's Reports* 7a, at 7b (1584).

22. Wolfe, *Rise of Modern Review*, p. 19.

23. Chief Justice Tindal, addressing the House of Lords in *The Sussex Peerage Case*, 11 Cl. and Fin. 85, at 143 (1844); quoted in Sir Rupert Cross, *Statutory Interpretation*, 2d ed. (London: Butterworth's, 1987), p. 14.

24. 96 U.S. 1 (1878).

25. Lord Diplock, in *Fothergill v. Monarch Airlines, Ltd.*, A. C. 251, at 279–80; quoted in Cross, *Statutory Interpretation*, p. 152.

26. Lord Wensleydale, in *Grey v. Pearson*, 6 H. L. Cas. 61, at 106 (1857), quoted in Cross, *Statutory Interpretation*, p. 16 (emphasis added).

27. 310 U.S. 534, at 543–44 (1940), quoted in Cross, *Statutory Interpretation*, p. 153 (emphasis added). See also Edward H. Levi, *An Introduction to Legal Reasoning* (Chicago: University of Chicago Press, 1949), p. 29.

28. Hart and Sacks, *Legal Process,* quoted in Calabresi, *Common Law,* pp. 203–4 n. 1.

29. Quoted in Lofgren, "Original Understanding of Original Intent?" p. 141. Referring to Madison's statement, Keith Whittington points out that "The 'early, deliberate & continued practice' of the first legislatures supplemented the text, the historic purpose of the text, and the 'comments prevailing at the time it was adopted' in providing the necessary material for a legal interpretation of the Constitution. Early practice did not indicate the fluidity of constitutional meaning or an avenue of constitutional change, but rather made express the implicit meaning of a complicated text. More recently, the Court has institutionalized this understanding as legally applicable doctrine. Thus, in a different context, Felix Frankfurter explained that the plain text must be understood in terms of the 'gloss' placed on it by 'systematic, unbroken executive practice, long pursued to the knowledge of the Congress and never before questioned, engaged in by Presidents who have also sworn to uphold the Constitution, making as it were such exercise of power part of the structure of our government' " (*Constitutional Construction,* vol. 2, *Divided Powers and Constitutional Meaning,* p. 326). See also *Youngstown Sheet & Tube Co. v. Sawyer,* 343 U.S. 579, at 610–11 (1952).

30. See generally Clinton, *Marbury and Review,* chap. 5.

31. 6 Cranch 78 (1810).

32. 4 Wheaton 518 (1819).

33. See generally Clinton, *Marbury and Review,* chap. 9.

34. 6 Wheaton 264 (1821).

35. See Clinton, *Marbury and Review,* pp. 94–97.

36. 4 Wheaton 316 (1819).

37. 9 Wheaton 1 (1824).

38. See Clinton, *Marbury and Review,* pp. 194–96.

10. THE RULES OF INTERPRETATION, STARE DECISIS, AND LEGAL FICTION IN CONSTITUTIONAL LAW

1. Guido Calabresi, *A Common Law for the Age of Statutes* (Cambridge: Harvard University Press, 1982), p. 13.

2. J. W. Hurst, *Dealing with Statutes* (New York: Columbia University Press, 1982), p. 33; quoted in Sir Rupert Cross, *Statutory Interpretation,* 2d ed. (London: Butterworth's, 1987), p. 28.

3. Cross, *Statutory Interpretation,* p. 28.

4. Gilbert K. Chesterton, *Orthodoxy* (New York: John Lane Company, 1908), pp. 84–86. See Chapter 2 n. 21 and accompanying text.

5. Lon L. Fuller, *Legal Fictions* (Stanford, Calif.: Stanford University Press, 1967), p. 9.

6. Ibid., pp. 9–10.

7. Frederic William Maitland, *Collected Papers,* ed. H. A. Fisher, 3 vols. (Cambridge: Cambridge University Press, 1911), 3:316; quote, p. 10.

8. Justice Holmes, in *New York Trust Co. v. Eisner,* 256 U.S. 345, at 349.

9. Michael Gagarin, *Early Greek Law* (Berkeley: University of California Press, 1986), p. 100.

10. Immanuel Kant, *Foundations of the Metaphysics of Morals,* trans. Lewis White Beck (Indianapolis: Bobbs-Merrill, 1959).

11. Henry Sumner Maine, *Ancient Law: Its Connection with the Early History of Society and Its Relation to Modern Ideas* (Dorset Press, 1986), pp. 27–36.

12. J. Walter Jones, *The Law and Legal Theory of the Greeks* (Oxford: Clarendon Press, 1956), pp. 133–35.

13. Gagarin, *Early Greek Law*, pp. 121–22.

14. Ibid., p. 131.

15. Calabresi, *Common Law*, p. 3.

16. Maine, *Ancient Law*, p. 20.

17. Karl N. Llewellyn, *The Bramble Bush* (New York: Oceana Press, 1951), pp. 64–69; portions reprinted in John Bonsignore et al., eds., *Before the Law: An Introduction to the Legal Process*, 3d ed. (Boston: Houghton Mifflin Company, 1984), pp. 13–14.

18. See Sir Rupert Cross, *Precedent in English Law*, 3d ed. (Oxford: Clarendon Press, 1977), pp. 23–26.

19. See Arthur R. Hogue, *Origins of the Common Law* (Indianapolis: Liberty Fund, 1985), p. 200.

20. Quoted in Cross, *Precedent in English Law*, p. 24; see also Hogue, *Origins of Common Law*, p. 200.

21. See Hogue, *Origins of Common Law*, pp. 200–201.

22. Quoted in Cross, *Precedent in English Law*, p. 26.

23. See Ibid., pp. 26–27.

24. Ibid., p. 28.

25. William Blackstone, *Commentaries on the Laws of England*, 4 vols. (Chicago: University of Chicago Press, 1979), 1:67.

26. Ibid., pp. 69–70.

27. Ibid., pp. 76–78.

28. Ibid., p. 71.

29. Thomas Aquinas, *Treatise on Law (Summa Theologica, Questions 90–97)*, ed. Stanley Parry (Chicago: Regnery Gateway), pp. 111–12. Indeed, according to Postema, custom is, for Aquinas, the *primary* source of law: "For the authority to 'order behavior to the common good' rests first in 'the whole people,' and derivatively in the *princeps*" (Gerald R. Postema, *Bentham and the Common Law Tradition* [Oxford: Clarendon Press, 1986], p. 45).

30. See Sir Frederick Pollock and Frederic William Maitland, *The History of English Law Before the Time of Edward I*, 2 vols., 2d ed. (Cambridge: Cambridge University Press, 1968), 1:16–17.

31. See ibid., 1:16.

32. Ibid., 1:17.

33. See Clinton, *Marbury and Review*, Part 1.

34. *Marbury v. Madison*, 1 Cranch (5 U.S.) 137 (1803).

35. See Clinton, *Marbury and Review*, Part 2.

36. 19 Howard 393 (1857).

37. See Clinton, *Marbury and Review*, chaps. 9–11.

38. See ibid., chap. 12.

39. Pollock and Maitland, *History of English Law*, 1:17.

40. Quoted in W. S. Holdsworth, *The Historians of Anglo-American Law* (Hamden, Conn.: Archon Books, 1966), p. 66. Nothing that I have said in this (or any other) chapter should be taken to imply that legal precedent should always be followed. Indeed, overreli-

ance on precedent can sometimes produce absurd or unjust results in particular cases, as in the examples discussed by Alan Watson, *Roman Law and Comparative Law* (Athens: University of Georgia Press, 1991), chap. 23. It should be noted, however, that it is arguable whether Professor Watson's examples reflect erroneous use of, rather than overreliance on, precedent (by the judges in the examples). It should also be noted that the examples show the power of legal tradition even more remarkably than would a long catalog of good results, precisely in virtue of the absurdity of the results that were reached by the judges in these cases.

II. POLITICAL PHILOSOPHY

1. See Eric Voegelin, *The Nature of the Law and Related Legal Writings*, in *The Collected Works of Eric Voegelin*, eds. Robert A. Pascal, James L. Babin, and John W. Corrington (Baton Rouge: Louisiana State University Press, 1991), 27:xiv.

2. See Plato, *Great Dialogues of Plato*, trans. W. H. D. Rouse (New York: Penguin Books, 1984). See also Plato, *The Republic*, trans. Desmond Lee, 2d ed. rev. (London: Penguin Books, 1987), esp. Part 9.

3. See Thomas Hobbes, *Leviathan*, ed. C. B. Macpherson (London: Penguin Books, 1968), esp. Part 1.

4. Ibid., esp. Part 2.

5. For a classic mathematical treatment of game theory, see R. Duncan Luce and Howard Raiffa, *Games and Decisions: Introduction and Critical Survey* (New York: John Wiley and Sons, 1957). For a less technical treatment, with applications in social science, see Henry Hamburger, *Games as Models of Social Phenomena* (San Francisco: W. H. Freeman and Company, 1979).

6. For a general treatment of two-person games, see Anatol Rapaport, *Two-Person Game Theory* (Ann Arbor: University of Michigan Press, 1966). For a discussion of the prisoner's dilemma as an n-person game, see Henry Hamburger, "N-person Prisoner's Dilemma," *Journal of Mathematical Sociology* 3 (1973): 27–48.

7. See Thomas Schwartz, *The Logic of Collective Choice* (New York: Columbia University Press, 1986), esp. pp. 254–59.

8. See Plato, *Republic*, Part 7, Sec. 7, pp. 316–25. Grotius and Pufendorf recognized the problem and attempted to resolve it by positing an innate "sociality" in human nature that might effectively stabilize the social contract once the condition of civil society was reached. See Hugo Grotius, *Prolegomena to the Law of War and Peace*, trans. Francis W. Kelsey (Indianapolis: Bobbs-Merrill, 1957) and Samuel Pufendorf, *On the Duty of Man and Citizen According to Natural Law*, trans. Michael Silverthorne, ed. James Tully (Cambridge: Cambridge University Press, 1991).

9. Ibid., Part 9, pp. 356–420.

10. William H. McNeill and Jean W. Sedlar, eds., *The Classical Mediterranean World* (New York: Oxford University Press, 1969), p. 15 n. 8.

11. See Alexandre Kojeve, *Introduction to the Reading of Hegel: Lectures on the Phenomenology of Spirit*, trans. James H. Nichols, Jr., ed. Allan Bloom (Ithaca, N.Y.: Cornell University Press, 1980), p. 4.

12. For the relation between "concepts" and "percepts" that undergird this discussion, see Mortimer J. Adler, *Ten Philosophical Mistakes* (New York: Macmillan, 1985), esp. chap. 1.

13. David Hume, *An Enquiry Concerning Human Understanding*, ed. L. A. Selby-Bigge, in *Great Books of the Western World*, ed. Robert Maynard Hutchins (Chicago: Encyclopaedia Britannica, 1952), 35:505. See also John Locke, *An Essay Concerning Human Understanding*, ed. Alexander Campbell Fraser, in *Great Books of the Western World*, ed. Robert Maynard Hutchins (Chicago: Encyclopaedia Britannica, 1952), 35:253–54, who denies the connection between external reality and the words we use to represent our ideas in language: "Words are often secretly referred, first to the ideas supposed to be in other men's minds. But . . . words, as they are used by men, can properly and immediately signify nothing but the ideas that are in the mind of the speaker. . . . Secondly, . . . they often suppose the words to stand also for the reality of things . . . though . . . it is a perverting of the use of words, and brings unavoidable obscurity and confusion in their signification, whenever we make them stand for anything but those ideas we have in our own minds."

14. Mortimer J. Adler, *Intellect: Mind over Matter* (New York: Macmillan, 1990), p. 85.

15. Immanuel Kant, *Critique of Pure Reason*, trans. J. M. D. Meiklejohn, 2d ed. (London: J. M Dent and Sons, 1934), p. 41.

16. Ibid., pp. 10–11.

17. Etienne Gilson, *Being and Some Philosophers*, 2d ed. (Toronto: Pontifical Institute of Mediaeval Studies, 1952), pp. 130–31.

18. Adler, *Ten Philosophical Mistakes*, chap. 1, Epilogue.

19. Ibid., pp. 32–37.

20. Thomas Aquinas, *Summa Theologica*, trans. Fathers of the English Dominican Province, rev. Daniel J. Sullivan, in *Great Books of the Western World*, ed. Robert Maynard Hutchins, vols. 19–20 (Chicago: Encyclopaedia Britannica, 1952), First Part, Quest. 85, Art. 2, 19:452. For a full and clear discussion of the Thomistic epistemology that underlies Aquinas's statement on this point, and on which Mortimer Adler's analysis appears to be largely based, see Etienne Gilson, *The Philosophy of St. Thomas Aquinas*, trans. Edward Bullough, ed. G. A. Elrington (New York: Barnes & Noble Books, 1993), chap. 13.

21. Adler, *Ten Philosophical Mistakes*, pp. 27–28.

12. LAW AND JURISPRUDENCE

1. See esp. Plato, *The Republic*, trans. Desmond Lee, 2d ed. rev. (London: Penguin Books, 1987), Books 8, 9; Aristotle, *The Politics of Aristotle*, trans. Ernest Barker (London: Oxford University Press, 1958), Books 3–4. See also Cicero, *De Legibus*, trans. Clinton Walker Keyes (Cambridge: Harvard University Press, 1977), 16:289–519; Augustine, *The City of God*, trans. Gerald G. Walsh, S.J., Demetrius B. Zema, S.J., Grace Monahan, O.S.U., and Daniel J. Honan, ed. Vernon J. Bourke (Garden City, N.Y.: Doubleday and Company, 1958).

2. Thomas Aquinas, *Treatise on Law (Summa Theologica, Propositions 90–97)* (Chicago: Regnery Gateway), esp. pp. 73–116.

3. See ibid., pp. 101–4.

4. For the argument of Thrasymachus, see Plato, *Republic*, Part 1, Sec. 3; for the argument of Callicles, see Plato, *Gorgias*, trans. Donald J. Zeyl (Indianapolis: Hackett Publishing Company, 1987), pp. 50 ff.

5. Niccolo Machiavelli, *The Prince*, trans. George Bull (New York: Penguin Classics, 1961).

6. See Thomas Hobbes, *The Elements of Law: Natural and Politic*, ed. Ferdinand Tonnies (Cambridge: Cambridge University Press, 1928), Part 2, chap. 10, pp. 150–51. See also Thomas Hobbes, *A Dialogue Between a Philosopher and a Student of the Common Laws of England*, ed. Josephy Cropsey (Chicago: University of Chicago Press, 1971), an excellent discussion of which may be found in James R. Stoner, Jr., *Common Law and Liberal Theory: Coke, Hobbes, and the Origins of American Constitutionalism* (Lawrence: University Press of Kansas, 1992), pp. 116–30. Hobbes's rejection of custom is not complete, for he allows that customs may be regarded as laws if "they are admitted by the sovereign" (Hobbes, *Elements of Law*, p. 151; Stoner, *Common Law and Liberal Theory*, pp. 85–91, 118–25).

7. Thomas Hobbes, *Leviathan*, trans. C. B. Macpherson (London: Penguin Books, 1968), Parts 1 and 2.

8. Eric Voegelin, *The Nature of the Law and Related Legal Writings*, in *The Collected Works of Eric Voegelin*, ed. Robert A. Pascal, James L. Babin, and John W. Corrington (Baton Rouge: Louisiana State University Press, 1991), 27:80.

9. William T. Tete, "The Secularization of Natural Law: Beyond the Furor of Ideology" (Paper presented at the annual meeting of the American Political Science Association, Chicago, September 2, 1995), p. 10.

10. On the role of the praetors, see Colin Kolbert's excellent introductory essay in Justinian, *The Digest of Roman Law: Theft, Rapine, Damage and Insult*, trans. C. F. Kolbert (London: Penguin Books, 1979), pp. 13–16.

11. 302 U.S. 319 (1937).

12. See Michael Gagarin, *Early Greek Law* (Berkeley: University of California Press, 1986), p. 116.

13. 391 U.S. 145 (1968), esp. note 10.

14. Ibid., at note 10; quoted in Wallace Mendelson, *The American Constitution and the Judicial Process* (Homewood, Ill.: Dorsey Press, 1980), pp. 253–54.

15. Echoing some of the themes emphasized in Part One of this book, William Casto notes the effect of modern legal positivism on the legitimacy of judicial review: "Today virtually all American lawyers believe that law is the expression of government policy. In addition, today's lawyers believe that judges are themselves lawmakers and that the judicial resolution of a particular case is largely an outcome of the judges' understanding of appropriate governmental policy. From this new philosophical viewpoint, the issue of judicial review entails a clash between the Congress's and the judiciary's conflicting views of appropriate constitutional policy. Certainly there is nothing in the Constitution that warrants an arbitrary preferment of judicial policy judgments to legislative judgments. The doctrine of judicial review is therefore more subject to theoretical objection than it was two hundred years ago" (*The Supreme Court in the Early Republic: The Chief Justiceships of John Jay and Oliver Ellsworth* [Columbia: University of South Carolina Press, 1995], p. 219).

16. See Robert Lowry Clinton, "Judicial Review, Nationalism, and the Commerce

Clause: Contrasting Antebellum and Postbellum Supreme Court Decision Making," *Political Research Quarterly* 47 (1994): 857–60. See also Howard Gillman, "The Struggle over Marshall and the Politics of Constitutional History," *Political Research Quarterly* 47 (1994): 877–86; Clinton, "John Marshall's Federalism: A Reply to Professor Gillman," *Political Research Quarterly* 47 (1994): 887–90. For a second round of discussion on this issue, see Wallace Mendelson, "John Marshall and the Sugar Trust—A Reply to Professor Gillman," *Political Research Quarterly* 49 (1996): 405–13; Howard Gillman, "More on the Origins of the Fuller Court's Jurisprudence: Reexamining the Scope of Federal Power Over Commerce and Manufacturing in Nineteenth-Century Constitutional Law," *Political Research Quarterly* 49 (1996): 415–37; Mendelson, "Nullification via Dual Federalism: A Second Response to Professor Gillman," *Political Research Quarterly* 49 (1996): 439–44.

17. John Austin, *The Province of Jurisprudence Determined*, Lecture 1, excerpted in *The Nature of Law: Readings in Legal Philosophy*, ed. M. P. Golding (New York: Random House, 1966), p. 77.

18. Voegelin, *Nature of Law*, 27:80.

19. Aquinas, *Treatise on Law*, p. 3.

20. Ibid., pp. 36–54.

21. Ibid., pp. 10–11.

22. Ibid., pp. 12–13.

23. Ibid., pp. 14–16.

24. Voegelin, *Nature of the Law*, 27:81.

25. Aquinas, *Treatise on Law*, pp. 19–22.

26. Ibid., pp. 17–19.

27. Ibid., p. 57.

28. Cicero, *De Legibus*, 16:319.

29. Aquinas, *Treatise on Law*, p. 111.

30. Ibid., pp. 111–12.

31. Quoted in ibid., p. 18.

32. Austin, Lecture 1, pp. 77–78.

33. Ibid., p. 81.

34. Austin, Lecture 2, excerpted in John Stuart Mill, *Utilitarianism, On Liberty, Essay on Bentham: Together with Selected Writings of Jeremy Bentham and John Austin*, ed. Mary Warnock (New York: Penguin Books, 1974), p. 322.

35. Ibid., p. 324.

36. Austin, Lecture 5, in Golding, ed., *Nature of Law*, p. 89.

37. Ibid., pp. 89–90.

38. Ibid., pp. 90–91.

39. Austin, Lecture 6, in Golding, ed., *Nature of Law*, p. 93.

40. See Thomas Aquinas, *Summa Theologica*, trans. Fathers of the English Dominican Province, rev. Daniel J. Sullivan, in *Great Books of the Western World*, ed. Robert Maynard Hutchins, vols. 19–20 (Chicago: Encyclopaedia Britannica, 1952), 19:, Part 1, Quest. 85, Art. 2, pp. 453–55; see also Mortimer J. Adler, *Ten Philosophical Mistakes* (New York: Macmillan, 1985), chap. 1. See Chapter 11.

41. Austin, Lecture 2, in Mill, *Utilitarianism*, pp. 336–37.

42. Ibid., p. 337.

43. Henry Sumner Maine, "The Limits of the Analytical System," in *The Nature of Law: Readings in Legal Philosophy,* ed. M. P. Golding (New York: Random House, 1966), pp. 98–103.

44. See Voegelin, *Nature of the Law.*

45. See Albert Venn Dicey, *Introduction to the Study of the Law of the Constitution,* 8th ed. (Indianapolis: Liberty Classics, 1982), Part 3.

46. Austin, Lecture 5, in Golding, *Nature of Law,* p. 90.

47. Etienne Gilson, *Being and Some Philosophers,* 2d ed. (Toronto: Pontifical Institute of Mediaeval Studies, 1952), p. 214.

13. NATURAL LAW AND THE CONSTITUTION

1. Thomas Aquinas, *Treatise on Law (Summa Theologica, Propositions 90–97)* (Chicago: Regnery Gateway), Prop. 91, art. 3, pp. 17–19.

2. John Austin, Lecture 2, excerpted in John Stuart Mill, *Utilitarianism, On Liberty, Essay on Bentham: Together with Selected Writings of Jeremy Bentham and John Austin,* ed. Mary Warnock (New York: Penguin Books, 1974), p. 337; see Chapter 12.

3. See, e.g., Leonard Levy, *Original Intent and the Framers' Constitution* (New York: Collier Macmillan, 1988), p. 136, who asserts that the early Supreme Court read natural law doctrines into the Constitution in order to protect property rights. In a blatantly ad hominem directed at conservatives who "do not know what they are talking about," Levy points to a "long history" of judicial activism and "result-oriented" constitutional jurisprudence: "From its earliest years . . . through the great constitutional cases of the Marshall Court, the Supreme Court played fast and loose with the Constitution, reaching the results preferred by the policy choices of the majority of the Court."

4. See John Locke, *Two Treatises of Government,* ed. Peter Laslett (Cambridge: Cambridge University Press, 1960), Book 2, esp. Secs. 4–15, 123–31.

5. Ibid., esp. Secs. 123–31, 211–43.

6. For a late-Roman description of the various kinds of property, including "common" property, see Justinian, *Justinian's Institutes,* trans. Peter Birks and Grant McLeod (Ithaca, N.Y.: Cornell University Press, 1987), p. 55. For a more modern perspective, see Mancur Olson, *The Logic of Collective Action* (Cambridge: Harvard University Press, 1971), esp. pp. 9–16.

7. Thomas Aquinas, *Summa Theologica* 2:2, Quest. 66, First Article, in Thomas Aquinas, *On Law, Morality, and Politics,* ed. William P. Baumgarth and Richard J. Regan, S.J. (Indianapolis: Hackett Publishing Company, 1988), p. 177.

8. Ibid., Second Article, p. 179. It is interesting to note that Blackstone, though usually considered a Lockean, seems to agree with Aquinas. According to Robert P. Burns, "The only divine right to property, unqualified, unmediated, and unmodelled by the civil law to be found in the *Commentaries* is the God-given right of all men to possess the earth in common" (Burns, "Blackstone's Theory of the 'Absolute' Rights of Property," *Cincinnati Law Review* 54 [1985]: 77). In the *Commentaries,* amid a discussion of forfeitures, Blackstone states that "all property is derived from society, being one of those civil rights . . . conferred upon individuals, in exchange for that degree of natural freedom which every man

must sacrifice when he enters into social communities" (1 *Commentaries* 299, quoted in Burns, p. 82).

9. On the connection between property rights in the early American republic and property rights in the laissez-faire era, see Robert Lowry Clinton, "Judicial Review, Nationalism, and the Commerce Clause: Contrasting Antebellum and Postbellum Supreme Court Decision Making," *Political Research Quarterly* 47 (1994): 857–60, and references contained therein.

10. See, e.g., Richard A. Epstein, *Takings: Private Property and the Power of Eminent Domain* (Cambridge: Harvard University Press, 1985; Bernard H. Siegan, *Economic Liberties and the Constitution* (Chicago: University of Chicago Press, 1980).

11. Epstein, *Takings;* see also Lane V. Sunderland, *Popular Government and the Supreme Court: Securing the Public Good and Private Rights* (Lawrence: University Press of Kansas, 1995), esp. chap. 5.

12. Sunderland, *Popular Government and Supreme Court,* chap. 5.

13. Ibid., chaps. 1–2.

14. Ibid., chap. 2.

15. Michael Lienesch, *New Order of the Ages: Time, the Constitution, and the Making of Modern American Political Thought* (Princeton, N.J.: Princeton University Press, 1988), p. 80.

16. Sunderland, *Popular Government and Supreme Court,* chap. 2.

17. Ibid., chap. 3.

18. See Matthew J. Franck, *Against the Imperial Judiciary: The Supreme Court vs. the Sovereignty of the People* (Lawrence: University Press of Kansas, 1996), chaps. 6–7.

19. 2 Dallas 304, at 311 (1795) (Paterson, J.); Franck, *Against the Imperial Judiciary,* p. 114.

20. 2 Dallas 386, at 388 (1798)(Chase, J.); Franck, *Against the Imperial Judiciary,* p. 119.

21. 2 Peters 627, at 657 (1829)(Story, J.); Franck, *Against the Imperial Judiciary,* p. 146.

22. *Calder v. Bull,* 2 Dallas 386, at 388 (1798)(Chase, J.).

23. 9 Cranch 43 (1815)(Story, J.); Franck, *Against the Imperial Judiciary,* p. 142, quoting Gary L. McDowell, *Equity and the Constitution: The Supreme Court, Equitable Relief, and Public Policy* (Chicago: University of Chicago Press, 1982), p. 75.

24. 12 Wheaton 213, at 332 (Marshall, C. J.); Franck, *Against the Imperial Judiciary,* pp. 136–37.

25. 6 Cranch 87, at 139 (1810)(Marshall, C. J.); Franck, *Against the Imperial Judiciary,* p. 131.

26. 3 Cranch 87, at 143 (1810)(Johnson, J.); Franck, *Against the Imperial Judiciary,* p. 132.

27. Franck, *Against the Imperial Judiciary,* pp. 134–35, 138; see *Ogden v. Saunders,* 12 Wheaton 213, at 290 (1827)(Johnson, J.).

28. Franck, *Against the Imperial Judiciary,* esp. chap. 7.

29. John Stuart Mill, *On Liberty,* in Mill, *Utilitarianism,* p. 135. See also James Fitzjames Stephen, *Liberty, Equality, Fraternity,* ed. Stuart D. Warner (1874; Indianapolis: Liberty Classics, 1992), p. 6.

30. Mill, *On Liberty,* pp. 139–40. See also Stephen, *Liberty, Equality, Fraternity,* p. 7.

31. Stephen, *Liberty, Equality, Fraternity,* p. 12.

32. Ibid., p. 77.

33. Ibid.

34. John Stuart Mill, *Three Essays on Religion: Nature, The Utility of Religion, and Theism,* ed. Helen Taylor, 2d ed. (London: Longmans, Green, Reader, and Dyer, 1874).

35. Ibid., pp. vii–xi.

36. Mill, "Theism," pp. 123–257.

37. See Mill, "Utility of Religion," pp. 69–122.

38. Mill, "Theism," in pp. 242–57, esp. p. 256. See also Stephen, *Liberty, Equality, Fraternity,* pp. 174–75.

39. Mill, "Theism," p. 256.

40. Ibid., pp. 256–57.

41. Mill, "Nature," p. 52.

42. Ibid., p. 54.

43. See *Everson v. Board of Education,* 330 U.S. 1 (1947); see also *United States v. Carolene Products Co.,* 304 U.S. 144 (1938), n. 4.

44. See Chilperic Edwards, ed., *The Hammurabi Code, and the Sinaitic Legislation,* trans. C. Edwards (Port Washington, N.Y.: Kennikat Press, 1971).

45. See, e.g., Plato, *The Laws of Plato,* trans. Thomas L. Pangle (Chicago and London: University of Chicago Press, 1988); Katherine Fischer Drew, ed. and trans., *The Burgundian Code* (Philadelphia: University of Pennsylvania Press, 1949); Edgar Bodenheimer, John Bilyeu Oakley, and Jean C. Love, *An Introduction to the Anglo-American Legal System: Readings and Cases,* 2d ed. (St. Paul, Minn.: West Publishing Company, 1988).

46. See, e.g., Plato, *Laws;* Cicero, *De Legibus,* in *Cicero: In Twenty-Eight Volumes,* vol. 16, trans. Clinton Walker Keyes (Cambridge: Harvard University Press, Loeb Library, 1977); Aquinas, *Treatise on Law.* See Chapter 12.

47. See Justinian, *Institutes,* pp. 39–55 on the Roman law of persons.

48. *Everson v. Board of Education,* 330 U.S. 1 (1947).

49. See, e.g., *Engel v. Vitale,* 370 U.S. 421 (1962); *School District of Abington v. Schemp,* 374 U.S. 203 (1963); *Wallace v. Jaffree,* 472 U.S. 38 (1985); *Lee v. Weisman,* 60 U.S. L. W. 4723 (1992); *Allegheny County v. American Civil Liberties Union,* 492 U.S. 573 (1989).

50. See, e.g., *Wallace v. Jaffree,* 472 U.S. 38 (1985).

51. See *West Virginia State Board of Education v. Barnette,* 319 U.S. 624 (1943).

52. See, e.g., *Spence v. Washington,* 418 U.S. 405 (1974); *United States v. O'Brien,* 391 U.S. 367 (1968); *Cohen v. California,* 403 U.S. 15 (1971); *Tinker v. Des Moines School District,* 393 U.S. 503 (1969).

53. See, e.g., *Yates v. United States,* 354 U.S. 298 (1957); *Scales v. United States,* 367 U.S. 203 (1961); *Brandenburg v. Ohio,* 395 U.S. 444 (1969).

54. See, e.g., *Memoirs v. Massachusetts,* 383 U.S. 413 (1966); *Roth v. United States,* 354 U.S. 476 (1957); *Jenkins v. Georgia,* 418 U.S. 153 (1974).

55. *Stanley v. Georgia,* 394 U.S. 557 (1969).

56. See, e.g., *Griswold v. Connecticut,* 381 U.S. 479 (1965); *Eisenstadt v. Baird,* 405 U.S. 438 (1972); *Roe v. Wade,* 410 U.S. 113 (1973).

57. See *Planned Parenthood of Southeastern Pennsylvania v. Casey,* 112 S. Ct. 2791 (1992).

58. See *Munn v. Illinois,* 94 U.S. 113 (1877).

59. See *United States v. Carolene Products Co.,* 304 U.S. 144 (1938), n. 4.

60. See *Baker v. Carr,* 369 U.S. 186 (1962); *Reynolds v. Sims,* 377 U.S. 533 (1964); *Avery v.*

Midland County, 390 U.S. 474 (1968); *Hadley v. Junior College District*, 397 U.S. 50 (1970); *Lucas v. Forty-Fourth General Assembly*, 377 U.S. 713 (1964).

61. See *Reed v. Reed*, 404 U.S. 71 (1971); *Frontiero v. Richardson*, 411 U.S. 677 (1973); *Califano v. Goldfarb*, 430 U.S. 199 (1977); *Los Angeles Department of Water and Power v. Manhart*, 98 S.Ct. 1370 (1978).

62. See *Graham v. Richardson*, 403 U.S. 365 (1971); *In re Griffiths*, 413 U.S. 717 (1973); *Sugarman v. Dougall*, 413 U.S. 634 (1973); *Plyler v. Doe*, 457 U.S. 202 (1982).

63. See *Levy v. Louisiana*, 391 U.S. 68 (1968); *Trimble v. Gordon*, 430 U.S. 762 (1977); *Clark v. Jeter*, 486 U.S. 456 (1988).

64. See *Everson v. Board of Education*, 330 U.S. 1 (1947), reported in Wallace Mendelson, *The American Constitution and the Judicial Process* (Homewood, Ill.: Dorsey Press, 1980), p. 649, where Justice Black says, in effect, that the establishment clause requires virtually absolute separation of church and state, using Jefferson's famous "wall of separation" metaphor, and then violates both his rhetoric and his principle by upholding the challenged law.

65. See Augustine, *The City of God*, trans. Gerald G. Walsh, S.J., Demetrius B. Zema, S.J., Grace Monahan, O.S.U., and Daniel J. Honan, ed. Vernon J. Bourke (Garden City, N.Y.: Doubleday and Company, 1958), on the "mixing" of secular and religious authorities (and their respective clienteles) in the world. See also Graham Walker, *Moral Foundations of Constitutional Thought: Current Problems, Augustinian Prospects* (Princeton, N.J.: Princeton University Press, 1990), esp. chaps. 3–5.

66. See, e.g., *Braunfeld v. Braun*, 366 U.S. 599 (1961); *McGowan v. Maryland*, 366 U.S. 420 (1961); *Engel v. Vitale*, 370 U.S. 421 (1962); *School District of Abington v. Schemp*, 374 U.S. 203 (1963); *Wallace v. Jaffree*, 472 U.S. 38 (1985); *Lee v. Weisman*, 60 U.S. L. W. 4723 (1992); *Epperson v. Arkansas*, 393 U.S. 97 (1968); *Edwards v. Aguillard*, 482 U.S. 578 (1987); *Thornton v. Caldor, Inc.*, 472 U.S. 703 (1985); *Larkin v. Grindel's Den, Inc.*, 459 U.S. 116 (1982); *Lynch v. Donnelly*, 465 U.S. 668 (1984); *Allegheny County v. American Civil Liberties Union*, 492 U.S. 573 (1989); *Edwards v. Aguillard*, 482 U.S. 578 (1987). The problem is not so much the particular decisions in these cases but the secularism that is the main ground of decision running through them. For example, even though *McGowan* and *Braunfeld* upheld Sunday closing laws and thus might be thought by some observers to be proreligion decisions, the Court's basis for upholding the laws was their "secular purpose." Secular purpose is the first of the famous "three-pronged" test announced by the Court in *Lemon v. Kurtzman*, 403 U.S. 602 (1970) for use in establishment clause cases. From any point of view that takes seriously the historical basis of the establishment clause, the "secular purpose" prong of *Lemon* is utterly counterfactual. See M. E. Bradford, *Original Intentions: On the Making and Ratification of the United States Constitution* (Athens: University of Georgia Press, 1993), chap. 7. See also Ellis Sandoz, "Philosophical and Religious Dimensions of the American Founding," *Intercollegiate Review* 30 (1995): 27–42.

67. Etienne Gilson, *Being and Some Philosophers*, 2d ed. (Toronto: Pontifical Institute of Mediaeval Studies, 1952), p. 210.

68. Ibid.

69. G. K. Chesterton, *Saint Thomas Aquinas* (New York: Doubleday, 1956), p. 148.

70. See Stephen, *Liberty, Equality, Fraternity*, chap. 2.

71. See Mortimer J. Adler, *How to Think About God* (New York: Macmillan, 1980), chaps. 14–15.

72. See Kenneth J. Arrow, *Social Choice and Individual Values*, 2d ed. (New Haven and London: Yale University Press, 1963). See Chapter 5.

14. THE GNOSTIC ALTERNATIVE

1. See Hans Jonas, *The Gnostic Religion: The Message of the Alien God and the Beginnings of Christianity*, 2d ed. (Boston: Beacon Press, 1963).

2. See Eric Voegelin, *Science, Politics, and Gnosticism* (Chicago: Henry Regnery Company, 1968).

3. See Eric Voegelin, *Autobiographical Reflections* (Baton Rouge: Louisiana State University Press, 1989).

4. See Eric Voegelin, "What is History?" in *What is History? And Other Late Unpublished Writings*, ed. Thomas A. Hollweck and Paul Caringella, vol. 28, in *The Collected Works of Eric Voegelin* (Baton Rouge: Louisiana State University Press, 1990), p. 51.

5. On Augustine's reaction to the gnosticism of the Manichees, see Peter Brown, *Augustine of Hippo: A Biography* (Berkeley and Los Angeles: University of California Press, 1969), pp. 53–60. On Augustine's doctrine of grace, see Augustine, *De Quaestionibus ad Simplicianum*, trans. John Burleigh, in *Library of Christian Classics*, vol. 6 (Philadelphia: Westminster Press, 1953); Augustine, *De Correptione et Gratia*, trans. Peter Holmes and Robert Wallis, in *Nicene and Post-Nicene Fathers of the Christian Church*, ed. Philip Schaff, vol. 5, *The Anti-Pelagian Writings* (Grand Rapids, Mich.: William B. Eerdmans, 1959); Augustine, *De Dono Perseverantiae*, trans. Peter Holmes and Robert Wallis, in *Nicene and Post-Nicene Fathers*, vol. 5; Augustine, *De Praedestinatione Sanctorum*, trans. Peter Holmes and Robert Wallis, in *Nicene and Post-Nicene Fathers*, vol. 5; Augustine, *Enchiridion*, trans. Albert Outler, in *Library of Christian Classics*, vol. 7 (Philadelphia: Westminster Press, 1955).

6. See John Stuart Mill, "Theism," in Mill, *Three Essays on Religion: Nature, The Utility of Religion, and Theism*, ed. Helen Taylor, 2d ed. (London: Longmans, Green, Reader, and Dyer, 1874), Parts 2 and 5.

7. See Mill, "Nature," in *Three Essays*, p. 29, quoted and discussed in Eugene August, *John Stuart Mill: A Mind at Large* (New York: Charles Scribner's Sons, 1975), p. 248.

8. See Mill, "Utility of Religion," in *Three Essays*, pp. 109–22. I am indebted to Christopher Budsisz for calling my attention to the significance of the Comte-Mill connection. See Budsisz, "John Stuart Mill, August Comte and the Religion of Humanity" (Master's thesis, Southern Illinois University, 1996).

9. See John Austin, Lecture 2, in John Stuart Mill, *Utilitarianism, On Liberty, Essay on Bentham: Together with Selected Writings of Jeremy Bentham and John Austin*, ed. Mary Warnock (New York: Penguin Books, 1974), pp. 322–42.

10. William F. Harris II, *The Interpretable Constitution* (Baltimore: Johns Hopkins University Press, 1993).

11. Ibid., esp. pp. 11–16.

12. Ibid., esp. pp. ix, 29–31.

13. Ibid., esp. chap. 1.

14. Ibid., esp. pp. ix–xiii.

15. Ibid., esp. pp. 84–96.

16. Ibid., esp. pp. 98–113.

17. Ibid., esp. chap. 2.

18. Ibid., esp. pp. 46–70.

19. Ibid., pp. 144–58.

20. Ibid., p. 145.

21. Ibid., p. 148 (quoting Justice Joseph Story).

22. Ibid., p. 150.

23. Ibid., p. 152 (quoting Justice Thurgood Marshall).

24. Ibid., p. 152 (quoting Justice William O. Douglas).

25. Ibid., p. 161.

26. See ibid., p. 147 n.17 (on Raoul Berger's subordination of text to intent); see also William Blackstone, *Commentaries on the Laws of England*, 4 vols. (1765; Chicago: University of Chicago Press, 1979), 1:58–62.

27. Harris, *Interpretable Constitution*, p. 160.

28. Ibid., pp. 160–61.

29. Eric Voegelin, *Order and History*, vol. 5: *In Search of Order* (Baton Rouge: Louisiana State University Press, 1987), p. 65.

30. Ibid.

31. Harris, *Interpretable Constitution*, p. 163.

32. Ibid., pp. x–xi.

33. Ibid., p. 1.

34. Ibid., p. 1 n.1.

35. Ibid., p. 14.

36. Mortimer J. Adler, *How to Think About God: A Guide for the 20th-Century Pagan* (New York: Macmillan, 1980).

37. Harris, *Interpretable Constitution*, p. 129.

38. Ibid.

39. John Locke, *An Essay Concerning Human Understanding*, ed. Alexander Campbell Fraser, in *Great Books of the Western World*, 35:85–395 (Chicago: Encyclopaedia Britannica, 1952), esp. Book 3.

40. Ibid., p. 258.

41. Ibid.

42. Ibid., pp. 253–54.

43. Ibid., pp. 251–52.

44. Harris, *Interpretable Constitution*, p. 14.

45. Alexandre Kojeve, *Introduction to the Reading of Hegel: Lectures on the Phenomenology of Spirit*, trans. James H. Nichols, Jr., ed. Allan Bloom (Ithaca, N.Y.: Cornell University Press, 1980), p. 75.

46. Ibid., p. 91.

47. Ibid., esp. pp. 88–99.

48. Ibid., p. 89.

49. See ibid., pp. 89–90.

50. See ibid., p. 91 n.4.

51. See ibid., pp. 92 ff.

52. John 1:1 (translation mine).

53. See Eric Voegelin, "What is History?" in *Collected Works*, 28:35–39.

54. See ibid., 28:41 ff.

55. Leo Strauss, "On Natural Law," in *Studies in Platonic Political Philosophy*, ed. Strauss (Chicago: University of Chicago Press, 1983), p. 144, quoted in Franck, *Against the Imperial Judiciary*, p. 182.

56. See Austin, Lecture 1, in Golding, *Nature of Law*, pp. 77–89.

57. Voegelin, *The Nature of the Law and Related Legal Writings*, in *Collected Works*, 27:82.

58. Of course, there were exceptions—most notably Jefferson who, according to Dennis R. Nolan, held "a gnostic view of history, believing it to be a continuing struggle of good against evil, Saxon against Norman, Whig against Tory, Republican against Federalist" (Nolan, "Sir William Blackstone and the New American Republic: A Study of Intellectual Impact," *New York University Law Review* 51 [1976]: 749).

59. Stoner, *Common Law and Liberal Theory*, chap. 13.

60. Harris, *Interpretable Constitution*, p. 107.

61. Ibid., p. 95.

62. Ibid., p. 84.

63. Ibid., p. 74.

15. THE GOD OF THE COSMOS AS A WHOLE

1. Graham Walker, *Moral Foundations of Constitutional Thought: Current Problems, Augustinian Prospects* (Princeton, N.J.: Princeton University Press, 1990), p. 58.

2. See Mortimer J. Adler, *Ten Philosophical Mistakes* (New York: Macmillan, 1985), pp. 191–93.

3. Ibid., p. 197.

4. See ibid., pp. 192–93.

5. Mortimer J. Adler, *How to Think About God: A Guide for the 20th-Century Pagan* (New York: Macmillan, 1980), p. 148.

6. Ibid., p. 149.

7. The debate is reprinted in John Hick, ed., *The Existence of God* (New York: Macmillan, 1964), at pp. 167–91; this excerpt is from pp. 174–75.

8. See Alfred Jules Ayer, *Language, Truth and Logic*, 2d ed. (New York: Dover Publications, 1952), p. 31. Ayer explicitly derives his doctrine from those of Russell, Wittgenstein, Berkeley, and Hume. See also Hick, ed., *Existence of God*, pp. 217–24.

9. See John Hick, "Theology and Verification," in Hick, ed., *Existence of God*, pp. 253–74.

10. See Thomas Aquinas, *Summa Theologica*, Part 1, Quest. 2, Art. 3 ("Fifth Way"), in Thomas Aquinas, *On Law, Morality, and Politics*, ed. William P. Baumgarth and Richard J. Regan, S.J. (Indianapolis: Hackett Publishing Company, 1988).

11. Ibid. ("Third Way").

12. See J. J. C. Smart, "The Existence of God," in *New Essays in Philosophical Theology*, ed. Anthony Flew and Alisdair MacIntyre (New York: Macmillan, 1955), pp. 38–39. See also Hick, ed., *Existence of God*, pp. 224–28.

13. See Hick, ed., *Existence of God*, p. 81.

14. See Immanuel Kant, *Critique of Pure Reason*, trans. J. M. D. Meiklejohn, 2d ed., (London: J. M. Dent and Sons, 1934), p. 188. See Chapter 11.

15. Aquinas, *Summa*, First Part, Quest. 2, Art. 3.
16. Adler, *How to Think About God.*
17. Ibid., p. 19.
18. Ibid., pp. 6–7.
19. Ibid., p. 79.
20. Ibid.
21. Ibid., p. 93.
22. Ibid., pp. 113–16.
23. Ibid., pp. 116–20.
24. Ibid., pp. 123–24.
25. Ibid., p. 125.
26. Ibid., p. 126.
27. Ibid., p. 131.
28. Ibid.
29. Ibid., pp. 136–37.
30. Ibid., chap. 15.
31. Ibid., p. 133.
32. Ibid., p. 140.
33. Ibid., p. 133.
34. Ibid., pp. 142–43.
35. Ibid., pp. 143–44.
36. Ibid., pp. 144–45.

16. THE GOD OF THE COSMOS AND ITS PARTS

1. Mortimer J. Adler, *How to Think About God: A Guide for the 20th-Century Pagan* (New York: Macmillan, 1980), Parts 5 and 6.
2. See Mortimer J. Adler, *Ten Philosophical Mistakes* (New York: Macmillan, 1985), esp. pp. xiii–xx.
3. Adler, *How to Think About God*, Part 4.
4. Mortimer J. Adler, *Intellect: Mind over Matter* (New York: Macmillan, 1990), p. xiii.
5. Ibid., p. 53.
6. Adler, *How to Think About God*, p. 117.
7. Ibid., p. 124.
8. Ibid., p. 133.
9. See Adler, *Intellect*, esp. chap. 4.
10. See Mortimer J. Adler, *The Angels and Us* (New York: Macmillan, 1982), esp. chap. 7.
11. Ibid., p. 106.
12. Ibid., p. 109.
13. See ibid., esp. chap. 12.
14. Ibid., p. 188.
15. See ibid., p. 109.
16. Etienne Gilson, *Being and Some Philosophers*, 2d ed. (Toronto: Pontifical Institute of Mediaeval Studies, 1952), p. 74.
17. Ibid. (emphasis added).

18. See Adler, *Intellect*, chap. 5.

19. See F.C. Copleston, *Aquinas* (Harmondsworth, U.K.: Penguin Books, 1955), chap. 4.

20. Plato, *Parmenides*, trans. F. M. Cornford, in Plato, *The Collected Dialogues of Plato: Including the Letters*, ed. Edith Hamilton and Huntington Cairns (Princeton, N.J.: Princeton University Press, 1961), pp. 924–31.

21. Ibid., pp. 931–56.

22. Eric Voegelin, *Order and History*, vol. 5, *In Search of Order* (Baton Rouge: Louisiana State University Press, 1987), p. 86.

23. Plato, *Timaeus*, trans. Benjamin Jowett, in *Great Books of the Western World*, ed. Robert Maynard Hutchins (Chicago: Encyclopaedia Britannica, 1952), 7:447.

24. See ibid., 7:456–58; see also Voegelin, *In Search of Order*, pp. 91–107.

25. Voegelin, *In Search of Order*, p. 93.

26. Gilson, *Being and Some Philosophers*, p. 165.

27. Ibid., chap. 5, esp. pp. 160–84.

28. Ibid., p. 175.

29. Ibid., pp. 185–86.

30. Thomas Aquinas, *Summa Theologica*, trans. Fathers of the English Dominican Province, rev. Daniel J. Sullivan, Part 1, Quest. 50, Art. 5, in *Great Books of the Western World*, ed. Robert Maynard Hutchins (Chicago: Encyclopaedia Britannica, 1952), 19:274.

31. See Adler, *Intellect*, pp. 48–53; see also chapter 10.

32. Voegelin, *In Search of Order*, p. 107.

33. See Adler, *Intellect*, esp. chap. 5.

34. Adler, *How to Think About God*, p. 148.

35. See Plato, *Phaedo*, in Plato, *The Trial and Death of Socrates: Four Dialogues*, trans. Benjamin Jowett (New York: Dover Publications, 1992), esp. pp. 96 ff.

36. See Stanley L. Jaki, *The Road of Science and the Ways to God* (Edinburgh: Scottish Academic Press, 1978), chap. 2, esp. pp. 19–20, where Jaki suggests that Socrates' preoccupation with purpose in his rejection of Anaxagoras in *Phaedo* was essential, though problematic, for scientific development.

37. Immanuel Kant, *Critique of Pure Reason*, trans. J. M. D. Meiklejohn, 2d ed. (London: J. M. Dent and Sons, 1934), p. 188 (emphasis added).

38. Ibid., p. 13 (emphasis added).

39. A. D. Lindsay, Introduction, in Kant, *Critique of Pure Reason*, p. xix.

40. Ibid., pp. xix–xx.

41. Alfred Jules Ayer, *Language, Truth and Logic*, 2d ed. (New York: Dover Publications, 1952), p. 31.

42. Kant, *Critique of Pure Reason*, p. 286.

43. Eric Voegelin, "What Is History?" in Voegelin, *What Is History? And Other Late Unpublished Writings*, ed. Thomas A. Hollweck and Paul Caringella, in *The Collected Works of Eric Voegelin* (Baton Rouge: Louisiana State University Press, 1990), 28:6.

44. See Adler, *Intellect*, chap. 7; see also Adler, *Ten Philosophical Mistakes*. See Chapter 11.

45. See Kant, *Critique of Pure Reason*, p. 304; see also Adler, *Intellect*, chap. 8, esp. p. 99.

46. Chesterton, *Saint Thomas Aquinas*, p. 147.

47. Ibid., pp. 145–46; see also Adler, *Intellect*, p. 86.

48. Chesterton, *Saint Thomas Aquinas*, p. 146.

49. Eric Voegelin, *The Nature of Law and Related Legal Writings*, in *The Collected Works of Eric Voegelin*, ed. Robert A. Pascal, James L. Babin, and John W. Corrington (Baton Rouge: Louisiana State University Press, 1991), 27:xiv.

50. Stephen C. Meyer, "The Origin of Life and the Death of Materialism," *Intercollegiate Review* 31 (1996): 24-25.

51. Ibid., p. 24.

52. George Gilder, "The Materialist Superstition," *The Intercollegiate Review* 31 (1996): 6.

53. Ibid.

54. Meyer, "Origin of Life."

55. Ibid., p. 32.

56. Ibid., p. 33.

57. Ibid.

58. Jacques Maritain, *Man's Approach to God* (Latrobe, Pa.: Archabbey Press, 1960), pp. 2-3.

17. THE IMPLICATIONS OF BELIEF

1. Augustine, *Confessions*, trans. R. S. Pine-Coffin (Middlesex, UK: Penguin Books, 1979).

2. See Immanuel Kant, *Foundations of the Metaphysics of Morals*, trans. Lewis White Beck (Indianapolis: Bobbs-Merrill, 1959). Kant says that "in morals, the proper and inestimable worth of an absolutely good will consists precisely in the freedom of the principle of action from all influences from contingent grounds which only experience can furnish" (p. 44). According to Kant, neither the free will nor its obligations may be surrendered, since by the idea of freedom, rational beings are "involuntarily impelled" out from "the determining causes of the world of sense" into an "intelligible world" (p. 74). See also Kant, *Critique of Practical Reason*, trans. L. W. Beck (Indianapolis: Bobbs-Merrill, 1956), pp. 52-59, for the explanation of how this idea leads to that of the free will as a *causa noumenon*.

3. See Peter Brown, *Augustine of Hippo: A Biography* (Berkeley and Los Angeles: University of California Press, 1969), esp. chap. 5 (on Manichaeism), chaps. 19-21 (on Donatism), and chap. 29 (on Pelagianism).

4. Eric Voegelin, "The Beginning and the Beyond," in *The Collected Works of Eric Voegelin*, ed. Thomas Hollweck and Paul Caringella (Baton Rouge: Louisiana State University Press, 1990), 28:203.

5. Ibid., 28:200.

6. Ibid.

7. Ibid. See Plato, *Gorgias*, trans. Donald J. Zeyl (Indianapolis: Hackett Publishing Company, 1987).

8. Voegelin, "Beginning and Beyond," 28:201.

9. Ibid.

10. Ibid.

11. Ibid., 28:203.

12. Ibid., 28:202-3.

13. Ibid., 28:201-2.

14. Quoted in G. K. Chesterton, *Saint Thomas Aquinas* (New York: Doubleday, 1956), pp. 144–45.

15. Plato, *Gorgias*, p. 67.

16. Plato, *Phaedo*, in Plato, *The Trial and Death of Socrates: Four Dialogues*, trans. Benjamin Jowett (New York: Dover Publications, 1992), pp. 98 ff.

17. See John Ralston Saul, *Voltaire's Bastards: The Dictatorship of Reason in the West* (New York: Free Press, 1992), p. 327.

18. See Ronald Dworkin, *Taking Rights Seriously* (Cambridge: Harvard University Press, 1977). Lane V. Sunderland, in *Popular Government and the Supreme Court: Securing the Public Good and Private Rights* (Lawrence: University Press of Kansas, 1995), chap. 4, demonstrates the manner in which Dworkin subordinates all other principles to that of "equal concern and respect."

19. See Chapter 7 for a discussion of two examples provided by Michael S. Moore; see also *Colautti v. Franklin*, 439 US 379 (1979).

20. See Mortimer J. Adler, *How to Think About God: A Guide for the 20th-Century Pagan* (New York: Macmillan, 1980), p. 98.

21. Immanuel Kant, *Critique of Pure Reason*, trans. J. M. D. Meiklejohn, 2d ed. (London: J. M. Dent and Sons, 1934), p. 188.

22. Adler, *How to Think About God*, pp. 98 ff.

23. Ibid., p. 153.

24. Ibid., p. 148.

25. See Eric Voegelin, *The New Science of Politics: An Introduction* (Chicago: University of Chicago Press, 1952), for an elaborate discussion of the underlying basis of this way of thinking about constitutions.

26. See Sunderland, *Popular Government and the Supreme Court*, esp. chap. 2.

27. See Matthew J. Franck, *Against the Imperial Judiciary: The Supreme Court vs. the Sovereignty of the People* (Lawrence: University Press of Kansas, 1996), esp. Part 2.

28. Soterios A. Barber, "Review," *American Political Science Review* 85 (1991): 634–35.

29. Eric Voegelin, "What Is History?" in Hollweck and Caringella, eds., *Collected Works of Eric Voegelin*, 28:38–39.

30. Ibid., esp. 28:13–20.

31. See Max Hamburger, *The Awakening of Western Legal Thought*, trans. Bernard Miall (London: Allen and Unwin, 1942).

32. Voegelin, "What Is History?" esp. 28:47–51.

33. Eric Voegelin, *The Collected Works of Eric Voegelin*, ed. Robert A. Pascal, James L. Babin, and John W. Corrington (Baton Rouge: Louisisana State University Press, 1991), 27:81.

34. Ibid., 27:82.

35. Ibid.

36. Michael Gagarin, *Early Greek Law* (Berkeley: University of California Press, 1986).

37. Sir Henry Sumner Maine, *Ancient Law: Its Connection with the Early History of Society and its Relation to Modern Ideas* (1861; Dorset Press, 1986), esp. pp. 311 ff.; see also Maine, *Lectures on the Early History of Institutions* (London: John Murray, 1880).

38. F. W. Maitland, *The Forms of Action at Common Law: A Course of Lectures*, ed. A. H. Chaytor and W. J. Whittaker (1909; Cambridge: Cambridge University Press, 1989), esp. chaps. 1–2.

39. Maine, *Ancient Law*, pp. 27 ff. See also Arthur R. Hogue, *Origins of the Common Law* (Indianapolis: Liberty Fund, 1985), pp. 200–201.

40. See Justinian, *Justinian's Institutes*, trans. Peter Birks and Grant McLeod (Ithaca, N.Y.: Cornell University Press, 1987), esp. pp. 23–26.

41. Martin Shapiro, *Courts: A Comparative and Political Analysis* (Chicago: University of Chicago Press, 1980); see also John Henry Merryman, *The Civil Law Tradition: An Introduction to the Legal Systems of Western Europe and Latin America*, 2d ed. (Stanford, Calif.: Stanford University Press, 1985).

42. Guido Calabresi, *A Common Law for the Age of Statutes* (Cambridge: Harvard University Press, 1982).

43. See Hogue, *Origins of Common Law*, esp. chap. 9; see also T. F. T. Plucknett, *The Legislation of Edward I* (Oxford: Oxford University Press, 1949).

44. See Gagarin, *Early Greek Law*, p. 116.

45. Ibid., p. 117.

46. J. Walter Jones, *The Law and Legal Theory of the Greeks* (Oxford: Clarendon Press, 1956), pp. 90–92.

47. See Plato, *Trial and Death of Socrates*, pp. 19–41, (*Apology*), pp. 43–54 *(Crito)*.

48. See A. R. W. Harrison, *The Law of Athens*, 2 vols. (Oxford: Clarendon Press, 1968), vol. 1.

49. See Justinian, *Justinian's Institutes*, p. 61.

50. See Jones, *Law and Legal Theory of the Greeks*, pp. 302–3.

51. Ibid., pp. 298–303.

52. Ibid., pp. 271–72.

53. Ibid., p. 274.

54. Ibid. See also *Macpherson v. Buick Motor Co.*, New York Court of Appeals, 217 N.Y. 382, 111 N. E. 1050 (1916).

55. Eric Voegelin, *The New Science of Politics* (Chicago: University of Chicago Press, 1952), p. 1.

Bibliography

Adler, Mortimer J. *The Angels and Us*. New York: Macmillan Publishing Company, 1982.

——. *Desires Right and Wrong: The Ethics of Enough*. New York: Macmillan Publishing Company, 1991.

——. *How to Think About God: A Guide for the 20th-Century Pagan*. New York: Macmillan Publishing Company, 1980.

——. *Intellect: Mind over Matter*. New York: Macmillan Publishing Company, 1990.

——. *Ten Philosophical Mistakes*. New York: Macmillan Publishing Company, 1985.

——. *Truth in Religion: The Plurality of Religions and the Unity of Truth*. New York: Macmillan Publishing Company, 1990.

Aquinas, Thomas. *On Law, Morality, and Politics*. Edited by William P. Baumgarth and Richard J. Regan, S.J. Indianapolis: Hackett Publishing Company, 1988.

——. *Summa Theologica*. Translated by Fathers of the English Dominican Province. Revised by Daniel J. Sullivan. In *Great Books of the Western World*. Vols. 19–20. Edited by Robert Maynard Hutchins. Chicago: Encyclopaedia Britannica, 1952.

——. *Treatise on Law (Summa Theologica, Questions 90–97)*. Edited by Stanley Parry. Chicago: Regnery Gateway.

Aristotle. *Metaphysics*. Translated by W. D. Ross. In *Great Books of the Western World*. Vol. 8. Edited by Robert Maynard Hutchins. Chicago: Encyclopaedia Britannica, 1952.

——. *Physics*. Translated by R. P. Hardie and R. K. Gaye. In *Great Books of the Western World*. Vol. 8. Edited by Robert Maynard Hutchins. Chicago: Encyclopaedia Britannica, 1952.

——. *The Politics of Aristotle*. Translated by Ernest Barker. London: Oxford University Press, 1958.

Arrow, Kenneth J. *Social Choice and Individual Values*. New Haven: Yale University Press, 1951. 2d ed. New Haven and London: Yale University Press, 1963.

August, Eugene. *John Stuart Mill: A Mind at Large*. New York: Charles Scribner's Sons, 1975.

Augustine. *The City of God*. Translated by Gerald G. Walsh, S.J., Demetrius B. Zema, S.J., Grace Monahan, O.S.U., and Daniel J. Honan. Edited by Vernon J. Bourke. Garden City, New York: Doubleday and Company, 1958.

——. *Confessions*. Translated by R. S. Pine-Coffin. Middlesex, U.K.: Penguin Books, 1979.

———. *De Correptione et Gratia*. Translated by Peter Holmes and Robert Wallis. In *Nicene and Post-Nicene Fathers of the Christian Church*. Vol. 5, *The Anti-Pelagian Writings*. Edited by Philip Schaff. Grand Rapids, Mich.: William B. Eerdmans, 1959.

———. *De Dono Perseverantiae*. Translated by Peter Holmes and Robert Wallis. In *Nicene and Post-Nicene Fathers*. Vol. 5.

———. *De Praedestinatione Sanctorum*. Translated by Peter Holmes and Robert Wallis. In *Nicene and Post-Nicene Fathers*. Vol. 5.

———. *De Quaestionibus ad Simplicianum*. Translated by John Burleigh. In *Library of Christian Classics*. Vol. 6. Philadelphia: Westminster Press, 1953.

———. *Enchiridion*. Translated by Albert Outler, In *Library of Christian Classics*. Vol. 7. Philadelphia: Westminster Press, 1955.

Ayer, Alfred Jules. *Language, Truth and Logic*. 2d ed. New York: Dover Publications, 1952.

Bader, William D. "Some Thoughts on Blackstone, Precedent, and Originalism." *Vermont Law Review* 19 (1994): 5–18.

Ball, Terence, and J. G. A. Pocock, eds. *Conceptual Change and the Constitution*. Lawrence: University Press of Kansas, 1988.

Barber, Soterios A. "Michael Perry and the Future of Constitutional Theory." *Tulane Law Review* 63 (1989): 1289–1303.

———. *On What the Constitution Means*. Baltimore: Johns Hopkins University Press, 1984.

———. "Review." *American Political Science Review* 85 (1991): 634–35.

Bassham, Gregory. *Original Intent and the Constitution: A Philosophical Study*. Lanham, Md.: Rowman and Littlefield, 1992.

Bentham, Jeremy. *A Comment on the Commentaries*. Edited by J. H. Burns and H. L. A. Hart. London: Athlone Press, 1977.

———. *A Fragment on Government*. Edited by J. H. Burns and H. L. A. Hart. London: Athlone Press, 1977.

———. *Of Laws in General*. Edited by H. L. A. Hart. In *The Collected Works of Jeremy Bentham*. Edited by J. H. Burns. London: Athlone Press, 1970.

Berger, Raoul. *Government by Judiciary: The Transformation of the Fourteenth Amendment*. Cambridge: Harvard University Press, 1977.

Berkeley, George. *The Principles of Human Knowledge*. In *Great Books of the Western World*. Vol. 35. Edited by Robert Maynard Hutchins. Chicago: Encyclopaedia Britannica, 1952.

Bickel, Alexander. *The Least Dangerous Branch: The Supreme Court at the Bar of Politics*. Indianapolis: Bobbs-Merrill, 1962.

———. *The Morality of Consent*. New Haven: Yale University Press, 1975.

———. *The Supreme Court and the Idea of Progress*. New York: Harper and Row, 1970.

Black, Charles. *The People and the Court*. New York: Macmillan, 1960.

———. *Structure and Relationship in Constitutional Law*. Baton Rouge: Louisiana State University Press, 1969.

Black, Duncan. *Theory of Committees and Elections*. Cambridge: Cambridge University Press, 1958.

Blackstone, William. *Commentaries on the Laws of England*. 4 vols. Facsimile of the First Edition of 1765–1769. Chicago: University of Chicago Press, 1979.

Bodenheimer, Edgar, John Bilyeu Oakley, and Jean C. Love, eds. *An Introduction to the Anglo-American Legal System: Readings and Cases.* St. Paul, Minn.: West Publishing Company, 1988.

Bonsignore, John et al., eds. *Before the Law: An Introduction to the Legal Process.* 3d ed. Boston: Houghton Mifflin Company, 1984.

Boudin, Louis. *Government by Judiciary.* 2 vols. New York: William Godwin, 1932.

Bradford, M. E. *Founding Fathers: Brief Lives of the Framers of the United States Constitution.* 2d ed. Lawrence: University Press of Kansas, 1994.

———. *Original Intentions: On the Making and Ratification of the United States Constitution.* Athens: University of Georgia Press, 1993.

Brest, Paul. "The Fundamental Rights Controversy: The Essential Contradictions of Normative Constitutional Scholarship." *Yale Law Journal* 90 (1981): 1063–1109.

———. "The Misconceived Quest for the Original Understanding." *Boston University Law Review* 60 (1980): 204–38.

Brown, Brendan F., ed. *The Natural Law Reader.* New York: Oceana Publications, 1960.

Brown, Peter. *Augustine of Hippo: A Biography.* Berkeley and Los Angeles: University of California Press, 1969.

Budsisz, Christopher. *John Stuart Mill, August Comte and the Religion of Humanity.* Master's thesis, Southern Illinois University, 1996.

Burke, Edmund. *Reflections on the Revolution in France.* Edited by Thomas H. D. Mahoney. Indianapolis: Bobbs-Merrill, 1955.

Burns, Robert P. "Blackstone's Theory of the 'Absolute' Rights of Property." *Cincinnati Law Review* 54 (1985): 67–86.

Calabresi, Guido. *A Common Law for the Age of Statutes.* Cambridge: Harvard University Press, 1982.

Cardozo, Benjamin N. *The Nature of the Judicial Process.* New Haven: Yale University Press, 1921.

Carter, Lief. *Contemporary Constitutional Lawmaking: The Supreme Court and the Art of Politics.* New York: Pergamon, 1985.

Casto, William R. *The Supreme Court in the Early Republic: The Chief Justiceships of John Jay and Oliver Ellsworth.* Columbia: University of South Carolina Press, 1995.

Chadwick, Henry. *The Early Church.* New York: Penguin Books, 1967.

Chesterton, Gilbert K. *Orthodoxy.* New York: John Lane Company, 1908.

———. *Saint Thomas Aquinas.* New York: Doubleday, 1956.

Choper, Jesse H. *Judicial Review and the National Political Process: A Functional Reconsideration of the Role of the Supreme Court.* Chicago: University of Chicago Press, 1980.

Cicero. *De Legibus.* Translated by Clinton Walker Keyes. Cambridge: Harvard University Press (Loeb Library), 1977.

Clinton, Robert Lowry. "Historical Constitutionalism and Judicial Review in America." *Policy Studies Journal* 19 (1990): 173–91.

———. "John Marshall's Federalism: A Reply to Professor Gillman." *Political Research Quarterly* 47 (1994): 887–90.

———. "Judicial Review, Nationalism, and the Commerce Clause: Contrasting Antebellum and Postbellum Supreme Court Decision Making." *Political Research Quarterly* 47 (1994): 857–76.

————. *Marbury v. Madison and Judicial Review.* Lawrence: University Press of Kansas, 1989.

Cochran, Clarke E. *Religion in Public and Private Life.* New York and London: Routledge, 1990.

Cochrane, Charles Norris. *Christianity and Classical Culture: A Study of Thought and Action from Augustus to Augustine.* Oxford: Oxford University Press, 1957.

Collingwood, R. G. *The Idea of History.* London: Oxford University Press, 1956.

Copleston, F. C. *Aquinas.* Harmondsworth, U.K.: Penguin Books, 1955.

Corwin, Edward S. "The Basic Doctrine of American Constitutional Law." *Michigan Law Review* 12 (1914): 247–76.

————. "The Supreme Court and Unconstitutional Acts of Congress." *Michigan Law Review* 4 (1906): 616–30.

Cross, Sir Rupert. *Precedent in English Law.* 3d ed. Oxford: Clarendon Press, 1977.

————. *Statutory Interpretation.* 2d ed. London: Butterworth's, 1987.

Cross, Sir Rupert, and J. W. Harris. *Precedent in English Law.* 4th ed. Oxford: Clarendon Press, 1991.

Descartes, Rene. *Meditations on First Philosophy.* Translated by Elizabeth S. Haldane and G. R. T. Ross. In *Great Books of the Western World.* Vol. 31. Edited by Robert Maynard Hutchins. Chicago: Encyclopaedia Britannica, 1952.

————. *Objections Against the Meditations, and Replies.* Translated by Elizabeth S. Haldane and G. R. T. Ross. In *Great Books of the Western World.* Vol. 31. Edited by Robert Maynard Hutchins. Chicago: Encyclopaedia Britannica, 1952.

Dicey, Albert Venn. *Introduction to the Study of the Law of the Constitution.* 1915. Reprint of 8th edition. Indianapolis: Liberty Classics, 1982.

Dickinson, John. *Administrative Justice and the Supremacy of Law in the United States.* Cambridge: Harvard University Press, 1927.

Drew, Katherine Fischer, ed. and trans. *The Burgundian Code.* Philadelphia: University of Pennsylvania Press, 1949.

Dworkin, Ronald. *Taking Rights Seriously.* Cambridge: Harvard University Press, 1977.

Edwards, Chilperic, ed. *The Hammurabi Code, and the Sinaitic Legislation.* Translated by Chilperic Edwards. Port Washington, N.Y.: Kennikat Press, 1971.

Elshtain, Jean Bethke. *Democracy on Trial.* New York: Basic Books, 1995.

Ely, John Hart. *Democracy and Distrust: A Theory of Judicial Review.* Cambridge: Harvard University Press, 1980.

Epstein, Richard A. *Takings: Private Property and the Power of Eminent Domain.* Cambridge: Harvard University Press, 1985.

Farquharson, Robin. *Theory of Voting.* New Haven: Yale University Press, 1969.

Fisher, William W. III, Morton J. Horwitz, and Thomas A. Reed, eds. *American Legal Realism.* New York: Oxford University Press, 1993.

Flew, Anthony, and Alisdair MacIntyre, eds. *New Essays in Philosophical Theology.* New York: Macmillan, 1955.

Franck, Matthew J. *Against the Imperial Judiciary: The Supreme Court vs. the Sovereignty of the People.* Lawrence: University Press of Kansas, 1996.

Frank, Jerome. *Courts on Trial: Myth and Reality in American Justice.* New York: Atheneum, 1963.

Frohnen, Bruce. *Virtue and the Promise of Conservatism: The Legacy of Burke and Tocqueville.* Lawrence: University Press of Kansas, 1993.

Fuller, Lon L. *Legal Fictions.* Stanford, Calif.: Stanford University Press, 1967.

———. *The Morality of Law.* New Haven: Yale University Press, 1964.

Fuller, Lon L., ed. *The Problems of Jurisprudence: A Selection of Readings Supplemented by Comments Prepared by the Editor.* Brooklyn, N.Y.: Foundation Press, 1949.

Gagarin, Michael. *Early Greek Law.* Berkeley: University of California Press, 1986.

Gellhorn, Ernest, and Ronald M. Levin. *Administrative Law and Process in a Nutshell.* 3d ed. St. Paul, Minn.: West Publishing Company, 1990.

Gilder, George. "The Materialist Superstition." *Intercollegiate Review* 31 (1996): 6–14.

Gillman, Howard. *The Constitution Besieged: The Rise and Demise of Lochner Era Police Power Jurisprudence.* Durham, N.C.: Duke University Press, 1993.

———. "More on the Origins of the Fuller Court's Jurisprudence: Reexamining the Scope of Federal Power over Commerce and Manufacturing in Nineteenth-Century Constitutional Law." *Political Research Quarterly* 49 (1996): 415–37.

———. "The Struggle over Marshall and the Politics of Constitutional History." *Political Research Quarterly* 47 (1994): 877–86.

Gilson, Etienne. *Being and Some Philosophers.* 2d ed. Toronto: Pontifical Institute of Mediaeval Studies, 1952.

———. *The Philosophy of St. Thomas Aquinas.* 3d ed. Translated by Edward Bullough. Edited by Rev. G. A. Elrington. 1924. Reprint. New York: Barnes and Noble Books, 1993.

Glendon, Mary Ann. *Abortion and Divorce in Western Law.* Cambridge: Harvard University Press, 1988.

Golding, M. P., ed. *The Nature of Law: Readings in Legal Philosophy.* New York: Random House, 1966.

Goldstein, Lawrence, ed. *Precedent in Law.* Oxford: Clarendon Press, 1987.

Goldstein, Leslie Friedman. *In Defense of the Text: Democracy and Constitutional Theory.* Savage, Md.: Rowman and Littlefield, 1991.

Graglia, Lino A. *Disaster by Decree: The Supreme Court Decisions on Race and the Schools.* Ithaca, N.Y.: Cornell University Press, 1976.

Green, Thomas Andrew. *Verdict According to Conscience: Perspectives on the English Criminal Trial Jury, 1200–1800.* Chicago: University of Chicago Press, 1985.

Green, Thomas Hill. *Lectures on the Principles of Political Obligation.* Ann Arbor: University of Michigan Press, 1967.

Grey, Thomas. "Do We Have an Unwritten Constitution?" *Stanford Law Review* 27 (1975): 703–18.

Grotius, Hugo. *Prolegomera to the Law of War and Peace.* Translated by Francis W. Kelsey. Indianapolis: Bobbs-Merrill, 1957.

Gunther, Gerald, ed. *John Marshall's Defense of McCulloch v. Maryland.* Stanford, Calif.: Stanford University Press, 1969.

Hale, Sir Matthew. *The History of the Common Law of England.* Edited by Charles M. Gray. Chicago and London: University of Chicago Press, 1971.

Hamburger, Henry. *Games as Models of Social Phenomena.* San Francisco: W. H. Freeman and Company, 1979.

———. "N-person Prisoner's Dilemma." *Journal of Mathematical Sociology* 3 (1973): 27–48.

Hamburger, Max. *The Awakening of Western Legal Thought.* Translated by Bernard Miall. London: George Allen and Unwin, 1942.

Harris, William F. II. *The Interpretable Constitution*. Baltimore and London: Johns Hopkins University Press, 1993.

Harrison, A. R. W. *The Law of Athens*. 2 vols. Oxford: Clarendon Press, 1968.

Hart, H., and A. Sacks. *The Legal Process: Basic Problems in the Making and Application of Law*. Harvard University, 1958. Typescript.

Hegel, G. W. F. *Hegel's Philosophy of Right*. Translated by T. M. Knox. London: Oxford University Press, 1967.

———. *Phenomenology of Spirit*. Translated by A. V. Miller. Oxford: Oxford University Press, 1977.

———. *The Philosophy of History*. Translated by J. Sibree. New York: Dover Publications, 1956.

Heidegger, Martin. *Identity and Difference*. Translated by Joan Stambaugh. New York: Harper and Row, 1969.

Hick, John, ed. *The Existence of God*. New York: Macmillan, 1964.

Hignett, C. *A History of the Athenian Constitution to the End of the Fifth Century B.C.* Oxford: Clarendon Press, 1952.

Hobbes, Thomas. *A Dialogue Between a Philosopher and a Student of the Common Laws of England*. Edited by Joseph Cropsey. Chicago: University of Chicago Press, 1971.

———. *The Elements of Law: Natural and Politic*. Edited by Ferdinand Tonnies. Cambridge: Cambridge University Press, 1928.

———. *Leviathan*. Edited by C. B. Macpherson. 1651. Reprint. London: Penguin Books, 1968.

Hoffer, Peter Charles. *The Law's Conscience: Equitable Constitutionalism in America*. Chapel Hill and London: University of North Carolina Press, 1990.

Hogue, Arthur R. *Origins of the Common Law*. Indianapolis: Liberty Fund, 1985.

Holdsworth, William S. *Charles Dickens as a Legal Historian*. New Haven: Yale University Press, 1929.

———. *The Historians of Anglo-American Law*. Hamden, Conn.: Archon Books, 1966.

———. *A History of English Law*. 16 vols. London: Methuen and Company, Sweet and Maxwell, 3d ed. 1945.

Hume, David. *An Enquiry Concerning Human Understanding*. Edited by L. A. Selby-Bigge. In *Great Books of the Western World*. Vol. 35. Edited by Robert Maynard Hutchins. Chicago: Encyclopaedia Britannica, 1952.

Hurst, J. W. *Dealing with Statutes*. New York: Columbia University Press, 1982.

Jacobsohn, Gary J. *The Supreme Court and the Decline of Constitutional Aspiration*. Totowa, N.J.: Rowman & Littlefield, 1986.

Jaki, Stanley L. *Brain, Mind and Computers*. New York: Herder and Herder, 1969.

———. *Cosmos and Creator*. Edinburgh: Scottish Academic Press, 1980.

———. *The Road of Science and the Ways to God*. Edinburgh: Scottish Academic Press, 1978.

Jonas, Hans. *The Gnostic Religion: The Message of the Alien God and the Beginnings of Christianity*. 2d ed. Boston: Beacon Press, 1963.

Jones, J. Walter. *The Law and Legal Theory of the Greeks*. Oxford: Clarendon Press, 1956.

Justinian. *The Digest of Roman Law: Theft, Rapine, Damage and Insult*. Translated by C. P. Kolbert. London: Penguin Classics, 1979.

———. *Justinian's Institutes*. Translated by Peter Birks and Grant McLeod. Ithaca, N.Y.: Cornell University Press, 1987.

Kahn, Ronald. *The Supreme Court and Constitutional Theory, 1953–1993.* Lawrence: University Press of Kansas, 1994.

Kammen, Michael. *A Machine That Would Go of Itself: The Constitution in American Culture.* New York: Alfred A. Knopf, 1987.

Kant, Immanuel. *Critique of Practical Reason.* Translated by Lewis White Beck. Indianapolis: Bobbs-Merrill, 1956.

———. *Critique of Pure Reason.* Translated by J. M. D. Meiklejohn. 2d ed. London: J. M. Dent and Sons, 1934.

———. *The Doctrine of Virtue: Part II of The Metaphysic of Morals.* Translated by Mary J. Gregor. Philadelphia: University of Pennsylvania Press, 1964.

———. *Foundations of the Metaphysics of Morals.* Translated by Lewis White Beck. Indianapolis: Bobbs-Merrill, 1959.

———. *The Metaphysical Elements of Justice.* Translated by John Ladd. Indianapolis: Bobbs-Merrill, 1965.

———. *Religion Within the Limits of Reason Alone.* Translated by Theodore M. Greene and Hoyt H. Hudson. New York: Harper and Row, 1960.

Kelley, Donald R. *The Human Measure: Social Thought in the Western Legal Tradition.* Cambridge: Harvard University Press, 1990.

Kelsen, Hans. *Pure Theory of Law.* Translated by Max Knight. 2d ed. Berkeley: University of California Press, 1970.

Kens, Paul. *Judicial Power and Reform Politics: The Anatomy of Lochner v. New York.* Lawrence: University Press of Kansas, 1990.

Kenyon, Cecelia, ed. *The Antifederalists.* Indianapolis: Bobbs-Merrill, 1966.

Kojeve, Alexandre. *Introduction to the Reading of Hegel: Lectures on the Phenomenology of Spirit.* Assembled by Raymond Queneau. Translated by James H. Nichols, Jr. Edited by Allan Bloom. Ithaca, N.Y.: Cornell University Press, 1980.

Kunkel, Wolfgang. *An Introduction to Roman Legal and Constitutional History.* Translated by J. M. Kelly. 2d ed. Oxford: Clarendon Press, 1973.

Lea, Henry Charles. *The Duel and the Oath.* Edited by Edward Peters. 1866. Reprint. Philadelphia: University of Pennsylvania Press, 1974.

Levi, Edward H. *An Introduction to Legal Reasoning.* Chicago: University of Chicago Press, 1949.

Levinson, Sanford. *Constitutional Faith.* Princeton, N.J.: Princeton University Press, 1988.

Levy, Leonard. *Original Intent and the Framers' Constitution.* New York: Collier Macmillan, 1988.

Levy, Leonard, ed. *Judicial Review and the Supreme Court.* New York: Harper and Row, 1967.

Lienesch, Michael. *New Order of the Ages: Time, the Constitution, and the Making of Modern American Political Thought.* Princeton, N.J.: Princeton University Press, 1988.

Llewellyn, Karl. *The Bramble Bush.* New York: Oceana Press, 1951.

———. *The Case Law System in America.* Translated by Michael Ansaldi. Edited by Alan Gewirth. Chicago: University of Chicago Press, 1989.

Locke, John. *An Essay Concerning Human Understanding.* Edited by Alexander Campbell Fraser. In *Great Books of the Western World.* Vol. 35. Edited by Robert Maynard Hutchins. Chicago: Encyclopaedia Brittannica, 1952.

———. *An Essay Concerning the True Original Extent and End of Civil Government (Second*

Treatise). In *Great Books of the Western World*. Vol. 35. Edited by Robert Maynard Hutchins. Chicago: Encyclopaedia Britannica, 1952.

———. *Two Treatises of Government*. Edited by Peter Laslett. Cambridge: Cambridge University Press, 1960.

Loury, Glen C. *One by One from the Inside Out: Essays and Reviews on Race and Responsibility in America*. New York: Free Press, 1995.

Luce, R. Duncan, and Howard Raiffa. *Games and Decisions: Introduction and Critical Survey*. New York: John Wiley and Sons, 1957.

Machiavelli, Niccolo. *The Prince*. Translated by George Bull. New York: Penguin Classics, 1961.

MacDowell, Douglas M. *The Law in Classical Athens*. Ithaca, N.Y.: Cornell University Press, 1978.

McNeill, William H., and Jean W. Sedlar, eds. *The Classical Mediterranean World*. New York: Oxford University Press, 1969.

Maine, Sir Henry Sumner. *Ancient Law: Its Connection with the Early History of Society and its Relation to Modern Ideas*. 1861. Reprint. Dorset Press, 1986.

———. *Lectures on the Early History of Institutions*. London: John Murray, 1880.

Maitland, Frederic William. *Collected Papers*. Edited by H. A. L. Fisher. 3 vols. Cambridge: Cambridge University Press, 1911.

———. *The Constitutional History of England: A Course of Lectures*. Edited by H. A. L. Fisher. Cambridge: Cambridge University Press, 1908.

———. *The Forms of Action at Common Law: A Course of Lectures*. Edited by A. H. Chaytor and W. J. Whittaker. Cambridge: Cambridge University Press, 1936.

———. *Selected Historical Essays of F. W. Maitland*. Edited by Helen M. Cam. Cambridge: Cambridge University Press, 1957.

Maitland, Frederic W., and Francis C. Montague. *A Sketch of English Legal History*. Edited by James F. Colby. New York: G. P. Putnam's Sons.

Maltz, Earl M. *Rethinking Constitutional Law: Originalism, Interventionism, and the Politics of Judicial Review*. Lawrence: University Press of Kansas, 1994.

Maritain, Jacques. *Christianity and Democracy*. Translated by Doris C. Anson. New York: Charles Scribner's Sons, 1950.

———. *Existence and the Existent*. Translated by Lewis Galantiere and Gerald B. Phelan. New York: Pantheon Books, 1948.

———. *Man's Approach to God*. Latrobe, Pa.: Archabbey Press, 1960.

———. *On the Use of Philosophy: Three Essays*. Princeton, N.J.: Princeton University Press, 1961.

———. *Saint Thomas and the Problem of Evil*. Milwaukee, Wis.: Marquette University Press, 1942.

Melone, Albert P., and George Mace, eds. *Judicial Review and American Democracy*. Ames: Iowa State University Press, 1988.

Mendelson, Wallace. *The American Constitution and the Judicial Process*. Homewood, Ill.: Dorsey Press, 1980.

———. "The Influence of James Bradley Thayer on the Work of Holmes, Brandeis, and Frankfurter." *Vanderbilt Law Review* 31 (1978): 71–87.

———. "John Marshall and the Sugar Trust—A Reply to Professor Gillman." *Political Research Quarterly* 49 (1996): 405–13.

——. "Nullification via Dual Federalism: A Second Response to Professor Gillman." *Political Research Quarterly* 49 (1996): 439–44.

——. *Supreme Court Statecraft: The Rule of Law and Men.* Ames: Iowa State University Press, 1985.

——. "Was Chief Justice Marshall an Activist?" In *Supreme Court Activism and Restraint.* Edited by Morton Halpern and Charles Lamb. Lexington, Mass.: Lexington Books, 1982.

Merryman, John Henry. *The Civil Law Tradition: An Introduction to the Legal Systems of Western Europe and Latin America.* 2d ed. Stanford, Calif.: Stanford University Press, 1985.

Meyer, Stephen C. "The Origin of Life and the Death of Materialism." *Intercollegiate Review* 31 (1996): 24–43.

Mill, John Stuart. *Three Essays on Religion: Nature, The Utility of Religion, and Theism.* Edited by Helen Taylor. 2d ed. London: Longmans, Green, Reader, and Dyer, 1874.

——. *Utilitarianism, On Liberty, Essay on Bentham: Together with Selected Writings of Jeremy Bentham and John Austin.* Edited by Mary Warnock. New York: Penguin Books, 1974.

Miller, Arthur S., and Ronald F. Howell, "The Myth of Neutrality in Constitutional Adjudication." *University of Chicago Law Review* 27 (1960): 61–95.

Milsom, S. F. C. *The Legal Framework of English Feudalism.* Cambridge: Cambridge University Press, 1976.

Moore, Michael S. "A Natural Law Theory of Interpretation." *Southern California Law Review* 58 (1985): 277–398.

Nagel, Robert. *Constitutional Cultures.* Berkeley: University of California Press, 1989.

Nedelsky, Jennifer. *Private Property and the Limits of American Constitutionalism: The Madisonian Framework and Its Legacy.* Chicago: University of Chicago Press, 1990.

Nelson, William E. *Americanization of the Common Law: The Impact of Legal Change on Massachusetts Society, 1760–1830.* Cambridge: Harvard University Press, 1975.

Newmyer, R. Kent. *The Supreme Court Under Marshall and Taney.* Chicago: Harlan Davidson, 1968.

Nicholas, Barry. *An Introduction to Roman Law.* Oxford: Clarendon Press, 1962.

Nolan, Dennis R. "Sir William Blackstone and the New American Republic: A Study of Intellectual Impact." *New York University Law Review* 51 (1976): 731–68.

Ogden, C. K. *Bentham's Theory of Fictions.* Paterson, N.J.: Littlefield, Adams and Company, 1959.

Olson, Mancur. *The Logic of Collective Action.* Cambridge: Harvard University Press, 1971.

Pangle, Lorraine Smith, and Thomas L. Pangle. *The Learning of Liberty: The Educational Ideas of the American Founders.* Lawrence: University Press of Kansas, 1993.

Pangle, Thomas L., ed. *The Roots of Political Philosophy: Ten Forgotten Socratic Dialogues.* Ithaca, N.Y.: Cornell University Press, 1987.

Pelikan, Jaroslav. *Jesus Through the Centuries: His Place in the History of Culture.* New York: Harper and Row, 1985.

Perry, Michael J. *The Constitution, the Courts, and Human Rights: An Inquiry into the Legitimacy of Policymaking by the Judiciary.* New Haven: Yale University Press, 1982.

——. *Morality, Politics, and Law: A Bicentennial Essay.* New York: Oxford University Press, 1988.

——. "Review." *Ethics* (October 1985): 202–3.

Plato. *Gorgias*. Translated by W. C. Helmbold. Indianapolis: Bobbs-Merrill, 1952.

——. *Gorgias*. Translated by Donald J. Zeyl. Indianapolis: Hackett Publishing Company, 1987.

——. *Great Dialogues of Plato*. Translated by W. H. D. Rouse. New York: Penguin Books, 1984.

——. *The Laws of Plato*. Translated by Thomas L. Pangle. Chicago and London: University of Chicago Press, 1988.

——. *Parmenides*. Translated by F. M. Cornford. In *The Collected Dialogues of Plato*. Edited by Edith Hamilton and Huntington Cairns. Princeton, N.J.: Princeton University Press, 1961.

——. *The Republic*. Translated by Desmond Lee. 2d ed., rev. London: Penguin Books, 1987.

——. *Timaeus*. Translated by Benjamin Jowett. In *Great Books of the Western World*. Vol. 7. Edited by Robert Maynard Hutchins. Chicago: Encyclopaedia Britannica, 1952.

——. *The Trial and Death of Socrates: Four Dialogues*. Translated by Benjamin Jowett. New York: Dover Publications, 1992.

Plucknett, T. F. T. *The Legislation of Edward I*. Oxford: Oxford University Press, 1949.

Pollock, Sir Frederick, and Frederic William Maitland. *The History of English Law Before the Time of Edward I*. 2 vols. 2d ed. 1895. Reprint. Cambridge: Cambridge University Press, 1968.

Postema, Gerald J. *Bentham and the Common Law Tradition*. Oxford: Clarendon Press, 1986.

Powell, H. Jefferson. *The Moral Tradition of American Constitutionalism: A Theological Interpretation*. Durham, N.C., and London: Duke University Press, 1993.

Pufendorf, Samuel. *On the Duty of Man and Citizen According to Natural Law*. Translated by Michael Silverthorne. Edited by James Tully. Cambridge: Cambridge University Press, 1991.

Rabkin, Jeremy. *Judicial Compulsions: How Public Law Distorts Public Policy*. New York: Basic Books, 1989.

Rakove, Jack N., ed. *Interpreting the Constitution: The Debate over Original Intent*. Boston: Northeastern University Press, 1990.

Rapaport, Anatol. *Two-Person Game Theory*. Ann Arbor: University of Michigan Press, 1966.

Rapaport, Anatol, and A. M. Chammah. *Prisoner's Dilemma*. Ann Arbor: University of Michigan Press, 1965.

Rawls, John. *A Theory of Justice*. Cambridge: Harvard University Press, 1971.

Robbins, Sara, ed. *Law: A Treasury of Art and Literature*. New York: Beaux Arts Editions, 1990.

Rohr, John A. *To Run a Constitution: The Legitimacy of the Administrative State*. Lawrence: University Press of Kansas, 1986.

Rostow, Eugene V. *The Sovereign Prerogative: The Supreme Court and the Quest for Law*. Westport, Conn.: Greenwood Press, 1962.

Rousseau, Jean-Jacques. *The Social Contract and Discourses*. Translated by G. D. H. Cole. Revised and augmented by J. H. Brumfitt and John C. Hall. London and Toronto: J. M. Dent and Sons, 1973.

Sandoz, Ellis. "Philosophical and Religious Dimensions of the American Founding." *Intercollegiate Review* 30 (1995): 27–42.

Saul, John Ralston. *Voltaire's Bastards: The Dictatorship of Reason in the West*. New York: Free Press, 1992.

Savigny, Frederick Charles von. *Of the Vocation of Our Age for Legislation and Jurisprudence*. Translated by Abraham Hayward. New York: Arno Press, 1975.

Schubert, Frank A. *Grilliot's Introduction to Law and the Legal System*. 6th ed. Boston: Houghton Mifflin Company, 1996.

Schwartz, Thomas. *The Logic of Collective Choice*. New York: Columbia University Press, 1986.

Shapiro, Martin. *Courts: A Comparative and Political Analysis*. Chicago: University of Chicago Press, 1980.

———. "The Supreme Court's 'Return' to Economic Regulation." In *Studies in American Political Development*. Edited by Karen Orren and Stephen Skowronek. Vol. 1. New Haven: Yale University Press, 1986.

———. *Who Guards the Guardians? Judicial Control of Administration*. Athens: University of Georgia Press, 1988.

Shils, Edward. *The Constitution of Society*. Chicago: University of Chicago Press, 1982.

Siegan, Bernard H. *Economic Liberties and the Constitution*. Chicago: University of Chicago Press, 1980.

Snowiss, Sylvia. *Judicial Review and the Law of the Constitution*. New Haven: Yale University Press, 1990.

Sosin, J. M. *The Aristocracy of the Long Robe: The Origins of Judicial Review in America*. New York: Greenwood Press, 1989.

Sowell, Thomas. *Black Education: Myths and Tragedies*. New York: David McKay Company, 1972.

———. *Civil Rights: Rhetoric or Reality?* New York: William Morrow and Company, 1984.

———. *Inside American Education: The Decline, the Deception, the Dogmas*. New York: Free Press, 1993.

Spinoza, Benedict de. *Ethics*. Translated by W. H. White. Revised by A. H. Stirling. In *Great Books of the Western World*. Vol. 31. Edited by Robert Maynard Hutchins. Chicago: Encyclopaedia Britannica, 1952.

Stenton, Doris M. *English Justice Between the Norman Conquest and the Great Charter, 1066–1215*. London: Allen and Unwin, 1963.

Stephen, James Fitzjames. *Liberty, Equality, Fraternity*. Edited by Stuart D. Warner. 1874. Reprint. Indianapolis: Liberty Fund, 1992.

Stimson, Shannon C. *The American Revolution in the Law: Anglo-American Jurisprudence Before John Marshall*. Princeton, N.J.: Princeton University Press, 1990.

Stoner, James R., Jr. *Common Law and Liberal Theory: Coke, Hobbes, and the Origins of American Constitutionalism*. Lawrence: University Press of Kansas, 1992.

Storing, Herbert J., ed. *The Complete Anti-Federalist*. 7 vols. Chicago: University of Chicago Press, 1981.

Story, Joseph. *Commentaries on the Constitution of the United States*. Edited by Thomas M. Cooley. 2 vols. 4th ed. Boston: Little, Brown and Company, 1873.

Strauss, Leo. *Studies in Platonic Political Philosophy*. Chicago: University of Chicago Press, 1983.

Sunderland, Lane V. *Popular Government and the Supreme Court: Securing the Public Good and Private Rights*. Lawrence: University Press of Kansas, 1995.

Tarcov, Nathan. *Locke's Education for Liberty*. Chicago: University of Chicago Press, 1984.

Taswell-Langmead, Thomas Pitt. *English Constitutional History from the Teutonic Conquest to the Present Time.* Edited by Coleman Phillipson. 8th ed. Boston: Houghton Mifflin Company, 1919.

Tete, William T. "The Secularization of Natural Law: Beyond the Furor of Ideology." Paper presented at the annual meeting of the American Political Science Association, Chicago, September 2, 1995.

Thayer, James Bradley. *Cases on Constitutional Law.* 2 vols. Cambridge: George H. Kent, 1895.

Tocqueville, Alexis de. *Democracy in America.* 2 vols. Translated by George Lawrence. Edited by J. P. Mayer and Max Lerner. New York: Harper and Row, 1966.

Tonnies, Ferdinand. *Custom: An Essay on Social Codes.* Translated by A. Farrell Borenstein. Chicago: Henry Regnery Company, 1971.

Tushnet, Mark. "Following the Rules Laid Down: A Critique of Interpretivism and Neutral Principles." *Harvard Law Review* 96 (1983): 781–827.

——. "Judicial Review." *Harvard Journal of Law and Public Policy* 7 (1984): 77–79.

——. *Red, White, and Blue.* Cambridge: Harvard University Press, 1988.

Twiss, Benjamin R. *Lawyers and the Constitution: How Laissez-Faire Came to the Supreme Court.* Princeton, N.J.: Princeton University Press, 1942.

Urofsky, Melvin I. *A March of Liberty: A Constitutional History of the United States.* New York: Alfred A. Knopf, 1988.

Vining, Joseph. *The Authoritative and the Authoritarian.* Chicago: University of Chicago Press, 1986.

Vinogradoff, Paul. *Common-Sense in Law.* New York: Henry Holt and Company.

Voegelin, Eric. *Autobiographical Reflections.* Baton Rouge: Louisiana State University Press, 1989.

——. *The Nature of the Law and Related Legal Writings.* In *The Collected Works of Eric Voegelin.* Vol. 27. Edited by Robert A. Pascal, James L. Babin, and John W. Corrington. Baton Rouge: Louisiana State University Press, 1991.

——. *The New Science of Politics.* Chicago: University of Chicago Press, 1952.

——. *Order and History.* 5 vols. Baton Rouge: Louisiana State University Press, 1956–1987.

——. *Science, Politics, and Gnosticism.* Chicago: Henry Regnery Company, 1968.

——. *What Is History? And Other Late Unpublished Writings.* In *The Collected Works of Eric Voegelin.* Vol. 28. Edited by Thomas A. Hollweck and Paul Caringella. Baton Rouge: Louisiana State University Press, 1990.

Walker, Graham. *Moral Foundations of Constitutional Thought: Current Problems, Augustinian Prospects.* Princeton, N.J.: Princeton University Press, 1990.

Walsh, William F. *A History of Anglo-American Law.* 2d ed. Indianapolis: Bobbs-Merrill, 1932.

Warmington, E. H., ed. and trans. *Remains of Old Latin: Lucilius, The Twelve Tables.* Cambridge: Harvard University Press, 1938.

Wasserstrom, Richard A. *The Judicial Decision: Toward a Theory of Legal Justification.* Stanford, Calif.: Stanford University Press, 1961.

Watson, Alan. *Legal Transplants: An Approach to Comparative Law.* Edinburgh: Scottish Academic Press, 1974.

——. *Roman Law and Comparative Law.* Athens: University of Georgia Press, 1991.

——. *Roman Slave Law*. Baltimore and London: Johns Hopkins University Press, 1987.

Wechsler, Herbert. "Toward Neutral Principles of Constitutional Law." *Harvard Law Review* 73 (1959): 1.

White, Edward J. *Legal Antiquities: A Collection of Essays upon Ancient Laws and Customs*. St. Louis: F. H. Thomas, 1913.

White, G. Edward. *Intervention and Detachment: Essays in Legal History and Jurisprudence*. New York: Oxford University Press, 1994.

Whittington, Keith E. *Constitutional Construction*. Vol. 1. *Interpretation and Original Intent*. Typescript. Department of Politics, Catholic University of America, Washington, D.C.

——. *Constitutional Construction*. Vol. 2. *Divided Powers and Constitutional Meaning*. Typescript. Department of Politics, Catholic University of America, Washington, D.C.

Wiecek, William W. *Liberty Under Law: The Supreme Court in American Life*. Baltimore: Johns Hopkins University Press, 1988.

Winfield, Richard Dien. *Law in Civil Society*. Lawrence: University Press of Kansas, 1995.

Wolfe, Christopher. *The Rise of Modern Judicial Review: From Constitutional Interpretation to Judge-Made Law*. New York: Basic Books, 1986.

Wood, Gordon. *The Creation of the American Republic, 1776–1787*. New York: Norton, 1972.

Index

Academic specialism, 7, 8
Adler, Mortimer J., 7, 142, 182, 192, 196,
   201, 202, 206, 207, 212, 221
   How to Think About God, 201, 202, 212
   Intellect, 202
Administrative Procedure Act, 43
Affirmative action, 32
American Founding, 129, 182
American Revolution, 72, 93
Anselm, Saint, 196, 218
Antinomies
   constitutional, 19
   cosmological, Kantian, 211
   public and private, 75
Aquinas, Saint Thomas, 1, 4, 7, 59, 72, 99,
   110, 125, 130, 131, 132, 138, 142, 145,
   150, 151, 157, 192, 194, 196, 202, 203,
   205, 211
   Summa Theologica, 1, 103, 142, 151, 194
   Treatise on Law, 145
Aristotelianism, 7, 100, 131, 189, 192, 206
Aristotle, 6, 59, 99, 105, 131, 145, 158, 192,
   197, 202, 203, 206, 207, 226
   Politeia, 145
Arrow, Kenneth J., 7, 45, 49, 50, 51, 53,
   55, 67, 76, 164
   impossibility theorem of, 45, 49–50, 51,
   52, 53, 56
   impossibility theorem of, conditions of,
   50, 51, 54, 76, 164
   Social Choice and Individual Values, 49

and social choice processes, 49, 50, 51,
   53, 55
Articles of Confederation, 19, 159
Atheism, 6, 213, 216
Atomism, 1, 188
   social, 1, 146, 188
August, Eugene, 176
Augustine, Saint, 7, 72, 131, 145, 168, 176,
   192, 216
   Civitas Dei, 145
   Confessions, 216
Austin, John, 4, 21, 100, 130, 137, 144, 150,
   153, 157, 177, 188
Ayer, A. J., 211

Barber, Soterios A., 9, 14, 16, 83, 84, 222
Becket, Thomas, 98
Behe, Michael, 214, 215
Being
   as composite of essence and existence,
   59, 205
   as formal essence, 205
Bentham, Jeremy, 129, 136, 145, 154, 219
Bergson, Henri, 212
Berkeley, George, 141
Bickel, Alexander, 34
Bill of Rights (American), 62, 101, 130,
   148, 161
Bill of Rights (English), 96
Black, Duncan, 52

Blackstone, William, 6, 73, 82, 92, 98, 110, 112, 124, 145, 179, 225
 Commentaries, 82, 92, 102, 225
 and Justinian's *Institutes*, 225
Book of Exodus (Old Testament), 216
Book of Judges (Old Testament), 227
Bracton, Henry de, 123
Brown v. Board of Education, 30

Calabresi, Guido, 66, 118
Calder v. Bull, 162
Callicles, 145
Calvinism, 102
Cardozo, Benjamin, 67, 99, 148
Case/controversy rule (Article 3), 26
Casto, William R., 102
Chase, Samuel, 162
Chesterton, Gilbert K., 55, 81, 119, 169, 211, 219
Chicago School (of Law and Economics), 160
Choper, Jesse, 35
Christianity, 6, 145, 175, 204
Cicero, Marcus Tullius, 100, 131, 138, 145, 153, 167
 De Legibus, 145
Civil War (U.S.), 26, 36
Clear case rule, 38
Coke, Edward, 71, 93, 98, 124, 145
 Institutes, 98
 and legal reason, 101
Coleridge, Samuel, 128
Command theory of law, 99, 172
Common law (English), 3, 5, 32, 71, 77, 82, 89, 91, 99, 147, 225
 and *ad similia* rule, 123
 and the American colonies, 96
 as blend of nature, custom, and reason, 102
 and cases of first impression, 77, 81
 and conventional morality, 78
 and custom, 81, 98, 125
 as custom of the realm, 73
 in formative era, 81, 147
 as highest reason, 100
 and juries, 94

and legal change, 119
and the legal profession, 105, 189
and lex non scripta as unwritten substance of, 100
medieval, 103
as perfection of reason, 100
and presupposition of underlying legal order, 104, 124
reception in American states, 91
and the rights of the English, 73
and Roman law, 92
and statutorification, 225
and the unity of legal reason, 100
Comte, Auguste, 165
Congress, U.S., 15, 20, 27, 38, 42, 97, 111, 127
 debates in, 15, 27
Conservatism, 26, 31, 35, 65, 107, 109, 127, 224
Constitutional amendment, 22, 31, 42
Constitutional commentators, 15, 18, 27, 45, 166
Constitutionalism
 as alternative to natural law and legal positivism, 178
 American, 3, 5, 6, 17, 23, 59, 71, 89, 93, 96, 98, 129, 159, 170, 181
 artifactual, 222
 blueprint, 11, 18, 19, 35, 45, 61
 British, 3, 72, 73, 156
 classical, as parallelism of psyche and polis, 73
 and the common law, 99, 189
 consensual, 42, 53, 62, 78, 222
 judicialized, 2, 7, 11, 13, 45, 54, 62, 79, 82, 215, 220, 227
 modern, 1, 3, 163, 187
 theistic, 2, 6
 and writtenness, 46, 58, 178
Constitutions, 2, 3, 5, 9, 15, 18, 19, 40, 45, 46, 47, 54, 56, 58, 59, 63, 64, 73, 80, 85, 89, 95, 98, 105, 109, 115, 116, 127, 131, 143, 156, 170, 178, 181, 202, 205, 208, 221
 American state, 58, 95, 98
 as Arrovian social choice processes, 49

British, and the common law, 98
rigid and flexible, 89
Constitutions, American federal, 9, 11, 14, 17, 18, 19, 23, 25, 29, 31, 33, 34, 39, 42, 44, 45, 46, 56, 58, 59, 63, 65, 67, 71, 82, 84, 90, 91, 96, 98, 108, 109, 115, 116, 148, 157, 159, 163, 170, 178, 181, 191, 225
commerce clause, 113
contract clause, 162
enumerated powers, 161
as *ex nihilo* creation, 178
as explicit rendition of Hobbesian social contract, 178
and interpretability as essence of linguistic readability, 178
and natural law, 157
as *novus ordo seclorum*, 187, 225
Constitutions, unwritten, 3, 18, 21, 24, 56, 58, 59, 63, 64, 89, 156, 189, 205
as decisional predisposition, 47, 60
democratic, 48
as self-definition of a polity, 170
as self-definition of individual, 47, 54
tyrannical, 48
Constitutions, written, 9, 18, 20, 23, 41, 46, 56, 58, 59, 64, 69, 73, 89, 95, 105, 115, 127, 178, 181, 221
Constitutions of Clarendon (1164), 98
Construction
Blackstone's First Rule, 110
Blackstone's Tenth Rule, 98
constitutional, 11, 24, 25
liberal, 25
rules of, 15, 113
statutory, 95, 98, 110, 111, 117
strict, 25
Convention, 16, 18, 26, 49, 55, 58, 61, 63, 74, 77, 81, 83, 96, 105, 108, 111, 150, 161, 222
legal, 16, 26, 83, 105, 111
moral, 2, 16, 46, 67, 74, 78, 81, 83, 135
social, 16, 74, 77, 83
Convention, constitutional, 61, 63
Conventionalism, 3, 16, 77, 83
legal, 16, 83

moral, 16, 83
Cooley, Thomas M., 127
Cooper v. Aaron, 27
Copleston, F. S., 193–94
Corwin, Edward S., 22
Courts, in Great Britain, 81, 91, 113, 116, 123
Court of Exchequer, 112
House of Lords, 96, 114
Courts, in United States, 13, 43, 65, 95, 98, 115, 116, 123
colonial, 91
D.C. Circuit Court, 43
New York Court of Appeals, 226
Supreme Court, 1, 2, 3, 4, 13, 17, 24, 26, 28, 34, 38, 54, 58, 62, 63, 65, 69, 75, 91, 107, 115, 117, 127, 148, 162, 167
Supreme Court, and natural law, 130, 159
Cross, Rupert, 114, 124
Custom, 49, 55, 58, 80, 81, 83, 98, 124, 132, 135, 141, 150
as intelligible reality, 125
legal, 121, 125
legal, and conventional morality, as foundation of normative ethics, 122
legal, and normativity of habitual community behavior, 121
social, 56, 135
Cynicism, 40

Dartmouth College v. Woodward, 116
Darwin, Charles, 213
Declaration of Independence, 66, 159
Declaratory theory of law, 19, 100, 123
and Marshall's constitutionalism, 59
and precedent, 125
Deconstruction, 18, 35
Demosthenes, 226
Dicey, Albert Venn, 64, 156
Dr. Bonham's Case, 98
Dred Scott v. Sanford, 31, 127
Dual federalism, 26, 67
Due process of law, 26, 39, 44, 62, 63, 66, 148
substantive, 26, 44, 67

Due process of law, *continued*
    substantive, and liberty of contract, 26,
        39, 65, 69, 75, 220
Duncan v. Louisiana, 148
Dworkin, Ronald, 219

*E. C. Knight v. Jones & Laughlin Steel
    Corp.,* 31
Ellsworth, Oliver, 102
Ely, John Hart, 35
English Act (1679), 97
Epistemology, 4, 129, 138, 143, 146, 149,
    154, 183, 211, 221
    coherence, 86, 143, 149, 184, 211
    correspondence, 86, 143
Epistemology, empiricist, 129
    and logical possibility, 195
    and natural science, 210
    and social science, 211
Epistemology, Kantian
    necessity and contingency, 195
    and positivism, 196
    reality of noumena, 210
    and subjectivism, 196
    unknowability of noumena, 195, 209,
        211
Epistemology, Lockean, 183
    and correspondence theory of knowl-
        edge, 183
    and ideas as objects of thought, 183
    and knowability of nominal essences,
        183
    and linguistic constructivism, 183
    and nominalism, 183
    and unknowability of real essences, 183
Epistemology, nominalist, 99, 146, 149,
    183, 211
Epstein, Richard, 160
Essence, 19, 22, 48, 58, 59, 64, 70, 87, 89,
    124, 135, 148, 151, 168, 183, 204, 205,
    219
    as absence of inner contradiction, 59,
        184
    constitutional, 22, 48, 58, 59
    formal, 59, 70, 184, 205
    legal, 154

material, 219
    moral, 87
    nominal, 59, 184
    real, 59
    as self-identity, 59, 184
    as tertiary abstraction, 70
Everson v. Board of Education, 167
Existence
    actual, 59, 64, 70, 99, 139, 140, 145, 184,
        197, 202, 205, 210, 219, 220
    as assumption, 194
    constitutional, 69
    as constitutive source of order, 192
    as givenness, 60, 205
    as independent, 196
    as infinite, 195
    as intransient, 195
    as necessary, 195
    as prediction, 194
    as presupposed by assumption of crea-
        tion, 198
    and relation to historical events, beliefs,
        and practices, 201, 208, 221
    and relation to individual beings, 201
    and science, 201
    as transcendent source of order, 208, 214
Existence, of cosmos in totality
    as givenness, and ingratitude for, 175,
        187
    as merely possible, 199
    and natural disinclination to persevere,
        198, 221
    as necessary, 199
    as radical contingency, 198, 208
    as whole of physical and non-physical
        existence, 207
    as whole of physical existence, 199, 203
Existence, of individual beings
    and efficient causation, 197, 202
    and natural inclination to persevere,
        197, 202
    and principle of inertia, 197, 202
    as superficial contingency, 197, 201
Existence, of supreme being
    and modern gnosticism, 191
    and rational obligation, 221

and reasonableness of inquiry on, 193
and relation to cosmos in totality, 200
as exnihilating preservative cause, 201
Experience
    as an aid to reason in the discovery of
        law, 104
    corporeal, 138
    and objects of perception, 139
    and pure concepts, 139
Experience, common, 5, 141, 147, 155, 172,
    221
    and external reality, 144
    as intersubjectively verifiable, 142
    of self-movement, 217
Experience, constitutional, 3, 20, 60, 64,
    67, 69, 89, 172, 180, 184
    as field of tensions, 65, 68, 73, 89, 168
    and symbolism, 3, 20, 46, 60, 64, 69, 75,
        89, 119
Experience, historical
    as field of tensions, 187, 222
    as recurrence, 222
Experience, legal, 8, 31, 92, 100, 104, 151,
    169
    of common property, 158
    as imposition of moral standards, 169
    and symbolism, 121
Experience, of transcendence, 145, 154
    and Augustine's conversion, 216
    and Jewish chosenness, 216
    and Kant's kingdom of ends, 216
    and theistically driven morality, 216
Experience, philosophical, 145
    as field of tensions, 204, 213

Federalists, 16, 28
Fictions, 48, 53, 111, 119, 122, 182
Fictions, constitutional, 53
Fictions, legal, 111, 120, 122
    in constitutional law, original intent and
        stare decisis, 121
    danger of, 120
    definition of, 120
    and the intention of a collective body,
        107, 120
    and reason, 121

as symbolization of normativity of tra-
    dition, 119
and truth, 121
utility of, 121
Fictions, political, 48
    utility of, 185
Fictions, scientific, 120
Fictions, theoretical, 182
Fletcher v. Peck, 162, 179
Forms, institutional, 16
Forms, legal, 20
Forms, of government, 14, 16, 23, 164
    democratic, 16, 27, 28, 36, 45, 48, 49, 51,
        53, 55, 66, 76, 81, 118, 161
    democratic-participatory, 36
    Jacksonian Democratic, 27
    Jeffersonian Republican, 27
    platonic, 203
    republican, 14, 23
Fourteenth Amendment, 26, 62, 66, 98,
    130, 148, 166, 172
Fourth Amendment, 106
Framers (American), 65, 160, 180, 187
    and classical legal thought, 189
    and common law foundation of Consti-
        tution, 189
    and constitutional solipsism, 189
    and Hobbesianism, 189
    and natural law foundation of common
        law, 189
Franck, Matthew J., 162
French Revolution, 99
Freud, Sigmund, 213
Fuller, Lon L., 120
Gagarin, Michael, 121
Gaius, 226
Game theory, 133, 135, 136
Gandhi, Mohandas, 216
Gibbons v. Ogden, 117
Gilded Age, 1, 26, 62, 127, 163
Gilder, George, 213, 215
Gilson, Etienne, 7, 59, 70, 87, 141, 156, 205
Gnosticism, 4, 89, 166, 175, 185, 211, 216,
    223
    and history, 176, 187
    and modern jurisprudence, 177

Gnosticism, constitutional, 4, 185
  and the American founding, 189
Gnosticism, philosophical, 175
  and behaviorism, 192
  in Comte and Marx, 216
  and existentialism, 192
  in Hegel and Heidegger, 175, 216
  and positivism, 192
  and rationalism, 80, 192
Gnosticism, political, 175
  and modern social engineering, 175
  and nazism, 192
  and socialism, 192
  and Stalin and Hitler, 216
Gnosticism, theological, 175
  as ancient heresy, 175
  as ingratitude for the cosmos as given,
    175, 187
  as possession of world-transformative
    knowledge *(gnosis)*, 175
Gorgias, 217
Gospel of John (New Testament), 187
Government
  functions, 23, 168
  functions, judicial, 13, 16, 27, 29, 38, 95,
    98, 127, 160
Graglia, Lino, 26
Griswold v. Connecticut, 31, 71, 179

Hale, Matthew, 99, 105, 123, 145, 189
  History of Common Law, 123
Hamilton, Alexander, 28
Hammer v. Dagenhart, 31
Hand, Learned, 76
Harris, William F. II, 4, 155, 178, 181, 211,
    222
  constitutional theory, 181, 182, 183
  theory of interpretation, 179, 180, 186
Hegel, G. W. F., 136, 175, 186, 205, 212
Heidegger, Martin, 175
Heraclitus, 69, 73, 136, 142, 189, 224
Heydon's Case, 112
History
  constitutional, 9, 11, 15, 17, 24, 27, 37,
    40, 53, 61, 69, 127, 186
  constitutional, American, 31

as context for all acts of knowing, 182
institutional, 8
and intelligible reality, 187
legal, 2, 7, 8, 17, 63, 90, 126, 129, 155,
    159, 166, 221, 223
legal, English, 156, 159
and normativity, 223
and objectivity, 222
of order, and experience of transcen-
    dence, 191
philosophy of, 8, 128, 187
and regularity, 223
and transcendence, 187, 223
Hobbes, Thomas, 1, 6, 20, 71, 73, 80, 99,
    129, 133, 135, 136, 144, 154, 158, 178,
    181, 209, 219
  Elements of Law, 145
  Leviathan, 133, 135, 146
  nominalism, 99
  theory of law, 99
Hobbesianism, 1, 4, 6, 40, 48, 71, 73, 99,
    129, 132, 133, 135, 136, 138, 163, 178,
    189, 211
  as opposition of individual and society,
    53, 135
  and social contract, 133
Holmes, Oliver Wendell Jr., 40
Holmes, Oliver Wendell Sr., 219
House of Representatives (United States),
    96
Hume, David, 139, 141, 183, 192
Hurst, J. Willard, 119

Ideas
  as intelligible abstractions, 71, 80, 122
  as objects of thought, 144, 157, 171, 183
  as tools of thought, 142, 144, 171
Injustice, 1, 2, 146, 151, 176
Intellect, 79, 139, 142, 145, 154, 202, 203,
    206, 207, 214
Intellect, immaterial, 141, 145, 202, 207,
    221, 226
  and angels, 208
  and distinction between appearance and
    reality, 142
  and efficient causation, 208

as incorruptible, 207
and intelligible reality, 99, 125, 138, 141, 142, 143, 145, 153, 171, 203, 207, 221, 226
in mode of being, 203, 206
in mode of operation, 203, 206
and rational obligation, 221
as regulative, 143
as self-moving, 217
as simple substance, 205
Intellect, material
as reducible to brain function, 202, 211
and sense perception, 142
Interpretation, constitutional, 2, 3, 6, 8, 11, 13, 16, 17, 23, 24, 25, 28, 30, 33, 34, 38, 45, 58, 61, 63, 69, 78, 84, 95, 106, 113, 116, 118, 178, 181, 191
and coherence epistemology, 184
congressional, 15
deconstructionist, 106
extratextualist, 179, 222
and gnosticism, 177
and history of order, 191
intentionalist, 35, 90, 105, 107, 110, 116, 118, 119
intentionalist, objective, 110, 113, 117, 118, 119, 180
intentionalist, original, 109
intentionalist, remedial, 109
intentionalist, subjective, 106, 111, 113, 119, 180
interpretivist, 6, 11, 29, 30, 35, 191
noninterpretivist, 6, 11, 30, 35, 179
originalist, 6, 29, 35, 82, 105, 107, 109, 122
presidential, 15, 27
textualist, 18, 23, 29, 59, 69, 179, 181, 191, 222
traditional, 77
and writtenness, 187
Interpretation, judicial, 30, 35, 40, 157, 179, 226
Interpretation, legal, 104
intentionalist, 6, 35, 59, 90, 111, 179, 187, 222
Interpretation, liberal, 26, 30

Interpretation, restrictive, 26
Interpretation, rules of, 3, 11, 18, 22, 30, 34, 40, 42, 55, 59, 77, 90, 109, 111, 116, 119, 127, 129, 226
golden rule, 112, 114, 117
mischief rule, 110, 111, 116, 118
plain meaning rule, 112, 179
traditional, 8, 31, 34, 40, 55, 129
Interpretation, statutory, 68, 82, 95, 109, 115, 116, 118, 179, 226
and constitutional law, 118
intentionalist, and acts of parliament, 119
Isidore of Seville, Saint, *Hispana,* 126

Jaki, Stanley, 209
James, William, 212
Jay, John, 102
Jefferson, Thomas, 22, 119, 167
Jenks, Edward, 93
Jones, J. W., 122
Judges, 2, 10, 11, 13, 16, 19, 24, 28, 31, 33, 34, 39, 41, 42, 45, 46, 54, 55, 59, 64, 66, 76, 77, 81, 85, 92, 96, 101, 106, 110, 112, 116, 122, 140, 142, 157, 163, 219, 226
Judicial activism, 4, 14, 19, 23, 26, 32, 43, 77, 107, 128, 149, 160
Judicial behavior, 18, 40
Judicial finality, 3, 4, 11, 15, 27, 28, 35, 42, 45, 54, 173, 181, 222
Judicial freedom, 3, 4, 11, 28, 30, 34, 42, 45, 54, 77, 181, 222
Judicialization, 2, 5, 7, 10, 11, 13, 42, 45, 54, 62, 64, 79, 82, 160, 215, 220, 225
of administrative law, 42
of constitutional law, 13, 44
of natural law, 160
of public law, 2
Judicial restraint, 26, 149
Judicial review, 2, 3, 6, 8, 11, 14, 16, 27, 29, 30, 34, 38, 43, 45, 61, 81, 82, 85, 95, 98, 127, 160, 220, 225
administrative law, 43, 44
constitutional law, 127
noninterpretive, 30
scope of, 33

Judicial supremacy, 3, 11, 14, 17, 24, 28, 34, 38, 45, 54, 55
  theoretical framework, 35
Judiciary Act of 1789 (Section 25), 117
Julianus, 99
Jurisprudence, 2, 3, 4, 8, 21, 36, 40, 45, 46, 71, 86, 90, 92, 98, 103, 106, 110, 122, 130, 144, 150, 153, 157, 159, 163, 172, 173, 177, 178, 219, 221, 224
  analytical, 21, 150, 156
  Christian, 147
  classical, 167
  constitutional, 2, 4, 21, 45, 46, 90, 130, 155, 166
  constitutional, compatibility of original intent and stare decisis, 90, 118
  English, 173
  equity, 93
  historical, 122, 173
  naturalistic, 5, 144
  and the nature of law, 155
  Roman, 173
  scholastic, 103
  and transcendent character of law, 223
Jurisprudence, Thomistic, 153
  common ownership, 158
  and custom, 125–26
  and definition of law, 151–52
  and divine law, 152
  and eternal law, 151–52, 157
  and human law, 152
  and natural law, 152–53, 157
  private ownership, 158
  private possession, 158
Justice, 1, 2, 40, 54, 65, 94, 114, 145, 148, 166
Justinian, 1, 93, 225

Kant, Immanuel, 53, 67, 84, 122, 139, 141, 192, 195, 197, 209, 216, 220, 227
  Critique of Pure Reason, 140, 209, 220
  and the law-morals distinction, 84
  moral imperative, 53
  pragmatic imperative, 53
Kantianism, 196, 216

Kelley, Donald R., 56
King, Martin Luther, 216
Kojeve, Alexandre, 186

Law, 14, 16, 20, 23, 34, 42, 56, 73, 80, 81, 89, 91, 96, 98, 99, 104, 118, 121, 123, 144, 145, 150, 157, 159, 223, 227
  common, 2, 3, 5, 32, 37, 43, 61, 66, 71, 73, 77, 81, 89, 91, 96, 98, 104, 109, 110, 112, 118, 119, 122, 129, 144, 148, 151, 182, 203, 225
  criminal, 120, 148, 225
  divine, 152, 190
  ecclesiastical, 126
  English, 63, 92, 96, 99, 124, 147, 167
  eternal, 138, 151, 157
  gentic, 95, 147, 151
  human, 125, 152, 216
  as institutionalized history, 3
  jurisdictional, 44, 77, 95, 117, 147
  as mixture of reason and experience, 99
  and morality, 3, 16, 46, 74, 84, 89
  of nations, 151
  as noumenal reality, 227
  positive, 80, 137, 145, 149, 150, 158, 188, 203
  private, 8, 36, 82, 93, 120, 148, 151, 225
  private, *res judicata*, 120, 226
  procedural, 8, 22, 41, 225
  public, 2, 8, 93
  Roman, 93, 96, 126, 147, 151, 167, 226
  substantive, 18, 22, 37, 41, 77, 91, 146, 151, 159, 225
  as traditional practice, 227
  as uniform legal reality, 105
  unwritten, 100, 124
  written, 110, 122
Law, administrative, 44, 61
  adjudication, 43
  Administrative Procedure Act, 43
  delegation of authority, 44
  jurisdictional, 44
Law, constitutional, 2, 3, 4, 8, 11, 13, 17, 19, 23, 25, 28, 32, 34, 39, 41, 42, 45, 54, 56, 64, 69, 74, 77, 82, 87, 91, 98,

105, 107, 116, 118, 119, 129, 130, 148, 157, 159, 163, 172, 179, 225

balanced government, United States, 161

case-controversy rule, 98

of criminal procedure, 148

as distribution of sovereign power, 46

equal protection, 67, 166, 168

establishment clause, and antitheistic interpretation by Supreme Court, 166–67

federalism, 26, 67, 70

freedom of expression, 166, 167

intellectual property, 226

as judicial gloss, 64

and morality, 81

and precedent, 129

and the public-private distinction, 93

separation of powers, 15, 30, 44, 70, 95

substantive, 22

Law, Greek

archaic, and virtue, 167

classical, and the use of precedent, 122

Draconian homicide statute, 148

Gortynian code, and habeas corpus, 225

Law, natural, 4, 36, 39, 86, 102, 130, 138, 144, 149, 150, 157, 159, 163, 172, 178, 188, 200, 203, 221, 224

classical, 138, 154, 163, 172, 188

conservative, 224

justiciability of, 162

modern, and social contract, 188

modern, Lockean, 130, 159

revolutionary, and social contract theory, 224

Law, statutory, 38, 116, 118, 226

of American states, 94

of Edward I, 225

remedial, 110

Legalism, 18, 20

Legal profession (United States), 15, 65

Legislative supremacy (United States), 160

Liberalism, 4, 6, 25, 30, 45, 50, 51, 53, 55, 71, 75, 80, 84, 129, 137, 166, 184

and common law, 72, 129

Liberalism, Lockean, 6, 160

Liberalism, Millian, 4, 75, 81, 130, 137, 163, 164

and academic freedom, 169

and division of spiritual and temporal spheres, 164

and egalitarianism, 168

and epistemological skepticism, 169

and "fundamental values" jurisprudence, 177

and gnosticism, 176, 177

and harm principle, 164

and libertarianism, 56, 170, 177

and lifestyle liberalism, 75, 164

and moral neutrality, 169

and principle of liberty, 164

and progressivism, 130, 177

and religion of humanity, 165, 177

and sentimentalism, 170

and utility of religious sentiment, 165

Liberalism, modern, and materialism, 137

Lienesch, Michael, 161

Lindsay, A.D., 210

Llewellyn, Karl, 82, 122

Lochner v. New York, 31, 62

Locke, John, 6, 57, 94, 136, 141, 158, 160, 183, 219

Lysias, 226

McCulloch v. Maryland, 61, 117

Machiavelli, Niccolo, 80, 137

Madison, James, 36, 116, 189

Magna Carta, 93, 97

Maine, Henry, 21, 122, 155

Maitland, Frederic William, 7, 92, 96, 121, 126

  History of English Law, 96

Maltz, Earl M., 105

Manichaeism, 165

Marbury Myth, 126, 128

Marbury v. Madison, 15, 17, 27, 33, 35, 38, 46, 58, 107, 115, 116, 126, 127

Maritain, Jacques, 214

Marshall, John, 16, 24, 36, 39, 46, 58, 59, 70, 97, 107, 116, 149, 162, 168, 179

Marshall Court, 36, 39, 70, 97, 116

Marx, Karl, 136, 175, 213, 216
Materialism, 1, 40, 80, 137, 143, 146, 172,
    175, 192, 202, 208, 209, 215, 216, 221
  and idolatry, 227
  Ionian, and search for fundamental con-
      stituent, 219
  metaphysical, 137, 172, 202, 209, 211,
      214, 217
  scientific, 137, 192, 209, 221
Mendelson, Wallace, 26
Metaphysics, 1, 197, 206
  Aristotelian, 196, 203, 202, 206
  essentialist, 70, 206
  existentialist, 192, 217
  Platonic, independence of form and
      matter, 203
Meyer, Stephen C., 213, 215
Mill, John Stuart, 4, 9, 75, 128, 136, 163,
    176, 219
  On Liberty, 9, 164
  Three Essays on Religion, 165
Milsom, S. F. C., 90
Ministerial responsibility (Great Britain),
    97
Molina, Luis de, 192
Moore, Michael S., 20, 76, 78, 83, 85

Nagel, Robert F., 13, 24
Naturalism, 2, 4, 11, 99, 130, 138, 144, 148,
    155, 157, 166, 177, 183, 224
  classical, 138, 145
  constitutional, 5, 109, 166
  legal, 2, 4, 130, 144, 151, 224
Nature, animal, 131, 138, 145, 188, 218
Nature, human, 5, 75, 85, 132, 144, 150,
    151, 164, 172, 175, 188, 219, 221, 224
  and classical natural law, 188
  as common, 144
  and contractarianism, 188
  and intellect, 207
  as knowable, 175
  and materialism, 219
  and reason, 125, 153, 158, 218
  and spirituality, 143
  as unchanging and distinctive, 172
Nature, state of, 4, 132, 135, 178, 188

Hobbesian, 133, 135, 157–58, 178, 188
  Lockean, 157–58
Necessary and proper clause, 26
Niebuhr, Reinhold, 192
Nietzsche, Friedrich, 175
Nihilism, 38, 169, 172, 175, 192, 211, 217
  metaphysical, 172, 175
Noumena, 131, 141, 146, 195, 209, 227
  as inaccessible to modern reason, 171

Ogden v. Saunders, 162
Olmstead v. United States, 107
Order, constitutional, 4, 6, 9, 18, 20, 23,
    24, 31, 40, 60, 63, 69, 74, 82, 104, 107,
    130, 170, 173, 185, 191, 220
  American, 107, 130, 173
Order, cosmic
  and accident, 214
  necessity and contingency, 193
  and transcendence, 133, 191
Order, divine, 4, 75, 136, 141, 156, 184,
    191, 200, 221, 226
Order, legal, 4, 6, 19, 66, 91, 102, 104, 122,
    148, 151, 225
Order, natural, 133
Order, political, 2, 14, 20, 23, 31, 41, 49,
    54, 58, 59, 66, 69, 132, 170, 178, 185,
    208, 220
Order, social, 9, 47, 50, 51, 55, 71, 76, 132,
    133, 135, 167, 208
  and status differentials, 170
Otis, James, 93

Palko v. Connecticut, 148
Parliamentary supremacy (Great Britain),
    95
Parmenides, 203, 204
Paterson, William, 162
Pensacola v. Western Union, 113
Perry, Michael J., 14, 30
Petition of Right (1628), 97
Phenomena, 8, 124, 131, 136, 138, 140, 143,
    146, 159, 166, 194, 209, 220, 227
Philadelphia Convention, 19, 41, 189
Philosophy
  classical, 146

classical, as love of wisdom, 20, 145
modern, as possession of wisdom, 186
Planned Parenthood of S.E. Penn. v. Casey,
    28, 32
Plato, 6, 10, 20, 47, 53, 56, 72, 100, 105,
    131, 132, 135, 138, 145, 167, 186, 195,
    203, 204, 207, 217, 224
    Apology, 131
    constitutional anthropomorphism, 48,
        53, 56, 73, 132, 136, 138, 141, 208, 226
    Crito, 131
    Gorgias, 145, 219
    Laws, 48, 56, 92, 100, 105, 167, 217
    Minos, 20
    Parmenides, 203, 204
    Phaedo, 219
    Republic, 135, 145, 188, 217, 224
    Timaeus, 186, 204
Platonism, 6, 50, 56, 102, 131, 142, 213, 217
Plessy v. Ferguson, 31
Political questions doctrine, 24, 27, 70
Political science, 7, 8, 18, 21, 38, 48, 136
Positivism, 4, 80, 99, 124, 130, 144, 149,
    154, 163, 175, 178, 183, 192, 217, 221,
    224
    and utilitarianism, 195
Positivism, Austinian legal, 80, 156, 163
    basis of in truncated human nature, 188
    and command theory of law, 153
    and common experience, 156
    and custom, 155
    and divine law, 153
    and natural law, 154
    and utilitarianism, 153, 157
Positivism, legal, 4, 80, 99, 130, 144, 148,
    154, 163, 172, 175, 178, 188, 217, 221,
    224
    as truncation of experience, 149
Positivism, logical, 221
    and metaphysical statements, 194
    and phenomenalism, 196
Postema, Gerald, 101
    and reason in common law theory, 102
Precedent, 16, 38, 66, 81, 90, 111, 116, 118,
    119, 122, 127, 128, 129, 225
    and the origin of written law, 122

ubiquity of, 225
President, U.S., veto of, 15, 27
Progressive historians, 40, 160
Protagoras, 142

Ratification, of U.S. Constitution, 25, 189
Rationalism, 79, 99, 128, 129, 138, 145, 192
    classical, 138
    as truncation of reason, 80, 172
Rationalism, modern, 79, 100
    and materialism, 79
    and moral authority, 79
    as truncation of reason, 79, 129, 137, 141
Rawls, John, 219
Realism, 2, 3, 7, 16, 20, 36, 46, 54, 56, 60,
    64, 69, 77, 80, 83, 99, 122, 136, 138,
    140, 145, 149, 154, 176, 183, 191, 212,
    218, 220
    constitutional, 6, 18, 24, 61, 63, 71
    legal, 36, 83, 122
    moral, 16, 76, 83
    moral, and constitutional interpretation,
        191
    philosophical, 2
Reason, 2, 19, 72, 99, 104, 124, 129, 131,
    132, 135, 136, 138, 140, 141, 144, 152,
    158, 169, 171, 175, 182, 192, 203, 204,
    208, 209, 210, 216, 221, 227
    abstract, 92
    classical, 100, 129, 132, 138, 141
    classical, and intelligible reality, 218
    classical, as foundation of distinctive hu-
        man nature, 172
    classical, as source of order in psyche,
        138, 141
    and the discovery of law, 104
    and faith, 208
    Hobbesian, 135
    practical, 100, 189, 210
    practical, Aristotelian, 100
    practical, in the American founding, 189
    speculative, 140, 147, 210
    speculative, and noumenal reality, 195
    speculative, limitation of, 210
    and transcendent source of order, 136
Reductionism, 80, 99, 106, 136

Reed, Stanley, 115
Relativism, 16
Rights
  constitutional, 29, 62, 137, 179
  conventional, 74
  economic, 75
  fundamental constitutional, 4, 83, 159, 163, 177
  human, 32, 83
  individual, 72, 73, 94, 98, 136, 161, 164
  natural, 36, 39, 100, 157, 160, 188, 221
  natural, protection of by majority rule, 160
  personal, 31, 75, 159
  personal, of equal treatment, 31
  personal, of freedom of expression, 31
  personal, of privacy, 31
  privacy rights and abortion, 28, 32, 62, 63, 68
  property, 31, 36, 40, 127, 136, 149, 158, 159, 163, 172, 177
  property, Lockean, 149, 159, 160
  property, personal, 32
  property, real, 32
Roe v. Wade, 31, 62, 63, 68
Roosevelt Court, 26
Rousseau, Jean-Jacques, 53, 165
Royal prerogative (Great Britain), 95
Russell, Bertrand, 171, 192, 193

Saul, John Ralston, 79
Scalia, Antonin, 28
School desegregation, 27, 32
Secularism, 1, 167, 172, 175, 218
Shapiro, Martin, 32, 43, 225
Sherman, Roger, 189
Skepticism, 2, 16, 21, 38, 75, 85, 140, 166, 172, 175, 213, 217
  epistemological, 172, 175
  moral, 16, 85
Slaughterhouse Cases, 65
Smart, J. J. C., 195
Snowiss, Sylvia, 38, 59
Social Darwinism, 75, 149
Socrates, 20, 101, 131, 209
  and the declaratory theory of law, 101

Sovereignty, 108
  American national, 161
  American state, 160
  and legitimacy, 145
  popular, 107
Spencer, Herbert, 40
Statute of Mortmain (1279), 97
Statute of Treasons (1352), 97
Stephen, James Fitzjames, 164
Stoner, James R., Jr., 71, 100, 110, 129, 189
Story, Joseph, 112, 162
Strauss, Leo, 188
Sunderland, Lane V., 70, 160

Taft, William Howard, 107
Taney Court, 149
Tenth Amendment, 26, 97
Terrett v. Taylor, 162
Thayer, James Bradley, 26
Theology, 1, 2, 173, 186, 192, 214, 217
Theology, rational, 192
  and argument from design, 194, 214
  and argument from motion, 217
  and cosmological argument, of Mortimer Adler, 198, 201
  and cosmological argument, of Thomas Aquinas, 194, 196, 198, 201, 202, 208
  and ontological argument, 196
  and scientific knowledge, 193
Theory, constitutional, 2, 3, 4, 6, 8, 11, 15, 17, 18, 22, 23, 25, 30, 35, 45, 61, 69, 77, 83, 89, 99, 105, 160, 166, 171, 177, 181, 182, 218, 222
  classical, 45
  and the common law, 105
  contemporary, 3, 11, 15, 22, 23, 25, 30, 77, 83, 89, 105, 177, 182, 222
  contractarian, and government by rational discourse, 185
  modern, liberal democratic, 45
Theory, legal, 2, 4, 99, 104, 123, 129, 136, 189
  common law, 101
Theory, moral, 6, 8, 80, 81, 83, 122, 192
Theory, political, 2, 4, 7, 8, 19, 20, 63, 71,

73, 80, 89, 107, 129, 131, 132, 136, 144, 152, 160, 178, 185, 212
  classical, 131
  modern, 132, 136, 188
  modern contractarian, 146
Theory, scientific, 99
Thomism, 7, 152, 157, 192
Thrasymachus, 145
Tiedeman, Christopher, 127
Tillich, Paul, 192
Tocqueville, Alexis de, 27, 82
Tradition, 5, 7, 8, 11, 14, 16, 18, 21, 28, 45, 49, 55, 58, 59, 63, 66, 69, 74, 80, 81, 90, 99, 105, 110, 121, 124, 129, 130, 132, 135, 137, 141, 147, 148, 163, 173, 182, 191, 223, 224
  constitutional, 14, 21, 45, 56, 58, 69, 74, 90
  constitutional, British, 90
  and democracy, 16, 56
  historical, 5, 9, 16, 79, 128, 163, 182, 200, 222
  as intelligible reality, 80
  philosophical, 227
  and reason, 222
  theological, 7
Tradition, legal, 5, 8, 56, 101, 110, 124, 130, 135, 147, 173, 224

  continuity of, 147, 173
  normativity of, 80, 121
  practice rules, 8, 25, 29, 31, 37, 63, 64, 77, 84, 115, 117, 180, 189, 191, 221, 227
Tully, 153
Tushnet, Mark, 15, 41

United States v. American Trucking Association, 115
United States v. Carolene Products, 40
Utilitarianism, 137, 154
  and law, 158

Van Horne's Lessee v. Dorrance, 162
Voegelin, Eric, 7, 19, 72, 151, 176, 180, 188, 204, 205, 207, 211, 216, 217, 223
  In Search of Order, 207
Voltaire (Francois Marie Arouet), 80, 99

Walker, Graham, 76, 191
Warren Court, 26
Watson, Alan, 92
Wechsler, Herbert, 34
Whittington, Keith E., 24, 107
Wilkinson v. Leland, 162
Wolfe, Christopher, 26, 38